PENGUIN BOOKS

# LIES AND THE LYING LIARS
## WHO TELL THEM

Al Franken is an Emmy Award-winning television writer and producer, Grammy-winning comedian, radio host, and bestselling author of *Rush Limbaugh is a Big Fat Idiot and Other Observations*; *Why Not Me?*; *Oh, the Things I Know!*; and *I'm Good Enough, I'm Smart Enough, and Doggone It, People Like Me!* In 2003, he served as a Fellow with Harvard's Kennedy School of Government at the Shorenstein Center on the Press, Politics, and Public Policy. He lives with his family in New York City.

# LIES

**(And the Lying Liars Who Tell Them)**

## A Fair and Balanced
## Look at the Right

## Al Franken

PENGUIN BOOKS

PENGUIN BOOKS

Published by the Penguin Group
Penguin Books Ltd, 80 Strand, London WC2R 0RL, England
Penguin Group (USA) Inc., 375 Hudson Street, New York, New York 10014, USA
Penguin Books Australia Ltd, 250 Camberwell Road, Camberwell, Victoria 3124, Australia
Penguin Books Canada Ltd, 10 Alcorn Avenue, Toronto, Ontario, Canada M4V 3B2
Penguin Books India (P) Ltd, 11 Community Centre, Panchsheel Park, New Delhi – 110 017, India
Penguin Group (NZ), cnr Airborne and Rosedale Roads, Albany, Auckland 1310, New Zealand
Penguin Books (South Africa) (Pty) Ltd, 24 Sturdee Avenue, Rosebank 2196, South Africa

Penguin Books Ltd, Registered Offices: 80 Strand, London WC2R 0RL, England

www.penguin.com

First published in the United States of America by Dutton 2003
First published in Great Britain by Allen Lane 2003
Published in Penguin with additional material 2004
4

Printed in England by Clays Ltd, St Ives plc

To my wife, Franni, who's been screaming about this stuff for years and believed in the book I love you so much. And even more importantly, you love me.

To Bill O'Reilly

# CONTENTS

**Although** I wrote this book in a spirit of dispassionate inquiry, I cannot expect my critics to respond in kind. My right-wing detractors will undoubtedly tell you that I'm an "obnoxious prick," a "smug asshole," and a "clear and present threat to our national security." I will not stoop to dignify such calumny with a response, except to say that Condoleezza Rice should watch her mouth.

More imaginative critics might charge that, "like Newt Gingrich, [I] had an affair with a Supreme Court justice." This kind of attack, which is totally irrelevant to the political content of this book, exposes how desperate my enemies have become. As the great Joseph Welch said to Joe McCarthy, "Have you no sense of decency, sir? At long last, have you left no sense of decency?"

Unlike Senator McCarthy and his intellectual heirs, Ann Coulter and Howard Stern, I *do* have a sense of decency. And that is why I've decided to reveal a "dirty little secret" about this book that my critics are too lazy and stupid to figure out on their own. I acknowledge—no, I *proudly* acknowledge—that I did not write this book alone.

No author ever writes a book entirely by himself. That would be impossible. Just ask Dennis Rodman or John Updike. Like making a movie or building a long suspension bridge, writing a book is very much a team effort. And that is why I think it's important to state clearly, right up front, the methodology used to research this book, and to give credit to the ragtag bunch of Harvard misfits I've come to affectionately call TeamFranken.

It all started when Harvard's Kennedy School of Government

asked me to serve as a fellow at its Shorenstein Center on the Press, Politics, and Public Policy. After my varied and celebrated career in television, movies, publishing, and the lucrative world of corporate speaking, being a fellow at Harvard seemed, frankly, like a step down.

I couldn't think of anything less appealing than molding the minds of tomorrow's leaders, unless it was spending fireside evenings sipping sherry with great minds at the Faculty Club. Yawn.

To my surprise and delight, though, all Harvard wanted me to do was show up every once in a while and write something about something. That gave me an idea.

"Would it be okay if I wrote a scathingly partisan attack on the right-wing media and the Bush administration?"

"No problem," Harvard said absentmindedly.

"Count me in," I replied. "From now on call me 'Professor Franken.'"

"No," Harvard said, "you're not a professor. But you can run a study group on the topic of your choosing."

"Great," I said. "I've got the perfect topic: Write My Son's Harvard College Application Essay."

"No," they said. "Harvard students already know how to write successful Harvard applications, Al. We want you to teach them something new."

Harvard was right where I wanted it. "How about if the topic is: How to Research My Book?"

"Sure," Harvard said. "Most of our professors teach that course. Why, in the Biochemistry department, most of the graduate level courses are—"

Harvard was boring me. "I gotta run, Harvard. Thanks."

From among the seven hundred students who applied for my study group, I chose fourteen intellectual heavyweights. Some undergraduates, some from the prestigious Kennedy School of Government, and one from the Harvard School of Dentistry, just in case. This was TeamFranken. Like the X-Men, each had his own special power. And each had a story.

There was Bridger McGaw, a Gore campaign veteran still sore from getting burned in Florida. Madhu Chugh, with a mind as insatiable as her name is unpronounceable. Emmy Berning, an ultra-feminist with a stunning résumé—and a figure to match. Ben Kane and Ben Wikler, "the Bens," TeamFranken's gay gladiators, whose fierce love for each other fueled their ceaseless advocacy of justice for gays, lesbians, the transgendered, bisexuals, and man-on-dog enthusiasts, such as Pennsylvania senator Rick Santorum. And the rest.

There were fourteen in all. Tough, smart, and deeply committed to coming to my Cambridge apartment once a week to eat a delicious hot meal cooked by my wife, Franni.

I felt like I had fourteen children. My fourteen Harvard research assistants. And like every good parent, I loved each in a different way. Some I loved like the irrepressibly mischievous child who doesn't do his homework. Others I loved like the good, deserving child who does all of his homework, mows the lawn, and ghostwrites the chapters. And still others I loved "more" than the rest, the way a parent secretly chooses favorites and undermines the self-confidence of the others.

No, I wasn't a perfect leader. But what counts for me, and I hope for you, the reader, is that this book brings to a new level the politics of personal destruction that have come to define our era. Because with fourteen researchers, I could do something that my targets seem incapable of doing—get my facts straight. Nothing highlighted the need for painstaking research and fact-checking more than the hiring process itself, which I had conducted on the basis of hearsay and guesswork. For example, the "Bens" turned out not to be gay. And one, Owen, wasn't even named Ben.

Thanks to TeamFranken, you can rest assured that almost

every fact in this book is correct. Either that, or it's a joke. If you think you've found something that rings untrue, you've probably just missed a hilarious joke, and should blame yourself rather than me or TeamFranken.

Enjoy.

**God** chose me to write this book.

Just the fact that you are reading this is proof not just of God's existence, but also of His/Her/Its beneficence. That's right. I am not certain of God's precise gender. But I am certain that He/She/It chose me to write this book.

This isn't hubris. I'm not saying this in an egotistical way. God didn't choose me because I'm the greatest writer who ever lived. That was William Shakespeare, whose work I have a passing familiarity with. No. I just happened to be the right vessel at the right time. If something in this book makes you laugh, it was God's joke. If something makes you think, it's because God had a good point to make.

The reason I know God chose me is because God spoke to me personally.

God began our conversation by clearing something up. Some of George W. Bush's friends say that Bush believes God called him to be president during these times of trial. But God told me that He/She/It had actually chosen Al Gore by making sure that Gore won the popular vote and, God thought, the electoral college. "THAT WORKED FOR EVERYONE ELSE," God said.

"What about Tilden?" I asked, referring to the 1876 debacle.

"QUIET!" God snapped. God was angry.

God said that after 9/11, George W. Bush squandered a unique moment of national unity. That instead of rallying the country around a program of mutual purpose and sacrifice, Bush cynically used the tragedy to solidify his political power and pursue an agenda that panders to his base and serves the interests of his corporate backers.

God told me that Bush squandered a $4.6 trillion surplus and is plunging us into deficits as far as God can see. And that Bush squandered another surplus. The surplus of goodwill from the rest of the world that he had inherited from Bill Clinton.

And this was pissing God off.

He/She/It was right. But it sounded like a lot of work.

"Look, God, I'm flattered, but I think you got the wrong guy. The kind of book you're talking about would require months of research."

And God said, "LET THERE BE GOOGLE. AND LET THERE BE LEXISNEXIS."

"Very funny, God. I use Google all the time."

"YES, I KNOW," God said. "FOR HOT ASIAN TEENS."

"You must be thinking of my son, Joe."

"AL? I'M OMNISCIENT."

"Okay, okay." I changed the subject. "It's just that I can't do this book myself."

"LEAVE THAT TO ME," God boomed.

And that's when Harvard called.


I had my Nexis, I had my Google, I had my Harvard fellowship, and I had my fourteen research assistants. I sat down to write. Nothing.

So I got on my knees and prayed for guidance. "How, God, can I best do Your work through this book? Who, dear Lord, is the audience for a book like this? And what's a good title?"

God answered, "YOU KNOW THOSE SHITTY BOOKS BY ANN COULTER AND BERNIE GOLDBERG?"

"The best-sellers that claim there's a liberal bias in the media?" I asked.

"TOTAL BULLSHIT," God said. "START BY ATTACKING THEM. HE'S CLEARLY A DISGRUNTLED FORMER EMPLOYEE, AND SHE JUST LIES. BY THE WAY, THERE'S SOMETHING SERIOUSLY WRONG WITH HER."

"That's pretty obvious."

"SO GO AFTER THEM, THE WHOLE LIBERAL BIAS MYTH, AND THEN GO AFTER THE RIGHT-WING MEDIA. ESPECIALLY FOX."

"Okay, God, I'm writing this down."

"THEN USE THEM AS A JUMPING-OFF POINT TO GO AFTER BUSH. YOU KNOW, BIG TAX CUTS FOR THE RICH, SURGING UNEMPLOYMENT, IGNORING EVERYONE BUT HIS CORPORATE BUDDIES, SCREWING THE ENVIRONMENT, PISSING OFF THE REST OF THE WORLD. THAT STUFF. AND THAT'S YOUR BOOK."

"Got it. One last thing. Title."

"HOW ABOUT *BEARERS OF FALSE WITNESS AND THE FALSE WITNESS THAT THEY BEAR*?"

"Hmm. I, uh, I'll work with that."

# 1
# Hummus

**Asking** whether there is a liberal or conservative bias to the mainstream media is a little like asking whether al Qaeda uses too much oil in their hummus. The problem with al Qaeda is that they're trying to kill us.

The right-wing media tells us constantly that the problem with the mainstream media is that it has a liberal bias. I don't think it does. But there are other, far more important, biases in the mainstream media than liberal or conservative ones. Most of these biases stem from something called "the profit motive." This is why we often see a bias toward the Sensational, involving Scandal, and, hopefully Sex or Violence, or please, please, *pleeeze*, both.

And there's the Easy-and-Cheap-to-Cover bias, which is why almost all political coverage is about process and horse race and not about policy. Why have an in-depth report on school vouchers when two pundits who've spent five minutes in the green room looking over a couple of articles Xeroxed by an intern can just scream at each other about the issue on the air?

There's the Get-It-First bias. Remember the 2000 election? I believe there were some problems there associated with that one.

Pack Mentality. Negativity. Soft News. The Don't-Offend-the-Conglomerate-That-Owns-Us bias. And, of course, the ever-present bias of Hoping There's a War to Cover.

Does the mainstream media have a liberal bias? On a couple of things, maybe. Compared to the American public at large, probably a slightly higher percentage of journalists, because of their enhanced power of discernment, realize they know a gay person or two, and are, therefore, less frightened of them.

By the same token, I'll bet the media were biased during the Scopes monkey trial. But they were professionals and gave the Noah's Ark side a fair shake.

But to believe there is a liberal political bias in the mainstream media, you'd have to either not be paying attention or just be very susceptible to repetition. Yes, we've heard it over and over and over again. For decades. The media elite is an arm of the Democratic National Committee.

Anyone notice the mainstream media's coverage of Clinton? For eighteen months, it was all Monica, all the time. There were just a few news organizations that did not succumb to this temptation, and I like to cite them whenever I can: *Sailing* magazine, *American Grocer Monthly, Juggs,* and *Big Butt* (which is ironic, because I think *Big Butt* had a story).

How about the 2000 presidential campaign? Remember in the first debate, Al Gore said he had gone down to a disaster site in Texas with Federal Emergency Management Agency director James Lee Witt? Actually, it turned out that he had gone to that disaster with a *deputy* of James Lee Witt. As vice president, Gore had gone to seventeen *other* disasters with James Lee Witt, but not that one. The press jumped all over him. There were scores of stories written about how Gore had *lied* about James Lee Witt. It was as if James Lee Witt had been the most popular man in the United States of America and Gore was lying to get some of that James Lee Witt magic to rub off on him.

Contrast that with the media's reaction to this Bush description of his tax cut in the very same debate. Bush said, "I also dropped the bottom rate from fifteen percent to ten percent, because, by far, the vast majority of the help goes to the people at the bottom end of the economic ladder."

"By far, the vast majority . . . goes to the people at the bottom." That is what George W. Bush told America. The truth is that *the bottom 60 percent got 14.7 percent.* Gee, that's a pretty significant misstatement, don't you think? More important than whether a Texas fire was one of the seventeen disasters you went to with American icon James Lee Witt. So what was the reaction of the liberal mainstream press?

Nothing.

Do I believe that this was because the mainstream media has a *conservative* bias? No. I just think the attitude of the press was "He doesn't know! He doesn't know! Leave the man alone! He doesn't know!"

But, of course, he did. Which is why George W. Bush said he doesn't mind being "misunderestimated." Because by "misunderestimated," Bush means being underestimated for the wrong reason. The media thought he was kind of stupid. He isn't. He's just shamelessly dishonest.

The mainstream media does not have a liberal bias. And for all their other biases mentioned above, the mainstream media—ABC, CBS, NBC, CNN, *The New York Times,* the *Washington Post, Time, Newsweek,* and the rest—at least *try* to be fair.

There is, however, a right-wing media. You know who they are. Fox News. The *Washington Times.* The *New York Post.* The editorial pages of the *Wall Street Journal.* Talk radio. They are biased. And they have an agenda.

The members of the right-wing media are not interested in conveying the truth. That's not what they're for. They are an indispensable component of the right-wing machine that has taken over our country. They employ a tried-and-true methodology. First, they concoct an inflammatory story that serves their political goals. ("Al Gore's a liar.") They repeat it. ("Al Gore lies again!") They embellish it. ("Are his lies pathological, or are they merely malicious?") They try to push it into the mainstream media. All too often, they succeed. ("Tall Tales: Is What We've Got Here a Compulsion to Exaggerate?" *New York Times,* October 15, 2000.) Occasionally, they fail. (Despite their efforts, the mainstream media never picked up the Clinton-as-murderer stories.) But even their failures serve their agenda, as evidence of liberal bias. Win-win. You got to admit. It's a good racket.

They used these tactics to cripple Clinton's presidency. They used them to discredit Gore and put Bush into office. And they're using them now to silence Bush's critics. Bush is getting away with murder—just like Clinton did. See? That's how insidious the right-wing *modus operandi* is. Even I bought into the Clinton murder thing there for a second. And that's my point. We have to be vigilant.

And we have to be more than vigilant. We have to fight back. We have to expose those who bear false witness for the false witness bearers that they are. And we have to do it in a straightforward, plainspoken way. Let's call them what they are: liars. Lying, lying liars.

Hence the title of this book: *Al Franken Tells It Like It Is.*

## 2
# Ann Coulter: Nutcase

**I know.** You think the chapter title is a little harsh. But, believe me, in Coulter's case, "nutcase" is more than justified. I should know. You see, Ann and I are friends.

I personally wasn't aware of that myself until I read it in the *New York Observer*. They did a profile of Coulter when her bile-filled, relentlessly ugly best-seller *Slander* topped *The New York Times* list. And for some reason—I guess to establish her bona fides as just a lovable gal about town—she told the writer from the *Observer* that she was "friendly with" Al Franken.

I found that odd. I have met Ann Coulter *once*. At a *Saturday Night Live* party. When she introduced herself to me, I made what in retrospect was a terrible mistake. Instead of saying, "Ann Coulter! You're a horrible person. Ooooh, I just hate you!" or something along those lines—instead, *I was cordial.* For maybe a minute or two.

That is the sum total of my personal interaction with Ann Coulter. And yet, to her, it was enough to include me on a very short list of people she's "friendly with." Pathetic, to be sure, but no more dishonest than every other word that comes out of this woman.

Coulter, for those of you lucky enough to not have been exposed to her, is the reigning diva of the hysterical right. Or rather, the hysterical diva of the reigning right. Coulter has appeared on shows like ABC's *This Week, Good Morning America, Hardball, Larry King Live,* and *The Today Show,* to complain, among other things, that conservatives don't get on TV enough. Her books, like her TV appearances, consist of nonstop rabid frothing. Her first, *High Crimes and Misdemeanors: The Case Against Bill Clinton,* put her on the radar as an up-and-coming liar.

Her next book, *Slander: Liberal Lies About the American Right,* argues that liberals use lies and shrill accusations to debase political discourse in America. It's a fascinating exercise in dishonesty, hypocrisy, and irony of the unintentional sort.

Let's get right to some examples. And there are examples and examples and examples. Take the dramatic conclusion of *Slander*. After 206 pages of accusing liberals of, among other awful things, being elitist snobs, she trots out her crowning piece of evidence: proof of *The New York Times*'s disregard and contempt for what real Americans care about.

> The day after seven-time NASCAR Winston Cup champion Dale Earnhardt died in a race at the Daytona 500, almost every newspaper in America carried the story on the front page. Stock-car racing had been the nation's fastest-growing sport for a decade, and NASCAR the second-most-watched sport behind the NFL. More Americans recognize the name Dale Earnhardt than, say, Maureen Dowd. (Manhattan liberals are dumbly blinking at that last sentence.) It took *The New York Times* two days to deem Earnhardt's death sufficiently important to mention it on the first page. Demonstrating the left's renowned populist touch, the article began, "His death brought a silence to the Wal-Mart." The *Times* went on to report that in vast swaths of the country people watch stock-car racing. Tacky people were mourning Dale Earnhardt all over the South!

Pretty powerful indictment, I have to admit. No mention for two days! One small problem. Dale Earnhardt died on February 18, 2001. On February 19, 2001, which by my calculation is the next day, the *Times* ran a front-page account of Earnhardt's death written by sportswriter Robert Lipsyte under the headline: "Stock Car Star Killed on Last Lap of Daytona 500." Here. Look at it.

Frankly, I think the fact that *The New York Times* did have a front-page article on Dale Earnhardt the day after he died kind of undercuts her point that they didn't. Don't you? I mean, if they didn't, that would have been something, huh? But they did.

*see!*

# The New York Times

Late Edition

NEW YORK, MONDAY, FEBRUARY 19, 2001

VOL. CL . . . No. 51,669

75 CENTS

## A Message in Eroding Glacial Ice: Humans Are Turning Up the Heat

By ANDREW C. REVKIN

At night, the Harlem block, with its lingering drug trade, can feel as it did in the old days.

## Beneath New Surface, an Undertow

By AMY WALDMAN

### AN AMERICAN BLOCK
Life on 120th Street

*Second of three articles*

## IN LAYOFF PLANS, REALITY IS OFTEN LESS SEVERE IN U.S.

### MANY CUTS ARE OVERSEAS

Attrition and Creation of New Jobs Help Limit Damage to Economy, Analysts Say

By DAVID LEONHARDT

## Clinton's Defense of Pardons Brings Even More Questions

By JOSEPH KAHN

WASHINGTON, Feb. 18 —

## Pakistani Tale of a Drug Addict's Blasphemy

By BARRY BEARAK

PESHAWAR, Pakistan, Feb. 15 —

## Stock Car Star Killed on Last Lap of Daytona 500

By ROBERT LIPSYTE

DAYTONA BEACH, Fla., Feb. 18 —

The No. 3 car of Dale Earnhardt Sr. hitting the wall at Turn 4 as Ken Schrader's car rams into it from behind during yesterday's Daytona 500.

*see!*

### INSIDE

**Balthus Dies**

The reclusive Internationally known painter, shown in a 1958 photograph and in a 1935 self-portrait titled the called "The King of Cats," was 92.   PAGE B8

**No Welcome for Kurds**

The 300 Kurds rescued from a beached freighter after a horrific voyage were expected to seek refuge in France, but officials were leery of granting it.   PAGE A9

**Eddie Mathews Is Dead**

The Braves' Hall of Fame third baseman, who hit 512 home runs and teamed up with Hank Aaron to form baseball's leading power-hitting combination, was 69.   PAGE B7

### News Summary

A-2

Arts                    C1-12
Business Day           C1-12
Editorial, Op-Ed      A24-25
National                A3-7
Metro                   B1-4
International            A8-9
SportsMonday           D1-16

Obituaries ... B7-8   Weather ... A28

Classified Ads ... C13   Auto Exchange ... D4

*Updated news: www.nytimes.com*

**William H. Masters, Expert on Sex, Dies**

Dr. William H. Masters, who with his co-researcher, Virginia E. Johnson, revolutionized the way sex is studied, taught and enjoyed in America, died Friday at a hospice in Tucson. He was 85.

*Obituary, Page B7.*

And, by the way, the article that Coulter refers to? The one written two days later? It was by Rick Bragg,[1] a Pulitzer Prize winner who grew up in Piedmont, Alabama. Boy, I hate those Piedmont snobs! It's always "Piedmont has the best this and Piedmont has the best that." Yeah, well, fuck you, Piedmont!

Where did Ann Coulter come from? Well, she's a lawyer, one of the "elves" who helped Paula Jones go after Bill Clinton. That's a feather in her cap. She was born in 1961. Or 1963. Depending on whether you believe her old Connecticut driver's license (1961) or her newer D.C. driver's license (1963). (The *Washington Post* looked into this.) Ann claims the D.C. license is correct, which means that when she registered to vote she was sixteen. (The *Post* checked with the New Canaan, Connecticut, registrar's office.) That, of course, would be voter fraud.

Either way, she lied on at least one of her driver's licenses, a government I.D., which is a violation of federal law under the Patriot Act. I believe she could be locked up indefinitely for that without being allowed to talk to a lawyer or a judge. Or Paula Zahn.

Now, lots of women lie about their age. But it raises a concern about Coulter (if that really is her name). Coulter's misstatements about her age make us question the veracity of the seemingly factual statements in her book, such as:

- "Liberals hate America."

- "Liberals hate all religions except Islam."

- "Democrats actually hate working-class people."

- "Liberals hate society."

---

[1]Bragg resigned from *The New York Times* after using an uncredited TeamBragg to research a story on oyster men in Apalachicola, Florida. Rick Bragg, the pride and subsequent shame of Piedmont, Alabama.

- "Even Islamic terrorists don't hate America like liberals do."

- "Democrats . . . will destroy anyone who stands in their way. All that matters to them is power."

- "Liberals can't just come out and say they want to take more of our money, kill babies, and discriminate on the basis of race."

- "Liberals seek to destroy sexual differentiation in order to destroy morality."

- "That's the whole point of being a liberal: to feel superior to people with less money."

- "Liberals are crazy."

All this seems the slightest bit odd considering that the first line of the first page of *Slander* is "Political 'debate' in this country has become insufferable." And she explains, "Instead of actual debate about ideas and issues with real consequences, the country is trapped in a political discourse that resembles professional wrestling."

So what is Coulter's contribution to civilizing our political discourse? Well, in the entire 206 pages, she never actually makes a case for *any* conservative issue. Not school vouchers, not supply-side tax cuts, not privatization of Social Security. The entire book is filled with distortions, factual errors, and vicious invective—slander, if you will—bolstered by the shoddiest research this side of the Hitler diaries.

Take, for example, this gem from page 68. To support her claim that the mainstream media is in the hands of lefties, Coulter makes the point that *Newsweek* Washington bureau chief Evan Thomas "is the son of Norman Thomas, a four-time Socialist candidate for president." Actually, Norman Thomas was the Socialist candidate *six* times, running first in 1928 with a radical proposal for something called "Social Security." It's odd that Coulter understates the number of times that Thomas was the Socialist party nominee, because that would make her argument that much stronger. *If* Norman Thomas had been Evan Thomas's father. Which he was not.

Now, in fairness to Coulter, this kind of research is tough to do. I asked TeamFranken how someone might be able to find out something like that. There were a number of suggestions. Google search. Nexis search. Go into *The New York Times* archives for the obit. Then one of the kids hit on a simple, yet quite brilliant idea. Why not *call* Evan Thomas?

Just for future reference, Ann, here's a transcript of my call with Evan Thomas:

> **ME:** Evan, thank you for taking my call.
>
> **EVAN THOMAS:** No problem, Al. What's up?
>
> **ME:** Was Norman Thomas your father?
>
> **EVAN:** No.

That sounds simple enough. But to protect my reputation for thoroughness, I didn't let Evan off the hook quite so fast.

> **ME:** Are you sure?
>
> **EVAN:** Yes.
>
> **ME:** And your father? What was his name?
>
> **EVAN:** Evan Thomas, Sr. I'm a junior.
>
> **ME:** Uh-huh? And your father, Evan Thomas, Sr., did *he* ever run for president?
>
> **EVAN:** No. He was in publishing.

**ME:** And you're sure?

**EVAN:** Yes. Al, is this about that Ann Coulter thing?

**ME:** Yeah.

**EVAN:** I heard about that. Is there something wrong with her?

Yes, there is. Particularly considering that when going after the book publishing industry, Coulter complains that "liberal jeremiads make it to print without the most cursory fact-checking." (Which reminds me, I really should be fact-checking this thing as I go along.)[i]

Actually, I do take great pains in my research. In my last book of this nature, a little number one *New York Times* best-seller entitled *Rush Limbaugh Is a Big Fat Idiot and Other Observations,* only one claim was arguably inaccurate, and I am pleased to be the first person to point it out publicly. In writing the book, I cited preliminary findings from a study by Kathleen Hall Jamieson regarding the political literacy of radio talk show listeners. In the final version of the study, the findings showed that people who listened regularly to political talk radio were able to identify the President more frequently than I had given them credit for. I regret the error.

Even John Fund, Limbaugh's ghostwriter on *The Way Things Ought to Be,* acknowledged to me, a bit grudgingly, that I had done an honest, though thoroughly vicious, job on his guy.

Coulter, however, has spawned a cottage industry of *Slander* debunkers, some of whom—dailyhowler.com, spinsanity.org, and Salon.com—I am cribbing from.

Coulter's defense, heard in countless appearances on talk shows, is "I have footnotes," or "There are thirty-five pages of footnotes," or "I have 780 footnotes," or "It's in the footnotes." There's a big emphasis on footnotes. Which brings me to:

# How to Lie with Footnotes

**HOW TO LIE WITH FOOTNOTES #1:**
**• DON'T HAVE FOOTNOTES**

Ann Coulter doesn't have 780 footnotes in *Slander*. She has zero footnotes. None. Not one footnote. She does have thirty-five pages of *endnotes*. Footnotes are easy to reference. They're at the bottom, or the "foot," of the page.[2]

Endnotes are much harder to reference.[ii] If you are using your "footnotes" to lie, make them endnotes.

**HOW TO LIE WITH FOOTNOTES #2:**
**• HAVE 780 OF THEM**

Coulter knows that her readers, the ones who buy her books out of an obsessive need to read stuff that reconfirms everything they already know or think they know, are probably not going to check one, let alone 780, of her endnotes.

Let me illustrate how Coulter exploits this simple principle of lying with footnotes (endnotes) from page 12 of *Slander*. This is a good one, and in a way, sort of sums up everything you need to know. (Just so there's no confusion, the endnote numbers are hers.)

> After Supreme Court Justice Clarence Thomas wrote an opinion contrary to the *clearly* expressed position of *The New York Times* editorial page, the *Times* responded with an editorial on Thomas titled, "The Youngest, Cruelest Justice." That was actually the headline on a lead editorial in the Newspaper of Record. Thomas is not engaged on the substance of his judicial philosophy. He is called a "colored lawn jockey for conservative white interests," "race traitor," "black snake," "chicken-and-biscuit-eating Uncle Tom,"[39] "house Negro" and "handkerchief head," "Benedict

[2]Like this.

Arnold"[40] and "Judas Iscariot."[41] All this from the tireless opponents of intolerance.

Okay. What percentage of Coulter's readers do you suppose read
this and thought, "My God! The *New York Times* called Clarence
Thomas 'a chicken-and-biscuit-eating Uncle Tom'! I knew the
*Times* was bad, but I never *dreamed* it was this bad!"? High
nineties? And what percentage do you think bothered to go to the
back of her book and wade through the endnotes to discover that
the quotes came from a *Playboy* interview with former Surgeon
General Joycelyn Elders and from a black leader at a meeting of the
Southern Christian Leadership Conference who was quoted in *The
New Yorker.*

The key here, of course, is the sleight of hand—". . . editorial
in the Newspaper of Record. Thomas is not engaged . . ."—that deliberately leads gullible readers to the conclusion that the *Times*
called Clarence Thomas "a colored lawn jockey." This should tell
us a couple things about Ann Coulter. First, she's dishonest. No
surprise there. But more importantly, it shows the contempt she
holds for her own readers.

**HOW TO LIE WITH FOOTNOTES #3:**
**• CITE A SOURCE, BUT TOTALLY MISREPRESENT**
  **WHAT IT SAYS**

She really works this one into the ground. Early in the book
she writes: "*New York Times* columnist Frank Rich demanded that
Ashcroft stop monkeying around with Muslim terrorists and con-
centrate on anti-abortion extremists." Except he didn't. In the column, written during the anthrax scare, Rich simply criticized
Ashcroft's refusal to meet with Planned Parenthood, which has
had years of experience with terrorism in the form of bombings
and sniper attacks from pro-life extremists. The piece doesn't include the words "monkeying" or "Islamic" or "Muslim," or make
any suggestion that Justice abandon its efforts against al Qaeda.

Coulter pulls this wild distortion, like so very, very many, directly out of her ass.

Just another quick one. On page 118 (by the way, when you see Coulter on TV, interviewers never ask her about anything past page 12. You've got to give me credit for being able to stomach the entire screed), she writes that when the media consortium study on the 2000 Florida vote was released, it showed "that Bush had won on any count." But the *Washington Post* story she cites says that the "Study Finds Gore Might Have Won Statewide Tally of All Uncounted Ballots." The reason there are so many capital letters in that quote is that it is from the headline of the story.

Don't you go to hell for this stuff?

**HOW TO LIE WITH FOOTNOTES #4:**
**• USE THE "ANY WORDS WRITTEN IN A NEWSPAPER**
  **CAN BE ATTRIBUTED TO THAT NEWSPAPER" TECHNIQUE**

(This can also be used to defame newscasts and magazines.) To show just how much the media elite hates Christians, Coulter writes:

> For decades, *The New York Times* had allowed loose associations between Nazis and Christians to be made in its pages. Statements like these were not uncommon: "Did the Nazi crimes draw on Christian tradition?" . . . "the church is 'co-responsible' for the holocaust. . . ."

Okay. The first quote ("Did the Nazi crimes draw on Christian tradition?") is from a 2000 *book review*. The *Times* reviewer, Paul Berman, was framing the question asked by the book he was reviewing, which was about a four-hundred-year-old play performed every ten years in Bavaria that portrays Jews as hateful and evil. Which, for the record, we are not.

The second quote is a *quote of a quote* from a 1998 *Times* article, "John Paul's Jewish Dilemma." The writer for the *Times* isn't saying that the church is "co-responsible" for the holocaust. He's quoting a critic of the church. In the same article, a Jewish historian is also quoted saying that "[Pope] Pius saved 750,000 Jews."

You really have to keep on your toes with Ann. In her next book, Coulter will probably write, "Al Franken says Jews are 'hateful and evil.'" Look for the endnote.

## HOW TO LIE WITH FOOTNOTES #5:
## • OVERLOAD A LEXISNEXIS SEARCH

For those of you unfamiliar with LexisNexis, it is a state-of-the-art research tool/journalistic crutch. Like any powerful instrument, LexisNexis searches can be manipulated to produce misleading results. It's like a chainsaw, which can be used productively (say, as a prop in a movie like *The Texas Chainsaw Massacre*), but can also be used for evil (such as in an actual chainsaw massacre). Throughout this book, I use LexisNexis productively. In *Slander,* Coulter uses it to dismember the truth. Introducing . . . the Overloaded LexisNexis Search.

On page 8 of *Slander,* Coulter refers to a controversial 1994 Christmas Day speech given by Jesse Jackson on British TV. "*The New York Times* did not report the speech," she complains. Checking the endnote reveals her methodology. "LexisNexis search of *New York Times* archives from December 1994 through January 1995 for 'Jesse Jackson and Germany and fascism and South Africa' produces no documents." Well, yeah.

A more reasonable search (Jesse Jackson and Christmas and Britain) shows that, yes, of course, the *Times* did run an article on December 20 about the controversy using excerpts of Jackson's speech, which was prerecorded.

Using Coulter's technique, I can prove that no newspaper has ever covered anything. For example, I can prove the *Washington Times* did not cover the incident in which George H. W. Bush threw up on the Japanese prime minister. A LexisNexis search from January 1992 for "Bush and Japan and prime minister and lap and cookies and tossed" produces no documents.

## HOW TO LIE WITH FOOTNOTES #6:
## • JUST MAKE SHIT UP

From page 134 of *Slander:* "Even during the media's nightly flogging of Iran-Contra, Reagan's approval ratings fell only 5 percentage points, from 80 percent to 75 percent." The endnote cites a *Christian Science Monitor* article from January 7, 1987. The article reports that "in last month's Gallup poll, Reagan's approval rating fell from 63 percent to 47 percent." And remember, this is from people who are not only Christian, but also scientists.

So that's how you lie with footnotes. Disgusting, huh? But it's not just you who thinks so. Even people Coulter considers friends say she's "a lying bitch,"[3] "a horror show of epic proportions,"[4] "oh, the poor thing,"[5] and "a bitch."[6]

---

[3]Me, to my wife.
[4]Ibid.
[5]My wife, to me.
[6]Me, to another friend.

# 3
# You Know Who I Don't Like?
# Ann Coulter

**I'm** sorry to do this to you. But I've just left so much good stuff out of the previous chapter. I told a friend that going after Coulter is like shooting fish in a barrel. He said, "I've never shot fish in a barrel. But I could imagine that after a while it could get boring."

So, I'll try to keep this short. First, a few more highlights:

- After 9/11, she wrote in her column, which now appears on the prestigious Internet: "We should invade their countries, kill their leaders, and convert them to Christianity."

- In the very same *New York Observer* article in which she called me a friend, Coulter joked to the reporter, "My only regret with Timothy McVeigh is he did not go to *The New York Times* building." Get it?

- To show there were no hard feelings, the *Times* invited her to comment on the Trent Lott controversy. She responded, "I don't remember liberals being this indignant about the 9/11 terrorist attacks."

Remember, this is coming from a woman who says "political 'debate' in this country is insufferable. . . . It's all liberals' fault."

Coulter believes that the rules don't apply to her. Anything she accuses liberals of doing, she can do herself, in spades.

Take her chapter, "The Joy of Arguing with Liberals: *You're Stupid!*" The premise: "If liberals were prevented from ever again calling Republicans dumb, they would be robbed of half their arguments. . . . This is how six-year-olds argue: They call everything 'stupid.'"

Let's look at some of the arguments this grown-up makes.

- Christie Whitman is a "birdbrain."

- Katie Couric is "an airhead."

- Adlai Stevenson was "a boob."

- Gerald Ford was "a little dumb."

- New Mexico Governor Gary Johnson is "truly stupid."

- Oh, in addition to being a "birdbrain," Christie Whitman is also a "dim-wit."

- Maine Senator Susan Collins is a "half-wit."

- And so is "half-wit" Jim Jeffords, the Vermont senator who defected from the Republican party. He's also "D-U-M-M."

And what really burns Coulter is that, in the fawning liberal media,

> Jim Jeffords's degree from Yale cannot be cited often enough. (And consider that Jeffords got into Yale long before the terrorizing regime of the SATs, back when admission to the Ivy Leagues turned on social class rather than stan-dardized tests.)

Quick. Yale, low SATs, social class? You thinking about who I'm thinking about?

Yet, on page 33, how does Coulter answer people who think our president may not be the brightest star in the firmament? Why, he "graduated from Yale College and Harvard Business School."

So consistency is not the woman's strong point. Take, for example, Chapter Two, "The Gucci Position on Domestic Policy," where we're told that "liberals thrive on the attractions of snobbery" and that "Democrats actually hate working-class people"!

Later Coulter calls the phrase "working families" "a euphemism for families in which no one works."

Does that seem maybe the tiniest bit elitist to you? And can you imagine just how hard Ann Coulter works! It takes time and effort to find stuff to take out of context, to make up or distort things that *The New York Times* did or did not print, to devise overloaded Nexis searches, to . . . wait a minute. No, that's wrong. I've been doing a lot of fact-checking and such (or at least Team-Franken has), and by God, it's a lot more work than just making shit up. No, come to think of it, Coulter is just plain lazy.

But then again, like any movement conservative, Coulter is a firm believer in the free market. By definition, anything that succeeds in "the marketplace of ideas," like her books, must inherently be of value. And, therefore, unlike members of working families, she really does work for a living.

Here's something to think about, though. A friend of mine works in the hotel industry. About 65 percent of the movies that are ordered in hotels are "adult movies." Clearly, two blondes going down on each other is a real winner in the marketplace of ideas. My all-time favorite stat: The average length of time those movies are on is . . . twelve minutes. That is my favorite statistic in life.

What Coulter writes is political pornography. She aims directly at her readers' basest instincts. Pornography may serve as a welcome release for Republican businessmen on the road, and as a profit center for Marriott, Hyatt, Sheraton, Radisson, and other big GOP donors, but it doesn't pretend to be something it's not. That's why the titles don't appear on your bill.

Though it may surprise you, I have a great deal of respect for many conservatives in the media. Terry Bradshaw, for example. And what shocked me most following the publication of *Slander* was the silence from those conservatives who complain about the ugliness of political discourse in this country.

Liberals don't hate America. We love America more than Ann Coulter does. I love it enough to engage my readers honestly.

As I was putting this book to bed, Coulter's new book, *Treason: Liberal Treachery from the Cold War to the War on Terrorism*, slithered onto the shelves. All indications are that it will be a best-seller. Based on TeamFranken's preliminary analysis, I can tell you she's done it again. But in lieu of a full-blown dissection, for now, I will dispense with *Treason* with a limerick.

> *A woman named Coulter cried "Treason."*
> *She did it without any reason.*
> *Though we know that she lied,*
> *'Twas perhaps justified:*
> *On her brain, I'm afraid, there's a lesion.*

I'm sorry if that sounds a little cheap, but I couldn't find a rhyme for "Julius Rosenberg."

# Addendum to Ann Coulter Chapter

**As** I mentioned, I was unable to submit *Treason* to the painstaking analysis that I had applied to *Slander*. I ended up sticking *Treason* into my office bookcase for a rainy day when I wanted to torture myself.

About a week after I had handed in *Lies,* my wife and I went out for an early dinner. Going out the back door, Franni decided she wanted to put on some lipstick and headed back to our bedroom. Standing in my office now, I noticed *Treason* directly in front of me at eye level. Andy Barr, one of TeamFranken's finest members, was working as my assistant for the summer, and was seated at his desk nearby.

Taking *Treason* from the bookcase, I said, "Andy, I'll bet you I can find a lie in this piece of shit before Franni gets her lipstick on." Andy knew just what to do. He cranked up Nexis, and we were on our way.

I told Andy, "There's a lie on every page of her books, so I'll just open to a random page." Boom. I opened to page 265 and scanned down the page and saw a paragraph beginning with the words *"New York Times."* Boom. There's always a lie when Coulter mentions *The New York Times*.

I read the paragraph aloud, so that Andy could start typing the Nexis search terms the instant we found the lie.

> New York Times columnist Thomas Friedman sniffed that
> racial profiling was not "civilized." He blamed twenty years
> of relentless attacks by Muslim extremists on—I quote—
> "religious fundamentalists of any stripe."

I didn't have to say a word. Andy was on it: *New York Times* AND Friedman AND religious fundamentalists of any stripe. Boom. Nexis kicked out one article: Tom Friedman's December 26, 2001, column titled "Naked Air."

Its premise. Make everyone fly nude. Nexis had bolded the search terms, so my eye went right to the relevant passage. Right there in the second paragraph.

> Think about it. If everybody flew naked, not only would you never have to worry about the passenger next to you carrying box cutters or exploding shoes, but no **religious fundamentalists of any stripe** would ever be caught dead flying nude . . .

"He blamed twenty years of relentless attacks by Muslim extremists on—I quote—'religious fundamentalists of any stripe.'" Wow! I don't think Franni had even done her top lip yet.

In October of last year, Coulter "responded" to my charges on her web blog, where she wrote: "It's interesting that the most devastating examples of my alleged 'lies' keep changing. As soon as one is disproved, I'm asked to respond to another." Huh?

She proceeded. "I shall run through a few of the alleged 'lies' from Franken's book that I have already been asked to respond to—and which have now been dropped by the Coulter hysterics as they barrel ahead to the next inane charge." Huh?

Let's take a quick look at Coulter's defense.

> FRANKEN'S VERY FIRST CHARGE AGAINST ME IS THAT I TOLD A REPORTER FROM *THE OBSERVER* THAT I WAS "FRIENDLY" WITH FRANKEN, WHEN IN FACT, WE ARE NOT "FRIENDLY."

> Needless to say, I never claimed to be friendly with Al Franken. Inasmuch as I barely know Franken, a normal person might have looked at that and realized the reporter misunderstood me.

This comes under the heading of the effective "It's not true, so I couldn't possibly have said it to the reporter" school of denying a lie. Next.

FRANKEN HYSTERICALLY ACCUSES ME OF "LYING" FOR
CALLING MY "ENDNOTES," "FOOTNOTES" IN INTERVIEWS
ON MY BOOK.

Yes, notes at the end of a book are technically "endnotes,"
not "footnotes." Franken will have to take his case up with
*The New York Times,* the *LA Times* and *The Washington Post*
and the rest of the universe—all of which referred to my
780 endnotes as "FOOTNOTES." Also, God for inventing the
concept of "colloquial speech."

Now, this comes under Coulter's tried-and-true technique of
misrepresenting something, then attacking the misrepresentation.
As you know, I simply pointed out the distinction between "footnotes" and "endnotes" to illustrate how Coulter deceives her readers into believing that *The New York Times* called Clarence
Thomas a "chicken-and-biscuit-eating Uncle Tom." This leads
nicely into this one:

I CLAIM EVAN THOMAS'S FATHER WAS THE SOCIALIST
PARTY PRESIDENTIAL CANDIDATE, NORMAN THOMAS.

Franken drones on and on for a page and a half about how
Norman Thomas was not Evan Thomas's father—without
saying that he was Evan's *grandfather.*

Of course, I do say that Norman Thomas was Evan's grandfather. *In my endnotes.* The rest of Coulter's blog is equally shoddy
and obnoxious and not worth the expense of any more space.

There were a number of other blogs that accused me of lying
in this book. The most common accusations were pretty hilarious.
For example, Chapter 16 of this book is entitled "Operation Ignore" because it chronicles how the Bush administration disas-
trously ignored the threat from al Qaeda from the transition to

9/11. The conceit of an actual Operation Ignore became the throughline of the chapter as on page 129 where I write:

> On its 172nd day, Operation Ignore suffered a major blow. Already, the operation was becoming more and more difficult to sustain as the intensity of terror warnings crescendoed. Now, on August 6, CIA Director Tenet delivered a report to President Bush entitled, "Bin Laden Determined to Strike in U.S." The report warned that al Qaeda might be planning to hijack airplanes. But the President was resolute: Operation Ignore must proceed as planned. He did nothing to follow up on the memo.

Never underestimate either the literalness or just plain thickness of a right-wing blogger, one of whom wrote on a website dedicated to exposing lies in *Lies:* "At no time did the Bush administration institute an Operation Ignore. This is a lie."

The second most common tidbit used to prove my horrible dishonesty is from Chapter 27, The Lying Years. I point out how Bush lied in his acceptance speech at the Philadelphia convention when he said, "If called on by the commander in chief today, two entire divisions of the army would have to report, 'Not ready for duty, sir.' "

A few days later in a Senate Armed Services Committee hearing, Bush foreign policy advisor Richard Armitage sheepishly admitted to its chairman Carl Levin that those two divisions were in fact ready for duty. In chapter 27, I note that Armitage admitted they were, "[b]ut instead of apologizing, Armitage bolted from the hearing room, knocking over veteran reporter Helen Thomas, breaking her hip and jaw."

One enterprising, if dense, blogger even wrote Thomas, who confirmed that a bolting Armitage never broke her hip and jaw.

# Liberals Who Hate America

**That's** me with John Glenn on the second of three USO tours I've done because I hate America. We had just choppered onto the deck of the USS *Harry Truman*, named for our thirty-third president, a liberal America-hater of the worst sort. Can you tell which of us is more accustomed to wearing flight gear?

There's just one reference to Truman in *Slander:* "Truman got the country into Korea and couldn't get us out for two and half years." That's it. No Truman Doctrine, no Marshall Plan, no NATO.

John F. Kennedy receives a similarly fleeting mention. "Kennedy got the country into a war in Vietnam after the disastrous Bay of Pigs invasion and then sat passively by while the Russians built the Berlin Wall."

FDR gets whacked around a bit because he "spent eight years failing to get the country out of the Depression but then had the skill and foresight to allow the nation to be taken by surprise at Pearl Harbor." That's all we get on Roosevelt except that he called Stalin "Uncle Joe."

She's tough on us Democrats and "their [our] beloved Soviet Union."

Ronald Reagan, however, "singlehandedly won the Cold War." In fact, Reagan "won the Cold War" on page 33 (the same page on which Bush graduated from Yale College and Harvard Business School), on page 34, on page 124, then again on 130, 131, 134, and finally again on page 197.

If Ann Coulter were genuinely interested in finding out who singlehandedly won the Cold War, she should have called my old friend Marshal Viktor Kulikov, the former Warsaw Pact commander. In 1992, Kulikov told *U.S. News & World Report* that "Reagan was a logical extension of what had started with Truman, a concentrated effort to weaken and intimidate the Soviet Union."

Other people give credit for ending the Cold War to the Polish pope, John Paul II; to Lech Walesa and his independent trade union, Solidarity; to Jimmy Carter, who put pressure on Moscow to respect the human rights of its people; and to the Soviet Union itself, which was collapsing under the crushing weight of its own failed system. Reagan, of course, did put the medium-range Pershing II missiles in Europe and began developing the Rube Goldberg Star Wars missile defense system which protects us to this day.

So credit where credit is due. Viktor told me that Reagan's aggressive posture unquestionably hastened the inevitable collapse of the Soviet Union by a week to ten days.

Personally, I believe it was the Beatles who set the whole thing in motion. Once *The White Album* made it over the border hidden in the false bottom of an Aeroflot pilot's briefcase, it was only a matter of time.

You do a lot of traveling on USO tours. John Glenn and I flew to Ramstein Air Force Base in Germany, to Aviano Air Base in Italy, to the *Truman* somewhere in the Mediterranean, and to Eagle Base in Tuzla, Bosnia, Camp Able Sentry in Macedonia, and Camp Bondsteel in Kosovo. At each stop, I entertained the troops with anti-American jokes.

I got to spend a lot of time with Senator Glenn and his wife, Annie. I'd kid him a lot. Whenever we were just taking off in some cargo plane or helicopter, I'd say, "So, John, you nervous?"

He'd laugh. And as I, a fellow Democrat, began to gain his trust, Glenn opened up to me about just how much he hates America. I mean, by Coulter's standards, he had been an extremely liberal senator: pro-union, pro-choice, pro–Social Security, pro-Medicare. You know, all those anti-American things.

On the flight from Europe back to Andrews Air Force Base, I asked him, "John, tell me. Are you kind of embarrassed about the fifty-nine missions you flew as a Marine pilot in World War II? And the ninety combat missions you flew in Korea? And the five Distinguished Flying Crosses and nineteen Air Medals you earned?"

"Yeah," he cringed, "I'd just as soon not be reminded of all that."

"How about being the first American to orbit the Earth?"

"It makes me ashamed just to think about it," he said, bowing his head as we touched down at Andrews.

Whenever I think back to that day and Glenn's slumped, heaving shoulders, Annie vainly trying to comfort him, I am always amazed at just how large a burden one man can bear for all the things he has done for the country he hates.

# 5
# Loving America the Al Franken Way

**If** you listen to a lot of conservatives, they'll tell you that the difference between them and us is that conservatives love America and liberals hate America. That we "blame America first." That we're suspicious of patriotism and always think our country's in the wrong. As conservative radio and TV personality Sean Hannity says, we liberals "train our children to criticize America, not celebrate it."

They don't get it. We love America just as much as they do. But in a different way. You see, they love America the way a four-year-old loves her mommy. Liberals love America like grown-ups. To a four-year-old, everything Mommy does is wonderful and anyone who criticizes Mommy is bad. Grown-up love means actually understanding what you love, taking the good with the bad, and helping your loved one grow. Love takes attention and work and is the best thing in the world.

That's why we liberals want America to do the right thing. We know America is the hope of the world, and we love it and want it to do well. We also want it to do good.

When liberals look back on history, we see things we're very proud of. And we also see some things, which might have seemed like good ideas at the time, but turned out to be mistakes. And some things we did, well, they were just bad. That doesn't keep us from loving our country—it's *part* of loving our country. It's called honesty. What do you think is more important to a loving relationship: honesty or lies?

Here's what I mean. I've made a list that takes a good, hard, if quick, look at our great nation's history, pointing out the good and owning up to the bad. It's not meant to be a complete list. For example, I've left out the Gadsden Purchase of 1853, which was something of a mixed blessing. The list is more a bittersweet love song to the world's only remaining superpower, that majestic, though slightly flawed, country that I call home.

- Salem witch trials—**bad**

- Revolutionary War—**good**

- Slavery—**bad**

- Ending slavery—**good, but hard**

- Civil War reenactments—**weird**

- Massacring Native Americans and breaking our treaties with them—**bad**

- Indian casinos—**?**

- Child labor during the Industrial Revolution—**bad**

- Child labor mowing lawns and baby-sitting—**character-building**

- Labor movement creating the weekend—**good**

- Land grant universities—**hot**

- Rural electrification—**hotter**

- Social Security—**hottest!**

- Dictating pop culture for the world—**mixed**

- Selling Saddam Hussein chemical weapons in the eighties—**in retrospect, bad**

- Louisiana Purchase—**bargain**

- Grand Canyon—**wonderful, though we really can't take much credit for it—no, wait:**

- National park system—**really good**

- Leading human genome project—**probably good**

- Genetically engineering super race of unstoppable killers—**bad, but probably inevitable**

- Winning World War II—**wow!!!**

- Creating democracy in postwar Germany and Japan; laying groundwork for European peace and prosperity in second half of twentieth century—**right on!**

- The Greatest Generation—**greatest!**

- *The Greatest Generation*—**best-seller**

- Liberty—**good**

- Justice for all—**would be nice**

- Bill of Rights—**great! but Second Amendment could have been clearer**

- Putting man on the moon—**awesome, if true**

- Supporting vile dictatorships in Iran, Indonesia, Iraq, Dominican Republic, Guatemala, Congo, Paraguay, Haiti, El Salvador, Bolivia—**bad**

- Parades—**wholesome fun for whole family**

- Gay parades—**exuberant expressions of individuality often featuring highly imaginative floats and costumes**

- Conducting horrific medical experiments on African-Americans in Tuskegee—**bad**

- Japanese internment camps—**good. Wait, what were these?**

- Truman Doctrine—**smart**

- Vietnam—**mistake**

- Winning Cold War—**credit all around, to postwar Republican and Democratic presidents alike**

- Gross human rights violations in name of winning Cold War—**credit all around, except to Jimmy Carter**

- Women getting the vote—**good . . . *for women!* Just kidding. It's good for everybody!!!**

- African-Americans getting the vote—**good . . . *for African-Americans!* Kidding again. Good for Democrats!!!**

- Making mistakes—**bad, but inevitable**

- Correcting mistakes—**good, but not inevitable**

- Calling those who point out mistakes "unpatriotic"—**itself unpatriotic**

- Owning up to our mistakes—**brave**

- America—**home of the brave**

# 6

# I Bitch-Slap Bernie Goldberg

**In** January of 2003, I was asked to appear on the MSNBC show *Donahue* with Bernard Goldberg, the former CBS correspondent whose best-seller, *Bias: A CBS Insider Exposes How the Media Distorts the News,* purports to take on the liberal media bias. *Slander* and *Bias* are the right's one-two punch against the effete lefty elite.

The *Donahue* show was going to be taped live in front of a studio audience at Rockefeller Center in New York. I was in San Francisco making big money with one of my hilarious and well-received corporate speeches, and I hate appearing on these shows via satellite. It puts you at a disadvantage. Still, I had read Bernie's book a few months earlier, and I had a few problems with it. So I said yes.

A couple weeks after I did the show, I was stopped by a TV news producer (not from CBS) who said, "Man, you really bitch-slapped Bernie Goldberg."

Yeah, I did. But I have to admit, I did it a little unfairly. I ambushed Bernie. With his own book.

I asked him about something from his chapter, "Liberal Hate Speech." (Coulteresque, huh?) In the chapter, he cites twelve examples of "liberal hate speech" from the past twelve years. Goldberg admits he got them from the Media Research Center, a right-wing media-watch group which sends out a regular newsletter chock-full of "outrageous" quotes from the liberal media. Now, considering the hundreds of thousands of hours of mainstream media coverage over that period, you'd think Goldberg would have some pretty choice examples to pick from, right?

One of the twelve examples was a quote from John Chancellor, the late, revered NBC anchor and commentator. Here's how it appeared in *Bias.*

It's short of soap, so there are lice in hospitals. It's short
of pantyhose, so women's legs go bare. It's short of snow-
suits, so babies stay home in winter. Sometimes it's short
of cigarettes, so millions of people stop smoking involuntarily. It drives everyone crazy. The problem isn't communism. No one even talked about communism this week. The
problem is shortages.

—*NBC Nightly News* commentator
John Chancellor on the Soviet Union,
August 21, 1991

After presenting the quote, Goldberg tears Chancellor a new one
for "his absurd observation that the problem in the old Soviet
Union wasn't communism, but shortages."

Hmm. The quote was from August 1991. So, on *Donahue*, I
read the quote, then asked, "Do you know what happened that
day in the Soviet Union, Bernie?"

He froze. Then came back with a good one: "Why don't you
tell me?"

I had learned how to handle that trick in the schoolyard back
in Minnesota. "No," I said, "why don't you tell me?"

Clearly, the man had no idea. I persisted, "What happened in
the Soviet Union that day?"

Bernie went white. Finally, "Well, I don't know what happened
that day."

So, I told him. Let's go to the videotape:

**FRANKEN:** That was the collapse of the coup, the hard-liner
coup at the parliament.

**GOLDBERG:** And?

**FRANKEN:** And that was huge. Do you know that perestroika
had been in effect for six years at that point? The point here

is, Bernie, you regurgitated a quote that you got from some right-wing media-watch group. And you did not care to look at the context of it. Listen to how Tom Brokaw opened that evening's news.

"Good evening. Wednesday, August 21, 1991. This is a day for bold print in history to be remembered and savored as the day when the power of the people in the Soviet Union proved to be greater than the power of the gray and cold-blooded men who thought they could return that country to the darkness of state oppression."

Boy, it sounds like a real pro-communist bias on NBC, doesn't it? But you know what, Bernie? You didn't even bother to find out what the context of John Chancellor—who, by the way, is dead, and couldn't defend himself. You had no interest in finding out the context of what he was saying.

I was talking into a camera in San Francisco, so I couldn't see Bernie. But when I watched the tape later, I have to admit I got a real kick out of watching Bernie sitting there silently, stewing. He knew he looked like a fool, because I was right. He had thrown something in his book without checking it. Frankly, when I had first read the quote in Goldberg's book, I hadn't known the context either. I'm a comedian. But I had a sneaky suspicion that John Chancellor had never been a Stalinist.

So, *I*, the comedian, bothered to look it up and get the transcript for the August 21, 1991, *NBC Nightly News* broadcast. Brokaw had asked Chancellor about Gorbachev's next move. And what Chancellor was saying was that Gorbachev couldn't use communism as an excuse because, by that point, he had completely dismantled communism in the Soviet Union.

Alan Greenspan would have agreed with what Chancellor was saying. And yet Goldberg had accused John Chancellor of "liberal hate speech."

Now I'm on the satellite, asking Goldberg to respond. And he can't. So Phil turns to another guest, a right-wing radio talk show host named Jeff Whitaker, "Now, Mr. Whitaker, you wanted to say briefly?"

And Whitaker says, "As many examples as Al can pull out, I can pull out a lot of leads into the nightly news." What the hell does *that* mean? I was talking about Goldberg's book.

And that's when I started yelling from San Francisco, "I want to hear Bernie. This is about accountability."

But nothing from Bernie. And as Phil goes to commercial, I'm still shouting, "Phil, why are you letting Bernie off?" When I watched the tape a few days later, I realized I may have appeared just a bit aggressive.

A little later in the show, Donahue took a caller.

**DONAHUE:** Billy from Tennessee. You waited. I thank you for your patience. What did you want to say?

**CALLER:** Phil, thank you. I think the main thing I wanted to say is I'm sad that the conservatives you have on tonight have done a poor job of articulating our conservative argument, which I think is another bias of the press is that you always pick very smart, astute liberals, like Al Franken, who are very articulate, and then you have conservatives who scratch their heads and can't come back with something.

**DONAHUE:** Oh , well . . .

*(Laughter.)*

Still later, Donahue turned to Bernie and said, "You know, I think you've been wounded tonight, kid."

He had been wounded. But unfortunately, because I was three thousand miles away, I wasn't able to shake hands with him after the show and take him out for a drink. If I'd been there, that's exactly what I would have done. And sipping my sake bomb, I would have explained to him what a travesty his book is.

It really should have been called *Bias: A CBS Insider Exposes How CBS Didn't Give Him the Career He Wanted.* On 72 of the book's 232 pages, Goldberg settles scores with his old boss Dan Rather. A representative sample: "If CBS News were a prison instead of a journalistic enterprise, three quarters of the producers and 100 percent of the vice presidents would be [Rather's] bitches."

Besides settling scores, Goldberg draws upon his twenty-eight years of broadcast journalism experience to relate a few telling anecdotes in which people in the newsroom said something

> **Point/Betterpoint**
>
> I think Goldberg's most valid point is that reporters tend to have more liberal views than the public on social issues. In one case, Goldberg cites an eighteen-year-old *Los Angeles Times* survey of three thousand journalists nationwide showing that they have more liberal views than the general public on things like *gun control* (78 percent of journalists favored tougher controls eighteen years ago, while only half the public did), *prayer in public schools* (74 percent of the public said yes eighteen years ago; 75 percent of journalists said no), and the *death penalty* (eighteen years ago, 75 percent of the public supported it, versus only 47 percent of journalists).
>
> He fails, however, to explain that editors and publishers—who have the final say over what goes out—tend to be conservative. According to a study made in *this* century by *Editor and Publisher* magazine, more than twice as many newspapers endorsed Bush as endorsed Gore. Bush-endorsing papers accounted for 58 percent of all national circulation.

liberal-sounding. Apparently, at 12:36 P.M. on April 14, 1999, during a routine *CBS Weekend News* conference call, producer Roxanne Russell had the temerity to jokingly refer to Gary Bauer as a "little nut from the Christian group." (Full disclosure—Gary's a friend of mine, is small, a Christian, and not a nut.) That was unfair.

Thank God, CBS didn't broadcast the conference call, because that would have been very biased.

I'll admit that, from among the hundreds of thousands of hours of broadcast news over the last three decades, Bernie is able to cobble together a few instances of liberally slanted reporting. But even when Goldberg seems to have a point, it still feels just the teensiest bit selective. It's like accusing a library of having a murder mystery bias after only going to the murder mystery shelf. They're all murder mysteries!

Worse, most of his examples are about as well researched as the John Chancellor quote.

Why, Bernie asks, if CBS identifies the Heritage Foundation as a "conservative" think tank, does it not identify the Brookings Institution as a "liberal" think tank?

I don't know. Bias? Or could it be because the Heritage Foundation's website says their mission is to "promote conservative public policies," while the Brookings website says it is committed to "independent, factual and nonpartisan research"?

Why, Bernie wants to know, is Phyllis Schlafly always labeled a "conservative"? Maybe because the official biography on her Eagle Forum website calls her a "national leader of the conservative movement."

Why, Bernie asks on page 57, is Rush Limbaugh referred to as a "conservative" talk show host, but Rosie O'Donnell is not always labeled a "liberal" talk show host? At first, I thought that one was a misfire. Rush spends three hours a day delivering his patented brand of right-wing folderol. But then I remembered a Rosie show where she interviewed Haley Joel Osment. The kid was supposed to be promoting *The Sixth Sense,* but he just wouldn't shut up about the Earned Income Tax Credit.

Bernie has a chapter called "The Most Important Story You Never Saw on TV." It's about latchkey kids and working moms. And it *is* an important story. But if you haven't seen it on TV, it's because you haven't been watching CNN (11 stories), CBS (11),

NBC (3), or ABC (10). When I see something only thirty-five times, I know the liberal media is trying to keep a lid on it.

You know, if there's one thing I associate with liberalism, it's anti-Semitism. And what else could explain the shocking media cover-up of the fact that many Arabs dislike Israel? Goldberg has the goods on this one. His smoking gun: "I learned much more about the atmosphere that breeds suicide bombers from one short article in *Commentary* magazine than I have from watching twenty years of network television news." The *Commentary* article discusses a hit song in Cairo, Damascus, and the West Bank entitled, "I Hate Israel."

"Why didn't I know this?" Bernie writes indignantly. "A computer check soon answered my question. On television, only CNN reported the 'I Hate Israel' story. On radio, NPR did a piece. So did the *Christian Science Monitor* and the *Chicago Tribune*. The *Los Angeles Times* ran a short wire service story."

So, in other words, except for CNN, NPR, the *Chicago Tribune*, the *Los Angeles Times,* and the wire services, *not one* of the liberal media outlets let us know about this important story—not Fox, not the *Wall Street Journal*, not the *Washington Times,* not even the *National Review*? Where are you, William F. Buckley, Jr.? You liberal anti-Semite?[1]

As I said, one of *Bias*'s biggest problems is its selectivity. The book came out in December 2001. Now, maybe Bernie doesn't follow politics, but there was a big election the previous year. Looking at the coverage of a presidential election might be a good way to test theories of media bias, don't you think? Say the media was liberal. Which candidate would it be nicer to? The Republican, George W. Bush? Or the Democrat, Albert Gore?

There's not one word in *Bias* about the 2000 presidential elec-

---

[1] Actually, a Nexis search reveals that the story was also mentioned in the *Washington Post, Boston Globe, Chicago Sun Times, Buffalo News, Milwaukee Journal Sentinel, Pittsburgh Post Gazette, Baltimore Sun, Phildelphia Inquirer, Atlanta Journal and Constitution,* etc. But still, William Buckley's silence on "I Hate Israel" speaks volumes.

tion. In my next chapter, I will try to fill in this gaping hole with a scientific analysis of just how liberal—or, perhaps, how *conservative*—that coverage was.

───────────

**Y**ou know, one of the joys of appearing on TV is going through the e-mail you get when you bitch-slap a Bernie Goldberg or a Bill O'Reilly. And boy, I got a lot of great e-mail from that *Donahue* appearance. Most of the comments were of the "way to get him" or "I liked your tie" variety, but quite a few were, shall we say, slightly negative.

One of my favorites:

> Saw you on Donahue with your liberal shit. Blow it out your ass, dickhead!

I've composed a standard response to e-mail like that:

> Thank you for your kind e-mail regarding my appearance on *Donahue*. As you can imagine, I've received so many positive responses that I cannot possibly answer them all personally. But, once again, thank you for your kind remarks.

The idea is to frustrate them. It's especially gratifying when they respond to my response. Like the "blow-it-out-your-ass" guy did:

> Hey, asshole. I know you read my e-mail, because you mentioned Donahue. Blow me.

So, I e-mailed him back again.

> Thank you for your kind e-mail regarding my appearance on *Donahue*. As you can imagine, I've received so many positive responses that I cannot possibly answer them all personally. But, once again, thank you for your kind remarks.

Sure enough, a few hours later, another e-mail from my new friend.

> Franken, you're a joke!

So, I e-mailed him back.

> Thank you for your kind e-mail regarding my jokes. As you can imagine, I receive so many positive e-mails regarding my jokes, that I cannot possibly answer them all. But once again, thank you for your kind remarks regarding my jokes.

Unfortunately, that was the last of our little correspondence.

# 7

# The 2000 Presidential Election: How It Disproved the Hypothetical Liberal Media Paradigm Matrix

**In** order to examine more closely the conservative claims of liberal media bias, TeamFranken constructed a hypothetical model. Let's say that during the 2000 presidential election, liberals controlled the media and used it in a biased manner.

In our hypothetical, we asked, how would this liberal media distort the news to ensure that the liberal candidate won the election over the conservative candidate?

At the risk of stating the obvious, one of our axioms was that negative press hurts a candidate running for election, while positive press helps. Ergo, if the liberal media wanted to help the Democratic candidate, it would run positive stories about him and negative stories about the Republican.

To illustrate our hypothetical paradigm, we commissioned this diagram:

**HYPOTHETICAL LIBERAL MEDIA PARADIGM MATRIX**

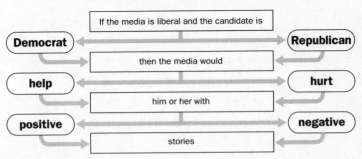

With this powerful new tool, the HLMP Matrix, developed here at Harvard with funds from the Bill and Melinda Gates Foundation for Social Justice, we were ready to evaluate in an analytical, unbiased way the media coverage of the 2000 campaign. Before we give you the results, let's look at what some of our friends have to say about the political slant of the media.

- Ann Coulter: "The public square is wall-to-wall liberal propaganda."

- Sean Hannity: "The evidence of bias is overwhelming."

- Bernard Goldberg: "They have a liberal bias."

Okay. Got it. Armed with both our Matrix and the reliable analysis of our friends, we knew what to expect. Lots and lots of negative stories about George W. Bush. And lots and lots of positive ones about Albert Gore.

So, you can understand why we were stunned when we saw an actual study on media coverage during the 2000 election. What actually happened during the 2000 election campaign blows to smithereens the predictions of our Hypothetical Liberal Media Paradigm Matrix. Get a load of this chart from the Pew Charitable Trusts Project for Excellence in Journalism.

**Tone of Coverage for Gore & Bush**

|  | Gore | Bush |
|---|---|---|
| Positive | 13% | 24% |
| Neutral | 31% | 27% |
| Negative | 56% | 49% |
| Total | 100% | 100% |

Holy shit! This makes no sense. The numbers for Gore, the *liberal*, were more negative and a *lot* less positive than the numbers for Bush. The media, which we just assumed to be liberal, because that's what we had heard so often, was actually *nicer* to the *conservative*! Could that possibly be true? Let's look at it again.

**Tone of Coverage for Gore & Bush**

|          | Gore | Bush |
|----------|------|------|
| Positive | 13%  | 24%  |
| Neutral  | 31%  | 27%  |
| Negative | 56%  | 49%  |
| Total    | 100% | 100% |

Holy *shit*!

A million questions raced through our minds. Who are these Pew people? Where do these numbers come from? Was this just another *liberal lie*?

No. It turns out that the Pew Charitable Trusts are among the largest, most prestigious foundations in America. Totally mainstream. Their Project for Excellence in Journalism comes out of the top-rated Columbia School of Journalism and is one of the few media research organizations without a political axe to grind.

And the numbers? Turns out they came from a comprehensive study examining 1,149 stories from seventeen leading news sources.

What could this possibly mean? Either there was something terribly wrong with our HLMP Matrix, or there is something terribly wrong with Ann, Sean, and Bernard.

**S**o what had happened? It turns out that TeamFranken had spent the 2000 election cycle locked away in its ivory tower. Any normal American who watched the news or read the papers that year would have noticed that the media just *hated* Al Gore.

Somewhere along the line, the pack decided that Al Gore was a sanctimonious, graspy exaggerator running against a likeable if dim-witted goof-off. Instead of covering the issues and how they might affect average Americans, the media looked for little scraps of evidence to support its story line of Gore the Exaggerator.

They found them in the unlikeliest places. For example, where he didn't exaggerate. Take his role in the creation of the Internet. In the 1980s, Gore was one of the handful of leaders who foresaw the tremendous potential of Arpanet, an emergency military computer network. As both a congressman and a senator, Gore fought tirelessly for the funding that would turn Arpanet into what is now the Internet.

The Internet, as you may know, became a big hit in the nineties and briefly enjoyed a great deal of media coverage. With this in mind, Gore told Wolf Blitzer in a 1999 interview, "During my service in the United States Congress, I took the initiative in creating the Internet."

What do you suppose he meant? That, late at night in his office in the Russell Building, after the other senators had gone home, he had written the PASCAL code that allowed packet switching? Probably not. No. What he seemed to be doing is what members of Congress do: He was taking credit for a program he championed and funded. In this case one that revolutionized the information infrastructure of the entire world.

What an asshole.

The phrase "invented the Internet" first appeared in a Republican Party press release and would be repeated by the "liberal" press thousands of times during the campaign. What should have been an enormous credit to the man's vision became a symbol of his insidious, compulsive dishonesty. Ironically, Gore was sometimes criticized via the Internet itself!

When a few people—like me—pointed out that he hadn't said that he had invented the Internet, Ann Coulter responded: "In point of fact, 'create' is a synonym for 'invent.' Any thesaurus will quickly confirm this." That may be true. But the very same thesaurus would show that "friendly" is a synonym for "intimate." So, when Ann told the *New York Observer* that she and I were "friendly," they knew it was her way of claiming that we are lovers, which we most certainly are not. I am not currently having an affair with any Republican woman, but if I were, it would be with Maine senator Olympia Snowe, whom I respect for voting her conscience.

Speaking of intimacy, let's get back to how Gore was buggered by his enemies in the media.

Take the *Love Story* story, which is really more of a *Hate Story* story. Or a *False Story* story. Read on, friend, for the true story of the false, hateful *Love Story* story.

In 1997, Gore was on Air Force II, chatting late into the night with a couple of reporters, including Karen Tumulty of *Time* magazine. The conversation turned, as conversations will, to movies and reminiscing about old friends. Gore mentioned that Erich Segal, the author of *Love Story,* had told the *Nashville Tennessean* that the characters of Oliver Barrett and Jenny Cavalleri had been based on him and Tipper. As Tumulty later recalled, "He said, 'all I know is that's what he [Segal] told reporters in Tennessee.'" She casually referred to this in her seven-page profile as follows: "Gore said [Segal] used Al and Tipper as models for the uptight preppy and his free-spirited girlfriend in *Love Story.*"

Was Gore lying? Imagine how embarrassing it would be if he were! Just thinking about it makes me embarrassed—not just for him, but for every vice president other than Spiro Agnew, and to a lesser extent Dan Quayle. Thank goodness, then, that in 1980 the *Nashville Tennessean* had indeed quoted Segal as saying that Tipper and Al had been the models for the star-crossed lovers. Phew.

But here's where it all starts to go terribly, terribly wrong. It turns out the *Tennessean* had *misquoted* Erich Segal. And when *The New York Times* contacted him, Segal confirmed that Oliver Barrett was based partly on Gore and partly on Gore's roommate Tommy Lee Jones (and, I like to think, a tiny bit on me)—but denied that Tipper was the model for poor Jenny Cavalleri. As anyone who has seen the movie knows, that character was based on Ali MacGraw.

The media went to town. An offhand remark, accurately quoting a seventeen-year-old story from his local paper, would be used against Gore more than a billion times over the next three years.

Here's an excerpt from the September 19, 2000, *Hannity and Colmes* program:

> **HANNITY:** This is a big picture we've got to look at. Al Gore once told the American people, told the crowd, *Love Story* was based on his life and Tipper's life. The author of *Love Story* says that's not true.
>
> **TALK SHOW HOST NANCY SKINNER:** No. That's not true, Sean—
>
> **HANNITY:** Absolutely, he's on record. . . . Did he create the Internet, Nancy?
>
> **SKINNER:** No, we're starting with *Love Story*. . . . Okay, Erich Segal said that indeed Al was the model for the male model—
>
> **HANNITY:** That's not true.
>
> **SKINNER:** But that he never said Tipper was, and that all that Al Gore had ever said—
>
> **HANNITY:** Not true—
>
> **SKINNER:** —is that he had read in the *Tennessean,* a newspaper, that, where Erich Segal had said that he and Tipper were the model. You know what? The *Tennessean* newspaper did write that. Erich Segal has confirmed that it was Al Gore, but not necessarily Tipper. So there was a minor difference that got blown into—
>
> **HANNITY:** I don't have a lot of time to refute every fact here.

Refute every fact? Sean, some of us are more concerned about refuting lies.

So Gore takes credit for a program he championed and funded.

And then he accurately quotes from a newspaper. Noticing a pattern here? An insidious, compulsive pattern? It gets worse.

In January of 2000, Gore spoke to a high school in Concord, New Hampshire, about how one individual can help change a community. He told a story about how the actions of one teenage girl from Toone, Tennessee, changed national policy. The girl had contacted Gore's congressional office about toxic waste in her hometown. Because of her initiative, Gore said, he "called for a congressional investigation and a hearing. . . . I looked around the country for other sites like that. I found a little place in upstate New York called Love Canal. Had the first hearing on that issue, and Toone, Tennessee—that was the one you didn't hear of. But that was the one that started it all." Gore pointed out that as a result, "we passed a major national law to clean up hazardous dump sites. . . . And it all happened because one high school student got involved."[1]

In other words, Gore told his audience of high school students that they should put aside their cynicism and get involved in the political process. Gore had a sterling reputation as an environmental crusader, but here he was handing credit over to an unheralded teenage girl from a little town called Toone. His speech was a beacon of hope for decency and humility in American politics.

A careful observer would have noted Gore's hands firmly gripping the podium, his ass extended behind him awaiting the brutal violation the media was about to administer.

First, both *The New York Times* and the *Washington Post* misquoted Gore, changing "*That* was the one that started it all" (referring to Toone, Tennessee) and making it into: "*I* was the one that started it all." The Republican National Committee helpfully fixed up the grammar, sending a fax to reporters stating that Gore had said, "I was the one *who* started it all."

---

[1] That law created Superfund, which has cleaned up countless hazardous waste sites in the intervening years. Bush has drastically slashed its funding.

Chris Matthews joined in the gang bang, accusing Gore of claiming to have "discovered" or even "invented" Love Canal. Even though *The New York Times* and the *Washington Post* issued corrections, the story was off and running. Rupert Murdoch, in the form of the *New York Post,* called it "a bald-faced lie." The *National Journal* said Gore was "mangling the truth for political gain." On NBC, ABC, pretty much everywhere, Gore the Exaggerator had done it again.

I mean, was the man *sick?* Yes, he *had* held the first hearing on Love Canal, and yes, those hearings *had* led to a major national law, and yes, he *had* told the story accurately. But, c'mon, Al! How many times do you have to be misquoted before you learn not to ever say anything to anyone that could possibly be taken out of context and changed to make you look bad? Like Oliver Barrett IV, Al Gore was learning the painful truth that being a reporter means never having to say you're sorry.

Meanwhile, over in the Bush camp, things weren't too rosy either. Anytime the candidate said something "stupid," it was jumped on as evidence that he might not be up to the job. Sometimes the criticism seemed fair, like when he said that "more and more of our imports are coming from overseas." Or when he said, "I know how hard it is for you to put food on your family." Or when he said, "I will have a foreign-handed foreign policy." Or when he said, "I know the human being and fish can coexist peacefully." Or when he said, "Families is where our nation finds hope, where our wings take dream." Stupid, stupid, stupid.

But sometimes, Bush, too, was the victim of a cynical, hypercritical press. Like when he was ridiculed for saying, "Rarely is the question asked, 'Is our children learning?'" But he was right. Until Bush had had the guts to ask it, I had *never* heard that question asked.

Or how about when he used the word "subliminable"? Not once, but four times. Personally, I think by using the word "subliminable," Bush was himself employing a subtle subliminal device. Think about it: "Subliminable . . . sublimin-able . . . subliminable . . . subliminally, I am *able* to be President." See? It took until this very moment for you to get it, didn't it?

But while the press may not have been picking up on his clever strategy of lowering expectations and subliminally manipulating the public, they were also ignoring some actual substantive lies.

Bush was lying throughout the 2000 campaign. And unlike Gore's lies about Love Canal, *Love Story,* and the Internet, Bush's lies weren't even true. Remember how Gore took credit for the Internet, which he funded? Bush took credit for a Texas Patients' Bill of Rights, which he *vetoed.*

Gore actually did conduct the first hearings on Love Canal. And in order to conduct these hearings, he not only showed up at them, but showed up at them every day. Plus, Gore wasn't using the hearings as a way to dodge the draft. Compare this to Bush's stint in the Air National Guard. In his autobiography, *A Charge to Keep,* Bush claims to have flown with his unit until 1973. But in a blow to Lady Truth, it seems that after getting Dad's help to pass over the poor slobs waiting in line for a safe spot protecting Texas from the Viet Cong, Bush managed to skip out on much of his duty. Assigned in May 1972 to the Tactical Reconnaissance Squadron in Montgomery, Bush had a perfect attendance record. Perfectly *bad.* Base commander Brigadier General William Turnipseed says of Bush that he is "dead-certain he didn't show up."

Regarding *Love Story,* at no time during that controversy did Gore ever get arrested for drunk driving. The contrast to Bush's 1976 arrest for drunk driving couldn't be more stark. More damaging still is the bold-faced **lie** Bush told reporter Wayne Slater of the *Dallas Morning News* months before the drunk driving arrest had been disclosed. According to Slater, their conversation went like this. I think you'll agree, it's unambiguous.

> **SLATER:** Governor, were you ever arrested after 1968?
>
> **BUSH:** No.

The drunk driving thing uncaged a whole zoo full of lyin'. Here's a good one from Bush spokeswoman Karen Hughes, fielding reporters' questions minutes after the announcement of Bush's unfortunate past as a drunk driver. I've added numbers to Karen's response for easy reference.

> **QUESTION:** Do you know why he was stopped, Karen? Was he driving erratically or anything?

> 1 **KAREN HUGHES:** I believe they—I don't know exactly, no. I
> 2 don't know. There was no—there was no incident—
> 3 there's—I don't know exactly. There was some discussion
> 4 that he appeared to have been driving too slow—too slowly.

The real answer? Bush was arrested because he *drove into a hedge.* That's what the arresting officer, Calvin Bridges, a former Kennebunkport policeman, told Portland, Maine's Fox-51 reporter Erin Fehlau the day the story broke. According to Fehlau, Bridges said that "he spotted Bush driving erratically . . . [and] says Bush ran off the road into some hedges."

Let's try to get into Karen's head, shall we? First off, it's pretty apparent that she didn't know. I derived that from the "I don't know exactly, no" (line 1), the "I don't know" (2), and the "I don't know exactly" (3). Why did she say this three times? I think she was stalling while her savvy political mind weighed the implications: Hmmm. Drunk driving? *Bad.* What's wrong with drunk driving? Kill people. People dead. *Very* bad. What would be the least deadly way to drive drunk? Erratically? No. Too fast? NO!!! Too slow? Yes! Too slow. That's it. "There was some discussion that he appeared to have been driving too slow—too slowly." That's good.

The media dutifully picked up on this, even following her line of reasoning. As a columnist in the *Washington Times* wrote: "As for Mr. Bush, it may be revealing that he was not speeding like so many people driving under the influence of alcohol, but was in fact, pulled over by the police because he was driving too slowly."

Great job, Karen!

And then there's the cocaine.

Back in 1979, the week after the release of radiation at Three Mile Island, I wrote a *Saturday Night Live* sketch with Tom Davis and Jim Downey called "The Amazing Colossal President." President Carter visits a nuclear plant during an "event," is irradiated, and grows to enormous size. At a press conference, a reporter asks the spokesman for the nuclear plant, "Is it true the President is over a hundred feet tall?"

"No, absolutely not! That is untrue!" the spokesman says indignantly.

"Is it true the President is over ninety feet tall?" asks another reporter.

"No comment."

You didn't have to be a genius to know that the Amazing Colossal President was somewhere between ninety and a hundred feet tall.

In the same way, it didn't take a genius to figure out that George W. Bush snorted cocaine sometime before 1974.

At first during the campaign Bush refused on principle to answer questions about cocaine. Then, because he was applying for a federal job (president) he had to fill out a form that asked if had used illegal drugs in the past seven years. Bush voluntarily told the press he was able to answer no.

A clever reporter asked whether he could have given the same answer when his father was president and federal forms asked about drug use for the prior fifteen years.

"Uh, let's see here . . . Yes, I could have," Bush said after a pause. Then, when asked again if he had ever used cocaine, Bush refused to give an answer. His dad was inaugurated in 1989. Therefore, using the "Amazing Colossal President" test, George W. Bush snorted cocaine between 1958 and 1974, assuming he didn't do coke before he was twelve.

So, we've got the Patients' Bill of Rights he vetoed, the draft-dodging, the drunk driving, and the cocaine. But what about the serious stuff? Like how he got rich? Like the Harken business—when, as a member of the audit committee, he dumped his stock just before it was about to tank and was eight months late in filing documents with the Securities and Exchange Commission? Like his ridiculously underanalyzed tax plan?

If this is too much to hold in your mind all at one time, here's a simple chart to summarize the raw material the media could have used to go negative against the candidates:

| Gore | Bush |
|---|---|
| Supposedly claimed to have discovered a canal | Skirted securities law by selling Harken Energy stocks while sitting on audit committee; *lied* about having supported Texas Patients' Bill of Rights and hate crime bill |
| "All I know is that's what he told reporters in Tennessee" | "By far the vast majority of my tax cuts go to those at the bottom end of the spectrum"[2] |
| Funded the Internet, which changed history forever | Snorted cocaine, dodged draft, drove drunk into a hedge |

In other words, both candidates made serious mistakes and legitimate questions could have been raised about their fitness for national office. Why then did Bush get twice as many positive stories and so many fewer negative stories? Hummus. That's right. Remember the oil in the hummus?

It's the other biases that killed Gore. Pack mentality. Once the

---

[2]Quote from February 15, 2000, debate with John McCain; repeated in various forms during debate with Gore and elsewhere.

pack had decided the story line on Gore, everybody jumped aboard and rode all the way to November. Also, laziness. That's a biiiiig bias. Why bother to check facts when you can quote yesterday's story about a story that ran the day before yesterday?

Negativity. What's more likely to hit the front page? Gore Tells Inspirational Story to High Schoolers? Or Gore Lies Again?

Plus, Bush was a *new* story. Gore was old. And the media just didn't like Gore. And by attacking him, reporters were safe from the accusation of having a liberal bias. Or were they?

Writing in the *Charleston Gazette*, Dan Radmacher cited a study by Howard Kurtz that found almost twice as many pro-Bush stories as pro-Gore stories on the front page of *The New York Times* during the campaign. An incredulous Ann Coulter could find only one explanation for a liberal newspaper implying a conservative bias in the *Times:* "The sheer joy liberals take in telling lies . . . They take insolent pleasure in saying absurd things."

I called Radmacher at his Charleston, West Virginia, office. TeamFranken transcribed the conversation.

**AL:** Hi, Dan. It's Al Franken. Did you know that Ann Coulter referred to one of your columns in her book?

**DAN RADMACHER:** Really?

**AL:** It was the one where you cited Howard Kurtz's study on media coverage during the election.

**DAN:** Oh God. What did she say?

**AL:** That's actually why I'm calling. She said that your column shows that liberals take sheer joy in telling lies. So I wanted to ask you: Do you take sheer joy in telling lies?

**DAN:** Yes. Yes, I do.

**AL:** Shoot. That proves her point, then. Also, she mentions insolent pleasure. Do you get insolent pleasure from lying?

**DAN:** Yeah. I guess so. But it's more the sheer joy.

**AL:** So more sheer joy than insolent pleasure?

**DAN:** Yeah. That's about right. By the way, we have a bet here in the newsroom about what exactly is wrong with Ann Coulter.

**AL:** I can't help you out. I don't claim to understand it. Anyway, thanks, Dan.

**DAN:** Sure, Al.

That's one of the nice things about this job. Making contact with fellow liberals and taking insolent pleasure and/or experiencing the sheer joy of lying to you, our readers. I'd made a friend for life.

# Conclusion: A Lesson Learned

**As** the application of TeamFranken's Hypothetical Liberal Media Paradigm Matrix amply demonstrates, there is no liberal bias in the media when it comes to politics. What a pity. I think a little liberal bias would make me feel better about all three branches of the government being controlled by the right.

Let's review.

- Politics—no liberal bias
- Social issues—trivial liberal bias (no mainstream journalist has ever bombed an abortion clinic)
- Sports—massive, but inconsequential, conservative bias.[1]
- The Funnies—funny bias, or in the case of *Family Circus*, funny and heartwarming bias

Am I overlooking anything important? I guess I'm done. That was easy. My second shortest book ever.

I guess I'll just check my stock portfolio. Money is so important to me.

Wait! That's it! Money! *That's* what I was forgetting. Economic issues. Nuts. I'm not finished, after all. Now I wish I hadn't dismissed TeamFranken. Well, I'll just have to get them back and assign them to do a massive amount of research on how the media covers economic issues, while I figure out some way to make that interesting.

Wait! I've got an idea . . .

---

[1] See Marv Albert's excellent book, *Curve Ball: An Insider Shows How Sportscasters Put a Rightward Spin on the Games You Love.*

# Five Get-Rich-Quick Tips
# the Wall Street Fat Cats Don't
# Want You to Know

**TIP #1**—Never option stock in a blue chip where the market cap is twenty times the I made this all up.

Economic issues can seem dry and technical for the average person. In fact, there is only one type of economic story that has proven to be universally captivating year after year. I am speaking, of course, of stories about lottery winners: where they bought their winning ticket; where they were when they heard that they had won; whether they plan to keep their job; and what kind of car they plan to buy.

I'll admit that stories about the unemployment rate, our national debt, and the balance of trade can seem a bit dry compared to a lottery winner. But look at it this way. A story about the unemployment rate is a story about whether you have a job. A story about the national debt is a story about whether or not you can afford the interest payments on your house. And that story about the balance of trade? Okay, that is a little dry.

So economic issues are just as important as stories about politics, social issues, and Whitney Houston. And the fact is the mainstream media has a bona fide conservative bias when it comes to economic issues.

Don't take my word for it. Because I sometimes include jokes in the things I write, my credibility can be suspect, compared to someone without a sense of humor, like Bernie Goldberg. Check out this 1998 study on the economic views of Washington journalists conducted by Dr. David Croteau of Virginia Common-wealth University.[1]

The survey found that while journalists consider themselves slightly to the left on social issues, they don't think they're liberal on economic issues. In fact, almost twice as many say they're to the right on economic issues as say they're to the left. And when it comes to Social Security, Medicare, free trade, corporate power, taxes, and health care, the study shows that journalists are significantly to the right of the general public.

Charts bore me. At least, *regular* charts bore me. That's why I've decided to pep this one up a little bit with some gentle humor (See next page).

So journalists are economically conservative. But this makes sense, given their position in society. Journalists have it made. Their lives are trouble-free. If you've ever met a journalist, you'll know what I mean. They're the happiest people on God's earth.

But put their contentment and good cheer to the side for a moment, and consider: Why is it that journalists are only one fifth as likely as the general public to have a negative view of NAFTA? And why does every major news outlet line up in favor of every opportunity to expand free trade?

It's simple, actually. Here's how free trade works. Tariffs on imports go down, and along with them go prices on products that journalists buy, like those fedoras you always see in the movies. That's the upside. The downside of free trade is that low-skilled

---

[1] Croteau surveyed 444 Washington-based journalists, including 31 bureau chiefs. Through four attempts to collect completed questionnaires, he assembled 141 responses. There was no statistically significant difference in profile between the respondents and those who did not respond. Croteau surveyed every journalist listed in the spring 1998 *News Media Yellow Book* under the assignment categories "Congress," "federal government," "national affairs," "politics," "White House," "business," "consumer issues," "economics," or "labor," and who had a Washington area code. Organizations receiving ten or more surveys included ABC News, the AP, Bloomberg News, CNN, Knight Ridder Newspapers, the *Los Angeles Times*, NBC News, *The New York Times*, Reuters, *Time*, *USA Today*, *The Wall Street Journal*, *The Washington Post*, *The Washington Times*, and I'm Impressed If You're Still Reading This.

| Issue | Journalists | Public | Comment and/or Witticism |
|---|---|---|---|
| Reforming Social Security by slowing spending should be one of our top few priorities | 56% | 35% | See how journalists differ from the public? |
| Protecting Social Security and Medicare should be one of our top few priorities | 39% | 59% | Might it be relevant that half of all journalists make six-figure salaries? |
| Too much power is in the hands of a few corporations | 24% strongly agree, 32% somewhat agree, 43% strongly or somewhat disagree | 62% strongly agree, 15% somewhat agree, 18% strongly or somewhat disagree | Maybe if more of the public worked for those corporations, they'd like them, too! |
| Agree that government should guarantee medical coverage for those without health insurance | 43% | 64% | Wait! That adds up to more than 100%! That's impossible! Oh, I see. Never mind. |
| Did NAFTA have more of a positive or more of a negative impact on the United States? | 65% positive, 8% negative, 27% don't know/not sure | 32% positive, 42% negative, 19% don't know/not sure, 7% no impact either way | Twice as many journalists like NAFTA! I'll bet you'll love the funny way I explore this one below. |

(now go back to previous page)

fedora-making jobs get exported overseas. So lower prices for consumers, but job insecurity for those with low skills.

Journalists are pro free trade precisely because they know that their jobs are not at risk for exportation. That's the same reason why I've always been pro NAFTA, pro GATT, and pro fast track authority. I know that a fourteen-year-old Bangladeshi might be able to sew my sneakers (and he did a great job), but there's no way he could write this book.

Or so I thought.

When I was explaining the idea for this chapter to my editor, Mitch, it gave him an idea. Why not save a few bucks and have a fourteen-year-old Bangladeshi boy write the book? Fortunately for me, his first attempt proved my point. Try as he might, Kharap Juta could not capture my hip, sophisticated New York sensibility. But judge for yourself.

# 10

# Chapter for American Book

*by Kharap Juta*

**My** job in the factory is very hard. I am made to stitch shoes for many hours. It is hard for me to stitch, but the men do not care. Yesterday, I punctured my finger on the machine. I tried to squeeze it, but the bleeding would not stop. When I asked the men to let me go see the nurse at the mission hospital, they hit me with insoles.

My twelve-year-old sister Choto began to yell at the men. I told her to be quiet and return to her work. The men told me that if she causes trouble again, they will fire her, and she will have to become a prostitute.

I am dizzy with hunger.

## 11
# I'm Funnier Than Kharap Juta

**See.** That isn't funny. Kharap's no threat to me. In professional comedy the technical term for writers like Kharap Juta is "talent-less hack." Kharap, a word of advice from a guy who's been in the business twice as long as you've been alive: As long as you're going for the easy laugh with your Choto gag, the word is "hooker." Never use "prostitute" when you can use "hooker." Unless you're doing a corporate gig. In which case, the phrase is "world's oldest profession." What I'm trying to get at here is: Keep your day job, kid. Or in your case, your day-and-night job.

There. I've put the kid in his place. The fact is, free trade may not be good for everybody. It may not be good for you, my reader, or for the Kharap Jutas of this world, of which there are three or four billion. But it is good for people in journalism and for people in the entertainment industry. People like me, Haley Joel Osment, and Bill O'Reilly.

# The Chapter on Fox

**They Distort, We Deride**

or

**We Retort, They Have Lied**

or

**They Purport, We Decry**

or

**They Are Short[1], We Have Plied[2]**

or

**Smorty Smort, Blort Deblort**

**Now** that TeamFranken has proven that there's no liberal bias in the mainstream media, we can move on to the right-wing media.

I should start by telling you that when I first proposed this book, my publisher turned me down flat. The year was 1986, and at that point, just about all the right-wing media was in print: the *Wall Street Journal* editorial page, the *Washington Times,* the *National Review,* et cetera. My publisher made the point that even the thousands of people who read books got most of their news from television. My book on the lies of the right-wing media would

[1] of Truth!
[2] the Truth!

have to wait until there was a whole network devoted to right-wing lies.

The Fox News Channel was launched by Rupert Murdoch on October 6, 1996, with Roger Ailes at its helm. Both Murdoch and Ailes are colorful men. In Murdoch's case, the color is green. Or magenta, the color of the Australian five-dollar bill. He has over two billion of these. *Forbes* magazine ranked him the fourth most powerful billionaire in the world. If you'll assume with me that billionaires are billions of times more powerful than normal people, you can see that the *Forbes* ranking means a lot.

In addition to the Fox News Channel, Murdoch's News Corporation owns *TV Guide.* You know how many people read *TV Guide?* Neither do I. But it must be millions. He also owns twenty-four other magazines, including *The Weekly Standard,* the neo-conservative periodical that tricked President Bush into going to war against Iraq. He also owns the Fox Broadcasting Network, which produced *Joe Millionaire,* a hit show. And HarperCollins publishing. Think about all those put together! Quite an empire, right?

But wait. He also owns 20th Century Fox, which owns the rights to over two thousand movies, including *Dr. Dolittle* and *Dr. Dolittle II. Dr. Dolittle II* didn't do as well as *Dr. Dolittle,* but Fox also owns *Titanic,* which was a *huge* hit. Plus, he has ownership or major interests in satellite services reaching Asia, Europe, North America, and South America. That's practically the entire world, excluding the "emerging" African market.

I would think that anyone would be satisfied with that much media. I know *I* would. Heck, I'd be happy with just *TV Guide,* HarperCollins, Fox Broadcasting, and the satellite companies. But even all this stuff doesn't satisfy K. Rupert Murdoch. No. He has to own the largest group of television stations in the United States, plus 130 English-language newspapers, including the *London Times* and the *New York Post.*

You might notice that many of these holdings have, shall we

say, a rightward cant. So you won't be surprised when I tell you that the cherry on top of Murdoch's corporate empire is the Los Angeles Dodgers, the most notoriously right-wing team in the history of Major League Baseball.

Plus he owns the Fox News Channel. Which brings us full circle.

But before I go into FNC, there's one other important thing you should know about Murdoch. He's evil. I defer to the august *Columbia Journalism Review:*

> Murdoch uses his diverse holdings . . . to promote his own financial interests at the expense of real news gathering, legal and regulatory rules, and journalistic ethics. He wields his media as instruments of influence with politicians who can aid him, and savages his competitors in his news columns. If ever someone demonstrated the dangers of mass power being concentrated in few hands, it would be Murdoch.

But evil? How about a specific example, Al? Okay. In 1993, Murdoch, a staunch anticommunist, began beaming programs into China from his Hong Kong–based Star TV satellite network. At the time Murdoch expressed the noble sentiment that "advances in the technology of telecommunications have proved an unambiguous threat to totalitarian regimes everywhere."

Angered by Murdoch's apparent lack of support for their totalitarian regime, China retaliated by banning the ownership of satellite dishes. Murdoch knew which side his rice was buttered on, and switched to a more, shall we say, pro-totalitarian point of view. "The truth is—and we Americans don't like to admit it—that authoritarian societies can work," he told critics. And to show the Central Committee that he had just been kidding about that "unambiguous threat" business, he cheerfully removed the BBC from his Star network. The BBC, it seems, had covered the Tiananmen

Square unpleasantness, and according to Murdoch "was driving them [the totalitarian Chinese regime] nuts." So, goodbye BBC, hello satellite dishes in the world's largest potential media market.

But some good came of this whole thing. Murdoch launched a multimillion-dollar joint venture with the *People's Daily*, the official state newspaper. The venture produced *ChinaByte*, an on-line news service that helped bring official Chinese government propaganda into the Digital Age.

Now, please understand that I'm not saying Rupert has a pro-communist bias. Just a pro-getting-money-and-power-no-matter-who-gets-hurt bias. Most of the time, this bias makes him indistinguishable from someone with a straight-up right-wing bias. He has been a tireless supporter of conservative politicians from Margaret Thatcher to Newt Gingrich, who have returned his favors with tax breaks and shady deregulations. But as you can see from his self-serving support of a murderous, Godless, communist regime, Murdoch's bottom line is less about politics and more about the bottom line.

Roger Ailes, however, is someone you can always rely on to stick to his conservative Republican guns. There is absolutely no question about this guy. He is a rock-ribbed, dyed-in-the-wool Republican through and through. Want a guy who will bash the Democrats with everything he's got? You want Roger Ailes.

That's why when Rupert Murdoch needed help starting a conservative cable news channel, he knew the right man for the job. The man who had been the GOP's preeminent political consultant. The man who had helped elect Nixon, Reagan, and George H. W. Bush. The man who's been called the Dark Prince of right-wing attack politics. It was Ailes, along with his Dark co-Prince, Lee Atwater, who directed the Willie Horton attack against Michael Dukakis (and it was Ailes who said "the only question is whether we depict Willie Horton with a knife in his hand or without it"). It was Ailes who produced Rush Limbaugh's ill-fated TV show. And so it was Roger Ailes who was the right choice for Murdoch's right-wing channel. Ailes would run the network, set its right-wing tone, guide its right-wing programming, choose its right-wing stars.

And, most importantly, pick its slogan: "fair and balanced."

And its tag line: "We report, you decide."

Tucker Carlson, the conservative co-host of CNN's *Crossfire*, has explained that the reason the Fox News Channel calls itself "fair and balanced" is "to drive liberals crazy." There are others who suggest that Ailes really believes that FNC is fair and balanced, but only looks right wing because the rest of the media is so far to the left.

This would be a plausible argument . . . *if* the rest of the media actually had a liberal bias. Or *if* Fox wasn't so obviously slanted to the right. Or *if* Ailes weren't a cynical Republican ideologue with no regard for fairness or balance. Any of those things would add a lot to that argument.

When Murdoch installed him at Fox, one of Ailes's first acts of "balance" was to clean house. Joe Peyronnin, then president of Fox News, told me the story.

"I had about forty people working for me," Joe told me, "and he asked some of them if they were liberal or not. There was a litmus test. He was going to figure out who was liberal or conservative when he came in, and try to get rid of the liberals."

Did Joe think this was appropriate? "I told him I didn't think it was appropriate."

Did Joe stay at his job? "I resigned."

So disgusted was Joe that he left English-language journalism altogether and is now executive vice president of news and information programming at Telemundo. Adios, Joe. Adios, fairness. *¡Hola, Señor Ailes!*

House clean, Ailes went to work hiring his team. For managing editor, he chose veteran journalist Brit Hume, a contributor to the ultraconservative *Weekly Standard* and the ultra-ultraconservative *American Spectator.* For Washington bureau chief, Ailes chose Brit's wife Kim, who was determined to change the tone of television journalism. Mainstream stories, she complained in 1997, are "all mushy, like AIDS, or all silly like Head Start."

Hubby also anchors the nightly news show, *Special Report with Brit Hume,* which concludes with Brit moderating a three-person panel of pundits. The most frequent panelist is prominent conservative Fred Barnes, executive editor of the *Weekly Standard.* Most often with Barnes are Mort Kondracke, centrist editor of *Roll Call* (a fiercely nonpartisan newspaper that reports on Capitol Hill), and Mara Liasson, a reporter for National Public Radio, who has been both a registered Democrat and registered Republican. In case you're counting, that's two hard-core conservatives and two centrists. Imagine a political game of seesaw, with two people sitting on one end, and two others sitting in the middle. See how balance works on *Special Report with Brit Hume?*

Fox's contribution to the Sunday morning political shows is *Fox News Sunday with Tony Snow.* Snow, a former speechwriter for the first President Bush, was editorial page editor for the *Washington Times* and is a frequent substitute host for the Rush Limbaugh radio show (which itself has been accused of having a right-wing bias).

Not all of Fox's stars are avowed conservatives. For example, Bill O'Reilly was an avowed independent when he joined FNC. I say "avowed" because he was actually a registered Republican. He lied about it. He's a big liar. That's why he's one of the lying liars featured on the cover of this very book. Take a look! There he is. Looking at you and lying. He should be called Bill O'*Lie*-lly. We'll get to him a minute.

If any program on the Fox lineup represents the network's credo "fair and balanced," it's got to be what has been called "the highest rated show in television"[1]: *Hannity and Colmes.* For those of you unfamiliar with the *Hannity and Colmes* dynamic, it's a conservative-versus-liberal talking head show, kind of a combination between *Crossfire* and a Harlem Globetrotters game. Han-

[1]It's not. But Hannity often says it is.

nity spins around on the floor, dribbling behind his back, tossing alley-oops to Peggy Noonan and Bill Bennett. Colmes, the lone Washington General, stumbles around confused until Ollie North hits him in the face with a bucket of confetti.

So there you have it. The Roger Ailes starting five. Hume, Snow, O'Reilly, Hannity, and Colmes.

The Fox News Channel is currently the number one twenty-four-hour news channel on television. It routinely beats CNN in the ratings. In just seven years, Fox has grown from a mere twinkle in Rupert Murdoch's bulging eye into a veritable all-news Death Star in his media Empire. And for that, I doff my hat to the Vader-like genius of one Roger Ailes, who has hit upon a winning formula: flag waving, martial musical stings, the whoosh, frequent advertisements for the Abdominizer, repetition of the "fair and balanced" slogan, and right-wing propaganda.

# Bill O'Reilly:
# Lying, Splotchy Bully

**Last** time I saw Bill O'Reilly in person, he called me an "idiot" and screamed at me to "shut up!" He also said I was "vicious, with a capital V," which I suppose means that I'm especially vicious. This all happened on national television, if you can call C-SPAN national television.

We were in Los Angeles at an annual publishing hootenanny called the BookExpo America. We were both there to promote our books. Bill was hawking his latest, *Living with Herpes*,[1] while I was promoting (with evident success) the book you are enjoying right now. We were on a panel with the wise, witty, and wonderful Molly Ivins, who was there to discuss her newest, *Bushwhacked: Life in George W. Bush's America.*

I was concerned there might be fireworks between me and O'Reilly. A preliminary cover of my book had been blown up and prominently displayed at the convention center. And based upon what I know about Bill, it occurred to me that having to walk past a giant foamcore book cover calling him a liar might light his notoriously short fuse. Also, as you may have noticed, the cover features an unflattering picture of O'Reilly looking splotchy and ill-tempered. Blown up ten times, he looked ten times splotchier. For the record, I had been hoping to get a better picture, or at least have the cover artist remove the splotches.

I first saw Bill when he charged into the green room and accused, not me, but Lisa Johnson, my 109-pound publicist, of doctoring the cover photo to make him look bad. "This is what I look

---

[1] Actually, the full title is *Living with Herpes in George W. Bush's America.*

like," he said angrily, pointing at his nose. "I've never looked like *that!* You responsible for this?" he said, leaning his six-foot-four frame toward her and jabbing his finger menacingly. "That's a doctored photo. *This* is what I look like," again with the pointing. Which seemed a little unnecessary, since both Lisa and I recognized him from his many appearances on television.

I tried to calm him down. "Bill, Lisa had nothing to do with the photo."

"This is what I look like."

"I know, I know."

"I've never looked like that."

"Bill, Bill. This is a preliminary cover." I explained that, in fact, I had *wanted* to have the photo doctored to take out the splotches. I'd even wanted them to retouch *my* photo. "Look," I said, "I want them to take about forty pounds off my ass." I thought that might lighten the mood.[2]

No sale. "I don't look like that. *This* is what I look like." Point. Point.

"Bill, we'd love to have a picture of you from *The Factor.* Something of you lying. Anything with your mouth open would work." Again, trying to lighten the mood. But I wasn't getting through.

By then the moderator of our panel, Pat Schroeder, was summoning us to the event, where seven hundred of America's best—our nation's booksellers—sat waiting for what promised to be a high-minded and civilized exchange of contrasting views between two men and a woman of letters.

Molly went first and enchanted us all with her tart Texas wit. Next up, O'Reilly. After talking about his book for about five minutes, he began to talk about mine. Seeking to contrast his style with my own, he said, "I don't call people names . . . I don't call anybody

---

[2]For the record, the ass on the cover belongs to male model Tyson Beckford. Thanks, Ty.

a liar. I'm not doing that. I'm trying to elevate the discourse . . . I don't call people big, fat idiots."

Nobody missed the reference to my book *Rush Limbaugh Is a Big Fat Idiot*.

Then it was my turn. Like the other panelists, I spent the first part of my allotted time describing my book in general terms. Then I got to O'Reilly. I felt a certain obligation to explain why a fellow panelist's face was on the cover of a book whose title included the words, "lies," "lying," and "liars."

So, I told a little story.


**A** couple of years ago, I was watching Bill O'Reilly on C-SPAN. He was being interviewed in front of an audience about his book *The No Spin Zone*. The interviewer reached back a few years into O'Reilly's career. "Now, you were the host of *Inside Edition*. That was kind of a tabloid show." (I'm paraphrasing here—I don't have this one on tape.)

"Tabloid show?!" O'Reilly was indignant. "We won two Peabodys!"

"Well, still. It was a tabloid show."

"I beg your pardon, but the Peabody is only the most prestigious award in journalism," O'Reilly answered with great umbrage.

"But you have to admit, *Inside Edition* was something of a tabloid show."

"So you want us to give the Peabodys back?" O'Reilly smirked. "We won two Peabodys, the most prestigious award in journalism."

Watching at home, I knew O'Reilly was right about one thing: The George Foster Peabody award *is* the most prestigious in broadcast journalism. But what on earth could *Inside Edition* have won a Peabody for? For its "Swimsuits: How Bare Is Too Bare?" story? Or maybe its three-part series on the father of Madonna's first baby, Carlos Leon?

So I went to my Nexis, and put in "Peabody Award" and "Inside Edition." I did get three hits.

They were *all* Bill O'Reilly claiming that *Inside Edition* had won a Peabody. Or two. If you read these *O'Reilly Factor* excerpts closely, you'll see an interesting progression.

*August 30, 1999:*

> **O'REILLY:** I anchored a program called *Inside Edition,* which has won a Peabody Award.

*May 8, 2000:*

> **O'REILLY:** Well, all I've got to say to that is *Inside Edition* has won, I—I believe two Peabody awards, the highest journalism award in the country.

*May 19, 2000* (with guest Arthel Neville):

> **NEVILLE:** You hosted *Inside Edition* . . .
>
> **O'REILLY:** Correct.
>
> **NEVILLE:** Which is considered a tabloid show.
>
> **O'REILLY:** By whom?
>
> **NEVILLE:** By many people.
>
> **O'REILLY:** Does that mean . . .
>
> **NEVILLE:** And even you . . .
>
> **O'REILLY:**  . . . we throw the Peabody Awards back? . . . We won Peabody Awards.

Next I went to the Peabody website, which lists all their winners throughout the years. No *Inside Edition.* Still, to be thorough, I called the Peabody people, and asked the woman on the other end of the line, "Yeah, did, by any chance, the show *Inside Edition* ever win a Peabody?"

She laughed. "No, *Inside Edition* has never been the recipient of a Peabody Award."

I decided to call Bill. He was nice enough to get right back to me.

"Yeah, Al, what can I do for you?"

"Well, first of all, Bill, congratulations on all your success."

"Thanks. What's up?"

"Okay. I saw you the other night on C-SPAN, and you said *Inside Edition* had won a couple of Peabodys."

"That's right. We won two."

"Well, maybe you should check that out with the Peabody people. Because they don't think you did."

There was a pause on the other end of the phone. Then, "I'll call you back."

About ten minutes later, Bill was on the line.

"It was a Polk."

"A Polk?" I asked.

"Yeah. Just as prestigious as the Peabody."

"So, there are *two* most prestigious awards in journalism?"

Bill didn't appreciate the sarcasm. "Al, it's a *very* prestigious award."

"Fine," I said. "But, Bill, don't you think it's little ironic that you got it wrong about a *journalism* award?"

"Okay, Al, go after me if you want," and he hung up.

And, by the way, that Polk? *Inside Edition* won it over a year *after* O'Reilly left the show.

I thought Bill's reaction was odd. He hadn't said, "Omigod! How embarrassing! I can't believe I've been saying that! Thank you so much, Al, for calling me. Now I won't humiliate myself by making that mistake again. Thank you so much for calling me rather than taking it public." Instead it was, "Go after me if you want."

So, I did. I called Lloyd Grove at the *Washington Post*'s Reliable Source column. Lloyd ran with it on March 1, 2001, after checking Nexis. He also offered Bill the opportunity to respond, and quoted him saying, "Al Franken is on a jihad against me. So I got mixed up between a Peabody Award and a Polk Award, which is just as prestigious."

Okay. So that was over. He got caught making a mistake, and was kind of a jerk about it. Fine.

Hang on.

A couple other papers picked up the Peabody story from the *Post. Newsday* ran a March 8 column by Robert Reno titled "Some Factors About O'Reilly Aren't Factual."

On March 13, O'Reilly introduced that night's Personal Stories segment: "Attack Journalism." "This is personal to me, because some writers are really violating every tenet of fairness in what they're saying in print about your humble servant."

His guest was Michael Wolff, the terrific media columnist for *New York* magazine. O'Reilly and Wolff began by discussing the definition of "attack journalism." O'Reilly, it was clear, considered himself an expert on attack journalism, but not for the reason you might think.

*March 13, 2001:*

**O'REILLY:** If you lie about someone it goes right up on the Nexis, where everyone can read it. . . . I'll give you an example. Guy says about me, couple weeks ago, O'Reilly said he won a Peabody Award. Never said it. You can't find a transcript where I said it. You—there is no one on earth you could bring in that would say I said it. Robert Reno in *Newsday,* a columnist, writes in his column, calls me a liar, all right? And it's totally fabricated. That's attack journalism. It's dishonest, it's disgusting, and it hurts reputations.

**WOLFF:** It's also incorrect journalism, if it's wrong . . .

**O'REILLY:** It is wrong.

**WOLFF:** Okay, well, then the guy made a mistake.

**O'REILLY:** No, come on. He made a mistake that's—lives forever in the Nexis. And did he write a column the next day saying he made a mistake?

**WOLFF:** Well, obviously, obviously, obviously he should— usually, I find, if someone's made a mistake, if you ask them to correct it, they do correct it.

**O'REILLY:** No, not in this society anymore.

So that was the story I told the seven hundred booksellers at the BookExpo America luncheon. Bill O'Reilly "mistook" one Polk that the show won, after he left it, for two Peabodys that, as he put it, "we" won. But then, not two weeks after conceding his error both to me and to the *Washington Post,* he attacked a journalist for accurately describing what he had done. I'd found four separate incidents where he had claimed to have won Peabodys, three of them in Nexis transcripts. O'Reilly bellowed: "Never said it. You can't find a transcript where I said it . . . it's totally fabricated. That's attack journalism. It's dishonest, it's disgusting, and it hurts reputations."

So, O'Reilly had lied to cover up his "mistake," and he had called an honest reporter a liar.

The entire crowd seemed to enjoy all the ironies of the story. With one exception. Bill O'Reilly, sitting three feet to my right, had become so angry he had developed another splotch. As I was telling the story I could see him stewing, gripping his pen with seething fury. My wife, watching on television three thousand miles away, thought that Bill was going to jam the pen through my eyeball and into my brain.

But I was having fun. Not because I enjoy attacking people gratuitously. But because O'Reilly is a bully and he deserved it. Everything I had said was true. On his show, O'Reilly cuts off anyone who disagrees with him. If they stand up for themselves, he shouts them down. But this wasn't his show.

When I concluded my remarks, O'Reilly went nuts. First, he called me an "idiot," fulfilling his earlier promise to "elevate the discourse." Then the King of the No Spin Zone, where spinning is prohibited, started deliberately mischaracterizing what everyone in the room and watching at home had just heard me say. "All he's got in six and a half years is that I misspoke, that I labeled a Polk Award a Peabody. He writes it in his book, he tries to make me out to be a liar . . ."

Of course, that wasn't the problem. The problem was what he did once he was confronted with his "misstatement." He went on the attack and lied. And here he was doing it again. "No, no, no," I tried to interject.

"Hey, SHUT UP! You had your thirty-five minutes." (I had spoken for twenty.) "SHUT UP!!!"

Tempers flared. A moment later, O'Reilly was spinning like Ari Fleischer's dreidel. "This guy accuses me of being a liar, ladies and gentlemen, on national television, because I misspoke and labeled a Peabody a Polk." Vintage O'Reilly. I had accused him of the ultimate sin. As he had said on a C-SPAN call-in earlier that day, "Once you lie, you're out of the box. That's the No Spin Zone."

He had said it to a Muslim caller who criticized *The Factor*.

**MUSLIM CALLER:** There's a lot of anti-Islamic rhetoric on there. For instance, you know, you compared the Koran to *Mein Kampf* . . .

**O'REILLY:** No, I didn't. That's a total lie.

Actually, it wasn't. The caller had been referring to a July 7, 2002, *Factor* regarding a controversy at the University of North Carolina. The school had assigned its incoming freshmen a book entitled, *Approaching the Qur'an: The Early Revelations.* O'Reilly was outraged:

> I don't know what this serves to take a look at our enemy's religion. See? I mean, I wouldn't give people a book during World War II on the emperor is God in Japan, would you? . . . I wouldn't read the book. And I'll tell you why: I wouldn't have read *Mein Kampf* either. If I were going to UNC in 1941, and you, Professor, said, "Read *Mein Kampf,*" I would have said, "Hey, Professor, with all due respect, shove it. I ain't reading it."

The Muslim caller tried in vain to explain his question. "Can I just finish, sir? Can I finish my question?"

"Whoa! Hold it. Hold it." O'Reilly interrupted. "No, you can't finish. Because once you lie, you're out of the box. That's the No Spin Zone. Get it? You can't say on national television, even if it is C-SPAN, 'You compared the Koran to *Mein Kampf.*' That's a lie, all right? So you're out of the box."

As distinct from Ann Coulter, whose lies are painstakingly crafted to serve her radical political agenda, Bill seems to lie for two reasons. One, to polish his own apple (Peabodys). And two, to attack anyone who's critical of him (Koran). Often, the two are related.

Take, for example, my favorite moment at the BookExpo luncheon. I questioned him about a claim he had made three minutes earlier about having "started out with nothing." See, O'Reilly always likes to crow about his hardscrabble childhood in working-class Levittown, Long Island. As he once told the *New York Observer,* "You don't come from any lower than I came from on an economic scale."

Trouble is, an inside source (O'Reilly's mother) tells a different story. Mrs. O'Reilly proudly told the *Washington Post* that the family regularly took vacations in Florida, and that little Billy attended private school, a private college, and that their home was in the affluent suburb of Westbury, not blue-collar Levittown.

So I asked Bill where he grew up. Was it Westbury or Levittown? Seemingly a hard question to spin. Backed into a corner, he replied with a crazy lie, saying that he had grown up "in the Westbury section of Levittown."

There is no Westbury section of Levittown. They are two separate villages several miles apart. It was like saying he had grown up in Brooklyn—the Manhattan section of Brooklyn.

O'Reilly's innumerable lies and distortions all feed a Big Lie: that he is a no-nonsense, bare-knuckled, working-class straight shooter who sticks it to the phonies and sticks up for the little guy. I ain't buyin' it.

In reality, O'Reilly is as phony as his Peabodys. Under the guise of his angry everyman persona, he uses a shopworn inventory of boorish tactics—bluster, bullying, and belittling—in order to advance a thinly disguised conservative agenda. It's not that O'Reilly is a Republican hack like Sean Hannity, whom we will meet in the next chapter. His position on issues is not doctrinaire movement conservative, and every once in a while I find myself in agreement with him, like when he says the government should stay out of the bedroom or when I'm drunk.

But his constant protest that he is an impartial observer and not an ideological conservative is just another lie. And it's another lie that he's had to lie about.

From the 1996 launch of *The O'Reilly Factor,* part of Bill's credentials as a non-ideologue was that he was a registered independent. Lie! NPR's Mike Pesca refuted this in his January 2001 profile of O'Reilly for *On the Media,* reporting that O'Reilly had been a registered Republican since 1994.

Calling the story "a hatchet job," O'Reilly claimed, "I've never heard of NPR's Mike Pesca."

In fact, Pesca had talked to O'Reilly for an hour and used portions of the taped conversation in the profile.

What about the party registration?

"Their accusation on my voting record is simply a lie," O'Reilly lied. "And I'm not surprised, since we've done a number of stories on NPR's left-leaning ways." Yes, O'Reilly admitted, he had been a registered Republican since 1994, but he had not been aware of it. It seems that there had been an innocent mistake. "When I registered in Nassau to vote in 1994, there was no box for an independent. I left all the boxes empty. Somehow, I was assigned Republican status."

Take a look. Reproduced below is his 1994 voter registration form from Nassau County. I have blocked out his home address and signature so that no one can steal his manufactured identity.

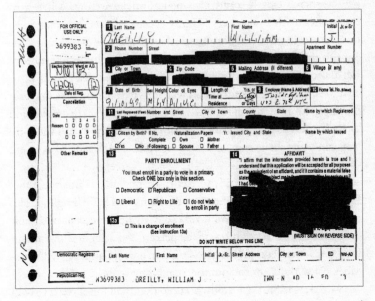

One thing we do know for sure. Bill O'Reilly is a registered Lie-o-crat.

**O**'Reilly is a right-wing blowhard of the schoolyard-bully variety. Even so, I found it curious when on his radio show the Monday following our BookExpo panel he told his audience: "Somebody calls you a liar to your face, you don't laugh that off. In the Old West that would have got you shot." More interesting, I thought, was his absolute *guarantee* that he would have won had we had a gunfight a hundred and fifty years ago. I found that especially odd since, as it so happens, during the summers, I do the entire state fair quick-draw circuit, and I happen to be third in the country. And I know damn well O'Reilly ain't first or second! Nevertheless, O'Reilly guaranteed that, and this is a quote, "I would have put a bullet right between his head."

There's no shame in screwing up a statistic every now and then. People make mistakes. It's just that somewhere deep in O'Reilly's psyche there's clearly a terror of being proved wrong. When he's confronted with a mistake, the bully comes out, and he bludgeons his guests with incorrect or just made-up facts and figures.

On the February 5, 2002, *Factor,* O'Reilly told his guest, National Organization for Women president Kim Gandy, that 58 percent of single-mom homes are on welfare. Actually, only 14 percent of single moms are on welfare. When Gandy challenged him, O'Reilly bloviated, "You can't say no, Miss Gandy. That's the stat. You can't just dismiss it . . . it's 58 percent. That's what it is from the federal government."

On February 26, 2001, O'Reilly defended Jeb Bush's "One Florida" program to State Senator Kendrick Meek. "All right, look, in the university system in Florida right now, 37 percent of the 10 universities are black. Thirty-seven percent." Black enrollment that year was 18 percent. When Meek tried to correct him, O'Reilly cut Meek off with "I got the numbers and they're dead on!"

On May 8, 2001, O'Reilly boasted that the United States gives "far and away more tax money to foreign countries than anyone . . . nobody else even comes close." Japan gives more. Not per capita. More. When his guest, Phyllis Bennis from the Institute for Policy Studies, pointed out that the U.S. gives a smaller fraction of its gross national product than any other developed country, O'Reilly bellowed, "That's not true." It is.

Bennis hung in there and said, "It's absolutely true on a per capita basis."

Clearly having no idea what he was talking about, O'Reilly flailed away. "Well, we have a three hundred million population base here and Sweden has three million, so that's skewed out." Sweden has about nine million people.

Now, like I said, there's no shame in occasionally messing up an obscure statistic like the population of a major industrialized nation. You probably didn't know it. I certainly didn't. But I would never insist that I did.

Even when an obnoxiously persistent guest catches O'Reilly dead to rights, Bill still manages to sow seeds of doubt in the viewers' minds. As you can see from this 1999 program with popular corporate speaker Al Franken.

FRANKEN: In '93 [Clinton] passed the budget deficit package with all Republicans voting against him.

O'REILLY: Clinton couldn't have passed it, Al, if all Republicans voted against him.

FRANKEN: Yes, he could. Well, every Republican voted against it in '93. Every one of—every single Republican.

O'REILLY: Is that—you—I might stand corrected there. We'll look it up.

FRANKEN: You might. You do. It is . . .

O'REILLY: I do stand corrected?

FRANKEN: Yeah.

O'REILLY: Are you sure?

FRANKEN: Absolutely. Every Republican . . .

O'REILLY: Okay. All right. We've got it on the tape.

Which, of course, they'll never rerun.

These are only a few examples, a few pearls dredged from the vast oyster bed feeding off the effluent flowing from the sewer of right-wing dishonesty.

This book is not intended to be the definitive account of Bill O'Reilly's lies and obnoxious behavior. Inevitably, when this book comes out, Bill will employ one of his standard gambits, one which has a certain crude effectiveness. He will say, "Is that all you got, Al? After six and a half years on the air, all you can find is my mistaking a Polk I didn't win for two Peabodys that never existed and then falsely accused a journalist of lying about it; that I physically intimidated your book publicist; that I freaked out about the splotchy photo; that I compared the Koran to *Mein Kampf* and then lied about it; that I lied about where I grew up; that I lied about my party affiliation; that I gave phony numbers on welfare moms, black university enrollment in Florida, and foreign aid; that I had no idea how Congress works; and that I threatened to shoot you between the head? Is that all you got, Al? Is that all you got?"

Well, no. Since you ask, there's also the fact that, every once in a while, you display such a depraved indifference to ordinary standards of decent behavior that it makes me wonder if I really was in danger there on the stage of BookExpo America.

On February 4, 2003, O'Reilly interviewed Jeremy Glick, whose father, a Port Authority worker, died in the World Trade Center attack. Glick had signed an advertisement opposing the war in Iraq, and O'Reilly invited him on the show to explain himself, which he did modestly and eloquently. Until, that is, O'Reilly cut him off.

> **O'REILLY:** I don't want to debate world politics with you.
>
> **GLICK:** Well, why not? This is about world politics.
>
> **O'REILLY:** Because, number one, I don't care what you think.

A little while later, O'Reilly told Glick to "shut up, shut up!" When Glick tried to explain his point, O'Reilly told his engineer: "Cut his mic. I'm not going to dress you down anymore out of respect for your father."

Once the microphones and cameras were off, Glick later told *Harper's* magazine, O'Reilly sent him on his way with some words of fatherly advice: "Get out of my studio before I tear you to fucking pieces!"

Rap artist Ludacris never had the pleasure of being a guest on O'Reilly's show. But as Ludacris himself might say: This member of the hip-hopcracy was a victim of the man's hypocrisy.

After Pepsi featured Ludacris in an ad for their world-famous soft drink, Pepsi, O'Reilly called on his viewers to start a boycott.

> I'm calling for all responsible Americans to fight back and punish Pepsi for using a man who degrades women, who encourages substance abuse, and does all the things that hurt particularly the poor in our society. I'm calling for all Americans to say, Hey, Pepsi, I'm not drinking your stuff. You want to hang around with Ludacris, you do that, I'm not hanging around with you.

The clarion call brought an immediate result. As he said the next day on his show, "Because of pressure by *Factor* viewers, Pepsi-Cola late today capitulated. Ludacris has been fired."

Now, I don't hold any brief for Ludacris. My son loves his stuff, as do many members of TeamFranken. Also, my daughter dated him for a while, and I have to say, he seemed like a nice enough fellow.

It's just that, ignoring the obvious evidence of his name, O'Reilly insists on taking Ludacris's profane lyrics about prostitutes, street violence, and drug use at face value. According to my son, Joe, what he enjoys about Ludacris is his gift for playful and irreverent hyperbole. That's how Joe put it in his tenth-grade essay, "Ludacris and *The Mayor of Casterbridge*," for which he received a B+.

In his own artistic efforts, however, O'Reilly doesn't display the same deft touch. Especially when writing about teen crack whores, pimps, vicious murders, and something that O'Reilly calls "fellatio."

I'm referring to his 1998 suspense thriller, *Those Who Trespass*, about "a serial killer who will exact revenge on everyone who has sabotaged his rising TV career." Believe it or not, this is a real book written by the real Bill O'Reilly.

Here is one of my favorite scenes, in which the killer, Shannon Michaels, seduces Ashley Van Buren, a tabloid reporter. I should warn you, because of the turgid, pedestrian prose and frank sexual nature of the following, young children and English majors might want to skip ahead.

> Ashley was now wearing only brief white panties. She had signaled her desire by removing her shirt and skirt, and by leaning back on the couch. She closed her eyes, concentrating on nothing but Shannon's tongue and lips. He gently teased her by licking the areas around her most sensitive erogenous zone. Then he slipped her panties down her legs and, within seconds, his tongue was inside her, moving rapidly.

In Ludacris's hit album *Word of Mouf*, which my son tells me means "word of mouth," there are depictions of four murders. In *Those Who Trespass*, there are six murders, one of which involves jamming a spoon through the roof of the victim's mouth and up into his brain stem. O'Reilly's book also depicts a fifteen-year-old crack whore performing this "fellatio" business on her pimp, Robo. ("Say, baby, put that pipe down and get my pipe up.") While

Ludacris, like O'Reilly, enjoys describing oral sex scenes, there are none on his album involving a teen crack whore.

However, when it comes to the use of the words "fuck" and "bitch," O'Reilly simply can't compete, managing a mere 51 variants of both words. Ludacris, on the other hand, achieves a commanding lead with 109 "fucks" and "bitches," a better than two-to-one advantage.

Perhaps, in light of their similar taste for profanity, oral sex, and hos, O'Reilly had second thoughts about his jihad against Ludacris, because five months later, O'Reilly denied that he'd ever called for a boycott. "I simply said I wasn't going to drink Pepsi while that guy was on their payroll," he said. "No boycott was ever mentioned by me."

I think Bill O'Reilly unquestionably has talent. And not just a talent for lying. And I'll admit I sometimes find his program entertaining, especially when he runs circles around a particularly inept guest, like a man with a lazy eye and a speech impediment who's come on *The Factor* to demand rights for child molesters. That can be good sport.

But at the end of the day, you have to ask yourself if it's worth the emotional capital necessary to try to change Bill O'Reilly.

I believe it is. I dare to hope that Bill O'Reilly can be saved. From himself. Because, frankly, I don't think Bill O'Reilly likes Bill O'Reilly. Although he clearly has no love for me, I want him to know that I love him, and that when this book comes out, I would be delighted to reach out to Bill O'Reilly by coming on his program and giving him a chance to apologize for his lies and his lies about lies. I know it would be cathartic.

When the last lie had been apologized for, the world would see a new Bill O'Reilly: fair, open-minded, genuinely impartial. Perhaps this new Bill O'Reilly's TV program would not be as successful as his old one. But the important thing is that if he doesn't calm the raging storm inside, the man may well be headed for a crack-up.

**O**h, one last thing. About the splotchy photo. I'd been planning to have it desplotched by the top guy in the field. But three days after our BEA encounter, Bill's publisher and agent called my publisher and said that he was threatening to sue if I didn't take his picture off the cover.

Good move.

So there you are, Bill, in all your splotchy glory.

What was it, anyway? Sun poisoning? A touch of the Irish flu? An allergic reaction to some shellfish you'd eaten at a Heritage Foundation event? Not that I'd believe you if you told me.

# Addendum to O'Reilly Chapter

**Since** this book came out in hardcover, O'Reilly has been accusing me of "defamation" and of being a "smear merchant." I have asked O'Reilly repeatedly to come up with anything in this chapter that is not true. He has been unable to.

To tell you the truth, I don't like being called a "smear merchant." But I'm a big boy, and I have a public platform. But there is someone that O'Reilly has gone after repeatedly that has no platform, and so I'd like to use this paperback edition to address a terrible wrong that O'Reilly has perpetrated against Jeremy Glick, the student whose father died in the World Trade Center. You know, the young man who O'Reilly had on his show and told to "get out of my studio before I tear you to fucking pieces."

In October 2003, Terry Gross asked O'Reilly about the incident on her NPR show *Fresh Air*.

> **GROSS:** I want to ask you about one of the famous interviews that you did on your show. It—this has gotten a lot of—this has been mentioned a lot in the press. And actually it was reprinted in *Harper's Magazine*. You were interviewing the son of a man who was killed in the World Trade Center attack on September 11. And he had signed an ad that was critical of the United States. This ad, while condemning the terrorists' actions, also criticized the United States for actions it had taken in Baghdad and Vietnam. You invited him to give his point of view on your show. And then you kept telling him to shut up. And I'm wondering how much of that is like theater and showmanship? Do you know what I mean?
>
> **MR. O'REILLY:** None.
>
> **GROSS:** Uh-huh.

**MR. O'REILLY:** None. If you read the transcript of that interview—have you read the transcript of it?

**GROSS:** Yes, I have. I read the transcript of the excerpt, not the—

**MR. O'REILLY:** No, I mean, outside of *Harper's*—outside of *Harper's*.

**GROSS:** No, I haven't read the complete interview. I read the transcript that was in *Harper's*.

**MR. O'REILLY:** Okay. Well, you should. You should get the full transcript. And it's easily available. You'll see that person came into the show and said that the attack of 9/11 was an "alleged" attack. All right? **And then he proceeded to blame President Bush and his father, Bush the elder, for orchestrating the attack on their own country. Now once you get into that realm—we were surprised. We thought he was going to be a rational person. I—it is my duty, all right, to say, "Can you prove that? Do you have any evidence to demonstrate what you're saying?" He had none. So, then I aborted the interview . . .** [my bolding] Now, *Harper's* and the left-wing press, you know, would do what they always do. They took it out of context. They didn't print the whole interview, to show what the guy's wild allegations were; defamatory allegations, by the way. And it is so irresponsible. And this is what happens all the time. I mean, these hit books, these slander books, smear books, that's what they do.

O'Reilly is right on one point. The transcript of the Glick interview on *The O'Reilly Factor* is readily available. It's easy to find on Google or on Nexis. I had done that in early 2003 to research this chapter. So, when I listened to the Terry Gross interview, I knew that, again, O'Reilly was lying. Nowhere, *nowhere* in the interview does Glick say anything about Bush or his father having pre-knowledge of, let alone "orchestrating," the attack on 9/11.

And therefore, of course, at no point did O'Reilly ask him for evidence.

Glick e-mailed me through my publisher soon after O'Reilly's *Fresh Air* interview to ask me for help. He wrote me: "It's very difficult to lose your dad in such a violent fashion, and even harder to have your love for your family questioned so abrasively by such right-wing hacks as O'Reilly."

Jeremy then thanked me for including his story in my book. But then he moved on to O'Reilly, who evidently had been spouting lies about what Glick had said for some time.

> He has been defaming me almost weekly. . . . He is telling the press that I said that "Bush knew about the WTC." We never even gestured toward the question of prior knowledge and anyway, I don't believe Bush "knew." . . . This is obvious to anyone who saw the episode or read the full transcript. This is very damaging for me. I'm a Ph.D. candidate and freelance writer. It doesn't help me to get gigs being painted as some sort of conspiracy nut.

O'Reilly was smearing a guy whose only crime was losing his father in the World Trade Center. All his family had of their father was his thumb.

Jeremy wanted my advice. Was there any way to sue O'Reilly for slander? I called up Floyd Abrams, my lawyer in the Fox lawsuit. Floyd told me that Glick would not only have to prove that O'Reilly was lying (easy to do), but that O'Reilly *knew* that he was lying. The fact that O'Reilly had lied so pathologically in the past would make that hard to do. His advice was "don't sue."

I figured the next best thing was to get O'Reilly to stop defaming Jeremy. I called a producer of O'Reilly's show and asked him/her to tell O'Reilly diplomatically that he was, shall we say, in error about the content of Jeremy's interview on *The Factor*. Could he perhaps stop saying that Jeremy was a conspiracy nut? The producer told me, "I can't do that. It wouldn't do any good."

A few weeks later, C-SPAN taped a speech I gave at the University of Missouri. I decided to use that platform to air this disgraceful story. Jeremy tells me that O'Reilly has since stopped.

What a guy!

Oh, one last thing. O'Reilly walked off *Fresh Air* before his interview with Terry Gross was over because he felt she was too tough on him. Evidently, it's okay to ask the tough questions in *The No Spin Zone*. But outside the *Zone* you have to toss nice, plump softballs so little Billy can make contact and run all the way to first base, where he can jump up and down while his mother cheers him on.

Anyway, the next day on *The Factor*, Billy complained that "Mrs.[sic] Gross tried to embarrass me." What's worse is "that I paid for it. And so did you. The Corporation for Public Broadcasting, which funds NPR, gets a billion dollars a year in taxpayer money."

Now, forget for a moment that when you pay your cable bill, you're paying for Fox whether you watch it or not. The fact is that the Corporation for Public Broadcasting received 377.8 million dollars in taxpayer money that year. But what's being off by almost a factor of three? Maybe that's why he calls it *The Factor*.

Did O'Reilly retract the lie? No. But that makes sense. Because, remember, as O'Reilly himself constantly reminds his audience, "We've never had to retract a story here on *The Factor*."

I repeat. What a guy!

# Hannity and Colmes

**As** we said before, there's no better examplar of the Fox News Channel's credo than its leading left/right debate show, *Hannity and Colmes*. According to Rush Limbaugh, "Hannity's vigor and clarity inspires." As hard as TeamFranken tried, they couldn't find a similarly glowing quote from anyone about Colmes, but I told them to keep looking and hopefully have one for the paperback edition.

To give you some idea of the show's fair balance, I picked a representative episode: the broadcast immediately following President Bush's 2003 State of the Union address. The point-counterpoint pretty much broke down like this:

"This is a big vision. This is a bold agenda!"

vs.

"President Bush did a magnificent job!"

**Q**uick. Which one of the critical sentiments was expressed by the liberal? If you guessed "magnificent job," you're a winner. And you know what's also a winner? Fair and balanced news coverage.

The show's first guest that day, former Reagan speechwriter Peggy Noonan, was struck with how, like Churchill, Bush seemed imbued with a special destiny. Hannity gushed:

**HANNITY:** There were two lines that we just played that I really loved in the speech. That "we will not ignore, we will not pass along our problems to other Congresses, other presidents, other generations. We'll focus on them with clarity and courage."

NOONAN: We will do it now. We won't pass off to anyone
else. We'll do it now. I think "do it now" was a strong kind
of sub-theme in the whole speech. I got to tell you this was
a big and powerful and important speech.

Lost in all the talk about not passing problems off to future
generations was that Bush was passing off to future generations a
projected ten-year deficit of $1.8 trillion dollars on top of the ex-
isting $6.4 trillion national debt. (Since then, the projected ten-
year deficit has risen to $4 trillion.) That might have been
something for Colmes, representing the liberal side, to comment on.
Instead, he asked Peggy if there were any great lines in the speech
that might live on in the public memory. Thanks for manning the
barricades, Alan.

Colmes's rhetoric may not be fiery, but at least there's not much
of it. In the State of the Union show, TeamFranken did a little rudi-
mentary content analysis: they counted how many words Hannity said, and then counted how many words Colmes said. Then we
compared them:

# HANNITY     COLMES
## 2,086         1,261

It makes sense that Sean Hannity is the alpha male to Alan Colmes's
zeta male. After all, Hannity got to pick his li'l partner himself.
Roger Ailes, who has a real eye for talent, personally chose the
telegenic, soon-to-be superstar Hannity to head up a show in
prime time on his newly created Fox News Channel. According to
*The New York Times,* the show's working title was *Hannity and
Liberal to be Determined.* After Hannity, a self-described "arch-
conservative," chose Colmes, the former stand-up comedian and self-
described "moderate" ("I'm quite moderate," he told a *USA Today*
reporter), Colmes and his lawyer demanded that the name of the

show be changed. It would be the last argument that Colmes would ever win.

When I first met Hannity, I had no idea who the hell he was. It was 1996, in a green room at Fox News. I had just finished my first appearance on *The Factor* to promote *Rush Limbaugh Is a Big Fat Idiot,* and was about to pick up my coat when I was confronted by what appeared to be an angry, Irish ape-man.

Hannity did not like the title of my book

"I don't believe in making ad hominem attacks," he said, thrusting his jaw in a characteristic display of simian aggression.

"Oh. That's why I titled it *Rush Limbaugh Is a Big Fat Idiot.* It's an ironic comment on the fact that Rush makes ad hominem attacks all the time. You see?"

Evidently not. "I've never heard him make an ad hominem attack." As I would later learn, this was in keeping with Sean's seasoned ability to lie and believe it. Or at least just lie.

"Really? How about when he called Chelsea Clinton 'the White House dog'? Would that qualify?"

This was a very famous incident. On Rush's TV show in 1993, shortly after Clinton took office and years before Buddy joined the First Family, the show put up a picture of Socks, the cat. "Did you know that the Clintons not only have a White House cat," Rush said coyly, "but they also have a White House dog?" Then, on screen came a picture of a thirteen-year-old Chelsea.[1]

Sean was ready for that one. "That was a mistake. A technician accidentally put up the wrong picture."

---

[1] Coulter, in her own deeply perverse idiom, weighs in on the issue of insulting women for their appearance. "There is nothing so irredeemably cruel as an attack on a woman for her looks. Attacking a female for being ugly is a hideous thing, always inherently vicious . . . so which women are constantly being called ugly? Is it Maxine Waters, Chelsea Clinton, Janet Reno, or Madeleine Albright? No, none of these. Only conservative women would have their looks held up to ridicule because only liberals could be so malevolent. A blind man in America would think the ugliest women ever to darken the planet are Paula Jones, Linda Tripp, and Katherine Harris. This from the party of Bella Abzug." Nicely done, Ann! Triple bank shot. Attacking Democrats for being irredeemably cruel while pointing to five, count 'em five, supposedly unattractive Democratic women.

"Really? Okay, then tell me, what was the joke? 'The Clintons not only have a White House cat'—picture of Socks—'they also have a White House dog.' What's the joke? What picture was supposed to come up?"

Alan Colmes was standing nearby. "You know, he's got a point, Sean. There's no joke without the picture of Chelsea."

But Sean would have none of it. "It was a *mistake!* A technician put up the wrong picture. That's what Rush said. And I believe Rush."

"Okay. Let me ask you this. It was a taped show. Taped hours before it aired. If it was a technical mistake, why didn't they fix it with the correct picture, whatever that possibly could have been?"

Sean kept arguing his indefensible position, instead of just giving up and admitting that his pal Rush had crossed the line, at least in that one instance. After a couple of trips around the barn, I accused Sean of intellectual dishonesty.

"Intellectual dishonesty?" he shot back. "How about the Democrats saying Gingrich wants to cut Medicare spending?"

"You're changing the subject, Sean."

"When actually it's a seven percent *increase* in spending! Increase!"

"Right. Look, could you just admit that Rush deliberately insulted a thirteen-year—"

"I mean, talk about intellectual dishonesty!"

For some reason, that set me off, and before long we were screaming at each other. I had never in my life hated a person more than I hated Sean Hannity at that moment. Finally, Colmes broke us up, and I left, shaking my head. Who was that asshole?

Fast forward seven years, and that asshole now has the second most popular radio talk show in America, right after the guy who made the Chelsea joke. Eight million listeners regularly sharpen their minds on the whetstone of his rough, sturdy tongue. One of those listeners e-mailed me a couple of months ago. Hannity, it seems, had told the story of our green room fracas. Only he embellished a little. According to Sean, I had been "escorted out by Fox security."

Another lie from Sean Hannity. Or was it? It occurred to me that I *had* been escorted out—by Colmes. In addition to being Sean's liberal on-air punching bag, maybe, just maybe, Colmes also worked security detail at Fox. In fact, now that I thought about it, as the only liberal at Fox, Colmes probably did a lot of other odd jobs around the network.

As it turns out, I was right. In the "Odd Jobs" chapter in Alan's new autobiography, *Back to You, Sean: The Alan Colmes Story,* we learn that Colmes's duties as cohost of *Hannity and Colmes* include adding toner to the copiers and printers, loofah-ing Roger Ailes in his personal steam room, and ordering Chinese food for editors working on misleading video packages. A scrupulous removal of lint from Sean's jacket using Alan's trusty lint roller, and it's show time. After another fabulous show, Hannity may be headed home, but Alan Colmes's day is just beginning. There're floors to be mopped, plants to be watered, light bulbs to be replaced, and coffee to be ground for the morning. It's lonely being the only liberal at Fox, but Alan doesn't mind. There is so much satisfaction to be had, not just from occasionally getting a word in edgewise on his own show, but from hearing Roger Ailes's chuckle when he sees the little paper strip reading "Hannitized for Your Protection" that the former comedian carefully placed across the seat of the toilet in his private bathroom.

If you haven't heard of Colmes's book, it may be because it's been overshadowed by Hannity's own page-turner, *The New York Times* best-seller *Let Freedom Ring.* The book lays out the conservative party line on everything from A to Z, where A is for abortion and Z is for zupply-zide zeconomics. Amazon.com reviewer Reagan Ohendalski of Huntsville, Texas, gives the book five stars and calls Sean "the new conservative genius." In his review, he goes on, "Don't listen to these other jerks who are only rating the book with 1 star to bring down the average."

Whether or not *Let Freedom Ring* deserves one star or five depends very much on how one judges books. If one relies on the uninformed, or "Ohendalski," approach, a five it is! However, TeamFranken used a more sophisticated approach. We asked questions like "Is what the book says true?" and "How could Hannity be so incredibly obnoxious?" and "Why would any sane person buy this book?"

To arrive at our rating, TeamFranken weighted the first question, "Is what the book says true?" 85 percent more heavily than the other two questions combined. This may seem unfair to Mr. Hannity, who, as we will demonstrate below, does not understand percentages.

You'd think, according to our weighting system, we'd start with the lies. But instead, for reasons too technical to be explained here, I'll just start with the incredibly obnoxious stuff.

Here's a doozy: pages 145 to 146. Hannity is ranting about the "absolute abomination" that is the New York City public school system. After rattling off some grim statistics about test scores, he says:

> City and state education officials didn't seem to have a clue about what was going wrong. "Is it teaching?" asked state Education Commissioner Richard Mills. "Is it teaching practice? Is it the material? Is it the work students are doing? What are they reading? What are they writing? What kind of math problems are they doing?"
>
> *What are these people doing with our tax dollars if they don't even know the answers to these questions?* [Italics in original.]

You should know, dear reader, that as I read these right-wing books, I often scrawl notes in the margins. When I reached this particular nugget, I wrote:

"Rhetorical question, asshole!"

It sure seemed like Mr. Mills was dramatically illustrating his commitment to examining every aspect of the state's educational system in his quest for excellence and higher standards, and that Hannity, full of contempt for both his readers and the truth, was twisting this good man's words into a noose of lies. In fairness, however, I went back to the article Hannity was quoting, and examined Mr. Mills's words for myself. Was he, as Hannity implied, bumbling around, hoping that someone would tell him what the kids in his schools were doing all day? I'll report. You decide. Here's how Mr. Mills starts:

> "When you look at schools in relation to the accountability system, New York City schools have a long way to go."

Now for a little context. Richard Mills was the person who had *created* that accountability system. In fact, just the year before, Mills had been presented with the prestigious Corning Award for Excellence because, among other things, he had set tough new academic standards and required rigorous testing of all students' progress. The difficulty of the tests that Mills himself had imposed had led to the low test scores Hannity cited. Back to the article:

> "There's no simple fix," he said. "I would peel the onion. I would ask questions about all the fundamentals that go on in school."

And that's where Hannity started quoting him—when Mills started asking questions about all the fundamentals. So when Mills asked "Is it teaching?" or "What are they reading?" he didn't mean it *literally.* He was using what's called "a rhetorical device."

But you knew that, Sean. And still you presented it as if the man had no clue what was going on in his schools. Do you see why that's obnoxious? And not just obnoxious, but also dishonest? And, frankly, stupid?

Let's do another one. During one of his endearing liberal-bashing jags, Hannity spits out: "They tell us that fuel-burning SUVs are bad for America, but flag-burning SOBs aren't." Well, Sean, fuel-burning SUVs burn fuel. And there are about fifty million of them. They contribute to global warming and our dependence on oil from countries like Saudi Arabia, which fund the very terrorism you *profess* to be so upset about. Flag-burning, on the other hand, is relatively rare. And what's more, Saudi Arabia does not produce American flags. Most American flags are made in Taiwan, a staunch ally.

Here's another ridiculous thing he says. In keeping with his uncompromising stance against terrorism, Hannity takes a tough principled stand against John Walker Lindh, the American Taliban. I'm with Hannity when he calls Lindh a traitor, but what really irks me is when he uses Lindh to malign an entire county. No one man can represent an entire county, unless that county is Climax County, Montana, which does indeed have a single resident— Gerard Wagner of County Rd. 1. Ho there, Gerard.

Here's Hannity:

> Named after John Lennon,[2] John Lindh was born in Marin County, a wealthy, liberal suburb of San Francisco.[3] He grew up in a veritable ideological Disneyland of moral relativism, political correctness, and not-too-subtle anti-American multiculturalism, the kind that preaches that America is a racist, sexist, bigoted, imperialist, homophobic, and thus fundamentally evil and oppressive nation.

It's a wonder that Marin produced only one American Taliban and not thousands, isn't it? We're lucky al Qaeda didn't establish a training camp right there in Sausalito. Hannity keeps hacking away:

---

[2]Who was named after John the Baptist.
[3]Actually Lindh was born in Washington, D.C., and moved to Marin when he was ten. Was Hannity lying? I don't think so. I think this is a simple case of what we at TeamFranken call "pulling an Uma." You see, as we like to joke, when you assume, you make an ass out of Uma Thurman.

> He grew up feeding his mind on *The Autobiography of Mal-
> colm X,* not Moses or Peter or Paul . . . In time, Lindh con-
> verted from anything-goes liberal agnosticism to hardcore
> Middle Eastern radical Islam.

Before reading this, I had never considered the direct line between
liberal agnosticism and hard-core, radical Islam. But Hannity has
a strong case. So many of my liberal, agnostic women friends from
college gradually relinquished their freedoms and decided to spend
the rest of their lives in chadors, avoiding the gaze of men.

In contrast to Lindh's depraved childhood environment, Hannity trumpets his Long Island childhood in the protective embrace
of the Catholic Church. Gee, nothing weird happened to cute little boys in the Catholic Church, eh, Sean? Nothing that would explain your bizarre fixation with our nation's homosexuals.

Throughout *Let Freedom Ring,* amid the half-truths about tax
policy and the pabulum about national security, we find page upon
page of denunciations of homosexuals, homosexuality, and homosexual practices—including, believe it or not, on page 158, a graphic
description of what he calls "fisting."

Speaking of formative experiences, Hannity tells us about one of
his great early inspirations. On page 43, he outlines the life story of
his embattled hero. He's talking about how his champion was
keyed in to the gravity of the terrorist threat even back in the eighties. He says:

> Ollie North—decorated for courage and bravery in Vietnam
> with the Silver Star, the Bronze Star, two Purple Hearts, and
> three Navy Commendation medals—helped plan the Rea-
> gan administration's liberation of Grenada. He helped plan
> the raid against Libya, in response to repeated rounds of
> Libyan terrorism. He helped the President wage a relentless
> campaign for freedom and democracy in Central America.

> And for his efforts, Ollie and his family were not heralded as American heroes. They were targeted—first by Libyan terrorists, and then by liberal Democrats.

On page 263, he tells the full story:

> Ollie North—decorated for courage and bravery in Vietnam with the Silver Star, the Bronze Star, two Purple Hearts and three Navy Commendation medals—was also keyed in to the gravity of the terrorist threat. He helped plan the Reagan administration's liberation of Grenada. He helped plan the raid against Libya, in response to repeated rounds of Libyan terrorism. He helped the Reagan-Bush administration wage a relentless campaign for freedom and democracy in Central America. And for his efforts, Ollie and his family were not heralded as American heroes. They were targeted—first by Libyan terrorists (physically) and then by liberal Democrats (politically and legally).

From this, I gleaned a couple of things. First, that Oliver North was decorated with the Silver Star, the Bronze Star, two Purple Hearts, and three Navy Commendation medals, was involved in the military actions in Grenada, Libya, and throughout Central America, and was targeted both by Libyan terrorists and by liberal Democrats. Secondly, that Hannity must have been paid by the word. As I am. Look for more on Oliver North's medals throughout this book.

Why, exactly, was North targeted by liberal Democrats (and moderate Democrats, and moderate Republicans) in the 1980s? Was it for his bravery and courage, which won him the Silver Star, the Bronze Star, two Purple Hearts, and three Navy Commendation medals? No, it was because he *broke the law* and then *lied to Congress about it.*

It was the Iran-Contra hearings that first got Hannity excited about politics. "Like nothing before it," he says, "the Iran-Contra hearings struck a chord of discontent and urgency in me. It was as if they were calling me to action."

You've got to wonder about a guy whose interest in politics was inspired by the illegal funding of terrorists.

Back to our book-rating system. The initial idea, if you recall, had been to separate the analysis into three categories: obnoxiousness, "Why would any sane person buy this book?" and *lies*. I now realize the hubris of this approach, since there's so much overlap between these categories. So far, I've tried my best to maintain a laserlike focus on incredibly obnoxious material, though I've perforce slipped into instances of naked dishonesty and strong reasons to question the sanity of anyone who bought this thing.

Similarly, as I move into the "lying" section, I will be unable to strictly adhere to the rigid boundaries of our initial model. I apologize.

## LIE #1: I CAN'T "VOUCHER" FOR HIS EXAMPLES OF VOUCHER SCHOOLS.

Where New York State Education Commissioner Mills noted that there is "no simple fix" to the problems of New York City schools, Hannity has found one—and not just for New York, but for every school in the country. Vouchers. It's about competition. If the government gives every student a voucher for tuition at the school of his or her choice, public, private, or parochial, schools will be forced to compete. The result? An education revolution. "You're going to see excellence in education, because the parents are going to send their kids to schools where there is discipline, where there are no problems, where their kids will get a good education, and we'd see test scores go through the roof," explains Hannity. Vouchers, says Hannity, will succeed because they will "break the nearly total government monopoly on K–12 education in this country."

The proof?

Hannity describes a couple of since-discredited studies and then quotes an editorial saying that "vouchers offer the only hope available to many poor students trapped in the worst schools." Now comes the lie. "Want more proof?" asks Hannity. "Come right here to New York."

He then trumpets *The Miracle in East Harlem: The Fight for Choice in Public Education*, a book that chronicles a remarkable success story in one of America's most troubled school districts. What happened in Harlem? A handful of teachers and principals in District Four reorganized their district into small, independently run alternative public schools to which neighborhood parents could choose to send their children. The result? Hannity puts it best: "small, innovative public schools having just a little more freedom than traditional public schools has paid such big and valuable dividends in the lives of children and their parents. . . . Kids are learning in Harlem."

Gives you hope, doesn't it? But not for vouchers. Because the "Miracle in East Harlem" didn't actually involve vouchers. There were no vouchers. None. Nobody got a voucher. Vouchers? Not a part of the miracle.

Even though he offers it as proof that "vouchers offer the only hope available," Hannity carefully avoids saying whether or not the East Harlem program uses vouchers. Suddenly, he switches to the term "school choice." The artful avoidance of a literal untruth makes this a particularly sneaky kind of lie. He's deliberately misleading his readers. When you have to mislead to make your argument, it's because you know you don't have a case.

The debate over vouchers isn't about school choice. It's about whether to divert money from public schools (where it can fund programs like this one) to private schools. The Harlem story is about innovation *within* the public school system and, specifically, about the proven benefits of reducing the size of large schools. The federal Smaller Learning Communities Program aims to replicate the Miracle of East Harlem nationwide. In his 2003 budget, however, President Bush put the program on his hit list for termination.

## LIE #2: THE NO-GROWTH NINETIES

This is a simple one. For some reason, in the midst of making a point about something or other on page 205, Hannity lets this one rip: "Decades of liberal no-growth policies have seriously endangered our economic and national security."

Here's a chance for you, the reader, to write your own joke. You might want to include a reference to how Clinton presided over the longest economic expansion in the history of the United States of America. I'm sure Hannity's publisher, HarperCollins, will get a kick out of seeing what you come up with.

Send your rib-tickler to:  HarperCollins Publishers, Inc.
10 East 53rd Street
New York, NY 10022

## LIES #3 THROUGH #7: THE CRAZY TABLE

During the first 190 years of our great democracy's existence, our government racked up $789 billion dollars in debt. That might sound like a lot. But during the eight years that Ronald Reagan occupied the White House, he managed to nearly triple that number. The day he left office, our national debt stood at $2.191 trillion dollars. That's a hard number to even comprehend. If it helps, picture a stack of 2,191 billion-dollar bills. Lot of money, huh?

It is a sacred tenet of the lying right that Ronald Reagan did not cause the massive budget deficits of the eighties. Republicans keep trying to find new and creative ways to disprove the truth on this one. A hallowed favorite is the old saw that, as Hannity puts it, "the deficits of the eighties were caused by the insatiable spending demands of congressional Democrats."

To prove it, Hannity pulls a table, not out of his ass, but out of his "e-ass." That is, he takes the trouble of going on the Arpanet—oh, I'm sorry, thanks to Gore, it's the Internet—and downloading a chart from "The Ronald Reagan Homepage." Lest you think

"The Ronald Reagan Homepage" is former President Reagan's actual official homepage, you should know it's not. It's the brainchild of Brett Kottman, who is also the webmaster of Brett Kottman's Reality Hammer, a page featuring occasional essays defending the Reagan legacy. Hannity plucks the table directly from the web and prints it on page 223 of his book. (Hannity alters the table slightly: He leaves out one key number, which I'll discuss below.)

The table proves, or should I say, "proves," or should I say, does not prove that Congress caused the deficit by inflating Reagan's spending. Here it is, just as Hannity presents it.

**Federal Budget Outlays Proposed (Reagan) and Actual (Congress), percent difference, and cumulative percent difference (in billions of dollars)**

| | Outlays | | | |
|---|---|---|---|---|
| Fiscal Year | Proposed | Actual | % Difference | (Cumulative) % Difference |
| 1982 | 695.3 | 745.8 | 7.3 | |
| 1983 | 773.3 | 808.4 | 4.5 | 12.1 |
| 1984 | 862.5 | 851.8 | -1.2 | 10.8 |
| 1985 | 940.3 | 946.4 | 0.7 | 11.8 |
| 1986 | 973.7 | 990.3 | 1.7 | 13.5 |
| 1987 | 994.0 | 1003.9 | 1.0 | 14.6 |
| 1988 | 1024.3 | 1064.1 | 3.9 | 19.1 |
| 1989 | 1094.2 | 1144.2 | 4.6 | 24.5 |
| **Totals** | $7357.6 | $7554.9 | | |
| **Average** | | | 2.8 | |

Source: http//reagan.webteamone.com/reaganbudgets.html.

If this is confusing, don't worry—it was meant to be. Stare at it for a while. In particular, think about the column on the right. Go ahead. Take a good long look. How ya doin'?

Perhaps it will help to read the sentence that Hannity uses to introduce the table: "In fact, had all of Reagan's budgets been adopted, federal spending would have been 25 percent less on a cumulative basis."

Let's parse that sentence. It seems to say that "had all of Reagan's budgets been adopted, federal spending would have been 25 percent less on a cumulative basis." In fact, that's exactly what it says.

What does that *mean*? Well, it seems to mean that if Congress had passed all of the budgets that Reagan proposed, then the government would have "cumulatively" spent 25 percent less money. That's a fair interpretation, right? And if true, that means Congress *was* responsible for the Reagan era deficits.

Now let's look at the "totals" section of the table. What appears to be the total of Reagan's proposals are about $200 billion less than what appears to be the total of Congress's budget-busting appropriations. Or, as the table says in the "average percentage difference" section, the difference is 2.8 percent (or, actually, 2.7 percent—if you're schooled in long division, as neither Hannity nor his source Kottman seem to be).[4]

How does that get us to the "cumulative" 25 percent? That seems to be where the right-hand column comes in. I stared and stared at the thing, and couldn't make a whit's worth of sense out of it. So I faxed the table to some good friends, and Ken Lay, former CEO of Enron, got back to me in a jiff.[5]

"He's compounding the difference, Al."

"I don't understand, Ken."

"It's simple. The first year the difference between Reagan's proposal and the actual number is 7.3 percent. The second year is 4.5 percent. So, he multiplies 1.073 times 1.045 and gets 1.121. Thus, a 12.1 percent 'cumulative' difference. And then on and on."

---

[4] $7554.9 \div 7357.6 = 1.0268158$. Since the original numbers are only precise to the tenth, we round the final answer to a difference of 2.7 percent.

[5] The dialogue with Ken Lay is fictional. He wouldn't even return my calls. Happy, Dutton lawyer?

"You know what's funny, Ken? Even over the phone I can hear the quotation marks around the word 'cumulative.' "

"Well, that's because what he's doing is completely meaningless. Remember how we just calculated a 12.1 percent cumulative difference? That assumes that when Reagan was making his second budget, he was somehow tied to the 'actual' number from the previous year. But he's *not* tied. He can propose whatever budget he wants."

"Hmmm. You see, that time I thought I heard quotation marks around 'actual.' "

"Oh yeah, there's no reason to trust any of the numbers from this guy. For example, he says that Reagan proposed 695.3 billion dollars in '82 and Congress approved a budget of 745.8 billion dollars. He got the Reagan number right, but Congress 'actually' approved 696 billion dollars in their concurrent budget resolution."

"Wow! How do you know all this stuff?"

"Hey, I didn't get to be the head of the world's largest energy trading company just by being a crook."

"So, wait. He's taking phony numbers, using them in a phony way, to make a phony point?"

"Yeah. You got this guy's number? I got a little start-up company cooking here, and I need a CFO who's willing to, you know, push the envelope."

"Gee, I don't have the number on me."

"Well, when you find it, give me a call on the Lear. Margie and I are flying to Aspen for the week. Gotta go."

You know, Ken Lay might have taken a real beating in the press, but if you need someone in a pinch to look at some shady number-crunching, he's a pal.

No sooner had I hung up with Ken, then I got a call from Thomas Mann at the Brookings Institution which (as you may remember) bills itself as an "independent, nonpartisan organization." Mann confirmed everything Lay had told me, but in a more boring, think tank-y way. He explained that Kottman had compared apples to oranges, or more precisely, apple lies to orange lies. An honest chart would compare Reagan's budget proposal to the budgets Congress actually passed. The Hannity/Kottman chart, by contrast, compares Reagan's budget to total spending. Here's the trouble: Once Congress passes a budget, what is actually spent can vary depending on economic conditions, non-budgetary policy changes, and estimation errors. This variance in spending cannot be entirely blamed on either Congress or the White House.

Thanks for the fucking civics lesson, Tom.

Okay, let's rewind. Remember how Hannity described his table? He said it proved that "had all of Reagan's budgets been adopted, federal spending would have been 25 percent less on a cumulative basis." Even if we ignore all the table's faults, this is still a whopper.

If you accept the bizarro cumulative percent differences, you can argue that eight years of Congressional budget increases would have yielded a 24.5 percent increase over the last year of Reagan's budget (1989). But Hannity, lyingly, makes the claim that it would have been 25 percent lower over the *entire period.* This is where Hannity left out one of Kottman's numbers. On Kottman's original table, he included an "average cumulative percentage difference" number, 3.1 percent. The fact that Hannity chose to omit this one specific number shows that, yet again, he knew he was lying.

Remember our first meeting, Sean? Remember, we discussed intellectual dishonesty?

Even if Kottman's numbers weren't phony, and even if Hannity were correctly interpreting the table, and even if the "cumulative" technique were something other than a laughable charade, then *still*, even then, Congress would have only passed $274 billion in extra spending in a period when the debt shot up $1,402 billion. So even in this loony right-wing fantasyland of a budget scenario, the deficits still weren't caused by Democratic congressional spending.

Still, I was curious. What *really* happened in the so-called "eighties"? So, at the risk of being bored, I called back Tom Mann, who put together an accurate table. Unlike the Hannity/Kottman table, which is the work of a hack, this table is the work of a scholar, which comes from the Latin *scholarum,* meaning "one who uses facts instead of *lies."* (Italics mine.)

**Actual Real Facts Table**

| Fiscal Year | Proposed | Actual | % Difference | (Cumulative) |
|---|---|---|---|---|
| 1982 | 695 | 696 | 0.1 | This |
| 1983 | 758 | 770 | 1.6 | is |
| 1984 | 849 | 859 | 1.2 | a |
| 1985 | 926 | 932 | 0.6 | totally |
| 1986 | 974 | 968 | -0.6 | bogus, |
| 1987 | 994 | 995 | 0.1 | piece- |
| 1988 | 1024 | 1041 | 1.9 | of- |
| 1989 | 1094 | 1100 | 0.5 | shit |
| **Totals** | $7314 | $7361 | | column |
| **Average** | | | 0.6 | |

Source: Budget of the United States, Fiscal Years 1982–1989;
Congressional Almanac 1982–1989.

Kudos to Tom for his excellent work on this one, especially the clearer right-hand column. Kottman, if you remember, styles himself "The Reality Hammer." Well, we Democrats have a few tools in our figurative toolbox as well. So let's apply our "Lie Detecting Plunger" to the lie-clogged toilet of Hannity's budget analysis.

**Lie #3:** The numbers on the chart are phony.
**Lie #4:** The "cumulative percentage difference" is presented as if it means something.
**Lie #5:** Hannity takes the cumulative percentage difference and,

confident in his readers' inability to interpret or think, intentionally mischaracterizes its already bogus conclusions. In for a penny, in for a pound!

**Lie #6:** The point that all these lies are intended to make (that spending-crazed Democrats, rather than Reagan, caused the deficits) is itself false.

**Lie #7:** Hannity uses "powerful arguments, clear thinking, and fact-based analysis." This is a quote from Newt Gingrich on the book's back cover.

## LIE #8: HANNITY MAKES IT SOUND LIKE IT WAS THE DEMOCRATS WHO WEREN'T INTERESTED IN INVESTIGATING THE CAUSE OF 9/11, WHEN ACTUALLY IT WAS THE REPUBLICANS, ESPECIALLY THE WHITE HOUSE, WHO DID EVERYTHING THEY COULD TO BLOCK AN INDEPENDENT PROBE INTO THE MASSIVE INTELLIGENCE FAILURE

No matter what Ann Coulter may say, 9/11 is no joking matter. On that we can all agree. After 9/11, I wanted to know what had gone wrong. So did most Americans. Except, Hannity claims, the Democrats in Congress. He says that "liberal Democrats at first showed little interest in the investigation of the roots of this massive intelligence failure."

If the Democrats were the bad guys, Hannity knows who the good guys were. Bush and his team, he says, "made it clear that determining the causes of America's security failures and finding and remedying its weak points would be central to their mission."

He must have been referring to the October 6, 2001, *New York Times* article "House Votes for More Spy Aid and to Pull in Reins on Inquiry," which said that "Democrats, who offered their own amendment, continued to push for a commission that would examine the events leading up to September 11 and the failure to stop the attacks." No, I guess that can't be it.

But you know, you can't trust *The New York Times* like you can trust the *Washington Times*. I guess Hannity must have been thinking of their May 24, 2002, "Bush Rejects Probe of 9/11: Will Not Give Up Sensitive Terror Papers." Wait! Bush "rejects"? That makes it sound like *Bush* was rejecting the probe instead of the Democrats.

So maybe Hannity was talking about the May 20, 2002, *New York Times* article "Cheney Rejects Broader Access to Terror Brief." That article began, "Vice President Dick Cheney said today that he would advise President Bush not to turn over to Congress the August intelligence briefing that warned that terrorists were interested in hijacking airplanes." Ooh. That almost sounds like the *opposite* of Hannity's point.

Wait. Must be the October 21, 2002, *Newsweek* article, "Cheney: Investigators, Keep Out." No. That doesn't sound too promising. But what about the first sentence? "Dick Cheney played a behind-the-scenes role last week in derailing an agreement to create an independent commission to investigate the 9/11 attacks." Hmm. Well, what about the article's last sentence? " 'There's just this general philosophical orientation that the less the world knows, the better,' says one GOP staffer."

Of course, the fact is the Bush administration fought a 9/11 commission every step of the way, even though the families of the victims were begging for an independent probe from day one.

When political reality finally forced the Bushies to give in, whom did they appoint to head the commission? The families' choice? Former New Hampshire Senator Warren Rudman, who cochaired the Hart-Rudman Commission on National Security? No. Rudman had backed John McCain in New Hampshire.

Instead, Bush picked Henry Kissinger. You can tell someone wants to get the truth out about cover-ups, mass killings, and mistakes made at the highest levels of government when they appoint Henry Kissinger to lead the investigation.

Critics complained that Kissinger had a history of being overly secretive and had potential financial conflicts of interest. When

Kissinger resigned a couple of weeks later, he said it was because he wanted to be secretive about his financial conflicts of interest.

So why does Hannity go out of his way to lie about who wanted to look into 9/11 and who didn't? It's because, like so many conservative henchmen, he is doing the dirty work for the Bush administration. Democrats, according to Hannity, wanted to cover up the intelligence failure that led to 9/11 because *it was all Bill Clinton's fault.*

# The Blame-America's-
# Ex-President-First Crowd

**Six** months after 9/11, the Gallup Poll of Islamic Countries found that an overwhelming majority of those surveyed believed the attacks on the World Trade Center and the Pentagon had not been the work of Arabs. Well-educated Egyptians and Saudis believed that the Israelis were behind the murder of three thousand innocents on 9/11, in large part because of articles in their countries' official state newspapers. One of the widely disseminated stories was that no Jews died in the collapse of the Trade Towers because they had received calls telling them not to go to work that day.

To tell you the truth, I got the Jew call. I had an office in the Trade Center where I used to do most of my writing. The call came from former New York mayor Ed Koch. "Al," he told me, "don't go to work on the twenty-third day of Elul."

**A**ctually, I watched the events of that awful day from Minneapolis, where I was visiting my mom. Mom's in a nursing home, so I was staying at a hotel. That morning, as I grabbed some coffee, I noticed people huddled around a TV. A plane had hit the World Trade Center. Must have been a commuter plane. Maybe the pilot had a heart attack or something. Then the second plane hit. It was sickening. Then came the Pentagon. We were under attack.

Somehow, I got through to my wife in Manhattan. She was fine, at home on the Upper West Side, about five miles north of the Trade Center. My son was at school on the Upper East Side. My daughter was away at college. As I watched the first tower collapse, I was stunned. But I still couldn't register the magnitude of what was happening, even as the second one went down.

I spent the rest of the day at the nursing home watching TV

with my mom. She didn't understand what had happened—as if any of us really did. A friend of mine watched with his elderly mother in Queens. As he left that evening, she said to him, "At least no one was hurt."

That night, like all Americans, I just kept watching. Giuliani was masterful. Bush seemed a little shaky.

On Wednesday, I couldn't reach my family. I desperately wanted to be home in New York. The airport was closed, of course. But Northwest said they'd start flying on Thursday, so instead of driving back, I played golf. In the charity tournament for my mom's nursing home where I had been billed as the celebrity guest. It was a very weird day for golf. Everyone was there to support the nursing home, but we all felt funny enjoying the beautiful day after the ugliest day in American history. At the closing ceremony, as I thanked the nurses who take care of my mom (she can be difficult), I started to choke up.

Thursday, I got a reservation on an afternoon flight to La-Guardia. Dropped my rental off at the airport Hertz. Just as I got to the Northwest ticket counter, they announced that the airport was closing down because of a security threat. I did a one-eighty and ran back to the Hertz counter, where I was told they were now charging $300 a day for cars. The world was falling apart, and I was being bilked.

"So, let me get this straight," I said. "Hertz is taking advantage of a horrific tragedy to jack up the price of your cars?" Yes. But the woman recognized me as the guy who had just turned in his car rented at the pre-terrorist-attack rate. So she gave me the same rate, plus a reasonable drop-off fee in New York. America was pulling together.

It was late afternoon. I left the Twin Cities, determined to drive straight through, listening to local radio and NPR. On September 11, 2001, NPR had more foreign correspondents abroad than any other network news organization in the United States. Americans, so the other networks thought (probably correctly), had lost interest in the world.

Listening to twenty straight hours of coverage as I drove alone through the heartland, I was overwhelmed with the enormity of what had happened. Friday afternoon, I pulled into a truck stop in Eastern Pennsylvania to watch President Bush lead a memorial service at the National Cathedral. For twelve bucks, I got a room with a bed, a shower, and a TV. I showered, changed into some clean underwear, and, lying in bed, watched the memorial and wept.

In times of crisis, people often respond by instinctively doing the things they find most comforting. For many Republicans, then, it is hardly surprising that their way of coping with the horror of 9/11 was to attack Bill Clinton.

Some attacks were more instinctive than others. A clearly rattled Orrin Hatch was all over the news that day, blaming Clinton because he had "de-emphasized" the military. Hatch was also the first to confirm al Qaeda's involvement by disclosing classified intercepts between associates of Osama bin Laden about the attack. Asked about it on ABC News two days later, a miffed Donald Rumsfeld said Hatch's leak was the kind that "compromises our sources and methods" and "inhibits our ability to find and deal with the terrorists who commit this kind of act." Thanks, Orrin.

So if it hadn't been for Hatch, we probably would've gotten bin Laden right away. The disclosure that al Qaeda was responsible did allow Representative Dana Rohrabacher (R-CA) to identify the "root of the problem" just hours after the attack: "We had Bill Clinton backing off, letting the Taliban go, over and over again."

The right-wing media followed suit. The *Washington Times* blamed Clinton. The *New York Post* blamed Clinton. You know who Rush Limbaugh blamed? Clinton. The *National Review*'s White House correspondent Byron York wrote that Clinton's "record is a richly detailed manual of how not to conduct a war on terrorism." Within two days, Newt Gingrich was blaming Clinton for the attacks because of his "pathetically weak, ineffective ability to focus and stay focused." You really got to give Gingrich credit for how hard he tried to disrupt Clinton's focus: His Republican-run House conducted dozens of hostile investigations against the President.

But it had kind of been a waste of Gingrich's time. Clinton, as I will demonstrate below, focused more on terrorism than any previous president. A month before Clinton left office, his administration was praised by two former Reagan counterterrorism officials. "Overall, I give them very high marks," Robert Oakley, who served as ambassador for counterterrorism in the Reagan State Department, told the *Washington Post.* "The only major criticism I have is the obsession with Osama, which made him stronger." Oakley's successor in the Reagan administration, Paul Bremer, disagreed slightly. Bremer, who is currently the civilian administrator in Iraq, told the *Post* he believed the Clinton administration had "correctly focused on bin Laden." Notice the word "focused" next to the words "on bin Laden." I'm talking to you, Newt. And all of you "Blame-Clinton-Firsters."

Right-wingers like to call us the "Blame-America-First Crowd." But they've blamed Clinton, who's not just an American, but was the President, virtually nonstop. And Clinton was not just the President. He was the last *elected* president, who received more votes than any other candidate running against him. In two straight elections! So who's blaming America? The left, which is blaming the terrorists? Or the right, which is blaming a twice-elected President of the United States?

But, you know what, I don't want to get into a whole partisan politics thing here. Not in this book, anyway. We'll leave that for my next book, *I Fucking Hate Those Right-Wing Motherfuckers!,* due out in October 2004. I'm hoping it will "fire up the troops" for the final weeks of the campaign season.

No, this book, the one you are reading now, is about giving both sides a fair shake and getting to the bottom of the big issues that face us all as America transitions into the twenty-first century. Who was to blame for 9/11, other than the terrorists? It's an important question, one that serious-minded people want answered. It's also one that less serious people like Sean Hannity are curious about. And I think it's time to go to the record with an open mind and, more important, an open heart.

Anyone with an open mind and an open heart must admit that, as with the budget deficit, Reagan's antiterror record was a disaster. Radical Islamic terrorists killed more Americans during his administration than during any before, and more than would die under Bush Sr. and Clinton combined. Between the 1983 embassy and Marine barracks bombings in Beirut and the destruction of Pan Am flight 103, nearly five hundred American lives were lost. Reagan's only direct response was a single bombing run against Libya in 1986.

To be fair, two days after the Marine barracks bombing, Reagan did invade Grenada. Although he cut and ran in Lebanon, which might have been interpreted as capitulation, I think his bold attack on Grenada sent a clear message to violent Muslim extremists: If you attack us, we'll invade a Club Med.

The Great Communicator scored another direct hit in the fight against terror by supplying arms to violent Muslim extremists among the Afghani Mujahedeen, as well as to his friends in Iran and Iraq. Crazy, you say? Crazy like a fox, say I!

Now, the Gipper wasn't the kind of president who saw terrorism just in terms of black and white. No, Reagan distinguished between good terrorists and bad terrorists. He loved his terrorist death squads in Guatemala, El Salvador, and most of all, Nicaragua. Enough to violate the Constitution to support the Contras as they raped and tortured nuns. Bad terrorists, on the other hand, were those who used terror irresponsibly. See, Reagan saw the shades of gray, where a less nuanced politician may have only seen unmitigated evil.

On to Bush Sr. No huge terrorist attacks, thank goodness. And there was no way he could have known that Ramzi Yousef and a vast network of violent Muslim extremists were planning the World Trade Center bombing that would take place February 26, 1993. You may remember that no one blamed Bush Sr. for this bombing of the World Trade Center by radical Islamic terrorists.

After all, it did happen on Clinton's watch. He had been president for thirty-eight days.

The only tiny little thing I fault Bush Sr. for is the way he handled Afghanistan. After he continued arming his violent Muslim extremist friends there, the Soviets eventually withdrew in early 1989. Bush promptly implemented the top-secret Project Neglect, which consisted of abandoning (or "neglecting") Afghanistan and allowing it to become a breeding ground for anti-U.S. terrorist training camps. As you will see, Project Neglect would prove a useful template for the far more extensive Operation Ignore put into effect during the first few months of his son's presidency.

In his four State of the Union speeches, George Herbert Walker Bush said the word "terror" only once, in the context of the "environmental terrorism" perpetrated when Saddam set fire to the oil fields. That was it. Bush Sr. cared even less about terror than he did about the *economy*. Stupid, stupid.


Thirty-eight days after taking office, when the World Trade Center was attacked the first time, the handsome, brilliant young President Clinton learned a painful lesson about the consequences of ignoring the terrorist menace. He swung into action. No, he didn't invade a Caribbean nation. Though later he did help restore democracy to Haiti. The way Clinton responded to the 1993 bombing of the World Trade Center was to capture, try, convict, and imprison those responsible. Ramzi Yousef, Abdul Hakim Murad, and Wali Khan Amin Shah are all currently behind bars. You can visit them and ask them if they think Clinton was tough on terror. I hear they enjoy having visitors.

You can ask them, too, about the Clinton administration's ability to thwart planned terrorist attacks. They were involved in further plots to kill the Pope and blow up twelve U.S. jetliners simultaneously. But neither happened. And neither did the huge attacks that were planned against the UN Headquarters, the FBI building, the Israeli embassy in Washington, the LA and Boston airports, the Lincoln and Holland tunnels, and the George Washington Bridge. Why? Because Clinton thwarted them. He thwarted them all. Why, he even thwarted a terrorist truck bomb plot against the U.S. embassy in Tirana, Albania.

That's a lot of thwarting. How did he do that? Well, for one thing he tripled the counterterrorism budget for the FBI. And doubled counterterrorism funding overall. And rolled up al Qaeda cells in more than twenty countries. And created a top-level national security post to coordinate all federal counterterrorism activity.

His first crime bill contained stringent antiterrorism legislation. As did his second. His administration sponsored a series of simulations to see how local, state, and federal officials should coordinate their responses to a terrorist strike. He created a national stockpile of drugs and vaccines (including forty million doses of smallpox vaccine). He coaxed, cajoled, and badgered foreign leaders to join in the fight internationally or to do more within their own borders. And a huge long list of other stuff.

"By any measure available, Clinton left office having given greater priority to terrorism than any president before him," Barton Gellman reported in his definitive four-part series for the *Washington Post*. Clinton's, he wrote, was the "first administration to undertake a systematic anti-terrorist effort."

Now, you know how Washington is. It's almost impossible to get anything done unless both parties are willing to put politics aside and work together. So, on this counterterrorism stuff, you're thinking the Republicans must have been cooperating the whole way. Isn't that what you're thinking? If so, I wish I lived in the same fantasy world as you. No, once the Republicans took hold of Congress, they fought Clinton with the same bitterness that the hostile Whig Congress fought President Polk during the storied second half of his first term. I still get angry thinking about that.

Just as the Whigs fought Polk every inch of the way on tariff reform, so did Republicans fight Clinton on counterterrorism spending. When Clinton asked for more antiterrorism funding in

1996, Orrin "Loose Lips" Hatch objected. "The administration would be wise to utilize the resources Congress has already provided before it requests additional funding."

The year before, after the horrific Oklahoma City bombing, Republicans rejected Clinton's proposed expansion of the intelligence agencies' wiretap authority in order to combat terrorism. Speaker Gingrich explained his opposition by questioning the FBI's integrity. On *Fox News Sunday,* Gingrich said, "When you have an agency that turns nine hundred personnel files over to people like Craig Livingstone . . . it's very hard to justify giving that agency more power." Gingrich, of course, was making a remark about Filegate, one of the many Fox-hyped investigations that yielded zip and then fizzled out. It is unusual to see a man of Gingrich's integrity compromise national security in order to score a cheap political point. Just proves that even the finest of our public servants can slip now and then.

Gingrich was more supportive in 1998, when Clinton struck targets in Sudan and Afghanistan with Tomahawk missiles in retaliation for terrorist strikes against our embassies in Kenya and Tanzania. "The President did exactly the right thing," said Gingrich. "By doing this we're sending the signal there are no sanctuaries for terrorists." See? He's not so bad.

And that's why I just know there must be some good explanation for why, on September 13, 2001, Newt said on Fox, "The lesson has to be that firing a few Tomahawks, dropping a few bombs is totally inadequate," and implored Bush to "recognize that the Clinton policy failed." On the surface this might seem to be a spitefully worded direct contradiction to his earlier position. But I think maybe Newt was having some trouble at home with his new wife, the former staffer he started porking while he was still married to his second wife. I mean, when good people say hurtful things, there's always something going on inside that none of us can truly know.

Immediately after the embassy bombings, Clinton issued a presidential directive authorizing the assassination of Osama bin

Laden. Assassinate bin Laden? Amen, I say. Sean Hannity, though, has devoted a substantial amount of time, both on the air and in his book, to pretending this never happened and criticizing Clinton for not having the balls to do it. On his show, he yammers a lot about Reagan's Executive Order 12333, which prohibits the assassination of foreign heads of state. Watch Hannity on TV, or listen to him on radio. He'll bring it up. It's one of the eleven things he knows.[1]

The fact that Osama isn't actually a foreign head of state and that Clinton issued his presidential directive to assassinate him didn't stop Hannity from writing in his book about a February 2001 episode of *Hannity and Colmes* on the topic. Guest racist David Horowitz is quoted as saying: "We can protect ourselves from terrorist threats like Osama bin Laden. It would be nice if the CIA were able to assassinate him."

Hannity writes about his own reaction: "Amen, I thought."

What is his deal, anyway?

**T**he final al Qaeda attack of the Clinton Era came on October 12, 2000. Al Qaeda terrorists attacked the USS *Cole,* killing seventeen of our sailors. Clinton decided to take the fight against al Qaeda to the highest level possible. Instead of funding and arming them like Reagan, or ignoring them like Bush, Clinton decided to destroy them. He put Richard Clarke, the legendary bulldog whom he had appointed as the first national antiterrorism coordinator, in charge of coming up with a comprehensive plan to take out al Qaeda.

---

[1]The other ten are: 1) Cutting taxes doubles revenues. 2) Democrats who oppose tax cuts for the rich are waging "class warfare." 3) Reagan won the Cold War by putting the Pershing II Missiles into Europe. 4) Democrats are on the wrong side of history. 5) Democrats, not Republicans, are the party of "race baiting," because Democrats accuse racists of racism. 6) A higher percentage of Republican than of Democratic senators voted for the 1964 Civil Rights Act, which means that the Republicans are the party of civil rights. 7) All education problems will be solved by vouchers. 8) Clinton gutted the military. 9) He's not going to sit here and listen to your talking points. 10) Clinton had a chance to get Osama bin Laden from the Sudan in 1996, but blew it. (See box.)

**Reliable Sources**

In *Let Freedom Ring,* Hannity outlines a charge that he frequently makes both on television and on the radio: that Clinton let bin Laden slip from his grasp. He writes,

> It's truly astonishing. Bill Clinton, Al Gore, and their liberal allies on Capitol Hill were offered Osama bin Laden by the Sudanese government, and they turned the offer down. They could have taken him into custody and begun unraveling his terrorist network almost six years ago. But they didn't. And now more than three thousand innocent Americans have paid with their blood.

That *is* astonishing. Hard to think of a more serious charge. You want to be damned sure you have that one locked down pretty tight before you put it in print.

But knowing what we already know about Sean Hannity and the standards to which he holds himself, what are the chances that this whole charge is just baloney?

His entire case comes from a guy named Mansoor Ijaz, a Pakistani-American who claims to have transmitted the offer as a middleman between the U.S. and Sudan. I got the story on Ijaz from former National Security Advisor Sandy Berger and from Daniel Benjamin, past director for counterterrorism on the National Security Council and now senior fellow at the Center for Strategic and International Studies.

Berger only had to meet once with Ijaz to form the opinion that he was an unreliable freelancer, pursuing his own financial interests. Ijaz was an investment banker with a huge stake in Sudanese oil.

Ijaz had urged Berger to lift sanctions against Sudan. Why the sanctions? Because Sudan was and remains a notorious sponsor of terrorism, harboring Hamas, Hezbollah, and al Qaeda. Also, the Sudanese regime is the leading state sponsor of slavery and is considered by many to be genocidal. And totally untrustworthy. Ijaz, however, was arguing their case. As Benjamin said of Ijaz, "Either he allowed himself to be manipulated, or he's in bed with a bunch of genocidal terrorists."

Ijaz said that Sudan was ready to hand over bin Laden. The U.S. does not conduct diplomacy through self-appointed private individuals. When the U.S. talked to Sudan, there was no such offer. The U.S. pursued every lead and tried to negotiate. Nothing.

The story does have a happy ending. Ijaz now has a job as foreign affairs analyst for the Fox News Channel.

*In his book, *Losing bin Laden: How Bill Clinton's Failures Unleashed Global Terror,* author Richard Miniter makes the same charge that Clinton rejected an offer from Sudan to turn over bin Laden. His proof? Well, he offered it on MSNBC's *Hardball:*

> **MATTHEWS:** Yes, but you're sure based on your writing, in fact in your writing, that there was, in fact, a clear-cut offer from the Sudanese government to turn over bin Laden and it was a credible offer that couldn't have been rescinded?
>
> **MINITER:** Chris, I talked to the Sudanese general who made the offer.
>
> **MATTHEWS:** Okay.
>
> **MINITER:** And you know . . .
>
> **MATTHEWS:** He had the power to deliver bin Laden.
>
> **MINITER:** He had the power to deliver bin Laden.

Okay. Let's remember who we're talking about here. A Sudanese general. The Khartoum regime is arguably the most brutal regime in the world. Worse even than Saddam's regime in Iraq. It has killed nearly two million Christians in southern Sudan, traffics in the slave trade, and is the definition of a state that sponsors terrorism.

Miniter's "proof" is like saying "I talked to Hermann Göring at the Nuremberg trials and he *swears* that he offered up Hitler at the 1936 Olympics to Jesse Owens. It was all arranged. All Owens had to do is run up to the reviewing stand and grab Hitler."

What unfolded became the subject of a shocking cover story in the August 12, 2002, *Time* magazine, which I will now take credit for having read.

Working furiously, Clarke produced a strategy paper that he presented to Sandy Berger and other national security principals on December 20, 2000. The plan was an ambitious one: break up al Qaeda cells and arrest their personnel; systematically attack financial support for its terrorist activities; freeze its assets; stop its funding through fake charities; give aid to governments having trouble with al Qaeda (Uzbekistan, the Philippines, and Yemen); and, most significantly, scale up covert action in Afghanistan to eliminate the training camps and reach bin Laden himself. Clarke proposed bulking up support for the Northern Alliance and putting Special Forces troops on the ground in Afghanistan. As a senior Bush administration official told *Time*, Clarke's plan amounted to "everything we've done since 9/11."

Remember how I mentioned that the *National Review*'s Byron York wrote that Clinton's "record is a richly detailed manual on how not to combat terrorism"? Well, if you take out the word "not," you get a pretty good description of the plan: "a richly detailed manual on how to combat terrorism." So Byron was just one word away from understanding the Clinton antiterror legacy.

But the plan was never carried out. In its place Clinton's successor, George W. Bush, and his national security team would conceive and execute a different plan entirely. A plan called Operation Ignore.

# Operation Ignore

**Bill** Clinton's far-reaching plan to eliminate al Qaeda root and branch was completed only a few weeks before the inauguration of George W. Bush. If it had been implemented then, a former senior Clinton aide told *Time,* "we would be handing [the Bush Administration] a war when they took office." Instead, Clinton and company decided to turn over the plan to the Bush administration to carry out. Clinton trusted Bush to protect America. This proved, nine months later, to be a disastrous mistake—perhaps the biggest one Clinton ever made.

Clinton's National Security Advisor Sandy Berger remembered how little help the previous Bush administration had provided to his team. Believing that the nation's security should transcend political bitterness, Berger arranged ten briefings for his successor, Condoleezza Rice, and her deputy, Stephen Hadley. Berger made a special point of attending the briefing on terrorism. He told Dr. Rice, "I believe that the Bush administration will spend more time on terrorism in general, and on al Qaeda specifically, than any other subject."

Which brings me to a *lie.* When *Time* asked about the conversation, "Rice declined to comment, but through a spokeswoman said she recalled no briefing at which Berger was present." Perhaps so, Dr. Rice. But might I direct our mutual friends, my readers, to a certain December 30, 2001, *New York Times* article? Perhaps you know the one, Condi? Shall I quote it?

"As he prepared to leave office last January, Mr. Berger met with his successor, Condoleezza Rice, and gave her a warning. *According to both of them,* he said that terrorism—and particularly Mr. bin Laden's brand of it—would consume far more of her time than she had ever imagined." (Italics mine.)

When I read this, my instinct was to shout for joy and dance around the room, naked, celebrating the finding of a lie. And I did.

"Badda Bing!" I cried, as I ran around the house, my genitals flopping wildly, embarrassing my wife and her bridge group.

After the dressing down from my wife, who really read me the riot act, it occurred to me that all I had really found was a contradiction between *Time* and the *Times*. Maybe *The New York Times* had it wrong. Maybe Dr. Rice, considered a paragon of integrity, had told *Time* magazine the truth—that her predecessor had never warned her about the impending threat from al Qaeda and its evil mastermind.

It was time for the Franken investigative juggernaut to assert itself. I called Dr. Rice's office, prepared to pierce the infamous White House veil of secrecy with a lance of white-hot journalistic enterprise. I left a message, and they called me right back with the answer. A White House official told me that Dr. Rice *had* met with Berger at a briefing, and he had told her about the seriousness of the al Qaeda threat.

Condi lied to *Time*! Badda Bing!

Anyway. After Berger left, Rice stayed around to listen to counterterrorism bulldog Richard Clarke, who laid out the whole anti–al Qaeda plan. Rice was so impressed with Clarke that she immediately asked him to stay on as head of counterterrorism. In early February, Clarke repeated the briefing for Vice President Dick Cheney. But, according to *Time,* there was some question about how seriously the Bush team took Clarke's warnings. Outgoing Clinton officials felt that "the Bush team thought the Clintonites had become obsessed with terrorism."

The Bushies had an entirely different set of obsessions. Missile defense, for example. The missile defense obsession proved prescient when terrorists fired a slow-moving intercontinental ballistic missile into the World Trade Center. If only Clarke had put his focus on missile defense instead of obsessing on Osama bin Laden.

Defense Secretary Donald Rumsfeld was obsessed with a review of the military's force structure, which had the potential of yielding tremendous national security dividends ten or fifteen years down the road. I, personally, am a longtime proponent of force structure review, as anyone who has had the misfortune to spend any time around me when I am drunk can attest. But I don't think it should be to the exclusion of everything else. Let me give you one little example: I also believe in FIGHTING TERRORISM.

While all the Bushies focused on their pet projects, Clarke was blowing a gasket. He had a plan, and no one was paying attention. It didn't help that the plan had been hatched under Clinton. Clinton-hating was to the Bush White House what terrorism-fighting was to the Clinton White House.

Meanwhile, on February 15, 2001, a commission led by former senators Gary Hart and Warren Rudman issued its third and final report on national security. The Hart-Rudman report warned that "mass-casualty terrorism directed against the U.S. homeland was of serious and growing concern" and said that America was woefully unprepared for a "catastrophic" domestic terrorist attack and urged the creation of a new federal agency: "A National Homeland Security Agency with responsibility for planning, coordinating, and integrating various U.S. government activities involved in home-land security" that would include the Customs Service, the Border Patrol, the Coast Guard, and more than a dozen other government departments and agencies.

The Hart-Rudman Commission had studied every aspect of national security over a period of years and had come to a unani-mous conclusion: "This commission believes that the security of the American homeland from the threats of the new century should be *the* primary national security mission of the U.S. government."

The report generated a great deal of media attention and even a bill in Congress to establish a National Homeland Security Agency. But over at the White House, the Justice Department, and the Pentagon, President Bush, Vice President Cheney, Attorney General Ashcroft, and Defense Secretary Donald Rumsfeld de-cided that the best course of action was not to implement the rec-ommendations of the Hart-Rudman report, but instead to launch a sweeping initiative dubbed "Operation Ignore."

The public face of Operation Ignore would be an antiterrorism task force led by Vice President Cheney. Its mandate: to pretend to develop a plan to counter domestic terrorist attacks. Bush announced the task force on May 8, 2001, and said that he himself would "periodically chair a meeting of the National Security Council to review these efforts." Bush never chaired such a meeting, though. Probably because Cheney's task force never actually met. Operation Ignore was in full swing.

Unbeknownst to Bush and Cheney, Richard Clarke was doggedly pushing his plan to put boots on the ground in Afghanistan and kill Osama bin Laden. Thanks to Clarke's relentless efforts, the plan was working its way back up the food chain, after having been moved to the bottom of the priority list, right below protecting the public from giant meteors.

On April 30, Clarke presented a new version of the plan to the deputies of the major national security principals: Cheney's chief of staff, Lewis Libby; the State Department's Richard Armitage; DOD's Paul Wolfowitz; and the CIA's John McLaughlin. They were so impressed, they decided to have three more meetings: one on al Qaeda, one on Pakistan, and a third on Indo-Pakistani relations. And then a fourth meeting to integrate the three meetings. Sure, scheduling these meetings would take months, and would delay the possibility of actually acting on the plan and eliminating al Qaeda, but, according to a senior White House official, the deputies wanted to review the issues "holistically," which as far as I can tell means "slowly."

On July 10, 2001, nearly five months after the Hart-Rudman report had warned of catastrophic, mass-casualty attacks on America's homeland and called for better information sharing among all federal intelligence agencies, Operation Ignore faced a critical test. Phoenix FBI agent Kenneth Williams sent a memo to headquarters regarding concerns over some Middle Eastern students at an Arizona flight school. Al Qaeda operatives, Williams suggested, might be trying to infiltrate the U.S. civil aviation system. He urged FBI Headquarters to contact the other intelligence agencies to see if they had information relevant to his suspicions. Had Williams's memo been acted upon, perhaps the CIA and FBI would have connected the dots. And had Hart-Rudman been acted upon, perhaps the memo would not have been dismissed. Operation Ignore, now in its 146th day, had proved its effectiveness once more.

The holdovers from the Clinton era—Clarke and CIA Director George Tenet—were going nuts. Bush administration insiders would later say they never felt that the two men had been fully on board with Operation Ignore. Tenet was getting reports of more and more chatter about possible terrorist activity. Through June and July, according to one source quoted in the *Washington Post,* Tenet worked himself "nearly frantic" with concern. In mid-July, "George briefed Condi that there was going to be a major attack," an official told *Time.*

Only *Time* would tell what happened next.

On July 16, the deputies finally held their long-overdue holistic integration meeting and approved Clarke's plan. Next it would move to the Principals Committee, composed of Cheney, Rice, Tenet, Secretary of State Colin Powell, and Rumsfeld—the last hurdle before the plan could reach the President. They tried to schedule the meeting for August, but too many of the principals were out of town. They had taken their cue from the President. August was a time to recharge the batteries, to take a well-deserved break from the pressures of protecting America. The meeting would have to wait till September 4.

No one understood better the importance of taking a break to spend a little special time with the wife and dog than President George W. Bush. Bush spent 42 percent of his first seven months in office either at Camp David, at the Bush compound in Kennebunkport, or at his ranch in Crawford, Texas.[1] As he told a $1,000-a-plate crowd at a fund-raiser in June, "Washington, D.C., is a

---

[1]The *Washington Post* reported in an August 7, 2001, article that Bush advisors first thought that his stints at the ranch would enhance his image as a "rugged outsider." But they later worried that the length and frequency of the getaways made it seem like the President was "loafing." To me this just illustrates the mental limitations of the Bush team. Who says a rugged outsider can't also loaf?

great place to work, but Texas is a great place to relax." That's why on August 3, after signing off on a plan to cut funding for programs guarding unsecured or "loose" nukes in the former Soviet Union, he bade farewell to the Washington grind and headed to Crawford for the longest presidential vacation in thirty-two years.[2]

On its 172nd day, Operation Ignore suffered a major blow. Already, the operation was becoming more and more difficult to sustain as the intensity of terror warnings crescendoed. Now, on August 6, CIA Director Tenet delivered a report to President Bush entitled, "Bin Laden Determined to Strike in U.S." The report warned that al Qaeda might be planning to hijack airplanes. But the President was resolute: Operation Ignore must proceed as planned. He did nothing to follow up on the memo.

Actually, that's not entirely fair. The President *did* follow up, a little bit. Sitting in his golf cart the next day, Bush told some reporters, "I'm working on a lot of issues, national security matters." Then, Bush rode off to hit the links, before dealing with a stubborn landscaping issue by clearing some brush on his property.

The next day, he followed up again, telling the press, "I've got a lot of national security concerns that we're working on—Iraq, Macedonia, very worrisome right now."

But Iraq and Macedonia weren't the only things on Bush's mind. "One of the interesting things to do is drink coffee and watch Barney chase armadillos," he told reporters on a tour of the ranch later in his vacation. "The armadillos are out, and they love to root in our flower bed. It's good that Barney routs them out of their rooting."

On August 16, the INS arrested Zacharias Moussaoui, a flight

---

[2]The importance of the loose nukes program (devised by Senators Nunn and Lugar) was explained to me by Jim Walsh of Harvard's Project for the Atom in the following amusingly straightforward way: "There are six hundred metric tons of highly enriched uranium and weapons-grade plutonium in Russia and the former Soviet Union. You cannot make a nuclear weapon if you don't have highly enriched uranium or weapons-grade plutonium. If you want to prevent a terrorist from getting a nuclear weapon, job one is securing all available highly enriched uranium and weapons-grade plutonium."

school student who seemed to have little interest in learning to take off or land a plane. The arresting agent wrote that Moussaoui seemed like "the type of person who could fly something into the World Trade Center." Trying to pique the interest of FBI Headquarters in Washington, a Minneapolis FBI agent wrote that a 747 loaded with fuel could be used as a weapon. If this information had been shared and analyzed, for example by a newly founded Homeland Security Agency, it might have sparked memories of the Clinton-thwarted 1996 al Qaeda plot to hijack an American commercial plane and crash it into CIA Headquarters.

On August 25, still on the ranch, Bush discussed with reporters the differences between his two dogs. "Spot's a good runner. You know, Barney—terriers are bred to go into holes and pull out varmint. And Spotty chases birds. Spotty's a great water dog. I'll go fly-fishing this afternoon on my lake." And you know something? He did just that.

Among those left to swelter in the D.C. heat that August was one Thomas J. Pickard. No fly-fishing for him. In his role as acting FBI director, Pickard had been privy to a top-secret, comprehensive review of counterterrorism programs in the FBI. The assessment called for a dramatic increase in funding. Alarmed by the report and by the mounting terrorist threat, Pickard met with Attorney General John Ashcroft to request $58 million from the Justice Department to hire hundreds of new field agents, translators, and intelligence analysts to improve the Bureau's capacity to detect foreign terror threats. On September 10, he received the final Operation Ignore communiqué: an official letter from Ashcroft turning him down flat. (To give Pickard credit for adopting a professional attitude, he did not call Ashcroft the next day to say, "I told you so.")

Clarke's plan to take the fight to al Qaeda lurched forward once more on September 4, 2001. Eight months after he had first briefed Condi Rice about it, and nearly eleven months after Clinton had told him to create it, Clarke's plan finally reached the Principals Committee that served as gatekeeper to the commander in chief. Bush was back from his trip, rested up, and ready for anything.

Cheney, Powell, Rice, Rumsfeld, and the other Principals debated the plan and decided to advise Bush to adopt it with a phased-in approach. Phase One, to demand cooperation from the Taliban and make fresh overtures to al Qaeda opponents such as the Northern Alliance, would begin the moment the President signed off on the plan. Phase Zero, however, came first: wait several days as the proposal made its way to the President's desk.

On September 9, as the plan cooled its heels, Congress proposed a boost of $600 million for antiterror programs. The money was to come from Rumsfeld's beloved missile defense program, the eventual price tag of which was estimated by the Congressional Budget Office at between $158 billion and $238 billion. Congress's proposal to shift $0.6 billion over to counterterror programs incurred Rummy's ire, and he threatened a presidential veto. Operation Ignore was in its 207th day.

On Operation Ignore Day 208, Ashcroft sent his Justice Department budget request to Bush. It included spending increases in sixty-eight different programs. Out of these sixty-eight programs, less than half dealt with terrorism. *Way* less than half. In fact, *none* of them dealt with terrorism. Ashcroft passed around a memo listing his seven top priorities. Again, terrorism didn't make the list.

On that day, I left for Minneapolis to visit my mom and play some charity golf.

On the next day, the world shook.

The day after that, they started blaming Clinton, covering their tracks, and accusing liberals of blaming America.

# Our National Dialogue on Terrorism

**Why** do they hate us?

> *They hate us because they're evil.*

That's it, huh? That's the entire story?

> *Yes. They're evil. And they hate us because of our freedoms.*

They hate us because of our freedoms?

> *But really because they're evil.*

I know they're evil. I was just thinking that maybe if we understood what specifically seemed to trigger the—

> *Why are you apologizing for the terrorists?*

I'm not. They're evil. You have no quarrel there. It's just that maybe if we understoo—

> *Why are you on the terrorists' side?*

I'm not! I hate the terrorists. I was just saying we might be able prevent the next—

> *Three thousand Americans dead. How can you defend al Qaeda?*

Believe me, I was not defending them. What they did was horrific and inexcusable. They're evil. I was just—

> *Then why are you apologizing for them?*

I'm not. I'm trying to say that maybe there are lessons we can—

> *Why do you hate America?*

# Humor in Uniform

**As** I said, I've gone overseas to entertain the troops on three separate occasions. And when I say the troops, I mean *our* troops. Whatever Ann Coulter would have you believe, I would never entertain any of our enemies. Besides, I'm mainly a verbal comedian. I doubt very much my stuff would translate to the North Koreans or Hamas.

Our men and women in uniform are the absolute best audiences I've ever worked in front of. Not because they love me. They like me. And they *really* appreciate that I bother to show up. But believe it or not, they're usually more excited to see the Dallas Cowboy cheerleaders. Or Jewel. Or Clint Black. Or almost anyone else I've traveled with.

On my last, hastily-thrown-together, post-9/11 trip, I went with three very game New England Patriots cheerleaders. Our forces had just begun the operation in Afghanistan, which President Bush at first called Operation Infinite Justice. Which was a mistake. So was his calling our response to 9/11 a "crusade." Not smart. I've always thought that in those first days, Karl Rove, the head of White House political operations, should have just gotten a Pakistani cab driver off the street in D.C. and run this stuff by him:

"Operation Infinite Justice?! Oh no! Please do not call it that! Only Allah can dispense infinite justice. Please, *please* do not call it that! . . . What else? . . . CRUSADE?!!! OH NO!!!"

So I'm flying across the Atlantic with the three New England Patriots cheerleaders at the start of what is now being called Operation Enduring Freedom. And I get an idea. Why not get some burkhas and introduce them as the Taliban cheerleaders?

I run the idea by Traci, the head cheerleader, and she thinks the idea is "wicked pissah." We work out the bit on the plane.

I announce, "Here, straight from Kabul, the Taliban cheer-leaders!" and they walk out covered head-to-toe in their burkhas.

"Ladies, could you do a number for us?"

Traci leans in, and she whispers through her hood into my ear.

"You're not allowed to dance?" I ask incredulously. "You're not even allowed to listen to music?"

Sadly, the three Taliban cheerleaders shake their heads "no."

"But you're not in Afghanistan anymore! You can do anything you want!" I turn to the troops. "Right, guys?!" The troops, pre-sumably, cheer.

The cheerleaders look at each other. Even through the burkhas, you can just feel the sense of renewed hope. They huddle, talking animatedly. They decide to go for it! Music kicks in: "Gonna Make You Sweat!" by C + C Music Factory, and the Taliban cheerlead-ers, still in their burkhas, do their raunchiest NFL bump and grind.

So, flying across the Atlantic, as Traci, Michelle, and Nicole work out the choreography, I ask one of our military attachés to call ahead to Ramstein Air Force Base for three burkhas.

**F**ive hours later we touch down in Germany and get the full mili-tary welcome. General Gregory S. Martin, Commander, USAF Europe, greets each of us as we hit the tarmac. There are phalanxes of airmen, lots of brass, including the commander of the 86th Air-lift Wing. He gives me a firm handshake and a warm smile.

"Mr. Franken, sir. I'm Brigadier General Mark Volcheff. Wel-come to Germany. Thank you so much for coming."

"My honor, sir."

"Could I talk to you for a moment?"

"Sure."

The general takes me aside and leans in confidentially.

"Mr. Franken, I understand that you put in a request for three burkhas, is that right?"

"Yes. I want to have the Patriots cheerleaders come out as

the Taliban cheerleaders." I grin, expecting a laugh. Instead, a pensive nod.

"Uh-huh. Mr. Franken, now this is entirely your decision. We certainly don't want to tell you how to do your job. But we are trying to make the point that this is not a war against Islam, and we think that the burkhas might send the wrong message to the Muslim world."

He's looking me square in the eye. The implication, basically, is that the Taliban cheerleaders bit could severely complicate our war against terrorism, perhaps leading to the deaths of thousands of innocent Americans.

"But it's funny!" As a comedian, that's always my immediate reaction. Somehow, though, I can't say, "But it's funny!" to the commander of the 86th Airlift Wing.

So the Taliban Cheerleaders bit? Gone.

Still, we had a great time, a whirlwind tour with stops at bases in Sicily, Bosnia, and Camp Bondsteel in Kosovo. It was my third trip in as many years to Kosovo. There's no airstrip at Bondsteel. So each time I went, we'd chopper in on Chinooks from Macedonia, flying over the rugged Sar Mountains, which tens of thousands of ethnic Albanians had traversed to escape the ethnic cleansing that President William Jefferson Clinton finally put an end to.

On my first USO tour, as we flew over the Kosovo countryside, we could see below us the burned out roofs of ethnic Albanian and Serbian homes that had been torched, right next door to homes with TV antennae on their intact roofs. That was Europe, 1999.

After Milosevic had thrown in the towel in June of that year, U.S. peacekeeping forces seized about a thousand acres of farmland not that far from the Macedonian border. On my first trip to Bondsteel, that December, the camp had been under construction. Soldiers slept in wooden barracks and used makeshift latrines. Brown

& Root, a subsidiary of Halliburton—a company you might have heard of—was the contractor.

Two years later, on my third trip, Bondsteel was looking like a base stateside, with twenty-five kilometers of roads and over three hundred buildings housing nearly seven thousand troops. There was even a Burger King. I was told that for every burger consumed by a GI at Camp Bondsteel, Brown & Root took a cut. And Dick Cheney received a coupon.

It reminded me of an exchange from the 2000 vice presidential debate. Citing the accomplishments of the Clinton/Gore years, Joe Lieberman alluded to Cheney's $20 million figure send-off from Halliburton: "And I see, Dick, from the newspapers, that you're better off than you were eight years ago."

That got a laugh. But Cheney came back with a topper. "And I can tell you, Joe, that the government had absolutely nothing to do with it." That got laughter and applause. Cheney had gotten the best of Lieberman. And in an election that was decided by 537 votes, you could reasonably point to that moment and say it changed the outcome.

Of course, what Cheney said was not entirely true. It was, in fact, a bald-faced lie. In addition to benefiting from the unprecedented expansion of the entire economy during the Clinton years, Halliburton had received $3.8 *billion* in government contracts and taxpayer-insured loans while Cheney was its CEO.

So "the government had absolutely nothing to do with it" had absolutely nothing to do with the truth, other than being the opposite of it. Also, I think it's fair to say that Cheney didn't become CEO at Halliburton because of his expertise in oil extraction. It just might have had something to do with his *government* experience, especially as secretary of defense during the war in the Persian Gulf. Which, in case you didn't know, is an area of the world that pumps a lot of oil.

And Halliburton did quite a lot of business with countries in that region during Cheney's tenure as CEO. Countries like Iran and Iraq. Small problem. Federal law prohibited U.S. companies from doing business with the two state sponsors of terrorism. Halliburton circumvented these restrictions by setting up subsidiaries in foreign countries. Such as Halliburton Products and Services, which has its "headquarters" in a Cayman Islands mailbox, and an office in Iran, an Axis of Evil stalwart.

In fact, a company brochure brags about its work on two offshore Iranian drilling contracts, saying that "we are committed to position ourselves in a market that offers huge growth potential." These deals may very well have been illegal. But for some reason, Bush's Department of Justice hasn't pursued the case.

From 1997 through mid-2000, Halliburton subsidiary Dresser Industries sold $30 million worth of water and sewage treatment pumps, spare parts for oil facilities, and pipeline equipment to Saddam Hussein's regime. Cheney lied about this on ABC's *This Week* on July 30, 2000, saying, "I had a firm policy that we wouldn't do anything in Iraq, even—even arrangements that were supposedly legal. . . . We've not done any business in Iraq since the sanctions [were] imposed, and I had a standing policy that I wouldn't do that." Cheney's lie on *This Week* was no Gore/James Lee Witt whopper, but still.[1]

**B**ack to Bondsteel 2001, and our show. One of the reasons I love military audiences is that they have a really sick sense of humor. This was their favorite joke:

> You know, a lot of Americans were really worried about you guys when we started our action here in Kosovo. In fact, I know that kind of constrained what you could do. And fortu-

---

[1]Explaining his remarks later, Cheney said that he hadn't known about his company's business with Iraq—but that if he *had* known, he wouldn't have done anything differently. Actually, he just said he didn't know—a defense later employed by Enron CEOs Ken Lay and Jeffrey Skilling.

nately, there were no combat casualties here. But you'll be happy to know, since 9/11, Americans are now willing to take casualties here in Kosovo.

They laughed because they knew it was true. Clinton's intervention in Kosovo, which prevented a genocide, did not have our country's wholehearted support. Americans did not like the Serbian atrocities they saw on their televisions, but they were in no mood to see our troops take casualties. Certainly not in Kosovo. And certainly not before 9/11.

The bombing campaign was particularly unpopular with certain Republicans, who had no qualms about expressing their objections while our troops were in harm's way.

> The President said if we did nothing, there would be an instability in the region. There would be a flood of refugees, Kosovars would die, and the credibility of NATO would be undermined. Well, Clinton's bombing campaign has caused all these problems to explode.
>
> House Majority Whip Tom DeLay—May 2, 1999

> This is President Clinton's war, and when he falls flat on his face, that's his problem.
>
> Senator Richard Lugar—May 3, 1999

> I had doubts about the bombing campaign from the beginning. I didn't think we had done enough in the diplomatic area.
>
> Senator Trent Lott—May 4, 1999

> They haven't prepared for anything in this. And they're running out of weapons to do it. And frankly, I don't think Clinton has the moral authority or ability to fight this war correctly.
>
> Sean Hannity—May 10, 1999

Thank God, Republicans are honorable and understand the patriotic value of constructive dissent. Otherwise, during this year's war in Iraq, guys like Hannity would have gone after any Democrats who were the least bit critical of President Bush.

Um, wait a minute. Here's Hannity on national television:

> Forty-eight hours we're sending our men and women in harm's way, and there's the leader of your party [Tom Daschle] in the United States Senate disgracefully attacking our president at a time when we're going to war. You ought to be ashamed. Every Democrat in this country ought to be ashamed of what this man did yesterday and what he repeated again today.[1]
>
> —March 18, 2003

> I mean the Democrats, I thought we would always would unite behind our troops with a pending conflict. And we have the Democratic leadership in the Senate daily attacking the President even now.
>
> —March 19, 2003

> You don't have to take cheap political partisan shots at the commander in chief and say to the world that he doesn't have the experience to lead when he is leading men and women into harm's way.
>
> —March 27, 2003

> Here we are in a conflict, in a war, and the President is trying to direct things, and they just can't put aside their partisanship for five minutes and support the troops and support the President, and these are the leaders of the Democratic Party.
>
> —April 6, 2003

[1] Daschle said, "I'm saddened that the President failed so miserably at diplomacy that we are now forced into war."

And a special shout-out to Colmes for never pointing out Hannity's shameless hypocrisy.

The bombing campaign in Kosovo ended on June 10, 1999, with the signing of a peace accord. Milosevic was kicked out of Belgrade a few months later and sent to The Hague, where he's now on trial for crimes against humanity. (I say "guilty.") And as I pointed out in my joke to the troops, there was not one American combat casualty during the entire campaign.

Back again to Kosovo, 2001. Flying out in the Chinooks, they made us wear flak jackets and helmets, which always made me feel silly. But on the last trip, as we were headed over the Sars Mountains, the Chinook did a quick turn, then dived. The pilot was taking evasive action. I could see tracers coming at us. We were being shot at. My first thought was about the joke I had told and how funny it would be if I were our first combat fatality in Kosovo.

Ah, the mind of a trained comedian.

# Who Created the Tone?

**"Scumbag**," "sociopath," "perpetual preener," "rapist," "unserious," "craven miscreant."[1] Sound like anyone you know? I mean, besides Steven Seagal?[2] Actually, it was the forty-second President of the United States, Bill Clinton, who was called all of these things. In my day, we never used such language to describe the President, unless he was a real asshole like Nixon.

Remember during the 2000 campaign how then Governor Bush kept saying he was going to "change the tone in Washington"? That really touched a nerve. The partisan rancor in D.C. had led millions of Americans to stop following politics and instead spend hours a day downloading pornography from the Internet.

Where did this malicious tone come from in the first place? I submit that it can be traced to a day in 1981, when billionaire Richard Mellon Scaife fielded a reporter's question about his financial backing of conservative groups.

"You fucking Communist cunt, get out of here," he said to Karen Rothmyer of the *Columbia Journalism Review.* He went on to tell her that she was ugly and that her teeth were "terrible." Of Ms. Rothmyer's mother, who was not present, he said, "She's ugly, too." Sensing that it was time to wrap up the interview, Ms. Rothmyer thanked Scaife for his time. He bade her farewell with a cheery "Don't look behind you."

That's the funny thing about tone. It's so subjective. Usually, I find it's enough to call someone a "fucking Communist cunt," without having to gild the lily by disparaging her teeth and issuing a veiled death threat.

---

[1] Scumbag—Representative Dan Burton to the *Washington Post;* sociopath—Craig Shirley in the *Washington Times;* perpetual preener, rapist, unserious—George Will in his syndicated column; craven miscreant—Michelle Malkin in the *Washington Times.*

[2] Just kidding. I have never heard of Steven Seagal being referred to as a "rapist," or a "sociopath." Or "unserious."

But then again, the *Wall Street Journal* has never called me "the financial archangel for the [conservative] movement's intellectual underpinnings." In total, Scaife's contribution to right-wing groups (more than a hundred of them) adds up to over $200 million dollars. That kind of money can buy a lot of tone. He's given $35 million to the far-right Heritage Foundation, backed the Federalist Society (a secretive conservative legal organization which feeds Bush his ultraconservative judicial nominees and political appointees), and donated to the Cato Institute, the Hoover Institution, Paul Weyrich's Free Congress Foundation, and the American Enterprise Institute. Moreover, he's funded the rise of the right-wing media apparatus, supporting conservative college newspapers and grown-up publications, from the eminently respectable *Public Interest* to the inarguably disreputable *American Spectator*. In the nineties, the *American Spectator* specialized in calling Bill Clinton a murderer.

So one could claim that Richard Mellon Scaife set the tone. But as I learned in the seventies, when I personally tried to set the tone of our political culture by repeatedly calling for "a return to niceness," it's hard for any one person to shape the character of our national discourse.

No, turning the public arena into a wasteland of personal destruction takes an entire army of like-minded ideologues hell-bent on shredding the already tattered standards of decency that once permitted reasonable discourse on matters of import.

The left, sadly, has no such army. Our attack dogs are a scrawny, underfed pack of mutts that spend half the time chasing their own tails and sniffing each other's butt. The right, by contrast, appears to have a well-oiled puppy mill for pit bulls, bred to kill and trained to go for the jugular. Or the balls.

David Brock was one of those pit bulls. Brock worked as a professional hate-spewer for the *Washington Times,* the Heritage Foundation, and the *American Spectator.* As aggressive dogs will, Brock left his mark everywhere: on Iran-Contra, the Bork nomination, the Thomas-Hill hearings, Troopergate, Paula Jones, Whitewater, and the Clinton impeachment. It was Brock who discredited the very sane, very staid Anita Hill as "a little bit nutty and a little bit slutty."

Later Brock had a change of heart and joined the forces of light. In his mea culpa, *Blinded by the Right,* Brock describes his days in the right-wing trenches: "I fought on the wrong side of an ideological and cultural war that divided our country and poisoned our politics."

Brock's revelations about his scandalous activities on behalf of the fanatical right are often discounted by his former compatriots, who make the uncharacteristically reasonable argument that he lied so much when he was working for them that nothing he says can be trusted now. Fair enough. We'll leave out Brock's tale of manufacturing Troopergate out of whole cloth, the bottom-fishing expeditions of the Scaife-funded Arkansas Project, and the payoffs to Whitewater witnesses. I'm not going to use it. Don't need it. While Brock does shed light on some of the clandestine dirty tricks used by what was, if not a vast right-wing conspiracy, at least a very, very large one, there were enough lies and baseless innuendos right out in the open to fill a book the size of Sidney Blumenthal's 802-page classic, *The Clinton Wars.*

For example, did you know that Hillary Clinton is a lesbian? And that, despite her homosexuality, she was having an affair with Vince Foster? Who then had to be murdered to cover up Whitewater? And did you know that Foster's execution was only one small part of a killing spree that claimed nearly forty lives, including those of former Commerce Secretary Ron Brown and the wife of an Arkansas state trooper who apparently didn't "get the message"? And did you know that Clinton, to finance his own gargantuan cocaine habit, had struck a deal with the CIA and the Contras to smuggle duffel bags filled with coke into Arkansas?

If you didn't, you weren't reading the *Wall Street Journal* editorial page, the *American Spectator,* or the *Washington Times.*

Typically, the *Spectator* would break the story, "forcing" the *Journal*, the *Times,* and the *New York Post* to comment on what was now a legitimate news item that was being ignored by the liberal-dominated media.

The *Journal* ran sixty-four editorials discussing Foster's death, systematically sowing sinister seeds of suspicion on his so-called "suicide." (I'm putting the right on notice that they don't own alliteration.) This continued even after two successive independent counsels (one of them, Kenneth Starr, a man not generally considered to be in the Clintons' pocket) concluded that Foster's death was, in fact, a suicide.

When readers threatened to tire of seemingly endless Agatha Christie–style discussions of the Foster case, the *Journal* ran a lurid account of the elimination of two Arkansas teens using that efficient murder weapon favored by Snidely Whiplash: a train. The *Journal* marshaled these facts: Two teenagers were killed by a train. The train was traveling through Arkansas. Bill Clinton was governor of Arkansas. Ergo, Bill Clinton murdered the boys with the train.[2] The *Journal* ran a series of pieces on the boys' deaths, and featured the story in their February 12, 1998, editorial "Obstruction and Abuse: A Pattern."

The *Journal* also used its blood-soaked editorial page to publish the 800 number for ordering *The Clinton Chronicles,* a piece-of-shit video that linked the Clintons to dozens of murders. *The Clinton Chronicles* sold over one hundred thousand copies, thanks in large part to the Reverend Jerry Falwell, who cofinanced, pub-

---

[2]To offer the *Journal* a courtesy that I'm sure they wouldn't reciprocate, I should explain that their editorial actually suggested that the boys were knifed to death and then put on the train tracks as an elaborate cover-up orchestrated by Clinton and his personal goon squad, the Arkansas state police.

licized, and distributed the video through an organization called Citizens for Honest Government (not to be confused with actual citizens who genuinely support honesty in government).

The tape casts the deaths of the two teenagers in a larger and more sinister context.

> **NARRATOR:** A number of people approached the police about Don and Kevin's murders and were subsequently murdered themselves.

Meanwhile, over at the *Washington Times,* a dedicated band of courageous journalists dared to expose the slaughter in Arkansas, heedless of the inevitable lethal consequences for themselves and their families. Their editor in chief, Wesley Pruden, led the charge. Pruden's September 18, 1998, editorial reads like a Bill O'Reilly suspense novel.

> Jane Parks was the wife then of Jerry Parks, who was the security chief of the Clinton-Gore campaign in Arkansas in 1992. His son, Gary, told Ambrose Evans-Pritchard of the *Sunday Telegraph* that he was watching a TV newscast with his father when Vince Foster's death was announced. The father went pale. "I'm a dead man," he told the son. "They're cleaning house." He told his wife Jane that he would be next. A few months later he was cut down in a volley of automatic-weapons fire on a Little Rock street corner.

And what would an O'Reilly-esque thriller be without some blow and a few underage babes?

> Jane Parks, the manager of a Little Rock apartment house, told the London *Sunday Telegraph* that Roger Clinton, the President's bad-boy brother, turned Apartment B-107 into a drug pad in the summer of '84, where it snowed every night

and young girls, some of them still in high school, were the bunnies who served themselves with the salad. The governor was a frequent visitor, so her story goes, and the rutting and snorting noises that drifted up through the vents occasionally got so loud she had to leave.

**A**fter Vince Foster, probably the most notorious of the Clinton murders was his airborne rubout of Commerce Secretary and long-time friend Ron Brown. Appearing on *Hannity and Colmes*, Christopher Ruddy, author of the delightful *The Strange Death of Vince Foster* and a reporter for the Scaife fishwrapper the *Pittsburgh Tribune-Review,* advanced the theory that Brown had been shot in the back of his head before his plane crashed in Croatia, killing all thirty-five aboard.

> **HANNITY:** Chris, welcome back. Let's—you know, by the way, Chris, you know that Mike McCurry, in a recent interview, singled you out as one of the people that—the haters of Bill Clinton, if you will. You have this report about Ron Brown that you've been going forward with. Medical examiners, including Lieutenant Colonel Cogswell, that he may have been shot. You're just reporting these things. Why would the spokesperson for the President single you out as—quote—one of those "haters"?
>
> **RUDDY:** Well, I think it's a great honor to be declared an enemy.

Hannity failed to point out that Colonel William T. Gormley, the Air Force pathologist who (unlike Cogswell) had actually examined Brown's body, said that "there is no doubt in anybody's mind who evaluated his case that this was a blunt-force injury and not a gunshot wound." X rays of the corpse showed no bone or metal fragments, no exit wound, and no bullet. And besides, the logic of shooting someone before crashing their plane escapes me. Though I will concede it does bear a highly suspicious resemblance to the earlier case of the teens who were stabbed before being run over by a train.

Which is perhaps why FNC's Brit Hume said of the Ron Brown shooting-crashing-dying conspiracy, "It's a story that's worth giving airtime to." And given airtime on Fox and ink in the *Washington Times*, the story inevitably made its way into the mainstream media (*New York Times, Washington Post, Time*, and ABC News) if only in reporting, as *Newsweek* put it, "The Life and Times of a Rumor."

Though outraged at Clinton's unquenchable thirst for murder, it was his career as a serial rapist which provided the bitterest grist for the right-wing rumor mill. "Who cares if our president is a molester, a rapist, even a serial rapist?" Joseph Sobran inquired rhetorically of *Washington Times* readers. The influential website NewsMax.com, available to most Americans thanks to Al Gore's visionary funding of the Internet, explained in their probing story-behind-the-story, "Bill's Biting Ways," why Clinton nearly bit Juanita Broaddrick's lower lip in two while raping her.

Bill O'Reilly deplored not only Clinton's alleged rape of Broaddrick, but also the mainstream media's rape of the American public in failing to report the alleged rape. In a 2001 interview with *Media Week*, O'Reilly declared that the *Los Angeles Times* was an abysmal paper, in part because "they never mentioned Juanita Broaddrick's name, ever. This whole [Los Angeles] area out here has no idea what's going on unless you watch my show."

Former *LA Times* editor Melissa Payton corrected O'Reilly by pointing out that her paper's archives contained twenty-one articles mentioning Broaddrick and that, contrary to O'Reilly's further claim, virtually her entire newspaper is devoted to information about "what's going on," including not only news, but movie times, and also free community events for the whole family, such as weekend puppet shows and please-touch nature walks at local parks.

I'm sorry. I got off the question of "Who set the tone?" and back onto the question of "Why does Bill O'Reilly lie so goddamn much?"

So let's follow the tone. It begins with Richard "fucking" Mellon "Communist cunt" Scaife, moves through the shadowy world of sleazy right-wing operatives, into the radical-right fringe press (*American Spectator*), over to the thinly disguised radical right-wing media (*Washington Times* and Fox News Channel), and onto the quasi-respectable right-wing press (*Wall Street Journal* editorial page). Gathering strength, the tone finally vaults into the mainstream media (*LA Times, Newsweek,* ABC, CNN, et cetera), where it is disseminated into the homes of millions of unsuspecting Americans.

But even as the right was spreading filth, sleaze, and bile through its media apparatus, a parallel effort was proceeding in the political arena. Ever hear of someone named Newt Gingrich? I know, it sounds like I made the name up. But he was once one of the most powerful men in America.

He was so powerful that he said, "People like me are what stand between us and Auschwitz." (Some believe Gingrich fell from power because of his grandiosity.)

One way Gingrich stood between us and Auschwitz was by being extremely mean and nasty. Sharing his secrets for success with Republican candidates, he sent out a letter advising them to characterize their Democratic opponents with words like "corrupt," "sick," "pathetic," "greedy," and "traitor."

Gingrich's recipe for success—"go negative early" and "never back off"—proved so successful that, in 1994, the Republicans captured the House and Senate by soundly defeating such pathetic traitors as Tennessee senator Jim Sasser.

Now in the majority, the Republicans were free to elevate the tone by shutting down the government and engaging in dozens of separate investigations of the Clinton administration.

Joe Lockhart, former Clinton press secretary, describes the GOP's SOBs' SOP:

> What they'd do is they would use the power of the subpoena
> to get document after document out of the White House that
> they could then distort and leak. And it was warfare. I mean,
> it was from the very first day Bill Clinton went in there, there
> was a declared war on him.

Why did they hate Clinton so much? I think it's because we—and by that I mean Bill, Hillary, and myself—I think we represented everything they despised. We were young. We were charismatic. Bill Clinton, for example, "was tall and handsome ... [and] had a vitality that seemed to shoot out of his pores."[3] The mauling of Clinton was payback for Nixon, Bork, Iran-Contra, and Clarence Thomas (every time we caught them doing something wrong, they got even madder), but more than that, it was payback for the sixties: Freedom Riding, bra burning, pot smoking, free loving, tree hugging, draft dodging, Woodstock attending, Woodstock overdosing, God not-fearing, and carrot cake. They've never forgiven us for carrot cake.

I don't defend everything that happened in the sixties. Just as I don't defend everything that happened in any decade. The current decade, for instance, is not off to the best of starts. But to the right, the Clintons embodied all of a generation's vices and none of its virtues. The Clintons' energy, their intellectual intensity, their compassion for those on the margins of society, their fundamental belief that the world could be made a better place—the right found all of these extremely irritating.

So they weren't content just to call him a murderer and a rapist. The fact that Clinton continued to be successful and popular left only one option. Clinton had to be removed. Determined not to sink to his level and have the President "conveniently" run over by a train, the Republicans took the high road and impeached him on blow job charges.

The story of Clinton's impeachment has been told many times

[3]Hillary Clinton, *Living History*. New York: Simon and Schuster, 2003.

and in many ways, though not yet in an opera, which I believe is the form to which it is best suited. One version of the story came from Kenneth Starr, who made his own perverse contribution to the tone in Washington with his gratuitously pornographic Starr Report, which my publisher says I cannot quote if I want this book sold in Wal-Mart.

The tone that Bush had promised to change had been created by his own party. His pledge to change that tone contained both a promise *and* a threat. Elect me and the tone will improve because I am a consensus builder, a uniter, not a divider, and a compassionate conservative. Elect Gore, and we'll nuke the living fuck out of him just like we did the last guy. America, the choice is yours.

# 20
# Did the Tone Change?

No.

# Why Did Anyone Think It Would Change?

**Everything** you need to know about the legitimacy of Bush's claim to the moral high ground can be summed up by the conduct of his campaign in the South Carolina Republican primary.

You may remember that Senator John McCain, like Bush a Vietnam-era fighter pilot (with one key difference—McCain actually fought in his fighter), had roundly defeated the Texas governor in New Hampshire. McCain's "Straight Talk Express" was gathering momentum. Something had to be done.

In February of 2000, lucky Republican voters in South Carolina began receiving phone calls assessing their feelings about a series of important issues. A typical call began like this:

> **CALLER:** Hi. I'm calling from an independent polling company and I was wondering if I could have a minute of your time to conduct a survey.
>
> **UNSUSPECTING VOTER:** Uh . . . sure.
>
> **CALLER:** Great! If you knew that Senator John McCain was a cheat and a liar and a fraud, and that he has fathered an illegitimate black child, would you be *more* likely to vote for him or *less* likely to vote for him?
>
> **UNSUSPECTING VOTER:** Hmm. Probably less.

As you might have gathered, the calls were not actually made by independent polling companies. Nor were they intended to gather information. They were a particularly insidious example of "push polling," a technique invented by Bush Sr.'s political guru, Lee Atwater.

**The Heartwarming Story of the Very First Push Poll**

Lee Atwater, a mentor to both Karl Rove and George Jr., ran the first push poll in 1978 against a friend of mine, Max Heller. I met Max and his wife, Trude, in Hilton Head in 1994. His intelligence, good humor, and obvious decency reminded me of my father, who had recently died.

Max told me his story.

In August of 1937, Max met his bride-to-be, Trude, at a summer resort near Vienna, where they were both born. Max fell in love with Trude immediately and told her that he would marry her someday, (she was fifteen at the time; he was eighteen). A few days later Max met an American girl named Mary Mills from Greenville, South Carolina, who gave him her address. When Hitler invaded Austria in March of 1938, Max decided it might be time to become an American. He wrote Mary, asking for help. She wrote, "I will help you. I have gone to see Shep Saltzman, who owns a shirt factory. He will send you the papers necessary to come to America." He did, and in July 1938, Max arrived in Greenville.

The young immigrant refused dinner and a room from Saltzman, and insisted on going to work an hour after his arrival in Greenville, sweeping out the factory warehouse. Trudy didn't make it to the U.S. until 1940. They married in 1942 and prospered. Eventually Max became the beloved mayor of Greenville, and in 1978 ran for Congress against an Atwater client, Republican Carroll Campbell.

Heller was ahead until Atwater commissioned a series of polls to discover how voters in the district would feel about "a foreign-born Jew who did not believe in Jesus Christ as the Savior." (The polls revealed a certain antipathy to such a person.)

Max lost.

Push polls are a sneaky way to spread lies about your opponent while appearing to keep your own hands clean. To my knowledge, McCain has not fathered any illegitimate children of any race. He and his wife Cindy did, however, adopt a Bangladeshi girl, Bridget, who has dark skin and appeared regularly with her parents at campaign events, thus granting the rumor an especially sinister veneer of plausibility. Nice work, Bush campaign!

(By the way, I myself suggested a retaliatory push poll to a friend in the McCain camp. It went like this: "Hi, we're an independent polling company. If you knew that, during the five and a half years that John McCain was being tortured in Hanoi, George W. Bush snorted five and a half kilograms of cocaine, would you be *more* likely to vote for Governor Bush or *less* likely to vote for Governor Bush?")

Other rumors about McCain that began circulating around this time were that he was gay (he's not); that he was pro-abortion (he isn't); that his wife had outstanding arrest warrants for giving alcohol to minors (she didn't); that he had voted for the largest tax increase ever (he hadn't); that he had been reprimanded by the Senate Ethics Committee (he hadn't); and that he had fathered an illegitimate child with a North Vietnamese woman, which was why he'd gotten special treatment from the Viet Cong. (This one's true. McCain's illegitimate child John McCain Vu Khaon is currently Minister of Bicycles of the Socialist Republic of Vietnam.)

Despite the fact that the sliming of McCain could have benefited no one but Bush (and possibly the distant also-ran Alan Keyes, who himself was facing allegations of having fathered three black children), the Bush campaign repeatedly protested its innocence.

However, in a candid moment captured by C-SPAN on February 12, Dubya tipped his hand to South Carolina State Senator Mike Fair. They didn't know the camera was on them as they spoke about McCain.

> **SENATOR FAIR:** You haven't hit his soft spots.
>
> **BUSH:** I know. I'm going to.
>
> **FAIR:** Well, they need to. Somebody does, anyway.
>
> **BUSH:** I agree. I'm not going to do it on TV.

The mastermind behind Bush's dirty tricks campaign in South Carolina and beyond was a man by the name of Karl Rove, whose fleshy and formless physique belies a heart as cold and steely and deadly as a discarded refrigerator with the door still attached.[1] Rove, whose official White House title is Senior Political Advisor, has so much influence over the President that he's been described as "Bush's brain" in the book *Bush's Brain: How Karl Rove Made George W. Bush Presidential.* Any student of Rove's personal history would not be surprised by the chicanery in South Carolina.

In 1970, while still a teenager, Rove pretended to be a campaign volunteer for the Democratic candidate for Illinois state treasurer, Alan J. Dixon. He swiped Dixon's letterhead and sabotaged the opening of Dixon's campaign headquarters by sending out over one thousand copies of an invitation offering "free beer, free food, girls, and a good time for nothing" to homeless shelters and soup kitchens. He now refers to this as "a youthful prank" that he regrets.

A few years later, a rapidly maturing Rove conducted training sessions for College Republicans on the nuance and technique of Nixon-style dirty tricks. George Bush, Sr., who was then head of the Republican National Committee, had to send the FBI to question the up-and-coming scam artist. Bush was so impressed that he later gave Rove a job.

In 1986, while working on the Texas gubernatorial race, a fully blossomed Rove dramatically "discovered" a mysterious electronic bug in his office. Instead of calling the police, he called a press conference. The timing of Rove's discovery was particularly fortunate: It was the morning of the only televised debate between his candidate, William Clements, and the Democratic governor, Mark White. White was forced to answer questions about the bug instead of about the issues, and subsequently lost. The Travis County D.A.'s office and the FBI later concluded that the bug had been planted by Rove himself on the same day he discovered it. The fact that the maximum battery life of the bug was a mere ten hours (meaning that a spy would have to sneak in and replace it at least twice a day) may have been something of a giveaway.

---

[1] In an elementary school playground during a Minnesota winter.

Rove's innovative approach to campaign strategy propelled him rapidly up the ladder to the top of the state Republican party, where he orchestrated the most complete takeover of Texas since Sam Houston routed Santa Anna at the Battle of San Jacinto. (Sam Houston was later killed at the Alamo by terrorists.)

By 2000, Rove knew how to steal an election without leaving any fingerprints. According to McCain's then campaign manager, Rick Davis, Rove had a seasoned team of character assassins already in place, including Warren Tompkins (another Atwater disciple) and former Christian Coalition executive director Ralph Reed. Davis told me that Reed later claimed "I was the one who delivered South Carolina for W."

Phone banks, flyers, e-mails, church pulpits, and, in one undocumented case, telepathy—all these were used as "Weapons of McCain Destruction," as Bill Schneider might have called them on CNN's *Inside Politics*. One such e-mail came from Bob Jones University Professor Richard Hand (Rhand@BJU.edu), who wrote to fellow South Carolinians that McCain "chose to sire children without marriage." When Hand was told on CNN that there was no evidence Senator McCain had fathered illegitimate children, Hand, displaying the intellectual rigor for which Bob Jones University is justifiably esteemed worldwide, said, "That's a universal negative. Can you prove that?"

You may remember that it was at Bob Jones University that George W. Bush kicked off his South Carolina campaign. The ultrafundamendalist school was famously anti–Roman Catholic and had a quirky policy against interracial dating. "We had to send a message—fast—and sending him there was the only way to do it," Tompkins would later say. Bush was criticized nationally for not addressing the school's ban on interracial dating. You know who I think would have criticized their interracial dating policy? Thomas Jefferson.

Bush won South Carolina, went on to capture the Republican nomination, and came within a hair's breadth of winning the election.

_____

*The following scene is excerpted from* The Big Heist, *my novelization of the Republican conspiracy to steal the election in Florida. The book was inspired by Bill O'Reilly's* Those Who Trespass *and Jeffrey Toobin's* Too Close to Call: The Thirty-six Day Battle to Decide the 2000 Election. *Note: While the Republicans did* send *lobbyist Mac Stipanovich to baby-sit Florida Secretary of State Katherine Harris during the entire thirty-six day fiasco, the depiction of a sexual affair between the two of them is purely fictional. As far as I know.*

Florida. November. A forty-three-year-old woman named Katherine Harris paced back and forth on a colorless carpet in an office that smelled of sweaty seersucker and day-old perfume. Nearby, a trim, goateed man was fanning himself lazily with a Panama hat while lying on the couch. "I swear, Katherine, I'm sweating like a nigger on Election Day. Can't we crank up the AC in here?"

"Just tell me what to do, Mac. Just tell me what to do."

"I told you what to do, baby. I told you to turn up the AC. The important thing is that you don't lose your cool."

"Mac, you don't understand," Harris said, worrying a blood-red fingernail. "When I was elected secretary of state, I never suspected I'd actually have to *do* anything."

Stipanovich chuckled, then lifted a haunch and let out a long, rattling fart. "You have to bring this election in for a landing."[2]

"I'm not cut out for this, Mac. I've never stolen an election before," Harris said, her voice quavering on the edge of hysteria.

Stipanovich stood up sharply, took three long strides across the office, and slapped the trembling woman across the face. Hard. "I'm only going to say this once, Kathy. I'm not leaving this office until the Texan's in the White House. I'm here to take care of you, Kathy. In any way I can."

A wave of calm, mingled with desire, washed over Florida's

[2] Jeffrey Toobin, *Too Close to Call: The Thirty-six Day Battle to Decide the 2000 Election.* New York: Random House, 2001, p. 69: "You have to bring this election in for a landing." (Other dialogue is pure conjecture.)

highest-ranking election official. It was good to have a man around. A real man. Not one of those country club milksops, but a living, breathing, farting man. Everyone who mattered in Florida knew Mac Stipanovich. For corporate interests in the Sunshine State, Stipanovich was the man to see for the project that absolutely had to be approved, the bill that simply had to pass.[3] Stipanovich knew where the bodies were buried. Hell, he had buried more than a few of them himself.

"Hold me, Mac, I'm scared."

"I'll do more than hold you, baby," he said, crushing his mouth to her lips.

Harris recoiled at the acrid taste of cigars and rye. "You stink, Mac."

"I know, baby. And I know you love it."

"I can't do this, Mac. I don't have the power to deny the Gore request for recounts. It's not up to me. It's up to each county's three-member canvassing board, each of which is comprised of the local election supervisor, a county judge, and an elected county commissioner."[4]

Stipanovich pulled her close with his left hand and raised his right hand menacingly. "Listen to me good, sweetcheeks. Here's how we're gonna play it. You prohibit the manual recounts by issuing opinion letters. As the chief elections officer for the state, you offer binding interpretations of Florida election law."[5]

Harris sighed. "You're going to have to be strong, Mac, for both of us."

"I will. I am." Stipanovich smiled. He was thinking of that phone call that had pulled him away from a nice warm bar stool and an even warmer redhead. His old friends in the Bush campaign needed someone to baby-sit the secretary of state. That the secretary of state was one beautiful baby was icing on the cake. Stipanovich turned, walked to the desk, and refilled his tumbler from

[3]Ibid., p. 68.
[4]Ibid., p. 72.
[5]Ibid., p. 72.

the half-empty bottle of cheap hooch. He turned back and whistled softly. Those calls to the county canvassing boards would have to wait. Mac Stipanovich had work to do.

Harris was now wearing only brief white panties. She had signaled her desire by removing her shirt and skirt, and by leaning back on the couch. She closed her eyes, concentrating on nothing but Stipanovich's tongue and lips. He gently teased her by licking the areas around her most sensitive erogenous zone. Then he slipped her panties down her legs and, within seconds, his tongue was inside her, moving rapidly.[6]

That's how it happened. The true story of the stealing of the presidency. Oh, there was more to it than just a sweaty sexual encounter in a small office with a broken air conditioner. There was the Harris-directed purging of thousands of legitimate black voters from the rolls; the relentless legal and extra-legal efforts to prevent an accurate counting of the votes—including a manufactured mob of Republican congressional aides flown in from Washington to scream and pound on the doors of the Miami-Dade canvassing board; the double standard the Bush campaign applied to military ballots, stretching the law to accept those in Bush counties, even as they were challenging those in counties that went for Gore—all while accusing the Democrats of "going to war against the men and women who serve in our armed forces in an effort to win at any cost." Although Republicans controlled every lever of power in the state, they shrieked that the venal Democrats were subverting the system to steal the presidency.

But if there's one enduring symbol of the Florida coup d'etat, it is the tongue of Mac Stipanovich, the Republican lobbyist who was put in Harris's office to be her "minder."[7] That tongue not only brought almost unimaginable pleasure to Katherine Harris,

[6]Bill O'Reilly, *Those Who Trespass*, p. 153.
[7]Toobin, p. 69.

but also to Jeb Bush, Karl Rove, and George W. Bush. I'm not suggesting he had sex with the Bushes, or even Karl Rove. But I can't say for sure that he didn't. As BJU Professor Richard Hand would point out, that's a universal negative and impossible to prove.

**O**nce Clarence Thomas, after considering the matter dispassionately, had cast the deciding vote in *Bush v. Gore*, thereby allowing his wife to continue her work for the Bush transition team, the new president-elect addressed the nation.

> After a difficult election, we must put politics behind us and work together to make the promise of America available for every one of our citizens.
>
> I am optimistic that we can change the tone in Washington, D.C. I believe things happen for a reason, and I hope the long wait of the last five weeks will heighten a desire to move beyond the bitterness and partisanship of the recent past.
>
> Our nation must rise above a house divided. Americans share hopes and goals and values far more important than any political disagreements. Republicans want the best for our nation. And so do Democrats. Our votes may differ, but not our hopes.
>
> I know America wants reconciliation and unity. I know Americans want progress. And we must seize this moment and deliver. Together, guided by a spirit of common sense, common courtesy and common goals, we can unite and inspire the American citizens.

I couldn't sleep that night. Not from bitterness for having had the election stolen by human filth like Karl Rove, but because I, too, shared the President-elect's vision of a united America, reconciled by our shared dream of a better tomorrow. My optimism that we could put the past behind us and, yes, change the tone lasted the better part of three weeks.

## 2 2

# I Grow Discouraged
# About the Tone

**The** first hint that America was not headed for a golden age of reconciliation and unity of purpose might have been Bush's nomination of John Ashcroft to be the nation's chief law enforcement official. A ferocious opponent of a woman's right to choose to have an abortion, a man's right to choose to have sex with another man, and a third man's right to choose to film them, Ashcroft was Bush's sop to the religious right.

By the time the Bush team occupied the White House, it was clear the tone had indeed changed—for the worse. With all the gravity of the Talmudic scholar–cum–Hollywood agent he so closely resembled, press secretary Ari Fleischer addressed a story recently leaked to the *Washington Post*. Criminal elements within the departing White House staff had committed a despicable outrage at 1600 Pennsylvania Avenue.

Referring more in sadness than in anger to the "vandalism," Fleischer demurred, "I choose not to describe what acts were done that we found upon arrival, because I think that's part of changing the tone in Washington," thereby leaving it up to the press corps to imagine shits taken on desks, vomit in filing cabinets, and TP covering the Rose Garden. To paraphrase Groucho Marx, "Truth goes out the door when rumor comes innuendo."

"Whether things were done that were perhaps less gracious than should have been, it is not going to be what President Bush focuses on, nor will it be what his staff focuses on," said the high-minded Fleischer, who continued to flog the story for weeks.

Meanwhile, media outlets were receiving leaks from anonymous Republican sources sickened by the most extensive sack of the White House since the War of 1812. "Trash was everywhere," one told CNN. Phone and computer lines had been cut, expletive-ridden graffiti written on the walls, file cabinets glued shut, and pictures stolen. The *Washington Times* quoted a Matt Drudge story titled "White House Offices Left Trashed: Porn Bombs, Lewd Messages."

Unlike Matt Drudge, I've never experienced a porn bombing. I can only imagine that a porn bomb is a form of "dirty bomb," consisting of a conventional explosive surrounded by a thick coating of dirty books and pictures. When the bomb goes off, the filth, either images or bits of text, could contaminate schoolyards, churches, and even John Ashcroft's morning prayer meeting.

In the first week after the story broke, Fox brought up the vandalism story thirteen times. Uber-conservative Grover Norquist told CNN that:

> There have been reports coming out of the White House of damage up to $200,000. . . . There have been obscenities scrawled. People have called in and gotten answering machines with obscenities attached to them. There have been pornographic things in the computers, viruses in the computer. I got a call from somebody at the White House today who said, "You can't call me back. Phone lines have been cut and damaged. I'll try to reach you next week," just in the context of doing business. And "I'll give you my phone number but it won't work." I called in and it didn't work. So there's evidently been extensive damage. But I think while Bush—and he's instructed his people to be very, very low-key on this because it really reflects very poorly on the presidency and the White House and the previous occupants, that it is important to document what happened because if you don't take pictures of it, you don't document it, we know the Clintons will deny it ever happened.

In fact, Fleischer assured the press that, while there was no investigation, "what we are doing is cataloguing that which took place."

Of course, none of this horrible vandalism actually occurred. But Georgia firebrand congressman Bob Barr had not been clued in on the ruse. Outraged, he demanded an immediate investigation by Congress's General Accounting Office.

The GAO found no damage to the White House itself. When the General Services Administration, acting on behalf of the GAO, asked the Administration for their "catalogue" of vandalism, the Bushies admitted that they had "no record of damage that may have been deliberately caused by employees of the Clinton administration."

The White House *had* been damaged. But not by Bill Clinton. No, the vandals were Karl Rove, Ari Fleischer, and their lickspittles in the right-wing press. And while no shits were found, Grover Norquist could not have done more damage had he taken a dump in each of the White House's 132 rooms.

The Bush administration had established its game plan. Pretend to stay above the fray; use surrogates to lie, attack, and discredit; then get the media to report it. And, parallel to the campaign to get the message out, there was a no-less-vigorous effort to keep certain messages in.

Dana Milbank of the *Washington Post* incurred official disfavor by writing about the taboo subject of how much the President loves to lie. A prescient article in the fall of 2002 questioned several of Bush's overblown claims regarding an imminent Iraqi threat to America. In light of subsequent events (e.g., the fact that Saddam did not pose much of a military threat to Americans in Baghdad, let alone Cincinnati), one can see why Milbank aroused the ire of the White House press operation.

By withholding routine information such as travel itineraries from troublesome reporters like Milbank, the White House was able to prevent them from asking embarrassing questions. It's hard to ask the President embarrassing questions if you can't find him.

It wasn't just the White House. Over at the Pentagon, tough guy Donald Rumsfeld knew how to court-martial a nosy reporter. "This is by far the worst it's ever been," said Thomas Ricks of the *Washington Post,* a ten-year veteran of the Pentagon beat. When Ricks asked why he had been excluded from a trip on which American journalists were allowed to cover a Special Forces operation for the first time, a press affairs officer told him: "We don't like your stories, and we don't like the questions you've been asking."

Since that incident, the only question Ricks has asked is "What kind of story would you like to see in the *Washington Post* tomorrow?"

A top news executive at one of the three major networks who spoke with me through an intermediary on the condition of anonymity for both of them and who insisted that I give no distinguishing information about him or her, said off the record, "This is the most cowed White House press corps in history."

Those early months were heady days for George W. Bush. Emboldened by his landslide victory, Bush passed a $1.6 trillion tax cut which went primarily to the rich, pulled out of the Kyoto Protocol, delayed rules that would reduce acceptable levels of arsenic in the drinking water, and implemented the enormously successful Operation Ignore.

Ironically, it took a man of Bush's own party to bring his extended honeymoon to a close. Jim Jeffords, an obscure senator from a little known state called "Vermont," had been on the receiving end of a series of petty slights, provoked by his bothersome habit of voting his conscience. To punish Jeffords, the cagey Karl Rove had decided not to invite him to a White House ceremony honoring one of Jeffords's own constituents, Michele Forman of Middlebury, as the Teacher of the Year.

Boy, did that backfire! As I can tell you from experiences with my wife's family, and particularly her Uncle Ray, New Englanders are a singularly cranky and short-tempered group of people. Not being invited to a Teacher of the Year ceremony is just the type of thing that would piss them off. Jeffords quit the Republican Party, throwing control of the Senate to the Democrats.

Emboldened by Jeffords's example, the Washington press corps suddenly found its pecker again. Stories critical of Bush's handling of the Teacher of the Year ceremony, of the secret Cheney energy task force, and of the President's interminable vacations, began to appear not just in the German media, but in some American papers as well.

Suddenly on the defensive, Karl Rove counterattacked with a series of photo ops of the President reading *The Very Hungry Caterpillar* to kindergartners. Which is exactly what he was doing when Operation Ignore came to an abrupt and disastrous conclusion.

After being chased around the country by imaginary terrorists for nine hours, Bush returned to Washington and addressed a jittery nation. Far from comforting the American people, the President, who appeared to be genuinely terrified himself, further unsettled the country by stammering through a pallid and perfunctory statement.

Nine days later, having overcome his panic, the President capped an astonishing recovery by delivering an inspiring speech to a joint session of Congress. It was only in retrospect that I realized that the skillfully crafted address contained the seeds of a Manichean view that divides the world into good and evil. Us and them. Black and white. American and "other."

In the immediate aftermath of 9/11, the American people put aside their differences over, for instance, whether cutting a billion dollars from the Environmental Protection Agency was a good idea or not, and got behind our president—as well we should have. After winning a swift victory in Afghanistan with Bill Clinton's military, Bush's approval rating shot up to an unprecedented 112 percent.

The media's testicles instantly shriveled and retracted back into their abdominal cavities, making a slurping sound as they did so. Afraid to appear unpatriotic or treasonous, even left-leaning periodicals like the *Daily Worker,* the *Young Spartacist,* and *The New York Times* wrote glowing articles about the President.

Instead of using this unique moment of national unity to usher in a new American century founded upon a reasonable measure of shared sacrifice, Bush and Rove decided to ask nothing of average Americans other than that they silently acquiesce to their eventual enslavement by a corporate hegemon.

Wealthy Americans, however, would be asked only to accept larger and larger tax cuts, and ever-weaker oversight from the underfunded Securities and Exchange Commission.

Ordinary citizens *were* asked to do their part in the war on terrorism by remaining alert and reporting suspicious packages and neighbors. A new color-coded alert system was instituted for purposes of alarming Americans with fine-tuned precision. At the orange level, the second-highest level of alert, people are still encouraged to go to the mall. At the red level, the highest state of alert, the President suggests that you stay away from public places, and instead shop on-line.

These days, at airports, Americans stand cheerfully in line—at the Cinnabon counter. Nearby, another, longer line of slightly less cheerful air travelers waits patiently to surrender their nail scissors, even though it seems extremely unlikely that the terrorists will strike in that precise way again. Personally, I think they're more likely to get us with a porn bomb.

First of all, there's no way the hijackers could ever get past the reinforced cockpit door. Secondly, every guy in first class has now deputized himself. Desperate to support the floundering airline industry and make a few bucks on the corporate lecture circuit, I flew often in the months following September 11. Invariably, when I sat down, the guy next to me would say something like: "I played high school football, how 'bout you?"

"I wrestled," I would reply.

"Any trouble, we'll kill 'em, right?"

"Yeah. Kill 'em."

Actually, and this is totally true, for the first six months after 9/11, I put three baseballs in my carry-on bag. I am blessed with an unusually accurate throwing arm, and wanted more than anything to thwart a hijacking by beaning a terrorist. How American is that!? I imagined the *New York Post* headline: "Franken Beans Hijacker: Terrorist Hit in Face with More Balls than Elton John."

In its October 19, 2002, issue, the conservative British newsmagazine *The Economist* wrote that "Mr. Bush is as partisan a president as America has ever had." That includes George Washington, whom the British have little reason to love.

A window into just how exclusively political the thinking is at the Bush White House was opened by University of Pennsylvania professor John DiIulio, whom the President had appointed to head the White House Office of Faith-Based and Community Initiatives. DiIulio quit the office in February of 2002 after only one of its initiatives, the Faith-Based Bureau of Weights and Measures, came to fruition. (The FBBWM had some success in reintroducing the cubit by requiring that the biblical unit of measurement be used in plans for new federal buildings.)

DiIulio stupidly wrote a seven-page letter to *Esquire*'s Ron Suskind to provide background for Suskind's article on Karl Rove's role as senior advisor in the Bush White House. "There is no precedent in any modern White House for what is going on in this one: a complete lack of a policy apparatus," DiIulio admitted in the soon-to-be-much-regretted letter. "What you got is everything— and I mean everything—run by the political arm. It's the reign of the Mayberry Machiavellis."

DiIulio contrasted the Bush White House with Clinton's, where "every domestic [issue] drew multiple policy analyses that certainly weighted politics, media messages, legislative strategy, et cetera, but also strongly weighted policy-relevant information, stimulated substantive policy debate, and put a premium on policy knowledge. That is simply not Bush's style."

Several paragraphs later, DiIulio gave what might very well be the key to the Bush administration's startling lack of accomplishment in the domestic sphere other than budget-busting, deficit-bloating tax cuts. "On social policy and related issues, the lack of even basic policy knowledge, and the only casual interest in knowing more, was somewhat breathtaking."

According to DiIulio, Bush's staff "consistently talked and acted as if the height of political sophistication consisted in reducing every issue to its simplest, black-and-white terms for public consumption, then steering legislative initiatives or policy proposals as far right as possible."

Of Rove, DiIulio said, "Karl is enormously powerful, maybe the single most powerful person in the modern, post-Hoover era ever to occupy a political advisor post near the Oval Office." (Evidently, DiIulio never met a poised young woman in the Clinton White House by the name of Dee Dee Myers!)

"**We** will fuck him. Do you hear me? We will *fuck* him. We will ruin him. Like no one has ever fucked him." Now, I like a little dirty talk as much as the next fellow. The only difference between me and Karl Rove is that I like to keep it in the bedroom. Rove's "fucking" quote was reported by Suskind, who overheard the meltdown while waiting outside Rove's office. The name of the man about to be fucked may never be known, but it's safe to say that he was fucked like no one had ever fucked him.

One person not afforded the courtesy of being fucked in private was Tom Daschle, who, because of Jeffords's defection, was now Senate majority leader.

One GOP official told the *Washington Post* that orders to crush Daschle had come directly from the West Wing. Rush Limbaugh, a wholly owned subsidiary of the Republican Party, began referring to Daschle as "El Diablo." Limbaugh's Spanish-speaking listeners got the message. Daschle was either "*a* devil" or "*the* devil." (No one on TeamFranken ever took Spanish.)

In the fall of 2001, ads began to appear comparing the somewhat liberal El Diablo to more radical political figures, such as Osama bin Laden, Saddam Hussein, and American Taliban John Walker Lindh.

"What do Saddam Hussein and Senate Majority Leader Tom Daschle have in common?" asked a newspaper ad that juxtaposed the two men. "Neither man wants America to drill for oil in Alaska's Arctic National Wildlife Refuge." (Also, both men are Libras.)

**A**fter 9/11, the balance between civil liberties and national security would be put to a severe test. Fortunately for those who came down heavily on the national security side, John Ashcroft was the one making most of the close calls. Could we round up immigrants and not let them see lawyers? Sure. Could we conduct all their hearings in secret? Yes. Could we detain Muslims who had done nothing wrong by calling them "material witnesses"? Fabulous idea. Could we keep people locked up for months in horrifying conditions without letting their families know they'd been detained? Why not?

Those who came down on the civil liberties side had to watch what they said. As Ashcroft told the Senate Judiciary Committee on December 6, 2001, "To those who scare peace-loving people with phantoms of lost liberty, my message is this: Your tactics only aid terrorists—for they erode our national unity and diminish our resolve. They give ammunition to America's enemies." This wasn't a nutcase like Ann Coulter shouting, "Treason!" This was the attorney general of the United States.

Who is also something of a nutcase.

In his book *Lessons from a Father to His Son,* Ashcroft explains that he anointed himself with oil before being sworn in for each of his two terms as Missouri's governor, in the tradition of "the ancient kings of Israel, David and Saul, [who] were anointed as they undertook their administrative duties." Ashcroft also anointed himself before being sworn in as senator with—swear to God—a bowl of Crisco, a trick that used to be popular in gay bathhouses.

Then there was the thing with the statue. The attorney general gives his press conferences from the Great Hall of the Department of Justice Headquarters. Behind the podium, visible over the AG's right shoulder, stands a statue of a woman that represents the Spirit of Justice. The eighteen-foot aluminum statue has her arms raised and a toga draped over her body, leaving her left breast exposed. So, according to ABC News, Ashcroft ordered the Spirit of Justice's tit draped at a cost of $8,000. He didn't like being photographed in front of another boob.

What does that mean? What is it like for John Ashcroft when he takes a trip to Rome? Does he walk around with an erection all the time?

And $8,000? I have a better idea for what to do with that money. USE IT TO FIGHT TERRORISM!!! Buy the FBI a new computer! Remember how, during the Senate-House Intelligence Committee hearings on the FBI, agents testified that the Bureau's computers could not do the equivalent of a Google search? Because of a security measure known as "stovepiping," they cannot search for two words at a time.

They can't search for "al Qaeda." To search for al Qaeda, they first have to go through every "Al." They go through me, they go through Al Gore, they have to read every Weird Al Yankovic lyric.

By contrast, someone searching with Google can go straight to the al Qaeda home page, with its valuable searchable member database.

The White House had fought hearings on the intelligence agencies until it was shamed into them after Americans learned of the President's August 6, 2001, briefing regarding al Qaeda's unwholesome intentions. That information had been leaked as part of an escalating feud between the FBI and the CIA over which was more to blame for 9/11. In keeping with the spirit of Operation Ignore, the Bush administration had done nothing to encourage cooperation between the two agencies. As Jim Walsh, an expert on terrorism at Harvard's Kennedy School of Government, told me, "We expected another attack, but we didn't do the first thing you'd do to prevent it."

One highlight of the hearings was the testimony of agent Colleen Rowley, a courageous whistleblower from the Minneapolis bureau, who reminded the country how the Bush administration had committed the cardinal sin of dropping the ball while failing to connect the dots.

In a desperate bid to change the subject, President Bush proposed the most sweeping reorganization of the federal government since the Truman administration. Suddenly, after arguing against it for nine months, Bush and Rove made an about-face and decided to create a cabinet-level Department of Homeland Security. John DiIulio described it as "remarkably slapdash" and "a politically-timed reversal" which had received little more than "talking-points deliberation."

Immediately, Democrats like Joe Lieberman and Georgia Senator Max Cleland, who had months earlier written legislation urging just such a reorganization, fell into line behind the plan. Bush had turned the lemons of embarrassment into the lemonade of a popular idea.

Little did the Democrats suspect that this seemingly bipartisan lemonade would be served with a date-rape pill.

The pill came in the form of a provision to deprive the new department's employees of civil service protection. It was a brilliant move. Democrats were put in the awkward position of voting against a Homeland Security Department or betraying one of their most loyal constituencies, one that needed to be insulated from coercive political pressures. As Cleland would put it, "I don't think you make America more safe by making the workers that protect America more unsafe."

When Senate Democrats voted against the legislation, President Bush didn't hesitate to debase the debate. "The Senate is more interested in special interests in Washington and not interested in the security of the American people," Bush railed at a fund-raiser in New Jersey. The tone was set for the 2002 midterm elections.

When you think of someone who isn't interested in the security of the American people, you think of Senator Max Cleland wheeling his merry way through the marble halls of the Capitol. You see, Max left three of his limbs in Vietnam. They were blown off by an American grenade accidentally dropped by a fellow soldier.

Cleland is a war hero. Conservative Georgians first elected him to the Senate in 1996 on the basis of his unquestionable integrity and selfless loyalty to his country. And yet he lost his bid for re-election in 2002 largely because of attacks on his patriotism.

Cleland's opponent, Saxby Chambliss, was not a war hero. He got out of Vietnam because of a bad knee. Cleland has never had a bad knee. Before the war, he had two good ones. Afterward, he would never have to worry about his knees for the rest of his life.

Chambliss ran one of the great attack ads of the 2002 cycle, one that warmed even Karl Rove's icy heart. It featured images of Osama bin Laden, Saddam Hussein, and . . . Max Cleland.

The ad savaged Cleland's votes against the "President's vital homeland security efforts." The tag line: "Max Cleland says he has the courage to lead. But the record proves Max Cleland is just misleading."

To recap quickly. Cleland loses three limbs in Vietnam. Cleland authors Department of Homeland Security legislation. Bush blocks it. Bush proposes politicized version of same legislation to trap Democrats. Cleland stands on principle and votes against it. Bush says senators "not interested" in security of American people. Chambliss compares Cleland to Osama and Saddam and attacks Cleland's courage.

Chambliss wins. Republicans take Senate. Bush credits victory to change in tone.

I grow discouraged.

## 2 3
# I'm Prudenized

**Every** once in a while, it's a good idea to think about Korea. And not just on Korea Day. We fought a war there and lost thirty-three thousand brave Americans. Fifty years later, we still have thirty-seven thousand troops deployed on the Korean peninsula, which might give you an inkling of how long we could be occupying Iraq. Oh, and North Korea has nuclear weapons and has threatened to turn Seoul into "a Sea of Fire."

Still, let's remember some of the things Korea has given us. Samsung, for example. Also, the Reverend Sun Myung Moon's Unification Church.

The Reverend Moon has proclaimed himself "the Savior, Messiah, and King of Kings of all humanity." Frankly, I don't think he's any of those things. But the folks over at the *Washington Times* do. They think he is the incarnation of Himself, and agree with him when he says, "I will conquer and subjugate the world."

After all, he's their boss. That's why, since 1982, employees of the *Times* have been forced to marry other *Times* employees in mass weddings conducted by the Reverend Moon. This May, for example, Moon paired off the men in the subscription department with the women in classifieds and married them on the *Times*'s five-color printing floor.[1]

So it's probably no surprise that the *Times* has not only reflected Moon's worldview (e.g., "I am the King of it"), but doctored stories involving South Korea and those dealing with the reverend's felony convictions for tax evasions. (The Messiah spent time behind bars in Connecticut.) Let's face it, you might be willing to alter wire service copy about a guy who has the power to force you to marry the gal in ad sales with a hump.

[1]The quotes are real. The *Times*' mass wedding is unconfirmed.

Most of the doctoring, though, has not been about Moon or Korea, but about American politics. And much of that was done at the behest of the *Times*'s executive editor, Wesley Pruden. Pruden is an Arkansan whose father was chaplain of the White Citizens' Council, an adjunct of the KKK. (The Ku Klux Klan, not the Korean King of Kings.) I'm not sure what the chaplain does in the White Citizens' Council. My guess would be he provides comfort and religious counseling to troubled members after a particularly traumatizing assault on black people.

According to *Times* writer and *Blinded by the Right* author David Brock, "There were endless controversies and resignations over what became known as 'Prudenizing' news copy—slanting it in a conservative direction." Which brings me to 1999, the year I was Prudenized. That spring, I give a speech to the White House Photographers Association. It's one of those big Washington dinners like the White House Correspondents Association dinner, only not so prestigious. Sort of like the Polk is to the Peabody. I mean, c'mon, they're just photographers.

So I'm doing my usual great job (Note: there is no reason ever to believe a comedian's self-report on how he went over— nevertheless, I was killing), and I go into a bit about John McCain.

A short sidebar about me and John McCain. I met John in 1996 when he gave a beautiful eulogy at the funeral of a mutual friend, David Ifshin, who died of cancer. Ifshin had been a Vietnam antiwar protester and, in 1970, went to North Vietnam (sans Jane Fonda), where he denounced our involvement in the war on Radio Hanoi. David's denunciation was piped into the Hanoi Hilton, where McCain got to hear it in his tiny solitary cell.

Cut to: 1984. Ifshin has become a mainstream Democrat and is serving as counsel on the Mondale campaign. McCain, now a congressman from Arizona, angrily denounces Mondale for having Ifshin on his staff. Ifshin goes up to the Hill, marches into McCain's office, finds him, and says, "I owe you an apology."

But McCain says, "No. I owe you an apology. You had every

right to do what you did." So they shake hands, become fast friends, and together (with others) work successfully toward normalization of relations between Vietnam and the United States.

In his eulogy, John said that Ifshin had taught him to see the best in everyone.

So I like John McCain.

Anyway, I'm doing the White House Photographers Dinner, and I go into my little McCain riff. "Hey, I like John McCain. And I really think he's courageous. I mean, his stance on campaign finance reform and tobacco. Wow. That takes guts. But this whole 'war hero' thing—I don't get it. I mean, as far as I'm concerned, he sat out the war. I mean, *anyone* can get captured! Am I wrong, but isn't the idea *to capture the other guy*?"

Big laughs. It's called irony, and whatever TV, radio, and print correspondents may say, photographers love irony.

The next day, in the *Washington Times*, I read a column by John McCaslin. And he gives me the "Boo of the Week."

> After several mocking references to Jews, Christians, and Christian doctrine, Mr. Franken scoffed at the war-hero credentials of John McCain, who was shot down over North Vietnam, tortured and held in mostly solitary confinement at the notorious hellhole called the Hanoi Hilton for more than five years.
>
> "Anybody could get captured," Mr. Franken said, and waited in vain for laughs. But he kept trying: "Essentially, he sat out the war." A few scattered boos. "Well, isn't the idea to capture the other guys?"

I call McCaslin and get him on the phone. "That bit killed! Were you even in the same room?" I ask indignantly.

"Uh, no," he says. Actually, he hadn't been at the event.

"What?! Then how could you write that?"

"I didn't." It turned out McCaslin hadn't even been aware that the "Boo of the Week" had been in his column. "Wes Pruden probably added it."

"Who?" (At this point in my life, I wasn't as up on my right-wing media.)

"He's the editor. I'm pretty sure he was at the dinner last night."

"So the editor can add stuff to your column? Without your knowing it?"

"Yeah," McCaslin said with just a twinge of resignation. "It happens all the time."

I'd never heard of such a thing. This editor had deliberately put my routine through the "de-irony-izer" to make me, a Democrat, look unpatriotic, and thereby serve his own sick political agenda. *And* he put it under a columnist's byline without even consulting him. I had no idea what to do with this. A letter to the editor seemed kind of futile.

So I sit on it. Waiting for just the right time to lay open this scandalous breach of journalistic ethics.

And two years later, I get my opportunity. I'm asked to be the keynote speaker at the American Society of Newspaper Editors. Maybe, I think, I can get the *Washington Times* expelled from the association.

But I realize I was relying on just one source: McCaslin. To be fair, I at least had to check with the editor for his version of the story. What was his name again?

I call the *Washington Times* and ask for their managing editor. I get a guy named Bill Giles. Giles tells me that there is *no way* that McCaslin's story is true. He's adamant. An editor would *never* insert something into a columnist's copy without consulting him. It would be a total violation of every journalistic tenet.

Well, that threw me for a loop. So I call McCaslin, and he says no, it wasn't the *managing* editor who inserted the copy. It was Wes Pruden, the *executive* editor. My next call is to Pruden, who answers his own phone.

I tell him who I am and explain the situation. And I ask him, "Do you ever insert copy into a column without consulting the columnist?"

A pause. Then, "Yes, we do that."

I thank Pruden and call back Giles. "Yeah, I just talked to Wes Pruden. And he confirmed McCaslin's story. You know that policy you said you had? Your paper evidently violates it all the time."

There was silence on the other end of the line. Then, "Okay. Thanks. That's good to know."

"One other thing," I say. "When do you plan to tender your resignation?"

Another beat of silence, then, "Thanks. Thanks for calling."

So I went to the dinner, told the group the same story I just told you. There was sort of a collective shrug that said: "Yeah, that's the *Washington Times.*"

# Paul Gigot Is Unable to Defend an Incredibly Stupid *Wall Street Journal* Editorial

**Sometimes** you read something so stupid it just takes your breath away. You can't quite believe that someone actually wrote what's on the page. The effect is heightened when the source is, if not necessarily reliable, at least literate and usually capable of masking its distortions beneath a patina of institutional credibility borrowed from its news division.

On February 3, 2003, the *Wall Street Journal* wrote an editorial so startlingly dumb that it may, in fact, be the single most idiotic piece of writing my fourteen Harvard research assistants found during their many, many hours of labor. (With the obvious exception of the entire Hannity book.)

Now, I don't want to bore you with the entire editorial. It starts reasonably enough, praising Attorney General Ashcroft for putting criminals who use guns while committing crimes behind bars. Their point, I gather, is that it's better to enforce gun laws than *not* to enforce them. Kudos.

Then the editorial makes one slightly stupid point, as if to foreshadow the tsunami of stupidity that is to come. It cites increased prosecutions of federal gun crimes as evidence of Ashcroft's effectiveness against crime. The problem with this point is that prosecutions tend to go up whenever crime rates go up. Which started happening the moment Bush took office.

But this is just standard *Wall Street Journal* distortion. It's in the next paragraph of their editorial that things really get weird. The *Journal* charges that the Clinton administration "spent its time devising new ways to keep average citizens from getting guns, while leaving bad guys on the street." In other words, Clinton's crime policies, especially on gun violence, failed—and Ashcroft's were working. To clinch their case, they cite a statistic that they claim is an indictment of Clinton's approach and "a vindication for Mr. Ashcroft." Are you ready for Mr. Dumb? Here he comes!

"In reality," the *Journal* writes, "gun violence has declined from 12% of violent crime in 1993 to 9% in the most recent Justice statistics. Any gun control advocates out there care to apologize?"

Okay, reader. Let's take a moment to test your political IQ. Who became president in 1993 when gun violence comprised 12 percent of violent crime? Was it George W. Bush? Or was it Bill Clinton? If you said Bill Clinton, give yourself a point.

Now, the "most recent Justice statistics" mentioned in the editorial came from the year 2001. Who ended his presidency in 2001? George W. Bush? Or Bill Clinton? Again, a point for Clinton.

This next question is a two-pointer, because it involves a logical deduction. Here it is. If Clinton was president during the time when gun violence rates dropped, is that a vindication for George W. Bush's attorney general? Or is it a vindication for Clinton and his advocacy of gun control? The correct answer is at the bottom of the page, written upside down so that you can't cheat.

Add up your score. If you got four points, your political IQ is somewhere between 40 and 200. If you, like the editorial writers for the *Wall Street Journal,* got between zero and three points, your political IQ is between 0 and 39.

Dolphins are about a 36. But they're cute. And friendly, too.

I think Paul Gigot, who has edited the *WSJ*'s editorial page since 2001, is kind of cute. Or, as he prefers, "handsome." But, as I learned when I called to ask about this editorial, he is not friendly. I left a message, and, to his credit, Paul called me back. To his discredit, he refused to discuss the editorial. Even worse, he got angry and attacked me personally, impugning my motives.

"You just want to be able to say that you called Paul Gigot

Clinton.

Paul Gigot

and that he couldn't defend his editorial, so you can put it in your book to sell more copies," he said.[1]

Frankly, I was hurt. Nobody had ever spoken to me that way before. My actual intention was totally innocent. My purpose in calling Gigot was to discuss the editorial and, in a civil manner, find out why he chose to publish something so mind-blowingly asinine. I would have thought that he would have

*loved* an opportunity to defend his work product against a mere comedian with only a passing knowledge of current events. Oh well.

One unfortunate result of Gigot's intransigence was that he did not have the opportunity to address some other questions I had. Since the statistics cited in the editorial seemed to vindicate Clinton's gun control policy, I had taken the liberty of having TeamFranken check out the *Wall Street Journal*'s coverage of the Brady Bill debate. The Brady Bill, which passed in late 1993 and took effect in early 1994, required background checks and a five-day waiting period for gun purchasers.

As I suspected, the *Journal* opposed Brady *and* the assault weapons ban. But what I wanted to talk to Gigot about was the tone of the anti–gun control editorials. For example, in their January 26, 1994, piece, the *Journal* wrote, "An awful lot of innocent Americans have had to be robbed, beaten, stabbed, raped, tortured, and murdered to arrive at the point where a Bill Clinton could feel compelled to get tough on crime."

I hope I'm not being overly partisan in suggesting that this was maybe just the slightest bit unfair to Clinton, who ran on an anti-crime platform, announced in his first State of the Union address his intention to put one hundred thousand more police on the

---

[1] I hate to break this to Paul, but I doubt my publisher will be building the promotional campaign for the book around the Franken-Gigot incident.

street, and successfully fought to reduce crime every single year of his presidency.

The *Journal*'s December 10, 1993, editorial was no kinder to "liberals" in general: "To date, their outrage over violent deaths has been a pose." Ouch! They nailed us there. I personally remember expressing mock outrage in 1993 over a brutal bludgeoning in Missouri I had read about. But I was really just posturing to make it seem like I was a decent person with actual feelings for human beings.

So what did the *Journal* editorial page say about gun control while it was being debated? In May of 1994, the editorial page wrote, "Democrats in Washington are bursting their buttons over two big contributions to the war on crime: Enacting the Brady Bill and voting in the House recently for a ban on 'assault weapons.' We're not impressed."

They spent most of the editorial questioning the feasibility and constitutionality of Brady and pointing out that "assault weapons" are "used in less than 1% of crime."[2]

Then the *Journal* concluded with a challenge: "Democrats now think that with their bans they have 'done something' about crime. We hope someone will be keeping score on the results."

Well, someone did keep score. And that score was presented in the shit-for-brains 2003 editorial: "Gun violence has declined from 12% of violent crime in 1993 to 9% in the most recent Justice statistics."

But let's take a more comprehensive look at Clinton's remarkable record on crime, using statistics from the FBI's Uniform Crime Reports. Violent crime had gone *up* nearly every year of the Reagan and Bush Sr. administrations. It went *down* every year during the Clinton administration, especially after his crime bill went into effect. Would you like to see it in chart form?

---

[2]Not "violent crime," but "crime." Since roughly 43 million crimes were committed in 1993, this means that, using their logic, assault weapons were used in up to 430,000 crimes that year. Even assuming that in, say, half of those 430,000 crimes, the assault weapon was merely brandished and not fired, that's still a lot of scary shit going down. (Their logic is wrong—assault weapons were used in less than 1 percent of *gun* crimes.)

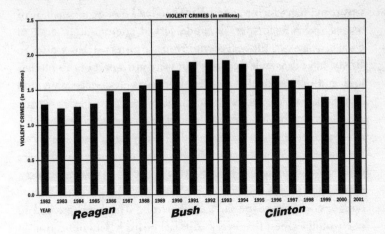

Now would you like to see it in a chart that, while technically accurate, is slightly and intentionally misleading? The kind the *Wall Street Journal* would use?

To be fair to opponents of gun control, there were a lot of other things Clinton did to achieve this remarkable, un-Reagan-like drop in crime rates. He put more cops on the street; he instituted community policing; he aggressively enforced the Community Rein-

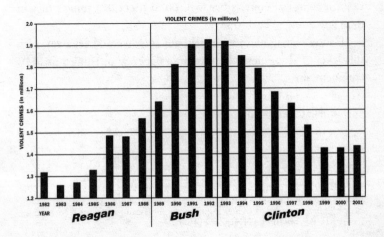

vestment Act, which requires banks to lend money to small businesses and homeowners in underserved communities; and, of course, he gave us the best economy in the history of the world. So Brady and the assault weapons ban were just a part of this incredible, and unprecedented, success in making America a safer and better place to live and raise our families.

Okay, maybe that sounds a little partisan. So let's go back to that original imbecilic editorial to see who's really right here. You know, the great thing about our society is that we have a free press, where different viewpoints can be expressed in a spirit of fearless inquiry. Sometimes, like in the case of the *Journal* and gun control, these opinions can prove to be badly, badly wrong. That happens. And no one would suggest that every editorial board has an obligation to admit when they've been wrong. Simply ignoring editorial mistakes is perfectly within the accepted practice of hack journalism.

But when an editorial page goes out of its way to print facts that prove it *completely wrong*, and then claims that these statistics prove it *completely right*, well, that is not just bad, it's downright weird.

In a way, this one little dumb-ass editorial is a microcosm of the *Journal*'s editorial page. How much is stupidity? How much is dishonesty, and how much is the *Journal* just trusting that its readers' rabid ideological convictions will blind them to gaping holes in their reasoning? Hard to say.

Can you imagine another field where you could get away with this level of sloppiness? Picture an ad agency pitching this SUV commercial:

VIDEO: CLIPS OF SUVs TIPPING OVER.

ANNOUNCER (VOICE OVER):
The new Ford Explorer. Like all SUVs, impossible
to tip over! Put your child in an Explorer today,
and see the results.

CUT TO: SHOT OF PARALYZED CHILD.

If you were Ford, you'd fire that agency, wouldn't you?

In conclusion, if I were Ford, I wouldn't hire the *Wall Street Journal* to make ads for any dangerous products I might want to foist upon an unsuspecting public. But that hasn't stopped the Bush administration from relying on the *Journal* to sell the public the most dangerous product of all: defective baby strollers that can collapse unexpectedly and crush a child.

Also, tax cuts.

# "This Was *Not* a Memorial to Paul Wellstone": A Case Study in Right-Wing Lies

**When** I do my corporate speeches, I normally talk to groups that are anywhere from 60 to, oh, 97 percent Republican. They know I'm liberal, and they're normally aware that they're conservative. So sometimes they're a little nervous that I'll do jokes that make them uncomfortable or angry. Here's how I defuse the situation.

I say, "As you probably can figure out from my book *Rush Limbaugh Is a Big Fat Idiot,* I'm a liberal. And I know you're conservative. And that's okay. See, I've discovered that Democrats can't afford me."

*Huge* laugh. They love this. It makes them feel rich.

Then I say, "So what I do is, I make fun of you. You laugh. And then you pay me."

Another huge laugh. Now I can say pretty much anything I want, and they'll just laugh and pay me. Everybody's happy.

Democrats are a different story. Unlike corporate events (which, by the way, I love—you can book me on the web), I speak to Democrats for free. I try not to do it too often, because a guy's gotta eat. So I pick and choose. And the Democrat I did the most speaking for over the years was Paul Wellstone.

Part of it was that I grew up in Minnesota. And Paul knew my folks. In Wellstone's first campaign for the Senate in 1990, my dad was part of a senior citizen theater troupe that did skits for Paul at nursing homes. That's pretty grassroots, don't you think?

My dad died in 1993, and my mom went downhill pretty fast. They had been married for fifty-one years. She got depressed, and about four years ago went into a severe psychotic depression, which brought with it an exciting element of paranoia.

One night at the hospital, I went up to one of the nurses and said, "Excuse me, it's kind of awkward to ask this, but I feel out of loyalty to my mom, I should."

"Go ahead," she said.

"Yeah. What I was wondering is, um, are you pumping poison gas into my mom's room? And are you videotaping her? And are you not really a nurse, but actually an actress who is trying to kill my mom?"

"No," said the kindly nurse.

"I didn't think so. But I felt I had to ask."

Fortunately, the doctors pulled Mom out of it with some miracle drug. But she's never really been the same.

The last time I saw Paul was in the late summer of 2002, about six weeks before he died in a plane crash. It was an evening event in the Twin Cities. Paul was in the middle of an intense, dead-even Senate race. He'd been targeted as vulnerable by the national Republican Party and money was flowing in from around the country for his opponent, a suit named Norm Coleman. Paul was fighting for his political life. The first thing he asked me was, "How's your mom?"

I told Paul I had just visited her. "It was tough. I couldn't even have a conversation with her."

Paul nodded, and said, "You know, touch means so much."

The next day I took my mom out into the nursing home garden in her wheelchair. It was a beautiful day. I sat next to her for a couple of hours with my arm around her. I can't tell you whether it meant a thing to her, but it meant a lot to me.

So, that was Paul. "Touch means so much" wasn't the kind of thing you'd hear from a Michael Dukakis. I, along with innumerable people, loved Paul Wellstone. For what he stood for, for what he fought for, and for who he was. I loved his wife Sheila, too. I don't think I ever saw Paul without Sheila by his side.

Paul died on October 25, 2002, when his plane went down in Northern Minnesota. Sheila; their daughter, Marcia; his driver, Will McLaughlin; two other close aides, Tom Lapic and Mary McEvoy;

and two pilots died with him. Four days later, C-SPAN, along with almost every Minnesota TV and radio station, carried a hastily-put-together memorial service for Paul, Sheila, Marcia, Will, Tom, and Mary. I was there. It was a beautiful memorial, sometimes incredibly sad, sometimes funny, sometimes rowdy, and sometimes political. Some people watching on television were offended. Some people were moved. But the right saw an opening. They took moments out of context, lied about the rest, and used it as a political club to attack the Democrats. It won them the Senate election in Minnesota and probably in Missouri, which means it gave Republicans control of the Senate.

This chapter is a case study of how the right lies and viciously distorts. It is the story of how the right-wing media repeats its fabrications until they echo into the mainstream press. It is a story of pure cynicism in the pursuit of power. It is the story of how the lying liars took the death of my friends and invented a myth that changed the 2002 elections.

And the best part is, it's hilarious! No, it's not. But read it anyway. You paid for the book.

**T**he Wellstone-Coleman campaign had been considered one of the most negative in recent memory. Coleman had called Wellstone a "joke." He told KSTP radio on July 7, "I run against a guy who I quite often think is just the lowest common denominator, the lowest common denominator." Coleman said that Wellstone "opposed any program that promised to move people from public assistance to private payrolls." Of course, that was a scurrilous lie. Paul's work in the Senate created jobs all over Minnesota.

But mainly it was Coleman's proxies who played it dirty. The National Republican Senatorial Committee (NRSC) ran an ad called "Pork" that hit the hypocrisy jackpot. It savaged Wellstone for voting "to spend thousands of dollars to control seaweed in Maui," claiming that he prioritized seaweed control over national defense. In fact, Wellstone *did* vote for S.1216, as did Strom Thurmond, Trent Lott, and eighty-four other senators. That bill did appropriate the seaweed control spending—but it also provided $21 billion for veterans' health care, $27 billion for veterans' compensation and pensions, and block grants to assist New York City's recovery from 9/11. The NRSC was chaired that year by Bill Frist, who later replaced Lott as Senate majority leader. Before the memorial, Frist spoke with the Wellstones' older son, David, who later recounted the conversation to me.

"I'm sorry about your parents and your sister," Frist told David.

"Did you authorize the seaweed ad against my dad?" David asked.

"Yes," said Frist.

"And did you vote for the seaweed bill?"

There was a pause. They both knew that the answer was yes. Finally, Frist said, "It wasn't personal."

"My dad took it personal," David said. "Thanks for coming to my family's memorial."

Four days earlier, the Wellstone candidacy had ended with the plane crash. The Coleman campaign changed its tone. Somewhat. According to a *Minneapolis Star Tribune* account of the thirteen days between the plane crash and the election, Vin Weber, a former GOP congressman and key Coleman strategist, started politicking mere moments after Wellstone's plane went down. Working his cell phone on his way to a meeting with Norm Coleman and the rest of the campaign brain trust, Vin tracked down his friends who had worked in John Ashcroft's 2000 campaign. He picked their brains about what to do when your opponent dies in a plane crash. What worked? What didn't? They told him that Ashcroft's decision to shut down his campaign and stay out of sight after the tragic death of his opponent, Mel Carnahan, had cost him the election.

A key decision was reached at the meeting. Coleman would not repeat Ashcroft's mistake. Instead of disappearing, Coleman's post-crash strategy would be, according to the *Star Tribune,* to "gravely and respectfully—but publicly—participate in the state's grieving process." The meeting ended at 2:30 P.M., about four hours after airport officials lost contact with Wellstone's plane.

Sure enough, at 4:15 P.M., Coleman told a throng of reporters, "I think our focus now is solely on bending our knees and being very reflective and very prayerful. . . . I am giving no thought to anything other than the memory of Paul and Sheila Wellstone and the others on that plane."

Coleman continued his new tactic by announcing that he was suspending his campaign until after Wellstone's funeral, and also by agreeing to appear that Sunday via satellite on ABC's *This Week.* After the show, he held what he called a "non-press-conference press conference." He was taking every possible opportunity to show voters that he was not exploiting Wellstone's death for political gain.

The Wellstone campaign was reeling. But the Democrats needed someone on the ballot. Former Vice President Walter Mondale approved a leak to the press that he was "highly likely" to run, but would not campaign until after a public memorial was held.

On Monday, Coleman went on national TV again, conversing with Judy Woodruff on CNN's *Inside Politics.* She asked him whether his campaign was gearing up. His response was right on message: "If I ruled the world, Judy, we'd all still be on our knees and saying some prayers."

The next guest was Harry Reid of Nevada, the number two Democrat in the Senate, who was unimpressed by Coleman's pieties. "Judy, Mr. Coleman is campaigning, and that's why he's on your program." He pointed out that Republicans had already starting polling in Minnesota. Worse, they had dispatched Newt Gingrich as a Coleman surrogate to bash Mondale on NBC's *Meet the Press.* "I just think this is so classless," said Reid.

Gingrich's attack on Mondale wasn't classless merely because it came so soon after Wellstone's death. It had the added classlessness of being a lie. Gingrich said:

> Walter Mondale chaired a commission that was for the privatization of Social Security worldwide. He chaired a commission that was for raising the retirement age dramatically. . . . If you want to raise your retirement age dramatically and privatize Social Security, Walter Mondale is a terrifically courageous guy to say that.

Mondale hadn't actually chaired the commission. He *co*-chaired it. More importantly, he disagreed with the commission's conclusions. While the majority did support raising retirement ages and privatizing government retirement programs, Mondale co-wrote (or *wrote,* as Newt might say) the dissenting opinion.

Had Gingrich searched on Google for "Mondale" and "Social Security," the first hit would have been an August 20, 2001, article entitled "Mondale Condemns Social Security Privatization."

The lie had its intended effect. About the same time the *Washington Post* was exposing Newt's lie on its website, Judy Woodruff was credulously repeating it for her national audience on CNN. "The Republicans say, Senator Reid, that . . . they're simply pointing out Walter Mondale's policy positions. That he chaired this commission last year that came out with a report recommending the privatization of Social Security."

**T**he Wellstone memorial was scheduled for Tuesday evening, October 29, at Williams Arena. I flew to Minnesota and met up with my brother to visit our mom. We left for the event three and a half hours early, but the arena parking lot was already full. When we finally got inside, the place was overflowing. Twenty thousand were packed into an arena meant for sixteen thousand.

The crowd at the event, which had been billed as a celebration of the lives of the deceased, had a raucous energy. From where I was sitting, it all seemed just incredibly natural and human, the way grieving people often jump between crying and laughing. A group of American Indians did some tribal drumming. A soul band called Sounds of Blackness played "Love Train" as dignitaries filed in. When the crowd saw Clinton on the Jumbotron, they went nuts. Same for Hillary, for Gore, and for Mondale, who was replacing Wellstone on the ballot. When Trent Lott's face appeared on the screen, a few people booed. It seemed like good-natured ribbing to me. Lott broke out in a grin and waved.

The event lasted three and a half hours. It opened with an ecumenical prayer led by the rabbi from the synagogue I went to as a child. Standing with the rabbi were dozens of clergy representing every religious tradition in the state. The first eulogy was delivered by a brother of Wellstone's driver, Will McLaughlin, and was one of the most beautiful I've ever heard. There were no celebrity speakers, even though many had offered. It was family, friends, and colleagues, who each gave moving testimony to the lives of those who died.

One of the eight eulogies that night, given by Wellstone's best friend Rick Kahn, ended with a political call to arms that went over the top. The first part of the speech, though, was dead-on. Kahn described how Wellstone had always said that it's not enough to believe in something if you don't act on it. Kahn exhorted the crowd to act on Wellstone's memory by "standing up for those who lack the strength to stand up on their own." Everyone stood up, which I thought was a very Minnesotan way to react. (We're very literal.) We cheered, too. With tremendous emotion. There was cheering and crying and stomping and applause all throughout the speech, even after Kahn's train left the rails.

The trouble began when Kahn put maybe too fine a point on what the crowd had to do to keep Paul's legacy alive. "We can redeem the promise of his life if you help us win this election for Paul Wellstone!" Huge cheers. He repeated variations of this several times, and the crowd stayed right with him. I could see how someone watching on TV might find this blatantly political battle cry just a bit too partisan for a memorial service.

Then Kahn named a number of Republicans in the audience: "Senator Domenici, Senator Brownback, Senator Lugar, Senator Hagel, and Senator DeWine, who are here tonight, are all Republicans for whom Paul had the utmost respect and whom he considered to be true friends." Cheers. Prolonged, warm, appreciative applause, as the crowd embraced the Republicans who had come to pay their respects. It seemed to me like things were back on track.

But it turned out that Kahn was going someplace I had never heard anyone go before. He said to the Republicans, "Can you not hear your friend calling you one last time to step forward on his behalf to keep his legacy alive and help us win this election for Paul Wellstone?"

That was bizarre, I thought. You can't ask Republicans to stump for Mondale. Still, the crowd kept cheering. This was three hours into the event, and the emotion was so intense that everyone was responding to everything. They had just cheered for Paul's friendship for the Republicans, and now they were cheering for the same Republicans to drop their own candidate like a hot rock.

Kahn ended his speech by repeating his final line three times: "We are gonna win this election for Paul Wellstone!" I looked at my brother, and he shrugged.

George Latimer, former mayor of St. Paul and emcee for the event, came back up and tried to do a little damage control by making a joke. "I was getting a little bit worried that the last speaker had a certain partisan tinge to his remarks," he said, "and I was glad that he concluded that with a call for bipartisanship." Big laugh. But some people watching at home had a sour taste in their mouths.

By one estimate, at least 630,000 people in Minnesota watched at least part of the memorial on TV. Reasonable people of goodwill were genuinely offended. And to people who only saw the ten-second clips that were later repeated and repeated on TV, it looked like Kahn and the crowd were just being foot-stompingly partisan—that Wellstone's death was being used for political gain.

But Kahn's speech was also full of phrases like "[our] hearts are now shattered" and "tonight we are filled to overflowing with overwhelming grief and sorrow." This speech was coming from someone who was crushed by the deaths of his best friend, his best friend's wife, his best friend's daughter, and three other very close friends. Yeah, it had some inappropriate moments. But I assumed that people would understand, and cut the man a little slack.

Governor Jesse Ventura, who by then was deeply unpopular in Minnesota, had chewed gum through the first three hours of the memorial. After Kahn's speech, Ventura walked out, saying that he was offended. Now, Jesse "the Body" is not a man easily offended. In his 1999 autobiography, *I Ain't Got Time to Bleed*, Ventura proudly describes his visit to Nevada's BunnyRanch, where he fornicated with what my feminist friends refer to as a "sex worker." In fact, he proudly wrote that he made money off the deal, by trading his belt made of machine gun shell casings to the sex worker for a trick and ten bucks. "All the girls look like *Playboy* playmates," the BunnyRanch website proudly quotes the Reform Party governor as saying. (He denies actually saying this, and I tend to believe him.)

Ventura had no problem with the BunnyRanch, but Kahn's speech was beyond the pale. In fairness, Ventura never described any of the sex workers as being overly partisan. Maybe he really was offended by the memorial and not just showboating the way he had every other moment of his public life.

So some people were offended, and some people were moved. I thought the story was over. The best summary of it all was Joe Klein's piece in *The New Yorker*.

The memorial service for Senator Paul Wellstone held last Tuesday evening in the Williams arena, on the University of Minnesota campus, was overlong, excessively partisan, unpretentious, emotional (without being maudlin), and, above all, egalitarian—in sum, an accurate reflection of the man being memorialized. . . . There was none of the glitz and few of the easy tears that have come to mark such public events. . . .

The emotions unleashed by his death—the tributes from even his staunchest political opponents—are certainly a consequence of Wellstone's, and his family's, bracing, un- varnished humanity; but, one senses, there is also a more general mourning for the politics of larger themes and for politicians willing to discuss them. It is, in any case, stun- ning that the death of one man has occasioned the only breath of life we've seen in this election year.

That was pretty much the way I saw it. (Though a lot less elo- quently.) What I didn't realize was that between the raucous crowd, Kahn's fiery speech, and the imprimatur of independent outrage provided by Ventura's walkout, the memorial service had created a sort of perfect political storm for Republican oppor- tunists.

The morning after the memorial, I picked up the *Minneapolis Star Tribune* and turned to the special section devoted to the event. It was titled "One Last Rally: Victims Remembered with Cheers and Tears," with a heartbreaking picture of Paul and Sheila's grand- daughter, Cari, crying. There were two stories on the front page. One was about the event itself: "Overflow Crowd Pays Tribute to Wellstone." The other was about GOP spin: "Republicans Decry Service as Political." With the stories side by side, it was as if two different events had taken place. The real one, and the lie one.

Vin Weber was framing the Republican story line. "This was NOT a memorial to Paul Wellstone. This was a political event." Weber said that the event was a "complete, total, absolute sham" and accused the Democrats of "exploit[ing] Wellstone's memory totally, completely and shamelessly for political gain."

This seemed almost surreally dishonest. I flipped to the real story and read an excerpt from the eulogies. This one from Paul and Sheila's younger son, Mark:

> The one thing that comes to mind when I think about my dad
> is how proud he was of everybody around him and how he
> wanted to shed light on everybody's accomplishments. It
> was never about him. It was never about Paul Wellstone. It
> was about the ideal; it was about the dream he had. . . .
> More than anything I just have a message to my dad. The
> message to my dad is, "Dad, we're okay. Dave and I are
> okay. The thousands and thousands of people that you left
> behind that care about you, we are okay. We will carry
> on. . . ." These are some of his favorite words that he ever
> spoke . . . "Never separate the lives you live from the words
> you speak."

That doesn't sound like a complete, total, *absolute* sham. In fact, it hardly sounds like a sham at all. That sounds like the kind of eulogy a father would love from his son. (Hear that, Joe?)

When I called Vin Weber to research this chapter, I asked him whether he had watched the whole event and whether he had seen any of the eulogies. He said, "Yeah, there was some very nice stuff." This candid Vin was a refreshing break from the lying Vin who talked to the *Star Tribune* in 2002. But Lying Vin had planted the story line: The memorial was a total sham, a political charade.

Going back to the lie story in the *Star Tribune,* I found a gem from a local Republican apparatchik.

> Republican political analyst and lobbyist Sarah Janacek said
> that what she found most outrageous were the screens in-
> side Williams Arena prompting audience reaction—when to
> laugh and how loudly to clap.

Janacek was referring to the *closed captioning* that the memorial's organizers had thoughtfully provided for the hearing impaired. Janacek, perhaps, was thinking impaired. Or, more likely, honesty impaired. On radio, she said that the text on the Jumbotrons was proof positive that the entire event had been scripted. She didn't mention that words appeared on the screen about five seconds *after* they had been spoken.

Janacek's insanely stupid and/or viciously dishonest claim was repeated over and over on local right-wing talk radio. But what's a local lie when you can have a national lie? On C-SPAN's *Washington Journal* that morning, Kellyanne Fitzpatrick Conway, one of the Republican party's most loyal flaks, picked up on the Jumbotron Lie and gave it a little more pizzazz:

> CONWAY: The *Star Tribune* covers the fact that the people who were in attendance were told by screen when to cheer and when to jeer, and they were told to cheer when the Clintons and Ted Kennedy were displayed, and they were told to jeer when Trent Lott and Rod Grams, former senator of Minnesota who lost in 2000, were displayed.

The Republican Lie Machine was whirring up to speed.

Driving to the airport, I happened to tune in to the Excellence in Broadcasting network. I don't normally listen to Rush Limbaugh—I felt I'd paid my dues while researching *Rush Limbaugh Is a Big Fat Idiot*—but I'd made a little bet with myself that I'd hear at least three lies before I reached the airport.

I won the bet, and I had to give myself ten bucks.

Almost the entire three-hour show was about the memorial. The first lie was sort of an overarching, background lie. Rush claimed to be absolutely "distraught" about the "appalling" spectacle he had witnessed the night before. He was "depressed," "embarrassed," and "feeling shame." He was "near speechless" because the whole thing had been "a giant setup." Wellstone (whom Rush used to refer to as Senator Welfare) had been used for "disgusting" and "ghoulish" political ends. The whole thing had "basically cheapened Wellstone's life." Limbaugh's entire three-hour show was based on his faked sorrow about the total absence of decency on the left.

Limbaugh's big lie, lie number two, was that this was all a calculated plot by the national Democratic Party to win a Senate election. "They pulled a fast one over everybody," Limbaugh blustered, pulling a fast one over his audience. "This was not a memorial service for Paul Wellstone, it was not. And that's to me what's so sad about it." Limbaugh was taking the high road, mourning Wellstone's death, just like Coleman. And the Democrats were a bunch of craven political opportunists.

A Democrat called in and asked if maybe there was a note of jealousy that twenty thousand people had come to the memorial.

"Oh, come on," Rush responded dismissively. "They were bused in by the AFL-CIO. I haven't even talked about the audience. Everybody knows it was a planted audience."

Wow. Ugly. Yes, there were some buses. Robert Richman, who took care of all the logistics for the memorial, arranged for buses for the families of those who died in the crash. The families weren't a "planted audience." Neither was the Apple Valley High School wrestling team, which came in on its bus because Mark Wellstone, Paul's younger son, was their assistant coach. And yes, some unions chartered their own buses to the memorial. That's because Paul had been fighting for unions since long before he went into politics. When he was a young professor, he took his students to walk the picket line for striking Hormel meatpackers in Austin, Minnesota. Oh, and some veterans' groups chartered their own buses as well, maybe because Paul wrote legislation to help homeless vets.

By four o'clock, a full hour before the event, there were so many people at Williams Arena that Twin Cities radio and TV had to tell people that if they hadn't already left their homes, there was no point in coming down. On top of the twenty thousand in the main arena, there were four thousand watching on screens in an adjacent gym, and thousands more standing outside watching an outdoor screen on a cold Minnesota evening.

It was the largest spontaneous display of grief in memory in Minnesota. As Joe Klein wrote in *The New Yorker,* "The most striking aspect of the evening was the crowd." He went on:

> Such crowds—indeed, crowds of any sort—have almost dis-
> appeared from American public life. Most political events,
> particularly in this election year, consist of a candidate, a mi-
> crophone, and a few television cameras. Often there will be
> more people standing behind the candidate—police officers,
> veterans, students, anyone who might seem evocative or
> picturesque—than in front.

"Everybody knows it was a planted audience." It was as if Limbaugh and Republicans in general couldn't believe that people
cared enough about a politician and what he stood for to actually
show up. And besides, spontaneous outpouring of grief didn't fit
the picture Limbaugh was trying to paint.

Back to my bet. Lie number three. "Who was the first to come
up with it?" Limbaugh mused to his twenty million listeners.
"Okay, Wellstone's plane goes down. Who was the first Democrat
whose eyebrows went up and whose eyes lit up? Said, 'Wow, what
an opportunity we've got now'? Ah, was it a call from Clinton,
whose eyebrows went up and whose eyes went up the soonest,
who saw this as an opportunity? Because somebody did. Somebody must have seen this as an opportunity for last night to have
even happened."

That's it, Rush. The old fallback. Blame Clinton. That always
works with your audience when you're trying to make something
up. (When I don't know something, I just tell a joke about Gingrich having a mistress.)

Rush, I know you have a three-hour show every day that leaves
precious little time for bothering to know what you're talking
about. So let me tell you how it happened. And let me tell you
how I found out: I called the people involved and asked them. Try
it sometime.

On Saturday, after David Wellstone had returned from the
crash site, he met with Jeff Blodgett, Wellstone's campaign manager. David said that he and his brother wanted a small service for
their parents and sister. But both realized the need for a larger pub-

lic memorial. The family and staff had been deluged by condolence calls, impromptu prayer vigils, and crowds at the makeshift "memorial wall" outside Wellstone campaign headquarters. So, Rush, it was Paul's son David who first saw this as an opportunity. An opportunity to honor the depth of feeling for his parents, his sister, and their friends.

They were under tremendous time constraints. It was now only eleven days before November 5, and they felt it would have been unfair to Coleman to schedule the memorial too close to the election. They settled on Tuesday, October 29. Blodgett knew that the campaign staff was a wreck. So he approached Ann Mulholland, whom he had worked with before she took time off to raise her three little kids, and asked her if she could give him three or four days to help plan the memorial. Ann had just accepted a new job at a nonprofit, but they agreed to let her start a little late. Ann told me what it was like when she went to work.

> The staff was a mess. They had lost not just their boss, their cause that they had been working for for months, years—but their best friends. They were all grieving. I didn't want to make a noise. No one else was functioning. I took a cell phone to the bathroom and called my husband, and told him, "I don't know how these people are standing."
>
> Anytime I'd sit down at a desk, someone would start crying and tell me, "That was Mary's desk"—so I'd move, and someone would start crying. "That was Tom's desk." You have to understand that Saturday, Sunday, Monday, and Tuesday, these people were going to funerals.
>
> Six people died. That was the overwhelming reality. Six people. Every one equal. We asked each family to choose someone to do the eulogy. At no point did it ever cross anyone's mind to read the speeches. The day before, the people from the hearing impaired group asked, "Do you have any of the speeches?" I just laughed. They wanted to type

the speeches in for the closed captioning, but we just didn't have anything.

On Monday night, our press guy said to me, "Oh my gosh—this is going to be on TV. Should we be thinking about something?" By then, it was just kind of too late.

So that was the huge Democratic Party conspiracy to use Paul Wellstone's death to gain advantage in the upcoming elections. Shame on you, Ann Mulholland.

Rush said, "There was nothing sacred about this last night at all, unless the only thing sacred to these people was the advancement of their own careers." I don't know, Rush. I'm not sure Ann's nonprofit felt one way or the other about her involvement.

Rush really got into the story line that this was all a preplanned, calculated power grab by the Democrats. He quoted Harry Reid saying that Gingrich's (lying) attack on Mondale had been "classless." Rush took this one for a ride:

Senator Reid, _you_ are the one to speak to classlessness. I mean, you obviously know it when you see it each day when you get up to shave. For Harry Reid to talk about classlessness knowing what he knew was coming, is illustrative of the sham that this whole thing last night was.

"Knowing what he knew was coming." "Sham." "Planted audience." "This was not a memorial service for Paul Wellstone." "Disgusting." Twenty million listeners.

On November 23, eighteen days after the election, Tim Russert interviewed Limbaugh on CNBC.

**RUSSERT:** Mark Penn, Bill Clinton's former pollster, said that 69 percent of Americans had heard about that memorial service before they voted all across the country.

**LIMBAUGH:** Oh, gotta say something about that.

**RUSSERT:** Go ahead.

**LIMBAUGH:** It was only broadcast on C-SPAN. How did they hear about it, Tim? CBS, ABC, Washington—there wasn't a whole lot of coverage of that in the mainstream press the next day.

**RUSSERT:** Talk radio?

**LIMBAUGH:** I think so. That's my point.

I don't know if Limbaugh can really take all the credit for the way coverage of Wellstone's memorial was cynically distorted for partisan political advantage. But the misinformation certainly reverberated into the mainstream. In fact, within hours of Rush's first broadcast about the memorial, CNN's Tucker Carlson was repeating and embellishing the story on *Crossfire*.

> The political world is still reeling tonight from yesterday's nauseating display in Minnesota, where a memorial service for the late Senator Wellstone was hijacked by partisan zealots and turned into a political rally. Republican friends of Senator Wellstone were booed and shouted down as they tried to speak.

Tucker had clearly seen a different memorial than I had. By that, I don't mean he had a different perspective on the same memorial. Because at *my* memorial, there was no open mic where friends could get up and reminisce about the dearly departed. No, the one I went to had a stage in the middle of a basketball arena with a preprinted program listing all the speakers, who had been chosen in advance by the families.

What exactly had Tucker been talking about? I called him six months later and asked.

"Did I say that?" he said.

"Uh-huh," I grunted in affirmation.

Tucker seemed genuinely embarrassed. "Gee, I try to always tell the truth, because I know people are watching and can catch me."

"No, Tucker," I assured him, "I know you tell the truth because it's the right thing to do."

Tucker seemed genuinely perplexed. He told me he had a tape of the memorial that he had watched, and he couldn't understand how he had gotten it so wrong. Still, he wanted me to know, he had found the memorial very disturbing—especially Rick Kahn's speech.

"Does it make any difference to you that he lost his best friend, his best friend's wi—"

"I don't know if he was his best friend. I heard he wasn't his best friend."

This was a wrinkle I hadn't come across. If Kahn *wasn't* Wellstone's best friend, but instead a cynical political operative, then maybe his speech really was just a shameless bid for votes rather than a misguided expression of raw pain. But then I thought back to the memorial, when George Latimer introduced Kahn with a quote from the acknowledgments in Wellstone's book, *The Conscience of a Liberal:* "Everyone should be blessed to have one friend like you. There is no one person outside my family that I admire and love so much." I wondered if Tucker had seen that on his tape of the memorial service.

Tucker was still stumped about why he'd said the thing about Republicans being shouted down as they tried to speak. He said he'd think about it and call me back. He didn't. A few weeks later I bumped into Tucker, and he promised again that he would call. A few more weeks passed. Finally, I called him and left a message. To his credit, he called back, and together we figured out what had happened.

It turned out that Tucker had gone on national TV October 30 and railed against Wellstone's memorial without actually having seen it. He didn't watch the tape until later that night, in preparation for the next day's *Crossfire*.

Tucker didn't mention to his viewers that he hadn't seen the memorial. Instead, he said, "It makes me sick" and "It is revolting" and "Republican friends of Senator Wellstone were booed and shouted down as they tried to speak." And, he said, "To politicize a man's tragic death is about as low as you can go, isn't it?" Yes, Tucker, it is.

The Republicans fell in love with the whole Lott-booing thing. Peggy Noonan said on *Hannity and Colmes* that "twenty thousand did it." (The *Star Tribune* called the boos a "smattering." On the TV broadcast they were almost inaudible.) Mort Kondracke said on Fox that Norm Coleman was booed. (He wasn't.) In the *Weekly Standard*, Christopher Caldwell wrote that, "The crowd of 20,000 *booed* [italics his] a succession of people who had come to pay their respects to a dead colleague: Senate minority leader Trent Lott, Minnesota governor Jesse Ventura, and former Minnesota senators Rod Grams and Rudy Boschwitz." (The *St. Paul Pioneer Press* said that "muted boos greeted the arrival of Lott, the Senate Republican leader, and Ventura." Rudy Boschwitz was not booed.)

Yes, a couple hundred people booed Trent Lott. As the *Star Tribune* reported, "Scattered boos greeted Senate Minority Leader Trent Lott, R-Miss., as he entered the arena. Lott smiled and waved." I thought it was good-natured booing, but maybe some or all of it wasn't. Who knows? Maybe he owed those people money.

I know this. If Newt Gingrich had died in a plane crash in early 1995, and Clinton had gone to his memorial in Marietta, Georgia, he would have been shot. I ran this theory by George Stephanopoulos, and he said, "Yeah, and then the press would have blamed him for coming."

In fact, that's exactly what happened when Hillary Clinton was booed at the Madison Square Garden memorial concert honoring the police and firefighters who died in 9/11. Most of the Republican talking heads who were "distraught" about the smattering of boos at Williams Arena were absolutely delighted by the deafening roar of jeers and taunts that silenced Hillary as she tried to introduce a film. "I think she got in large part what she deserved," said Sean Hannity. Rush Limbaugh was so distraught at the booing that he had the man who led it on his program as Dittohead Hero of the Day. Bill O'Reilly blamed Hillary for having the nerve to show up considering that "Mrs. Clinton has not visited one family that has been affected by the terror. Not one. She did not go to one funeral." Of course, this wasn't true.[3]

I made some more phone calls. First to former Reagan speechwriter Peggy Noonan, whose op-ed piece in the October 30 *Wall Street Journal* took the form of a memo from Paul Wellstone up in heaven criticizing his own supporters for being filled with "envy," "poison," "resentment," "revenge," and "hate." I wanted to know where Noonan had gotten the impression that "20,000 people" had booed Trent Lott.

She seemed very surprised to hear from me, but stayed on the phone long enough to make it clear to me that she had not actually seen Trent Lott get booed. When I told her that the boos were barely audible on the broadcast, she scoffed. I said, "Peggy, I've studied the tape. I've seen it fifty times."

"Oh, Al, we *all* have," she said in that condescending, unctuous, Peggy Noonan way.

"No, you haven't," I said. "And you want to know why? Because no one replayed it. Because you can't hear the booing."

"Oh, Al, Al."

"Tell you what. The whole memorial is on the Internet. It's at

---

[3]Senator Clinton met with victims' family members on eleven separate occasions between September 11 and when O'Reilly made this claim on November 15. On September 15, Senator Clinton attended and spoke at the funeral service for Fire Chaplain Mychal Judge, whom she had known. On October 6, she spoke at the funeral of a friend in Boston who had been on one of the planes that had struck the WTC. Senator Clinton said she didn't attend other funerals because she didn't want to inject herself into someone else's private grief or to cause a distraction. Which is what she was accused of doing at the Madison Square Garden event.

http://shows.implex.tv/Wellstone/. Lott gets booed at 01:18:22. Do yourself a favor. Start about two minutes before that, so you can hear what twenty thousand people sound like when they cheer for President Clinton."

Peggy promised to look at the website and call me back if she had anything to add. Now if you yourself go to the website and watch the infamous, almost inaudible booing, you might think that Peggy "20,000 people" Noonan would have called back to apologize for her misrepresentation. And she did. No, she didn't. She's awful.

Next call was to Christopher Caldwell, the *Weekly Standard* author of the "20,000 booed a succession of people" quote. Caldwell had written on behalf of the editors to give the official *Weekly Standard* take on the memorial.

He said that viewers "tuned in on television to watch a solemn commemoration and found a rally devoted to a politics that was twisted, pagan, childish, inhumane, and even totalitarian beyond their worst nightmares."

He compared Kahn's speech to "a Maoist reeducation camp," a "sinister incident, unexampled in recent American politics." He labeled the crowd a "mob." He said that "one of our major political parties, or at least a sizable wing of it, appeared to be dancing a jig on the grave of a particularly beloved fallen comrade."

"Most of those who watched this spectacle," Caldwell wrote authoritatively, "felt a disgust bordering on shame."

Huh. Why did he say "most of those" instead of "most of us"? Probably a question of style.

More bizarrely and libelously, Caldwell wrote, "The pilots and aides who died with him were barely treated at all." That was just crazy. There were long, beautiful eulogies about each of the aides. In fact, the speeches about Paul didn't start until nearly three hours into the broadcast. A friend who had watched on TV told me, "I was wondering when they would get to Paul already." (Yes, my friend is Jewish.)

How could Caldwell have overlooked the first three hours? It was all so puzzling. But then a question occurred to me. Tucker hadn't seen the memorial before he talked about it on national TV. Peggy, it seemed anyway, hadn't actually seen Trent Lott get booed. And as TeamFranken was researching this chapter, the whole nastiness with Jayson Blair hit *The New York Times*. Blair, as you will remember, was busted for making things up about events he hadn't actually seen. Could it be, I wondered, that Caldwell, writing on behalf of the editors of one of America's preeminent conservative journals, hadn't even seen the memorial?

Caldwell called me back. I asked him about the "pagan" characterization. Had he seen the ecumenical prayer at the beginning? No. I asked him about the "crowd of 20,000 booing." Had he seen that? No. How about the eulogies for the aides? Had he seen any of those? No.

"What *did* you see?" I asked him.

"I saw it on TV."

"On TV? Did you see it live?"

"No."

"Did you see a replay of it on C-SPAN?"

"No. Listen, I hate to sound like I'm trying to get off the phone, but I'm on deadline."

"Oh, I'm sorry. Thanks for calling back. Tell you what. When you need to get off, just tell me, and we'll end it there for now."

"Okay."

"So, did you see a tape of it?"

"No. I saw it on TV."

"On TV. What does that mean?"

"I saw it on TV."

"So . . . you saw clips of it on TV shows?"

"Yes."

"That's it? That's all you saw?"

"Listen. I got to go. I have two deadlines."

"Okay. Thanks. Good luck with your deadlines. One last thing, though."

"Sure."

"Your magazine is called the *Weekly Standard*. Doesn't that mean you should have high standards?"

"Actually, the 'Standard' refers to a flag or banner, you know, to rally around."

"Yeah. But I'll bet they come from the same root word."

"You're probably right. But I got to go."

"Okay. Thanks again. I'll call you."

"Sure."

That's the last I heard from him. I called him the next day, and then every business day for the next two weeks. He must have been in a real crunch on a book or something.

Clearly, Caldwell had written his entire piece based on the most damaging moments of the memorial: five-to-ten-second clips of Rick Kahn, and the one political moment from Paul's son Mark. Caldwell probably saw them on Fox, although the same clips were played on CNN and MSNBC. The right wing's story line played to the mainstream media biases of sensationalism, negativity, and laziness. Once the right wing had created its myth about what had happened, it became a lot easier to report the distortion than to report the truth. A journalist would just have to read a couple of op-ed pieces and watch the clips on TV, and he'd have his story. That's a lot easier than watching the tape of an emotionally wrenching four-hour memorial service or talking to people who were actually there.

Pretty soon, the story became the story. Predictions about the election noted the public reaction to the memorial myth rather than what happened at the memorial itself. The day before the election, Jeff Greenfield of CNN, one of the smartest and most thoughtful political commentators on the air, said, "Republican senators who had come there were booed by the crowd. It was a crowd of thousands."

When I called Jeff that day, he told me, "Al, the memorial backfired."

If the Wellstone people, or, worse, the Democratic Party, had tried to use the memorial for political gain, then, yes, it could be said to have backfired. Greenfield had bought the spin.

Jeff Blodgett told *Mpls/StPaul Magazine* about how the Democrats' dastardly plan had backfired so badly. "We had already been to five funerals. . . . We weren't thinking straight. If we had been preparing for a televised event that large numbers of voters would be watching, we would have scripted every minute. We would have known what every person was going to say."

"The ultimate irony," Wellstone field director Dan Cramer said, "was that what would later be billed as a political event came about because we didn't think about it in political terms."


It was the right, not the left, that tried to cheapen Paul Wellstone's life by dishonoring his death. It was the right-wing media, not the friends and family who spoke at the memorial or the people who came to it, that seized on an opportunity to use a tragedy for political gain. It was Rush, and the Republican Party, and the *Weekly Standard,* and the *Wall Street Journal,* and Fox—and then it was CNN and MSNBC and all the newspapers that wrote hundreds of articles—that got it wrong. Some of them did it maliciously. Some of them just picked up the story. Some were evil, some just lazy.

Sometimes I wonder why people do what they do for a living and how they feel about their work. What is it about their work that gives them a sense of a job well done? As a comedian, I know I've done my job when people laugh. David Wellstone builds low-cost housing for the poor. I think he feels a real sense of accomplishment when a family can move into its own home for the first time. What do you suppose gives Rush Limbaugh that warm glow?

Maybe it's when he gets into a real groove like he did the day after the Wellstone memorial. Maybe it was when he said:

> People took the occasion of his death and hijacked his soul
> last night and told us what was in it. For their own personal

gain. It was despicable. It was *despicable*. They wrenched Wellstone's soul right out of the grave, assumed it for themselves, and then used it for their own blatant selfish personal ambitions.

Or maybe it was when he said:

What about the man who's dead? And the wife? And the people? It was their memory last night, and their work, that was supposedly being heralded, and remembered, and memorialized. And that didn't happen last night. It didn't happen.

Or maybe he really got that natural high when he said:

Show me where the grief was. Where was the grief? Where were the tears? Where was the mourning? Where was the memorial service? There wasn't any of this.

It would be kind of funny if that's what made Rush feel great, because it made me want to cry. I was remembering the eulogies and the lives of those who had passed away. You've heard the right-wing story of what happened that night. Here's an excerpt from a eulogy by David McLaughlin. His younger brother Will was Wellstone's driver. Their late father, Mike McLaughlin, had been a well-known figure in state politics.

We have dealt with loss before. Quite a few years ago, we lost our father. And it was a difficult time but it was actually more of a celebration because so many people from our father's past came to share with us political battles won and lost. Some we should have won but lost, and some we should have lost but won because of my father. But really the most touching part of it, so many people including

George Latimer, who came up and had read about Dad in the paper, and said, "You know, I didn't know he had accomplished so many things because all he ever wanted to talk about was you kids . . ."

When Will went to work for the campaign, I think we were most proud of all. We did, however, have some concerns. William, being the youngest of nine kids, had long ago made the decision—he didn't much care for people telling him what to do or how to do things. And with his family, he had no qualms at all of telling us that. So we were genuinely concerned that here he went from being the big man on campus to basically being the driver and someone who needs to do what he was told. For people who have been in that role before, they said you often get blamed for things that aren't your fault and you just have to shut up and take it. That was not one of William's strong suits.

The funny thing is Will and Paul really did work well together. When other people would try and get Will a different assignment, Paul would overrule them and say, "No, Will is coming with me." I really do believe that that's why they became such great friends; both of them wanted to do things their way and they wouldn't do what people told them.

This is classic Will, knowing him he wouldn't settle for just doing a small job. He took it upon himself to be more than just a driver. To be the bodyguard, advisor, and the one who kept Paul going.

Will's sense of humor was not lost in the seriousness of the campaign. Driving Paul around in Will's now famous black SUV, whenever they would see a car with a Wellstone bumper sticker on it, Paul would insist: "Drive up next to them so I can wave." So they'd pull up next to the car and Paul would wave and wave and wave, and he'd sit back in the seat and say, "Huh, they didn't wave back."

And Will would smile and say, "Huh."

And this went on for a couple of days, and Will laughed to himself before he finally let the senator know, "The windows are tinted and they can't see you . . ."

We all know that Will was having the time of his life. He loved having great success with all he did. And he really enjoyed the importance of being with the senator. But what most of us don't know is that what Will loved most about the job was that he got to hear more stories about his dad. He truly loved being with Paul alone in the car, and Paul would tell Will stories of his dad's life that he hadn't heard before. . . . That's what he really loved about the job.

There are no words that any of us can come up with that would really justify Will's life, what he meant to us, as a family and our friends and his fraternity brothers. So I'm going to share with you some of Will's own words, from probably one of our proudest moments of him. When he was a senior in high school, just shortly after his father's death, he got up in front of the whole corps of cadets at St. Thomas Academy and did a very touching speech for us to see. Just as I have just a few moments to talk about Will's life, I'm going to share just a very small part of his speech:

"To my mother, you are the greatest. You have always been there for me, now it is time for me to be there for you. I love you very much. Thank you for everything you have done. To the family, in the words of our father, 'You done good.' Many times in our lives we take things, small and large, for granted. I always thought my father would be there for me when I needed him. He may not be there physically, but he will always be with me as the great memories we had. When I come home, I expect him to be there, but he is not. I guess in some ways I took him for granted, by not thanking him all the time or saying I love you.

"Take a minute today to think of those things that might not be there tomorrow. I love my family and friends, and I leave you with no quote or words of wisdom to live by. Just these simple words: 'I love my Dad.' "

William, we love you.

So you can see what Rush meant when he said, "It was despicable." And you can see what Jeff Greenfield meant when he said the event "backfired" for the Democrats. And you can see what Chris Caldwell meant when he said that Democrats were "dancing a jig on the grave of a particularly beloved fallen comrade."

You can see what Peggy Noonan meant when she wrote, "That memorial was a triumph of politics at the expense of the personal. At the expense of what makes you *human.*"

And you can see that the media has a liberal bias.

Yes, there's a difference between the left and the right. There's a difference between Democrats and Republicans. The day after the memorial, Rush Limbaugh told us his theory of what it is. "The point," he said, "is that these people are committed to mind control. And we are committed to freedom. That's the difference."

Tucker Carlson had a different theory. "You guys really believe," he told me, "that politics can change people's lives."

Well, I do believe that. Here's a real story about how politics changed a life. When my wife Franni was eighteen months old, her father, a World War II vet who fought in the Battle of the Bulge, died in a car accident. Her mother, at age twenty-nine, was a widow with no college education and five children. They lived in a house in Maine that they'd bought through a GI loan. Franni's mom worked in the produce department at a grocery store, which added just enough to her Social Security income to allow them to almost scrape by. Sometimes the heat was turned off or the phone was turned off. Franni's brother went into the Coast Guard, and the four girls all got college educations, thanks in part to Pell Grants and Department of Defense student loans.

There are millions of stories like this. Almost every American family has a story like this. What the hell was Tucker talking about?

I'm not saying that everything government does is good, or bad—it's just that it's not a game. Politics can be vicious and dirty and cruel. Or, for people like Paul Wellstone and those that loved him, it can be part of what makes us human.

At the memorial, they showed a short film about Paul's life that captured who he was and what he believed. It had a clip from a speech. In that passionate, exuberant cadence that everyone in the arena remembered from every time they'd heard him speak, Paul said:

> Politics is not about power. Politics is not about money. Politics is not about winning for the sake of winning. Politics is about the improvement of people's lives. It's about advancing the cause of peace and justice in our country and in our world. Politics is about doing well for people.

# I Attend the White House Correspondents Dinner and Annoy Karl Rove, Richard Perle, Paul Wolfowitz, and the Entire Fox News Team

I love the White House Correspondents Dinner. I've performed there twice. In 1994, it was the scene of my greatest triumph. (Buy *Rush Limbaugh Is a Big Fat Idiot* for details.) In 1996, Newt Gingrich almost slugged me. (Buy the paperback edition of *Rush*.)

This year we were at war, so instead of the usual comedian, the entertainment was Ray Charles. Judging from this year and from 1999, when Aretha Franklin sang, the Correspondents Association has decided that it's bad form to have a comedian during a war or an impeachment.

I came as a guest of *U.S. News & World Report,* and I was very excited. Three thousand people in tuxes and gowns (except the generals and admirals, who were in dress uniform) were gathered in the Washington Hilton ballroom. I thought of renting a four-star general uniform from a costume house in New York and wearing that, but, again . . . we were at war.

So there are all these senators and cabinet officers and White House officials and Fox News people. Frankly, I was salivating. The night before, I had done one of my wildly successful corporate gigs in Reno, Nevada, and I arrived at the Hilton just half an hour before dinner. After showering quickly, I nicked my chin shaving, then put some toilet paper on the cut so I wouldn't bleed on my tux shirt as I fiddled with the studs and cufflinks. I headed downstairs to make an appearance at the *U.S. News & World Report* cocktail party, holding a handkerchief to my chin to make sure I was sufficiently coagulated for the evening. On the way there, Matt Drudge said hi to me, and I said hi back. I bring this up not because I think you'll be impressed if I drop his name, but for a reason you'll see in a bit.

By the time I got to the dinner, my platelets had done their job, and I was looking quite dapper. I sat between the Irish ambassador, who had a delightful Irish brogue, and Jodie Allen, a managing editor of *U.S. News,* who is brilliant and charming and really beautiful. But as happy as I was between Jodie and Pat (Mike?), I was taking a good look around. At the table in front of us was Commerce Secretary Don Evans, one of the President's closest friends. At the table to our right was Richard Perle, the neo-con war profiteer who had recently resigned as chairman of the Defense Policy Board because of a financial conflict of interest, but had remained on the Board itself for reasons that will puzzle ethicists for centuries.

At a table to our left, the jackpot. Karl Rove. Karl Rove! And as the Marine band played "Hail to the Chief," we both stood, not two feet apart, both applauding the President as he entered the room and took his place on the dais. Rove took note and called out to a White House pal, grinning, "Hey, look, Franken's applauding the President!"

"Of course I am," I said, as I continued applauding heartily. "He's the President of the United States. He's my president; he's your president; he's the President, elected fair and squ— Well, he's the President."

"He was elected fair and square," Rove said, as we both kept applauding.

"I don't think so."

"Do you believe in the Constitution?" Rove asked me.

"Yes. I believe in the Constitution," I said with a firm nod.

"Then he was elected fair and square," he said.

"That doesn't necessarily follow," I answered. "I believe in the Constitution. But he wasn't elected fair and square."

That was fun. Then three thousand people, including me, drank a toast to the President, and sat down, and I learned a little about Ireland from Liam (Seamus?). Nothing interesting enough to tell you. I peeked at the program, which had a seating chart, and found Alan Colmes's table among all the Fox people. I had been watching a lot of *Hannity and Colmes* during the war in Iraq and had something I thought Alan could use against Hannity.

So, after my salad, I mosied over to table 251. As you can imagine, Don Evans, Richard Perle, and Karl Rove were at very nice tables dead center in front of the stage. Which meant I was sitting pretty, too. For some reason, Fox had lousy seats, as far to one side of the ballroom as possible. And when I reached the Fox tables, I saw that Alan was sitting directly behind a pillar. He had an obstructed view. I looked around the ballroom and saw that, in the entire place, there were four obstructed views. Alan Colmes had one of them.

Seated next to Alan was his fiancée, who is absolutely lovely. Alan introduced us, and I told him he's a very lucky man. Then I said, "Alan, I've been watching your show a lot during this war, and I think I have something that might help you."

"Oh, really? What?"

"Every day, Hannity goes after Democrats if they make even the mildest criticism of Bush. He says they're 'undermining the commander in chief while our men and women are in harm's way.' "

"Yeah," Alan nodded.

"Well, I did a Nexis on your show during Kosovo. And *every day* during Kosovo, Hannity was saying things a hundred times worse about Clinton than any Democrat has said about Bush. He said, 'Clinton can't be trusted. He's not following his advisors. He's doing a terrible job.' At one point he even said, 'We're running out of ammunition.' "

"That's interesting." Alan nodded.

"Interesting?"

"Yeah. I'll look it up."

"Look it up? You're going to use it, right?"

"Well, that's not the format of our show."

"Not the format of your show?"

"We don't go after each other. We go after the guests."

"But if he keeps repeating something so blatantly hypocritical, why can't—"

"That's not the format of our show."

"Look. I watch your show. Over and over Hannity keeps saying that ninety million Americans are going to get a thousand-dollar tax cut."

"And I've corrected him on that," Alan said.

"Yeah, once in a while—five minutes after he lies, you say something about how that's an average, not a typical family. But then the next day he says it again. Can you at least talk to him after the show, and tell him to stop?"

"Well, we don't really—that's not . . ."

The format of their relationship.

I understood for the first time the genius of their format. Hannity, a right-wing propagandist, gets to lie and distort show after show, and Colmes, a moderate milquetoast who doesn't lie and distort, is not allowed to call him on it. Perfect.

"So, basically, you're laying down," I said.

"No, I'm not laying down."

"Yes, you are. You're laying down!"

At that moment, a handsome young man who looked like a morning sports anchor came charging at me and got in my face. "Why are you bothering Alan?" he said menacingly. "What are you doing here?!"

There was only one thing to do. I moved in. An inch from his face. Narrowing my eyes, I asked, "Who are *you?!*"

He told me he was Brian Kilmeade (born Leslie Hochswenderson), the sports anchor on the FNC morning show, *Fox and Friends.* There we were, face to face, two fierce men: one about thirty and in very good shape; the other, fifty-one with chronic back pain. A classic standoff.

Time seemed to stand still.

Then some drunk from one of the Fox tables asked if he could get a picture. I said, "Sure," spun Brian around, and put my arm around his shoulders. "Smile," I told Brian, who seemed confused. Whoever has that picture, can I get it for the paperback?

I spent a few more minutes in the midst of the Fox people. Not arguing, really. It was more in the way of slightly hostile banter. Fun!

Back to my table. I sidled over to Rove. "I got a great idea for you," I said. "It'll really help the President. When they announce Ray Charles, have the President lead him out and play a trick on him. The President tells Ray he's leading him to his piano, but he takes him to the podium. Everyone will love it."

"No," Rove said curtly.

"Hey, this is one you might want to give a couple minutes' thought."

"No."

Back to my assigned seat for the entree, of which I have no memory. The Irish ambassador, Eoghan (?), told me something about something. After dinner, the President spoke. As you know, I don't like the man, but his remarks about the courage of journalists in Iraq and specifically about the deaths of Michael Kelly and David Bloom struck just the right note. No jokes. Good call.

The President didn't play a trick on Ray Charles. Unfortunately, the crowd did. The man may be a national treasure, but three thousand Beltway biggies were not very interested in listening to him sing. About five minutes into his set, folks were walking around, schmoozing, speaking loudly in order to be heard over the din. It must have been like playing the lounge at a Holiday Inn in Phoenix, but worse.

As a comedian, I make a point of being polite to other performers, and so I listened to and applauded each song, as people crisscrossed in front of me.

During the fourth or fifth number, I noticed Richard Perle, the former chair of the Defense Policy Board, talking to my friend Jonathan Alter of *Newsweek* at the next table. *The New York Times* had recently disclosed that Perle had been hired by Global Crossing to lobby the Pentagon, which the Defense Policy Board advises. Global Crossing wanted the Pentagon to allow a Hong Kong enterprise with close ties to the Chinese government to acquire the bankrupt telecom company. Perle's fee: $125,000. Plus, a $600,000 bonus if the deal went through. Conflict of interest? Yeah, kinda.

The *LA Times* found another icky one. As chair of the Defense Policy Board, Perle had received a classified briefing on Iraq and North Korea. A few days later, Goldman Sachs paid Perle to join a conference call with a select group of investors to tell them how to take advantage of this information. Oddly enough, I knew about this sleazy little arrangement before the *Times* broke it. A twenty-year-old TeamFranken member, who happens to be the scion of a ridiculously wealthy family, had been invited to be on the call. My TeamFranken member (let's call him "Horace Rockefeller") was sworn to secrecy, so I can't tell you what Perle said. But let's put it this way—I wouldn't invest in any real estate investment trusts with property along the Seoul subway line.

So screw Ray Charles! This was my chance to bother Richard Perle. I waited for a lull in the conversation and jumped in. "Mr. Perle, Al Franken."

He nodded.

"Say, how do I get in on this gravy train?" I asked. "I feel like I've missed the boat on this whole war."

"Invest in my fund," he said. I wasn't sure if he was serious. "I'll send you a portfolio." Like an idiot, I didn't take him up on it. That would have been juicy reading. Instead, I asked him about his threat to sue journalist Seymour Hersh, who had just exposed one of his shady deals in *The New Yorker,* for libel. Perle had called Hersh, "the closest thing American journalism has to a terrorist" and then threatened to sue him in Great Britain, where journalists aren't protected by our silly First Amendment. Weeks had passed without Perle suing, and it was becoming increasingly obvious that Perle had been bluffing just to save face while the story was big.

"Why don't you sue him here?" I suggested snarkily. "That'd really show everyone how strong your case is and how reckless Hersh had been." See, this is why I wouldn't make a good journalist. Here I could have gotten the portfolio for Perle's fund, and instead I had to go one step too far and piss the guy off.

Speaking of pissing off a neo-con: Later, at the after-party given by Bloomberg News, I went up to Paul Wolfowitz, the deputy secretary of Defense and the architect of the Bush preemption doctrine. "Hi, Dr. Wolfowitz. Hey, the Clinton military did a great job in Iraq, didn't it?"

He looked at me for a couple seconds, then said, "Fuck you."

Which I thought was funny. I think he was "kidding on the square," a phrase I hope will catch on. It means kidding, but also really meaning it. People do it all the time. "Kidding on the square." If this book does two things, I want it to get "kidding on the square" into the lexicon, and I want it to get Bush out of the White House.

Then Wolfowitz and I had a short argument. "The Clinton military never could have done this war," he said.

"Well, maybe they wouldn't have, but they could have."

This is a completely different military, he said. Then he talked about the influx of money since Bush's defense budget kicked in. (It kicked in during October 2002.)

I said, "Let me ask you. Did you guys actually make any of the machines that have been used in Iraq?"

That got him all pissed off again. So he got into how they've *reorganized* the military, and technical arguments on how they've changed the command structure. I mean, he *is* the deputy secretary of defense, and I have to admit he lost me.

But, of course, he was wrong. I was right. I'll get into all of this in a later chapter, entitled "Yeah? Well, Fuck *You.*" Actually, it's called, "Bush Can't Lose with Clinton's Military," and after you read it, I think you'll agree that Bill Clinton remains the greatest president of the twenty-first century.

As exciting as my little Noël Coward tête-à-tête was with Wolfowitz, I had my most interesting and perhaps most significant conversation that night with Commerce Secretary Don Evans. Evans is among Bush's closest friends and was featured heavily in Howard Fineman's *Newsweek* cover story "Bush and God." That was the top-selling *Newsweek* since 9/11.

As you probably know, until his fortieth birthday, Bush was a heavy drinker. Or, as we call them at Harvard, a "drunk." According to many accounts, Bush was also an "obnoxious drunk." Finally, Laura Bush laid down the law. Threatened with losing sex from his wife, Bush decided to quit drinking and turn to Christ. (That part about sex is not in the *Newsweek* article.)

It was Evans, a fellow oilman, who coaxed his old friend George into joining a Bible-study group in Midland. According to *Newsweek:*

> It was a scriptural boot camp; an intensive, yearlong study of a single book of the New Testament, each week a new chapter, with detailed reading and discussion in a group of ten men. For two years Bush and Evans and their partners read the clear writings of the Gentile physician Luke—Acts, and then his Gospel.

Now, I'm a Jew. And I grew up knowing zip about the New Testament and still know next to zip. But as it so happened, a few days before the Correspondents Dinner, I ran into economist Paul Solman at the Harvard gym. Paul, who teaches a course in business ethics, is also a Jew, but an educated one. So he knows the Bible. He, too, had read Fineman's cover story.

He told me he found it ironic that Acts was one of the two books Bush and Evans had studied. Acts, Paul told me, is Luke's account of the formation of the Church after Jesus' death. The book is almost a socialist tract, full of admonishment to the rich to share their wealth with the poor. The communist motto, "From each according to his ability, to each according to his need," is derived from Acts 4:32–35. Here's the whole passage:

> And the multitude of them that believed were of one heart and of one soul; neither said any of them that ought of the things which he possessed was his own; but they had all things common. And with great power gave the apostles witness of the resurrection of the Lord Jesus; and great grace was upon them all. Neither was there any among them that lacked: for as many as were possessors of lands or houses sold them, and brought the prices of the things that were sold, and laid them down at the apostles' feet: and distribution was made unto every man according as he had need.

In the Hilton ballroom, after Ray Charles had finished and received a perfunctory ovation, I saw Evans sitting alone at his table. I sidled into the seat next to him. "Mr. Secretary, do you mind if I speak with you?"

"Not at all, Al." I liked him immediately.

After some niceties, I steered the conversation toward Acts and how its message seemed at odds with the shape of the Bush tax cut. I led into it with "Did you read Howard Fineman's cover story in *Newsweek* on Bush and God?"

"Yes," Evans said.

"Did you like it?"

"Yes."

"So did I," I said. "So, you know what Acts is about."

Evans looked a little uncomfortable. Long pause. Then, "No."

> It was a scriptural boot camp; an intensive, yearlong study of a single book of the New Testament, each week a new chapter, with detailed reading and discussion in a group of ten men. For two years Bush and Evans and their partners

> read the clear writings of the Gentile physician Luke—Acts,
> and then his Gospel.

"No?"

No.

Based on what Paul Solman had told me and a subsequent glance at *The Complete Idiot's Guide to the Life of Christ,* I explained to the scriptural boot camp survivor what I understood Acts to be about. Then I went into my spiel about the unfairness of the tax cut.

"Ah," Evans smiled. "But Acts also has Jesus' Parable of the Talents."

"No," I said. "That's in Matthew."

The Parable of the Talents is a story Jesus told about a master giving three servants each a sum of money. When the master returns, two of the men have used the money to make more money. The other man buried the money in the ground. The master rewards the men who made money from the money and punishes the schmuck who didn't. Moral: God wants you to use your gifts. Conservatives tend to interpret the parable literally, as an exhortation to get rich.

It was a complete fluke that I had any clue at all about Talents. Last year my son, Joe, had been assigned some New Testament readings in his mostly Jewish private high school and had to write a short paper on, yep, Talents. He couldn't understand it and came to me. I couldn't make any sense of it either, so I called Gary Bauer. That's right. Gary Bauer, Goldberg's "little nut from the Christian group." As I said, Gary and I are friends. Honestly. It's a long story. But we like each other. And what better guy to explain a parable in Matthew? (Not Acts.)

Gary wasn't home, so his wife Carol, who's also a friend (though I think she has grave doubts about me), explained Talents.

Since then, I've noticed that the only Biblical parable supply-siders ever mention is Talents. And, for all I can tell, it might be the only one Evans knows. But even I was surprised Evans didn't know what book it was from.

What do you suppose those ten guys were really doing during their "scriptural boot camp"? Watching football? Eating pretzels? Plotting with Karl Rove how to use religious rhetoric to reassure the Christian right base that George W. was one of them?

**E**pilogue: Two days later, the right-wing website NewsMax.com ran a piece on me, "Al Franken Goes Fox Hunting at Correspondents Dinner," saying that I "accosted a table full of Fox News Channel personalities, causing a scene that threatened to erupt into physical violence."

> [Brian] Kilmeade said Franken's behavior was so deranged that some thought he was drunk, but that wasn't the case. . . . "I personally thought we'd end up coming to blows." **According to Internet scribe Matt Drudge, when witnesses spotted the liberal ranter later he was bleeding from the chin.** [boldface mine.] But Kilmeade said the altercation stopped short of throwing punches.

Drudge, remember, had seen me holding my handkerchief to my chin *before* the dinner. But these guys love to lie like Bill Bennett loves to gamble and Newt Gingrich loves to have mistresses.

I'm sorry. I don't know if Newt is really cheating on this new wife of his. I hope they're doing well. It's just a running joke I'm using. I think that the personal life of a public official should stay out of the domain of our national discourse unless it affects his or her job performance or reveals a particularly craven level of hypocrisy. And on the latter point, I think Newt qualifies. Hence the running joke. I'm kidding about Newt's infidelities. But, remember, I'm kidding on the square.

# The Lying Years

**I've** known since the 2000 Republican National Convention in Philadelphia that if Bush and Cheney were elected, their time in office would be remembered by history as "The Lying Years." That's because, for the first time since the Free Soil convention of 1852, both the presidential *and* the vice presidential candidate of a major political party lied in their acceptance speeches.[1]

Bush lied while claiming that Clinton had undermined the readiness of the military. He said, "If called on by the commander in chief today, two entire divisions of the Army would have to report, 'Not ready for duty, sir.' "

That was contradicted by the chairman of the Joint Chiefs of Staff, General Hugh Shelton; by Defense Secretary William Cohen; and by Bush's own foreign policy advisor at the time, Richard Armitage, who is now deputy secretary of State. The following is an excerpt from a hearing of the Senate Armed Service Committee held a few days later. Carl Levin was the committee's ranking member.

> **CARL LEVIN:** But I want to get back to the two divisions not being ready for duty, because Mr. Armitage has not answered that. Are those two divisions ready for duty, or aren't they?
>
> **RICHARD ARMITAGE:** I believe those two divisions, Senator, are ready for duty.
>
> **LEVIN:** That's not what Governor Bush said the other night, and that's why I think an apology is appropriate.

[1] In his acceptance speech at the 1852 Free Soil convention in Pittsburgh, presidential candidate John P. Hale grossly overstated the incidence of flogging in the United States Navy. His running mate, George W. Julian, falsely charged that Whig standard-bearer Winfield "Old Fuss and Feathers" Scott had personally flogged dozens of soldiers under his command during the Mexican War. This was particularly insidious given Scott's commitment to professionalizing the military.

But instead of apologizing, Armitage bolted from the hearing room, knocking over veteran reporter Helen Thomas, breaking her hip and jaw.[2]

Cheney's lie was more subtle, but I think more telling. After a speech bitterly denouncing the Clinton/Gore legacy of peace and prosperity, he switched to a more reflective tone and told a personal story. Describing the helicopter ride from Andrews Air Force Base to the Pentagon, a trip he had taken so often as secretary of Defense, Cheney invoked the great leaders and terrible sacrifices that forged this nation.

> You fly down along the Mall and see the monument to George Washington, a structure as grand as the man himself. To the north is the White House, where John Adams once prayed "that none but honest and wise men may ever rule under this roof." Next you see the memorial to Thomas Jefferson, the third president . . .

. . . blah, blah, blah . . .

> . . . Then you cross the Potomac, on approach to the Pentagon. But just before you settle down on the landing pad, you look upon Arlington National Cemetery, its gentle slopes and crosses row on row.
>
> I never once made that trip without being reminded how enormously fortunate we all are to be Americans, and what a terrible price thousands have paid so that all of us—and millions more around the world—might live in freedom.

I was starting to tear up by the time Cheney got to Arlington Cemetery. I'm a sucker for that kind of stuff. But when he said

---

[2]The Helen Thomas thing is a joke. In a number of right-wing blogs, this was cited as exhibit A in proving that my book is full of lies.

"crosses row on row," I flinched. The gravestones in Arlington National Cemetery are not crosses.

Had he really said that?

Cheney was lying. The graves in Arlington are marked with white rectangular headstones, rounded at the top. There are no "crosses row on row" that Cheney could have seen from his helicopter.

The phrase "crosses row on row" comes from a poem, "Flanders Field," about a World War I cemetery in Belgium. It seems

Flanders Field, Belgium

Arlington National Cemetery. See?

bizarre that a guy who made that helicopter trip so many times, particularly the secretary of Defense, would not remember the unforgettable sight of Arlington's vast gardens of stone. The most generous explanation I can think of is that Cheney had been watching *Saving Private Ryan* the night before he accepted the nomination, and had the cemetery from the last scene stuck in his head.

Can you imagine if Al Gore had said this? The media's reaction would have dominated the campaign for the next month.

"He is desecrating our war dead!"

"He says, 'I never once made that trip' without looking down at those graves—did he ever look even once? Did he ever visit the graves of America's heroes?"

"Has there ever been a more shameless attempt to wrap yourself in both God and country?"

"My Jewish father *died* defending Al Gore's religious freedom, and he is *not* buried under a cross. How dare he? How dare he?!"

But it wasn't Gore who said it. It was Cheney. And from the liberal media? Silence.

# Bush Can't Lose with Clinton's Military

Did Clinton gut the military because there was no evidence that countries like Iraq, Iran, North Korea, and an increasingly aggressive Communist China would represent serious future threats to America and our friends and allies? No. Rather, it was because he loathed the military.

—Sean Hannity, *Let Freedom Ring*

**Do** I continue to quote *Let Freedom Ring* because there is no evidence to support his claims? Partly. But mostly it is because I loathe Sean Hannity. And because I think he represents a serious threat to America and our friends and allies.

On page 82 of Hannity's ringing denunciation of the left, he produces what is quite simply the greatest table I've ever seen:

### COMPARISON OF DEFENSE BUDGETS

|  | Reagan-Bush 1986 | Clinton-Gore 1996 |
| --- | --- | --- |
| New tanks requested in president's budget | 840 | 0 |
| New tactical aircraft requested in president's budget | 399 | 34 |
| New naval ships requested in president's budget | 40 | 6 |

This is a table created by a child for children.

Where to start? First of all, in 1996 we didn't *need* any new tanks. The end of the Cold War had reduced the likelihood of an enormous tank battle across the plains of Central Europe to below zero. How many tanks do you think were requested in the first Bush-Cheney budget? Let's make a new chart, keeping Reagan but also comparing the final Clinton-Gore defense budget with the first Bush-Cheney defense budget.

## COMPARISON OF DEFENSE BUDGETS

|  | Reagan-Bush 1986 | Clinton-Gore 2001 | Bush-Cheney 2002 |
|---|---|---|---|
| New tanks requested in president's budget | 840 | 0 | 0 |
| New tactical aircraft requested in president's budget | 399 | 52 | 58 |
| New naval ships requested in president's budget | 40 | 6 | 5 |

Got it, kids? The contrast could not be more stark. Bush-Cheney ordered 11 percent more tactical aircraft than Clinton-Gore, but Clinton-Gore ordered 20 percent more ships than Bush-Cheney.

Did you know that in 1986 we were still fighting the Cold War? In current dollars, we spent $273 billion on defense in 1986 and $266 billion in 1996. Yes, that's 2 percent less, but then again, the Soviet Union no longer existed. The Clinton budget in 1996 was larger than the outgoing budget of the first Bush administration—a budget developed by then DOD Secretary Dick Cheney.

During the 2000 campaign, it was the Republican ticket that ran against our military. It was, according to Bush and Cheney, "hollowed out." Condoleezza Rice argued that Clinton had undercut our troops' ability to fight by sending them into what the Bush team called "useless" nation-building exercises. We were, George W. Bush said, at our lowest state of readiness since *Pearl Harbor*. I saw that movie, and let me tell you, our lack of preparedness caused some serious problems—not just for Ben Affleck, but for Josh Hartnett, as well.

Nine months after Bush took office, we went to war against the Taliban regime in Afghanistan. The Soviets couldn't conquer Afghanistan. Neither could the British in 1919. But somehow, we did it in a few weeks. With no new funding (the first Bush defense budget went into effect on October 1, 2002), Donald Rumsfeld had taken our "gutted" military and, with a little string and some baling wire, turned it into the greatest fighting force in the history of the planet.

The man is a fucking genius.

Or maybe Afghanistan (and then Iraq) was payoff for the "revolution in military affairs" in which Clinton invested so heavily. Take this scenario described by Fred Kaplan of the *Boston Globe*:

> A U.S. Special Forces soldier, sitting on horseback, spots a Taliban target. He types out the information on his laptop computer and transmits the data to a Predator, a new unmanned drone flying 25,000 feet overhead. The Predator relays the data to commanders in Saudi Arabia, who direct the drone to the target for a closer look—and take a look themselves through its real-time video transmission.
>
> The commanders then send the target's coordinates to a U.S. bomber pilot in the area, who punches the coordinates into the computer of a "smart bomb." The bomb is fired and explodes within 3 feet of the target.
>
> "This sounds like science fiction, but it's really happening," said William M. Arkin, a defense consultant and adjunct professor at the U.S. Air Force School of Advanced Air Power Studies. More striking still, the whole process—from finding the target to dropping the bomb—takes 19 minutes. During the Gulf War, assigning a particular bomb to a particular target took three days.

This is called Network Centric Warfare. Clinton's military brought it to fruition. It's about giving the on-scene commanders a much clearer picture of the battlefield. Let's take a look at how many tanks were involved: 0. Ships: 0. Yes, there was one tactical aircraft. But also a horse.

Quickly, let's compare the military budgets of Lincoln and Reagan.

**COMPARISON OF DEFENSE BUDGETS**

|  | Lincoln 1864 | Reagan 1984 |
| --- | --- | --- |
| New horses requested in president's budget | 188,718 | 3 |

Source: *The Photographic History of the Civil War* (10 vols.). Francis Trevelyan, ed. "The Cavalry." Theo S. Rodenbough © 1911, Patriot Publishing Co., Springfield, Mass.

Why did Reagan gut our military? Was it because there was no evidence that the Soviet Union represented a threat to America and our friends and allies? No. It was because Ronald Reagan loathed our military. After all, he did dodge the draft during World War II. He "served" in the filmmaking department, starring in the 1942 comedy, *Juke Girl* alongside Ann Sheridan. Its tagline: "Sure she's easy to meet . . . but try and forget her!"

In addition to falling down on the horse front, Reagan provided absolutely no funding for two of the other key elements of our war in Afghanistan. The Predator, a UAV (Unmanned Aerial Vehicle), which went into production in 1997 and which was first used in Kosovo, and the JDAM: the Joint Direct Attack Munition.

A word about JDAMs. During the first Gulf War, our "smart bombs" were laser-guided bombs that cost over $100,000 each. A JDAM, which costs $20,000, is a recycled Cold War "dumb bomb" that has a Global Positioning System guidance unit strapped to it. I'm not certain about this, but I was told that Roger Clinton got the idea for the JDAM while installing a LoJack on his '86 Camaro.

Maybe that's apocryphal. In any case, JDAMs were funded and stockpiled during the Clinton administration.

During the first Gulf War, less than 10 percent of the bombs and missiles dropped on Iraq were smart weapons. In our most recent war against Saddam, thanks to (Roger?) Clinton's JDAMs, that number jumped to over 70 percent. The result: fewer civilian casualties and less damage to infrastructure that might be needed for the "useless" nation-building that our troops are now undertaking in Iraq.

Captain Charles O'Brien, a company commander in Iraq, said that the Kosovo experience has given his soldiers a foundation in "stability support ops" (e.g., not getting killed by paramilitary forces, suicide bombers, et cetera). Turns out that those peace-keeping operations in the Balkans that Sean Hannity went to war against are now saving American lives.

Of course, there's a lot more to war than hardware and building on past experience. Every war brings with it a new set of tactical problems that have to be solved. Solving those problems speaks directly to the quality of our military leaders. As Don Rumsfeld noted, the credit for our battle plan in Iraq should go to General Tommy Franks. Franks was appointed to head the Central Command by the Clinton administration.

And it wasn't just the battle plan. "More important," as Lawrence J. Korb put it, was that "the military forces that executed that plan so boldly and bravely were for the most part recruited, trained, and equipped by the Clinton administration."

Who is Lawrence J. Korb? Well, he's currently director of national security studies at the Council on Foreign Relations. He goes on to say of our swift victory in Iraq: "The fact of the matter is that most of the credit for the successful military operation should go to the Clinton administration."

Oh. Korb was also assistant secretary of Defense during the *Reagan* administration. Maybe he's the guy who screwed up on the horses.

Let's review some quotes.

Did Clinton gut the military because there was no evidence that countries like Iraq, Iran, North Korea, and an increasingly aggressive Communist China would represent serious future threats to America and our friends and allies? No. Rather, it was because he loathed the military.

—Sean Hannity, *Let Freedom Ring*

If called on by the commander in chief today, two entire divisions of the Army would have to report, "Not ready for duty, sir."

—George W. Bush, August 3, 2000

Hi, Dr. Wolfowitz. Hey, the Clinton military did a great job in Iraq, didn't it?

—Al Franken

Fuck you.

—Paul Wolfowitz

A commander in chief leads the military built by those who came before him. There is little that he or his defense secretary can do to improve the force they have to deploy. It is all the work of previous administrations. Decisions made today shape the force of tomorrow. . . . And when that war [the first Gulf War] ended, the first thing I did was to place a call to California, and say thank you to President Ronald Reagan.

—Dick Cheney, the Southern Center for International Studies, August 2000

You suppose Clinton is waiting for Rumsfeld's call?

# Operation Chickenhawk: Episode One

**Unlike** some of my fellow Democrats, I hope the Bush campaign runs that footage of him strutting around the USS *Abraham Lincoln* in his flight suit. I hope they run it over and over.

You remember. The dramatic tailhook landing.

The President sitting in the S-3B Viking right beside the pilot who actually landed the plane.

Ari Fleischer saying that Bush couldn't arrive by helicopter because the *Lincoln* would "be hundreds of miles from shore" and impossible to reach except by jet.

The later reports explaining that, in fact, the *Lincoln* was so close to port that it had to go back out to sea, make lazy circles, and, finally, be positioned so that the cameras couldn't see the San Diego skyline looming behind him while Bush made his speech.

All that was fine by me. I just pray Bush uses the footage in his ads. That'll give us the excuse to run this response. Assume for a second that the Democratic nominee is John Kerry.

OPEN ON: QUICK CUTS OF: TAILHOOK LANDING ON USS *LINCOLN,*
BUSH IN COCKPIT GIVING THUMBS UP, MINGLING WITH SAILORS.

> KERRY (VOICE-OVER)
> You know, dress up and make believe are
> fun.

BUSH SWAGGERING AROUND IN THE FLIGHT SUIT, WINKING, ETC.

> KERRY (V.O.)
> But years ago George W. Bush had a chance to
> be a real fighter pilot in a war. Instead he let his
> dad get him into the Texas Air National Guard,

KERRY (V.O.) (continued)

passing over the other guys ahead of him in line.
Then he went AWOL for a year.

CUT TO: FOOTAGE OF LIEUTENANT KERRY IN VIETNAM.

KERRY (V.O.)

This is me in Vietnam. Sorry the footage is so
grainy. At the time, it was a little too dangerous
to get a camera crew in.

CUT TO: KERRY IN FULL PIRATE SUIT. BIG PIRATE MUSTACHE. BIG
PIRATE HAT. PARROT ON HIS SHOULDER.

KERRY

Yes. Dress-up and make believe *are* fun. But we
need a real president with real plans to protect
our nation, to get our economy going, and to fulfill the promise of our great country. Isn't that
right, Petey?

PARROT

AWWWK! That's right!

ANNOUNCER (V.O.)

Paid for by the Costume Designer's Guild of
America.

It's amazing, actually, how many hawkish Republicans found a
way to avoid military service. Every neo-con I can think of, for instance. Wolfowitz, Richard Perle, Bill Kristol—the guys who were
really, really gung-ho on Iraq.

Kristol, editor of *The Weekly Standard,* even said it wasn't such
a bad thing if we had a tough fight in Iraq. "In a certain way, the
willingness to stick it out would be impressive," he told the *Washington Post.*

In my book *Rush Limbaugh Is a Big Fat Idiot and Other
Observations,* I wrote a little flight of fancy called "Operation

Chickenhawk," placing some prominent Chickenhawks together in a squad in Vietnam.

There was Rush, who lied publicly about why he didn't go. He said he got a physical deferment because of a football knee, when in fact it was for a pilonidal cyst—a congenital incomplete closure of the neural groove at the base of the spinal cord. A pilonidal cyst can cause discomfort, but somehow Rush's dad managed to fight WWII with a pilonidal cyst. You know, Greatest Generation and all.

There was Phil Gramm—student and teaching deferments. George Will—student deferment. Clarence Thomas was 4-F. So was Pat Buchanan, who had a "bad knee." Though today he's an avid jogger.

Dan Quayle's father got him into the Indiana National Guard. Maybe that's why George Sr. picked Quayle in '88—reminded him of his boy.

Then there's Newt—grad school. But you gotta love him, because Newt's told us that he regrets not going to Vietnam because he "missed something."

In the original "Operation Chickenhawk" Ollie North drags the chickenshit squad kicking and screaming into battle and ends up single-handedly taking on a company of NVA regulars as his men cower and ultimately frag him. North loved the story so much he invited me on his radio show. Though I think he lied to me about how he came to read it. The piece had been reprinted in *Playboy,* but North told me a kid on a plane just happened to have a Xeroxed copy and handed it to him. Does that sound likely?

So I think it's time for another "Operation Chickenhawk." This one's a prequel, because Rush, Will, and Thomas eat it in the original one, and I wanted to use them again. Also, I've been following George Lucas's career, and prequels seem like a good way to keep the franchise alive.

There were so many great Chickenhawks to choose from. Like Saxby Chambliss, who defeated Max Cleland for the Senate in Georgia. Cleland lost three limbs in Vietnam, but Chambliss ran ads with Cleland's face next to Saddam Hussein's. Chambliss, it seems, had Buchanan's knee problem—the kind that gets better after you've gotten your 4-F.

There's Bill Bennett, who a few years ago said he has two regrets in his life: not meeting his wife earlier, and not going to Vietnam. I have the exact same regrets—I, too, wish Bennett had met his wife earlier and gone to Vietnam. I'll give you odds he's added a third regret.

There's a ton of these guys. Ken Starr got out for psoriasis. New Hampshire Senator Judd Gregg got out for acne. Acne! Ashcroft was teaching. Tom DeLay is a good one. According to a January 7, 1999, *Houston Press* article, DeLay once explained that there was literally no room in the military for him because so many minority youths had volunteered for the military to escape the ghetto.

I don't know why Bill O'Reilly didn't go into the military. As DeLay explained, it's such a great route out of the abject poverty of the Westbury section of Levittown.

Vice President Cheney has said that he didn't fight in Vietnam because at the time he "had other priorities." Coincidentally, that's exactly why I didn't go.

*Van Cong River: Mekong Delta, South Vietnam*
*August 1968*

The below-decks cabin was tight and smelled like men at war. Journalist Specialist First Class Al Gore studied Lieutenant Kerry's strangely Semitic features. The strong jaw, the deep-set eyes, the prominent nose that spoke of the Mittel-European shtetl and the seemingly unending tragedy of the Jewish people.

"This is going to be easy," thought Gore. Gore's editor at *Stars and Stripes,* Captain Ailes, had assigned him another by-the-numbers profile. Kerry, a lanky Swift Boat commander, had just been awarded the Silver Star, which made Gore all the more self-conscious of his only decoration, a good conduct medal for ghost-writing Captain Ailes's weekly column, "Why We Fight."

"Lieutenant, I was thinking of approaching this story from a different perspective, maybe writing from the point of view of the eleven VC you single-handedly killed. Sort of a postmodern thing."

Kerry already regretted allowing the overly solicitous Tennessean to tag along. "First of all, I didn't do it single-handedly. And, secondly, if I ever do wear the Silver Star, it'll be for the brave men I served with. It's their medal, too."

"That's great, that's great," Gore said, writing furiously. "Do you mind if I tell your crew what you said about their heroism?"

Kerry scowled, and picked a chip of paint off a rusting bulkhead. "Not this crew."

Something about Kerry's tone of voice aroused Gore's reporter's instincts. "So this is a new crew?"

"New?" Kerry scoffed. "That's a charitable way to describe them. Frankly, in my two tours, I've never seen a bigger bunch of pants-pissers."

Gore stopped writing. This wasn't the sort of angle Captain Ailes approved of. "So they're more heroes in the making than actual heroes?"

Before Kerry could answer, loud screaming broke out on deck. The lieutenant vaulted topsides, as Gore scrambled after.

All hell was breaking loose. The Swift Boat had pulled up alongside a fragile-looking sampan carrying two elderly Vietnamese women, baskets of fruit, and a small pig.

At the rail of the Swift Boat, two very agitated seamen were waving their M-16s and screaming.

"What's under the pig, dink bitch?!" shouted the smaller of the two in an accent somewhere between Midland, Texas, and Kennebunkport, Maine. "Pick up the fucking pig!"

The terrified old women began wailing in Vietnamese.

The stouter, bespectacled seaman snarled sarcastically, shouting, "What's wrong, Charlie, no speakee English? I bet you speakee Commie, don'tchee?"

"Bush, Cheney, stand down!" Kerry ordered.

"They're hostiles, Skipper!" Bush shrieked. "I've seen this trick a thousand times. Look at those grenades!"

"Those are mangoes, sailor." Kerry could tell that Bush was drunk again.

"What you got under that pig? Pick up the pig! PICK UP THE FUCKING PIG!" Cheney shouted, ignoring his commander.

As Gore watched helplessly, it almost seemed as if time stood still. He looked at the scene in front of him. The two panicked men with the M-16s. The lieutenant moving slowly toward them. And cowering behind some barrels, three other men, two white, one black, all scared out of their minds.

"Ashcroft, O'Reilly, Thomas! Get your asses out of there and give me a hand," Kerry shouted.

"If it's all the same to you, sir, we'll stay right here," said O'Reilly.

There's always a few bad apples in every unit, Gore reflected, but this was the first time he'd encountered a unit composed entirely of bad apples.

"WHAT YOU GOT UNDER THE PIG? PICK UP THE PIG! *PICK UP THE FUCKING PIG!*"

Cheney's trigger finger twitched. Shit was about to go very wrong.

Kerry edged closer to the pair of crazed sailors. He calmly held out his hand, speaking soothingly as if to a small child. "Gimme the gun, Cheney. C'mon, buddy. Gimme the gun."

Cheney responded by closing his eyes and squeezing the trigger. The M-16 belched lead and fire. The pig erupted in a blur of blood and guts. Bush followed suit, blindly spraying bullets into the sky.

Kerry tackled Cheney, and both men splashed into the water below. When Kerry surfaced, he saw that the women, though splattered with pig blood, were unhurt. He breathed a sigh of relief.

Next to him Cheney was thrashing around in the water, clutching his chest. "Help!" he gurgled. "Heart attack!"

On the boat, Bush jumped around hysterically. "Those dink bitches! They gave Dick another heart attack! You're not going to let them get away with it, are you, Skipper?" Bush pulled the pin from a hand grenade, dangled it above the sampan. Then lurching back drunkenly, he dropped it at his own feet. "Oh shit!"

As Ashcroft, O'Reilly, and Thomas dove off the far side of the boat, Gore rushed forward and scooped up the grenade. He threw it into the dense foliage lining the shore, where it rolled into a well-concealed machine-gun nest, killing three NVA regulars who were waiting in ambush.

"I just saved your lives," Bush shouted jubilantly. "I'm gonna get me a medal!" Then turning to Gore, he added, "Hey, reporter guy, gimme a beer."

"You see what I'm dealing with here?" Kerry asked, pulling on a dry shirt. "There's your article. I've got a headline for you: 'Commander Sent into Battle with Dangerous Morons.'"

"I don't think Captain Ailes will be too pleased with that. How about I just emphasize my own heroics in wiping out that machine-gun nest?"

"Sure, sure, fine. As long as you don't write about the mission. It's Top Secret." Kerry tossed an envelope marked "Operation Chicken Plucker" on the table in front of Gore. Kerry nodded, "Go ahead, take a look."

As Gore thumbed through the dossier, Kerry began to explain. "Eight months ago, a squad composed of raw recruits was sent to interdict VC supply routes along the Ho Chi Minh Trail."

"Slow down, slow down." Gore had begun writing again.

Kerry slapped the pen from the journalist's hand. "No! I told you, this is Top Secret."

"Sorry. I thought you winked at me."

Kerry continued. "The first time the squad was sent out, they came back two hours later without their lieutenant."

"Stepped on a mine?"

"That's what Gingrich and Limbaugh said. Private Buchanan said the officer was greased by a sniper."

"That doesn't make sense," Gore said, leafing through photos of the soldiers. Not a good-looking group. Private Phil Gramm, a sweaty, slack-jawed Southerner; Private Mortimer "Rush" Limbaugh, a corpulent and sweaty radio specialist; Private Newt Gingrich, a perspiring rifleman, also a few pounds north of fighting weight.

"That's what HQ thought. But they sent 'em out again with a freshly minted shavetail from the Point. This time they were back in twenty minutes, again without their officer."

"Twenty minutes? That doesn't smell right."

Kerry nodded. "According to Gingrich and Limbaugh, he stepped on a mine. Gramm said he fell into a pungee stick trap and died of an infection. But the fishiest story came from Private George Will."

"George Will? You mean Stoner?" Gore asked. "I know Stoner. I bought a bag of killer sticky icky off him."

"Yeah, same guy. He said the shavetail was eaten by a tiger."

Gore was putting it all together. "So these chickenshits were fragging their squad leaders?"

"It was obvious to everybody. Except General Westmoreland. He sent 'em out five more times. All told, they bagged four lieutenants, a sergeant , and two captains."

"Oh, man. So they killed all their officers?"

"All except Captain Max Cleland. They left him for dead, but he crawled back to base. That's when they went AWOL."

Gore shook his head in disgust, then looked back down at the dossier. He held up the picture of a young black man holding a *Playboy* and sweating. "This Private Clarence Thomas looks very familiar."

"That's because he's standing next to you," Kerry said with a bob of his head.

"Coke?" Thomas asked, holding out a can of Coca-Cola to Gore.

"Thomas here made military history. When he deserted from a group of deserters," said Kerry.

"I'm the first double-deserter since the Spanish-American War." Thomas beamed.

Gore felt that the young man's pride in his dubious accomplishment was more than a little displaced. "Keep your Coke, Thomas. You oughta be in the brig."

"I would be, but Colonel Scalia took a liking to me. He gave me a choice. Execution by firing squad, or lead the Skipper here upriver to my old unit's last position. And then Scalia'll give me a recommendation for law school on the GI Bill." Thomas strolled into the head with a magazine under his arm.

"So we're going to terminate our own men with extreme prejudice?" Gore asked, intrigued.

"No." Kerry said with obvious disappointment. "We made

" THIS PVT. CLARENCE THOMAS LOOKS VERY FAMILIAR. "

radio contact with Limbaugh and cut a deal with Gingrich. They're hiding in a cave fifty klicks upriver. We extract them, and they all go home with an honorable discharge and a unit citation."

"That hardly seems fair," Gore commented.

"HQ just wants the problem to go away. Bring 'em up on charges and we'll have a giant shitstorm."

"I still don't see why we can't just kill them."

"I hear ya. But I got my orders," Kerry said, idly picking a short, curly hair off the Coke can. "Thomas!" Kerry yelled over his shoulder. "Get out of there!"

**M**eanwhile, in a dank, foul-smelling cave fifty klicks upriver, Rush Limbaugh was eating his eighty-third raw snail of the day.

"At least pick 'em outta thair damn shells," Gramm said irritably.

"The fiber keeps me regular," Limbaugh snapped defensively.

"Regular? Eight dumps a day ain't regular," Buchanan shot back. "Maybe this cave wouldn't smell so bad if you ate newborn bats like the rest of us. Stoner here hasn't taken a shit in a week."

"That's because of the opium. And I told you, baby bats don't agree with me!" Limbaugh sniped, reaching for another snail.

"When are they getting us outta this fucking hole?" said Gingrich, as he nervously flicked the safety catch of his M-16 on and off. Click-click, click-click, click-click.

"Stop that!" Gramm and Buchanan hissed in unison.

Limbaugh threw the snail at Gingrich, hitting him in his generous belly. Gingrich leveled his rifle at the radioman. "I am *this close* to splattering you all over this cave. All of you!"

Just then, the radio crackled to life. "Foxtrot Romeo, this is Sea Lord." Kerry's voice echoed through the cave. "Come in, Foxtrot Romeo."

Limbaugh grabbed the handset. "Sea Lord, this is Task Force Brave Eagle. I told you 'Foxtrot Romeo' sounds faggy."

There was a pause. "Very well, Brave Eagle. Prepare for extraction at twenty-three thirty hours."

Limbaugh looked helplessly at Gramm, who shrugged. "Eleven-thirty at night, fatboy," scoffed Buchanan from the bottom of a fourteen-foot foxhole he had dug in the floor of the cave.

"Yeehaw!" Gramm shouted. "We're goin' to Saigon, boys! This time tomorrow we'll be knee-deep in slant-eyed pootie!"

"Uh, Brave Eagle, you're on an unsecure radio frequency." Kerry's disgust came through loud and clear. "And FYI, Four Corps Intel reports beaucoup Victor Charlie movement in your area."

Limbaugh shat himself.

"Jesus, Limbaugh," Gingrich gagged. Any suggestion of war or fighting always did that to Limbaugh. The acrid stench even penetrated Stoner's opium-induced delirium. He leaned over and vomited copiously into Buchanan's foxhole.

"Hey, Pat. Incoming," Gingrich shouted, cracking up both himself and Gramm.

"Listen up, Brave Eagle. When you approach the rendezvous point, remember the signal. Three clicks on the handset. Do you copy?"

Limbaugh clicked the handset three times. There was another pause.

"No, not now. At the rendezvous. Click the handset three times *at the rendezvous.* At twenty-three thirty. That's eleven-thirty at night. Sea Lord, over and out."

As dusk fell, wisps of mist began to rise from the slack brown water of the canal. At the helm, Kerry steered a middle course between the heavily jungled banks. In the fading light, Gore noticed that Kerry's mood seemed to darken as well.

"Sometimes I wonder if this war was such a good idea."

"What do you mean?" asked Gore guardedly. He had heard this kind of talk before, back at Harvard. Specifically, in a folksinging workshop taught by Pete Seeger, class of '42.

"I keep reading in Captain Ailes's column that victory is just around the corner. But for those of us in country, it just doesn't seem that way."

"I don't know, Lieutenant. If you imagine Asia as a row of dominoes, we've lost China, we've lost North Korea. If Vietnam falls, then Cambodia could be next, followed by Thailand, then Burma, Ceylon, India, Pakistan. Then . . ."

As Gore continued to list countries, Kerry's mind wandered. "I just wonder why we've lost the hearts and minds of the Vietnamese people."

"Give it back!" Thomas's squeal broke their reverie. "Give me back my magazine!"

Kerry and Gore jumped topsides and saw Ashcroft holding a cheaply printed magazine featuring teenage Vietnamese prostitutes putting hard-boiled eggs in their vaginas. "Filth!" roared Ashcroft. "Blasphemous filth!" He hurled the magazine into the swirling waters.

"Motherfucker!" shouted Thomas, preparing to dive after the egg magazine. But before he could, Kerry grabbed his arm in an iron grip.

"What's going on here?" the lieutenant asked as he hurled Thomas onto the deck.

"Let me explain, Big Guy," Bush said as he crumpled a beer can against his forehead. "Jesus Freak here's been gettin' on Bill Cosby 'bout his choice of reading matter."

"Skipper," said Ashcroft indignantly, "article eighteen, section twelve of the Uniform Code of Military Justice specifically forbids active duty personnel from possessing pornography. I plan to file a full report with your superiors when we get back."

"That's your prerogative, sailor. But until then, I'm ordering you to respect other people's right to privacy." Kerry and Ashcroft stared at each other. "Do you get me, Ashcroft?"

"Yes . . . sir," said Ashcroft, snapping off a sarcastic salute.

With a last hard look, Kerry turned and walked forward to the helm, where Gore was helplessly spinning the wheel, sending the boat in circles. "What was that about?" Gore asked as Kerry pointed the boat back upriver.

"Tell you what." Kerry said with a twinkle in his eye. "Maybe you want to go back and ask them about it. Might make a funny article for *Stars and Stripes.*"

**B**ack on the fantail, Thomas had confronted O'Reilly. "Why didn't you stick up for me? It's your magazine."

"Listen, Thomas, here's something you gotta know. Bill O'Reilly looks after one person and one person only. Bill O'Reilly. Besides, I was sick of that particular magazine anyway."

"Fucking pussy," Thomas said as he walked away angrily.

"What was that about?" Gore said to O'Reilly. "He call you a pussy?"

"Nah," O'Reilly said offhandedly. "He called me pushy. Tough. One thing you gotta know about Bill O'Reilly. He never walks away from a fight." Then, seeing Gore starting to write, he added, "Capital O, capital R, E, I, L, L, Y. O'Reilly. You know, I've won two Congressional Medals of Honor."

"As far as I know, no one has ever won two Medals of Honor. And, by the way, it *is* just Medal of Honor, not Congressional Medal of Honor. It's a common mistake."

"We'll just have to agree to disagree," O'Reilly said with a shrug. "I say it's Congressional Medal of Honor. And I say I've won two of them. You know, it's the most prestigious military decoration in the armed forces."

"Chow time!" Bush called as he approached with a tray of beers and a box of pills. "Journalist guy, Irish here been telling you 'bout his Congressional Medal of Honor?"

"Me*dals.* I've won two," O'Reilly corrected, as he swallowed a handful of the shiny black tablets.

"What are those?" asked Gore. "Food pills? That'd be a good invention."

"Wakey-wakeys. You know, pep pills, black beauties," said an already hopped-up Bush.

"I'm not sure that's wise." Gore said, taking care not to sound too disapproving.

"These are government issue," O'Reilly said, tossing one in the air and then catching it in his mouth like a piece of popcorn.

"Careful! You could choke," Gore said, trying not to sound too schoolmarmish.

"Yeah? Choke on this, pal," said O'Reilly, grabbing his crotch and kneading his balls.

Bush cracked up.


**W**ith the full moon glistening across the inky water, the Swift Boat idled slowly toward the rendezvous point. Kerry expertly nosed the bow through a dense tangle of vines and foliage, cutting the engine as he nestled the craft alongside the bank.

Without the regular throb of the engines, the jungle night came alive with sound. Hyped on their wakey-wakeys, the crew twitched nervously with every monkey shriek, every alligator splash, every lizard rustling through the undergrowth.

"Synchronize your watches. Cheney, what time you got?" Kerry asked in a whisper, knowing of the Wyoming native's fondness for expensive timepieces.

Cheney was too weak to answer, but Bush leaned over and read the glowing watch face. "About nine-thirty, Big Guy," Bush shouted.

"Sssshhhhhh. Quiet!" Kerry whispered urgently.

"Oh, right, right. Sorry." Bush said in hushed tones.

"And *about* nine-thirty doesn't help. Listen up. I've got twenty-one twenty-seven. That means we got two hours and three minutes till rendezvous. Remember, this is Charlie's side of the canal. Keep your eyes peeled. Your mouths shut. And your weapons ready."

Now, in the smothering heat and humidity of the tropical night, every man was alone with his thoughts.

Even though the temperature hovered in the nineties, Ashcroft shivered involuntarily. Before that night he had never taken anything stronger than the Vicks VapoRub his mother used to massage into his chest, invariably producing an erection. Like the VapoRub, the wakey-wakey had generated a deeply confusing blend of shame and excitement.

Thomas leaned over the gun tub toward O'Reilly, who was wedged behind the menacing barrels of twin .50-caliber machine guns. "You gotta help me, O'Reilly," Thomas whispered. "I'm so scared. The only thing that calms me down is porn."

"Does it have to be pictures? Or can I just tell you a dirty story?" O'Reilly murmured.

"Dirty story'll do."

"You want guy-girl, girl-girl, guy-girl-guy, or girl-guy-girl?"

Thomas thought for a moment. Just considering the options raised his spirits. "Hmm. How 'bout guy-girl?"

"Excellent choice," O'Reilly said, under his breath. He was equally grateful to have something to take his mind off his own gut-wrenching terror. After thinking for a moment, he began. "Ashley was now wearing only brief white panties. By removing her shirt and skirt, and by leaning back on the couch, she had signaled her desire. Now, she closed her eyes, concentrating on nothing but my tongue and lips. I gently teased her by licking the areas around her most sensitive erogenous zone. Then I slipped her panties down her legs and, within seconds, my tongue was inside her, moving rapidly."

A dozen feet away George Bush was oblivious to the amorous antics of Ashley and O'Reilly. Bush gazed up at the moon, thinking back to another moonlit night just six months ago and half a world away. He cursed the bad luck that had put those Mexican

day laborers in the bus shelter beside the dusty road that stretched between his favorite bar in Midland and his favorite bar in Lubbock. He didn't remember swerving around the school bus and hitting them. When Poppy bailed him out the next morning, he told his son the bad news. Because the Mexicans had died, the Air National Guard was now out of the question. Bush would have to serve in the actual military, and the sweet deal that would have allowed him to do his military service entirely by mail was now a thing of the past. Why? Why? Why did those dead Mexicans have to spoil everything?

Bush was rudely awakened from his self-pitying rumination by a hand suddenly clutching at his forearm. It was Cheney. The fear of having a heart attack had brought on another heart attack.

"Help . . . George . . ."

Cheney's face was white with fear. His pulse was weak and thready. His eyes seemed glazed. Bush's own heart skipped a beat. "Don't leave me, Dick! Don't leave me! I can't make it alone!"

"The pills. I need . . . a pill," Cheney sputtered.

"Nah. No more wakey-wakeys for you, pal."

"Not . . . wakey . . . wakeys," Cheney gasped, "ni . . . ni . . . nitro . . ."

Kerry rushed over and, pushing Bush aside, took the nitroglycerine tablets from Cheney's shirt pocket and slipped one into his mouth. As Cheney's breathing slowed and his color began to return to normal, Kerry grabbed Bush by the collar. "Listen. He has eighteen more pills. That's enough for eighteen more heart attacks. Give him the pill the moment you notice anything unusual."

"Yessir." This latest heart attack had clearly upset the annoyingly jocular Bush. "Sir?" he asked haltingly. "Sir, we're going to be okay, aren't we?"

"Sure, Bush. Everything's going to be fine."

"Skip? Do you ever get scared?"

Kerry smiled. "Let me tell you something Bush. Any man out here in the shit who says he's not scared is just crazy, a liar, or both."

"I'm not scared," said O'Reilly from his position deep inside the gun tub.


**T**ask Force Brave Eagle was late. Limbaugh blamed Buchanan, who had taken an extra forty minutes to climb out of his foxhole. Buchanan thought it was Gramm's fault for losing the flashlight. Gramm was sure that Gingrich was responsible, for wasting time arguing over who was going to take point. Gingrich, in turn, blamed Stoner, who, after taking point, kept wandering off in the wrong direction. Stoner, who had dropped acid, had decided to follow a hallucination of Ted Williams, whom he blamed for trying to lead him toward a secret fishing hole instead of the river. And all of them hated Limbaugh for the terrible smell that seemed certain to give away their position. Plus, somewhere along the way the exhausted fat man had set down the radio and intentionally forgotten to pick it up.


**"T**ask Force Brave Eagle. Come in, Task Force Brave Eagle." Kerry tried the radio again.

"Let's get the fuck outta here."

"Shut up, O'Reilly," Kerry shot back. "We're going to complete the mission."

"They're not coming! They're dead. Charlie got 'em. And Charlie's gonna get us, too!" Thomas wailed.

Kerry slapped him. "Thomas, get a grip on yourself."

Bush stepped forward. "I have a suggestion. Why don't we take a vote? All those in favor of leaving immediately, raise your hands."

Four arms shot up, while Cheney waved weakly to indicate his support as well. Only Kerry and Gore stood steadfast.

"Okay," said Bush. "Five to two. Let's get goin'."

"We're not going anywhere. Till I say so." Kerry was in Bush's face. After a moment, Bush backed down.

"Sure, Big Guy, you're the boss." Bush grinned. The reporter in Gore thought he noticed a hint of menace in Bush's voice.

Kerry nodded. "You're goddamn right I am. Now, get yourselves squared away and back to your posts."

As the men resumed their watch, Bush passed around the wakey-wakeys and handed Cheney another nitro pill, just in case.

"Skipper's gonna get us killed," O'Reilly whispered to Ashcroft.

But Ashcroft was staring intently into the jungle. "Ssssshhh. Did you hear that?"

Barely a hundred yards away, Ted Williams was leading Stoner directly toward the waiting boat. Suddenly, Stoner stopped in his tracks as the Red Sox slugger vanished and abruptly turned into Bertrand Russell, the distinguished British philosopher. Stoner screamed.

Later, it seemed to Ashcroft that he had squeezed the trigger even before the scream had begun. And that he had fired off the full clip before it had ended. The night erupted as the other men joined in a frenzy of lead and gunpowder. The foliage along the starboard side was shredded by the onslaught.

"Cease fire! Cease fire! Dammit!" Kerry shouted in vain over the furious barrage.

Task Force Brave Eagle may not have been the finest soldiers in the American Army, but they knew enough to lie flat on the ground when someone was shooting at them. All except for Bertrand Russell, who bravely marched into the line of fire despite the frantic entreaties of Stoner Will.

Gingrich was the first to return fire, aiming in the general direction of the canal. Astonished by his own boldness, he yelled at the others to do the same. Buchanan struggled to set up a mortar, as Gramm hurled a grenade from which he had neglected to pull the pin. It landed in the river with a satisfying plop. For the first time, Brave Eagle was fighting as a unit. Except for Limbaugh, whose weapon had become inoperable after being fouled repeatedly. And Stoner, startled by Bertrand Russell's transformation into a giant talking postage stamp.

Twelve feet directly below Gingrich, Colonel Binh Cao Nguyen of the People's Liberation Front was just beginning his nightly indoctrination class when the tunnel began to shake. Grabbing his AK-47, he ran down a short passageway, climbed a ladder, and stuck his head out of a well-concealed spider hole. There in front of him was a scene he could hardly have dared wish for. American soldiers shooting at American sailors. It was too good to be true. Silently, he led his platoon to a position directly behind the soldiers and gave the order to fire.

Red and white tracers crisscrossed over Gingrich's head. He looked behind him to see the shadowy outline of the VC as they fired from the trees. "Shit! We're in a crossfire!"

By now Gramm had caught sight of the Swift Boat. "Hey, I think those are our guys!"

"What?" said Buchanan as he fired a mortar round, which bounced off the tree canopy directly over his head and then ricocheted into the pilothouse of the Swift Boat.

---

The pilothouse was in flames. Gore grabbed the fire extinguisher only to find that Bush had used it to store several gallons of the highly flammable native liquor known as Mekong Moonshine.

"Medic!" yelled Bush, standing over Cheney, whose fragile heart was under attack as well. Bush reached into his own pocket and in the chaos fed Cheney a wakey-wakey instead of a nitro tablet. Cheney sat up, gave Bush a wink, and died.

"Noooooo!!!!" Bush poured the nitroglycerine tablets into Cheney's slack mouth. But it was too late.

The moment the mortar round exploded, Kerry knew it was American ordnance. They were taking friendly fire. But he also knew he had no choice but to shoot back with everything they had. He looked up to the gun tub, where O'Reilly stood frozen at the twin .50s. Kerry leapt up, shouldered O'Reilly aside, and unleashed the full fury of the machine gun in the direction of the incoming fire.

---

Gingrich sized up the situation: behind them, an entire platoon of crafty, dedicated Viet Cong; in front of them, a withering barrage of increasingly accurate fire that had them pinned down. Only a miracle could save them now.

Limbaugh stood up and turned around, facing the VC. "We surrender," he screamed in perfect Vietnamese, the only phrase he knew in that notoriously difficult language. Maybe this was the miracle Gingrich was hoping for.

Mai Nu Ky, a battle-hardened thirteen-year-old corporal, turned to her commander. "Comrade Colonel, shall we capture the American or kill him?"

Nguyen raised his arm in a signal to cease fire. The highly disciplined soldiers lowered their weapons as Limbaugh waddled toward them. Nguyen turned to Mai. "You may have the honor of executing the giant pig, Corporal." She raised her weapon and fired once, bringing Limbaugh down with a thunderous thud.

With surrender now out of the question, Gingrich could see only one chance to save his skin. He'd have to trick the other members of his unit into making a suicidal charge against the Swift Boat. With any luck, the Americans would kill each other off, leaving Gingrich with the boat and a chance to escape. "Charge!" Gingrich yelled.

"*You* charge," Gramm called back.

"Let's all charge together!" shouted Buchanan, planning to fake getting shot by falling to the ground and moaning.

"Ready?" yelled Gingrich. "One. Two. Three. Charge!" The three men stood up. Each took a half step before theatrically falling down.

"I've been hit!" They called in unison.

The tail end of Kerry's ammo ran through the .50s and clattered to the floor of the gun tub. "Gore, go below. Grab me some more ammo."

Gore jumped down into the cabin and opened the ammo locker to find . . . beer. Cases and cases of Lone Star. Putting two and two together, Gore cursed Bush for his reckless betrayal. While Gore understood that alcoholism was a disease and that, to some extent, Bush was not responsible for his own behavior, Gore still

THE THREE TOOK HALF A STEP BEFORE THEATRICALLY FALLING DOWN.

felt a deep-seated resentment that would take many years to heal. If he lived that long.

The silencing of the .50s put an end to the three men's extravagant charade. Gingrich called to the others. "Whatta you say we really charge this time?"

"Really really?" Gramm asked.

The approaching VC made up their minds for them. Buchanan was up first, running flat-out toward the boat and screaming his war cry. Gramm and Gingrich followed close behind, firing their weapons wildly. As they got within twenty feet of the boat, Kerry yelled at both sides to cease fire.

Buchanan was the first to climb aboard. "You're all my prisoners," he announced. Kerry grabbed Buchanan's M-16.

"Gimme that!" Kerry snarled.

Gramm clambered aboard and lay gasping on the deck. Ashcroft and Thomas pulled Gingrich up after him. "VC," Gingrich puffed. "They're right behind us. Gotta get outta here."

Sure enough, the VC were approaching. Without hesitation, Kerry hosed them down with Buchanan's M-16. Eleven fell dead, including Colonel Nguyen. The other twenty or so, now commanded by Corporal Ky, retreated to the safety of the jungle.

"Where are the other two?" Kerry asked Gramm. "Will and Limbaugh?"

"They're dead. Let's go!"

But at that moment Stoner emerged from the underbrush, carrying the head of a VC soldier on the end of a bayonet. He climbed aboard, handed the head to Kerry, went to sit by himself in a corner, and began rolling a thumb-thick doobie.

"Well, Limbaugh's definitely dead," Gingrich said. "I saw him go down. He took one in the throat."

"Help! Help me!" Kerry recognized Limbaugh's voice from the radio. "The fuckers shot me in the ear! I'm deaf! Oh, God, I'm deaf." Just then, Limbaugh stumbled out of the darkness, collapsing mere yards from the canal.

Kerry leapt off the boat to help the bloated radioman. Limbaugh threw his arms around the lieutenant's neck, almost pulling him to the ground. "Save me!" he cried pitiously. "Oh God, please save me."

Kerry hoisted Limbaugh's enormous bulk across his back in a fireman's carry. Staggering under the weight, he walked the last few feet to the boat and tossed him over the gunnels.

"Okay, you satisfied? Can we go *now?*" O'Reilly asked petulantly.

"Listen up, men. I need you to check your weapons. Then we're gonna split up into two squads and engage the enemy. Now, we don't have a lot of ammo, so we're going to have to use stealth and surprise. I'm taking you, you, you, and the guy who brought me the head. Are there any questions?"

Bang! A single shot ripped through Kerry's spine, exiting

"YEAH, I GOT A QUESTION. ANYBODY HERE SEE THAT? I DIDN'T THINK SO."

out his chest. His knees buckled; he was dead before he hit the deck.

Bush, his M-16 still smoking, grinned. "Yeah, I got a question. Anybody here see that? I didn't think so."

"Well, I certainly did," Gore said indignantly. "And I plan to make a full—"

Bang!

**A**s dawn broke over Vietnam, the party aboard Swift Boat PCF-73 was just getting into full swing. The men were ebullient. They were going home, or at least to Saigon. So they thought. It was only Stoner Will who noticed that the sun was rising on the wrong side of the river. But he didn't care. He had heard about the hash in Cambodia, and he was eager to try it out.

THE END

# Fun with Racism

**Strom** Thurmond is dead. The news came in just this morning as I sat down to write a chapter on the Bush family's close ties to the House of Saud, and, through them, to Osama bin Laden. Instead, to honor Thurmond's memory, I have decided to write on a topic close to his heart: racism.

You'll remember the ruckus caused by Trent Lott's ill-considered remarks at Thurmond's wild hundredth birthday party. Toasting the senator, Lott said, "When Strom Thurmond ran for president, we voted for him. We're proud of it. And if the rest of the country had followed our lead, we wouldn't have had all these problems over all these years."

*The New York Times,* the *Washington Post,* NPR, and the rest of the liberal media were all there. But none found this bald nostalgia for segregation remarkable enough to report on. NPR's *Weekend Edition* preferred to run another of Lott's well-crafted tributes: "Somebody once said, and I'm not quite sure where I got this, but I heard it, and I loved it, and it applies to Strom Thurmond: 'Youth is a gift of nature. Age is a work of art.' This, ladies and gentlemen, is a work of art." Sweet, don't you think? It's that old media bias for the "Awwwwww" moment.

Unfortunately for Lott, C-SPAN cameras captured the event for everyone to enjoy. While the "liberal" media filed it as a heart-warming human interest story, some more discerning viewers were aghast at Lott's paean to the Dixiecrats. Thanks to a few bloggers, the story took hold, and the controversy was up and running.

In some ways, I thought the whole thing was a little unfair to Lott. The Dixiecrat platform wasn't just about segregation. It also included a pro-poll-tax plank and a plank against anti-lynching laws. Plus, it called for stronger anti-miscegenation laws. Many people think of anti-miscegenation laws as being the same as segregation, but they're not. Miscegenation is about the "mongrelization" of the white race, which to this day is considered by some to be a crime against nature.

One of the things that I was most puzzled about during the Lott controversy was that no one asked *Thurmond* what he thought about Lott's comments. He was not invited on *any* of the major network news shows. Some may say this proves that they have a liberal bias after all. But my friend Norm Ornstein has a more sinister theory. Ornstein, a senior scholar at the American Enterprise Institute, believes that Thurmond may have died as long as three years ago, and that the Republicans have since been pursuing a *Weekend at Bernie's* strategy because the governor of South Carolina is a Democrat and the GOP wanted to keep the seat.

Once the controversy had gained momentum, almost no one was willing to defend Lott's remarks. Some conservative commentators couldn't resist using their de rigueur reprimands of Lott as a jumping off point for malicious distortions of the history of U.S. racial politics.

Sean Hannity was the poster boy for this conservative tic. "Segregation is the legacy of the Democratic Party," Sean would say over and over again. He and his clansmen (including Ann Coulter) based this on the true but fatuously disingenuous factoid that a higher percentage of Republican senators voted for the 1964 Civil Rights Act than Democrats. That's because racist Southern Democratic senators (like, say, Strom Thurmond) voted against the historic legislation. Southern Democrats. *Dixie*crats. Get it?

Sean knows very well that it was the liberal wing of the Democratic Party that ended segregation. He knows this because he lived in Newt Gingrich's ass from 1994 to 1998, so Sean had to have heard it when Newt declared, "It was the liberal wing of the Democratic Party that ended segregation." This was in Newt's historic speech to the House when he first took the gavel as Speaker.

When President Lyndon Johnson signed the 1964 Civil Rights Act, he is said to have turned to an aide and remarked, "We have just lost the South for a generation." The Republican Party became the home to Southern bigots and still is today.

While the Democratic Party lost the South that year, they did gain my dad. A lifelong Republican who voted for Herbert Hoover and every GOP presidential candidate through Nixon, Dad switched parties in 1964 because the Republican nominee, Barry Goldwater, had voted against the Civil Rights Act. Dad, a card-carrying member of the NAACP, always told us that Jews couldn't be against civil rights. He never voted Republican again.

Five weeks before Thurmond's birthday party, Georgia's Democratic Governor Roy Barnes lost his race for reelection. As governor, Barnes had reduced the size of the Confederate emblem on the state flag, and his opponent Sonny Perdue seized on it as an issue. One hundred and eighty thousand more rural white voters turned out in 2002 than had in 1998. I spoke with Max Cleland, who, in addition to being pictured with Osama bin Laden and Saddam Hussein, was buried by the racist avalanche in Georgia, and lost his Senate reelection bid. Here's how Cleland described it:

> Basically, when Roy Barnes changed the flag, that was it. That was the straw that broke the camel's back. And what happened was, Ralph Reed then took the hatchet and buried us. He took the hatchet that Roy Barnes gave him, by push-polling in the Republican suburbs, and in South Georgia, this question: The Democrats are trying to take away Georgia's culture. And it came off the charts, especially with white males. . . . And it quickly became a racial issue. And in the South, if all politics are local, all politics are racial in the South.

In January 2003, I gave one of my enormously popular corporate speeches to the South Carolina Bar Association in Charleston, where I learned that the Confederate flag is still a huge issue in the Palmetto State. That same day, I heard someone on Fox News call John Walker Lindh a traitor—which he was. He was a traitor because he fought against soldiers wearing the uniform of the United States of America. Terrible traitor.

You know who were the worst traitors in the history of our country? The Confederates. *They* took up arms against soldiers wearing the uniform of the United States of America. But they were much, much worse than John Walker Lindh. Because they killed hundreds of thousands of American troops. And for what cause? So they could whip and torture black people. Why would anyone want to put up a flag honoring *that*?

To give you some idea of just how evil and anti-American the Confederates were, here's a rough comparison between the American deaths caused by the Confederates and those caused by the most evil of our enemies today.

| Osama bin Laden | Saddam Hussein | Jefferson Davis |
| --- | --- | --- |
| 3,000 | 512 | 360,000 |

How could you possibly claim to be against traitors like John Walker Lindh, yet want to publicly display the battle flag of the most murderous, anti-American betrayers in history? No offense to my Southern readers and fans, but I don't get it.

I was talking to a Southerner about this the other day, and he said, "The Nazis were bad. But we drive around in Volkswagens."

I said, "Yeah, but we don't put a Volkswagen on top of the state capitol."

Don't get me wrong. Republicans aren't just racist in the South. Take California, where earlier this year, the highest-ranking African-American in the state GOP sent an angry e-mail to party leaders.

"Black Republicans are expected to provide window dressing and cover to prove that this is not a racist party, yet our own leadership continues to act otherwise," Party Secretary Shannon Reeves wrote to his fellow party board members.

Reeves wrote his comments because state Republican Vice Chairman Bill Back had sent out an e-mail containing an article by someone else suggesting that the nation would have been better off if the South had won the Civil War.

Reeves went on to describe some of his experiences as a black Republican. "As a Bush delegate at the 2000 convention in Philadelphia, I proudly wore my delegate's badge and [Republican National Committee] lapel pin as I worked the convention. Regardless of the fact that I was obviously a delegate prominently displaying my credentials, no less than six times did white delegates dismissively tell me [to] fetch them a taxi or carry their luggage."

It's no wonder that Republicans have a hard time attracting blacks to the party.

Being black and Republican can have its rewards, however. At the 2000 convention in Philadelphia, every Republican African-American elected official in the country got to speak from the podium. City councilmen, county executives, state legislators—they all got to speak. Except one guy. Morris Temple, the county coroner from London, Ohio. And he was pissed. I was covering the convention for ABC Radio and interviewed him.

> **TEMPLE**: Yeah, I'm angry. I'm damn angry. Every other black elected official in the whole damn country got to speak from that podium except me. Oh, the Bush people told me there was another guy, some motor vehicle commissioner from Maryland. Turns out the guy was Filipino![1]

In the 2000 presidential election, George W. Bush got 8 percent of the black vote. The African-American officeholders who were paraded on the podium in Philadelphia were not intended to attract black votes. They were presented for the consumption of suburban whites who don't want to vote for an overtly racist party, the kind of party that would deliberately purge the voting rolls in Florida of tens of thousands of blacks who should never have been purged. White suburban voters don't want to vote for a party that would

---

[1]Okay. I made up the whole Morris Temple story. Everything else here is true.

try to suppress black turnout in 2002 by putting out flyers in black neighborhoods saying:

> URGENT NOTICE. Come out to Vote November 6. Before you
> Come out to vote—Pay your parking tickets, motor vehicle
> tickets, your rent, and most important, ANY WARRANTS.

The election, of course, was November 5.

So it's a balancing act. Pursue Nixon's Southern strategy: flog the flag in Georgia and South Carolina, suppress votes in black neighborhoods, but feature the black Republican school board treasurer from Monroe, Louisiana, at your national convention.

And, by all means, anytime you can, flaunt Colin Powell and Condoleezza Rice.

In January, President Bush announced that his administration would file a pair of legal briefs against the University of Michigan's undergraduate and law school admissions programs. The White House told the *Washington Post* that Dr. Rice had been one of the "prime movers" behind the President's decision and that after "a series of lengthy one-on-one meetings with Bush, she drew on her experience as provost at Stanford University to help convince him that favoring minorities was not an effective way of improving diversity on college campuses."

The next day, *The New York Times* reported that a "dismayed" Rice was so "troubled by [the] article in the *Washington Post* that she announced that she believed universities should be able to use race as a factor in admissions policies, a view that may put her at odds with Mr. Bush." In other words, the White House had been lying to the *Post.* And while Bill Bennett and Sean Hannity told the Fox audiences that any use of race as a factor in admissions was "abhorrent," the only two blacks that Republicans ever point to, Rice and Powell, think it's an appropriate tool.

Perhaps Rice and Powell knew something about the world that the rest of the Bush administration doesn't know.

When I give my corporate speeches, almost invariably I open up with this line: "Looking out at your faces today, I can see that this group hasn't caved in to that whole affirmative action nonsense." Sometimes, the audience of mid-to-top-level executives will look around, see all the white faces, and laugh. Most of the time, they just burst out laughing right away.

I had a baseball coach pose this question to me: "You have two guys run down to first. They have equal times, but one has much better form. Which one do you choose?"

You choose the one with the bad form. You can coach him to use good form and he'll beat the other guy.

In the same way, blind adherence to SAT scores and GPAs is ridiculous. Take two kids, one white and one black. The white kid's in private school, has educated parents, opportunities to travel, intensive SAT tutoring. He takes the SATs three times and submits his highest score—1,280. The black kid is brought up by a single mom who didn't graduate from high school. No books in the house, works after school, shares a room with two brothers. No SAT tutoring, takes it once, gets an 1,120. You'd take the black kid, right?

Except, I forgot. The white kid's dad was your roommate in college. You spray-painted the dean's car together sophomore year. That was fun! Remember the look on Dean Whitehead's face? Oh, and your brother does a lot of business with the family. Hard not to take the white kid.

Of course, most white kids don't have these advantages. But almost *no* black kids do.

We don't live in a race-blind society. Two professors, one from M.I.T., the other from the University of Chicago, proved it with an elegant experiment. The professors selected 1,250 job advertisements in Boston and Chicago. To each employer, they submitted two pairs of made-up résumés. One pair of highly qualified candidates and one pair of average candidates. In each pair, one had a "black" name like Tamika or Tyrone and one had a "white" name like Amy or Brad. The professors found that the "white" names were 50 percent more likely to be called for an interview than the "black" names.

George W. Bush was the beneficiary of affirmative action. In more ways than we'll probably ever know. He got into Yale after a lackluster career at Andover. What people don't realize is that, like the University of Michigan, Yale had a point system when Bush applied in 1964. George W. received five points for being the son of a Yale graduate, twenty points for being the grandson of an extremely important Yale graduate, who was a U.S. senator and a Yale trustee, and a point for being a cheerleader at Andover. He almost didn't make it, though, because he lost ten points for showing up drunk to the interview. Fortunately, he got thirty points for being a Bush with over a 920 on his SATs, and he slipped through.

I'm not saying that all Republicans are racist or that all racists are Republican. That would be a reprehensible overstatement, akin to something Ann Coulter might say. But if Ann were a Democrat, she would point out that, after years of declining during Clinton, black poverty is now on the increase. And she would make great use of the fact that youth poverty among blacks is now at its highest level in the twenty-three years they've been keeping the statistic. And she'd blame it all on Bush. She'd claim it was because of overt, deliberate racism, rather than his more general bias toward the already privileged. She might even say that his tax cuts are inherently racist, because not only are blacks disproportionately likely to be at the bottom of the economic ladder, but they're disproportionately unlikely to be at the top.

But that's Ann. I personally would never accuse Bush's tax cuts of being racially motivated. I just think that, very generally speaking, they happen to hurt black people and help rich people. Who tend, again generally, to be white. That's all I'm saying.

During the whole Trent Lott mess, Gene Weingarten, a writer for the *Washington Post,* found a great website run by an obscure group called the African American Republican Leadership Council. The site, www.AARLC.org, seeks to dispel the myth that the Republican Party has lost touch with blacks and is determined to break the "liberal democrat stranglehold over Black America."

At the time, the group's official fifteen-person advisory panel included Sean Hannity, Grover Norquist, Gary Bauer, and Paul Weyrich. All but two of the fifteen members of the advisory panel of the African American Republican Leadership Council were white.

The site did list former Massachusetts Senator Edward W. Brooke III, a genuine African-American, as the panel's honorary chairman. So Weingarten called Brooke, who told the reporter that he had never heard of the group and had no idea why his name was on the site.

Weingarten called the man identified as the group's political spokesman and asked him why there weren't more African-Americans associated with the African-American advisory panel. The spokesman, Kevin L. Martin, said, "I'd like there to be more, but let's be honest, right now the Republican Party and African-Americans have a large rift."

I don't know about you. But I think it's a little sad that, since J. C. Watts left the House, the number one black leader in the Republican Party is Sean Hannity.

# 31

# I'm a Bad Liar

**I** never lie. That is, unless it's absolutely necessary. So the story I'm about to tell you is a little embarrassing.

It starts two and a half years ago. My son, Joe, a junior in a very high-powered, expensive New York City private high school, was beginning his college search. We started to put together a list of schools to visit during spring break. The boy wants to be an engineer, so M.I.T., Michigan, Washington University, and Princeton were early contenders.

My wife, who, I have to tell you, is not usually funny, had a hilarious idea. Why don't I take Joe down to Bob Jones University as a prospective student (which, technically, he was) and have fun at their expense?

Great idea, honey! Hilarious! We could ask them all kinds of snarky questions in the information session. Like about their interracial dating policy. Because of bad publicity, Bob Jones had changed the policy since Bush's visit. Now, according to news reports, they were allowing kids to date interracially *with their parents' permission*. "Yeah, um, I understand the students need their parents' permission to date other races. I was wondering. My wife is fine with Joe dating a black girl. But I'm against it. How would that work out?"

Or "Yeah, um, on your interracial dating policy, I have a theoretical question. Tiger Woods? Could he date *anyone*? Or *no one*? Could he even go out by himself?" Oddly enough, the answer to that last question, I would learn, was no, unless Tiger was leaving campus either to go home or on a mission.

Excited about all the comic possibilities, I immediately asked my assistant Liz to call BJU, which is what they call themselves. Find out when they have information sessions and tours. Liz called, and found the people in the BJU admissions office to be incredibly friendly. I mention this because it will become a leitmotif for the rest of this chapter.

Of course, there were plenty of information sessions and tours! Come down anytime! We'd love to get to know Joe! What's he interested in? Liz did her best—the boy's into history. Great!

That afternoon, when Joe got back from his fancy, two-thirds-Jewish high school, I told him the good news. We were going to go on a little comedy adventure. Joe—and in retrospect, this is to the boy's credit—was *absolutely appalled.* "No!"

"What?" I said incredulously. This was my son, who grew up in a comedy household. Didn't he recognize a great idea?

"Leave these people alone!" he said angrily. "What did they do to you?"

"Well, they're racist and nuts, and—"

"Dad, they just have a different belief system. Leave them alone."

And that, I thought, was that. What I didn't understand was that when you contact an evangelical organization, they will not stop mailing you shit. Did you know that BJU has quite a history department? Did you know that the BJU cheerleaders wear skirts down to their ankles? It's in their brochure.

And then there were the calls.

"Hi! Is Joe there?"

"Um, who may I say is calling?"

"Josie Martin from Bob Jones University."

"Oh. Joe's not here now."

"When will he be back?"

"Um, hmmm, I . . . don't know."

This happened a lot. A lot. And because I'm a busy man and my wife wasn't vigilant enough, Joe actually answered a few times, getting angrier and angrier at me because he was now being forced to lie. Something we Frankens don't do. Unless it's absolutely necessary.

The last straw was the call from a junior at BJU who was from Manhattan. "Where," he asked Joe, "do you go to church?"

"I don't go to church," Joe answered reflexively. On the other end of the phone, he heard a shocked GASP.

". . . in Manhattan," he quickly recovered. "I go to church on Long Island."

"Oh," said the very nice young man whom my son was lying to.

Joe charged out of his room and confronted me. "This has got to stop! I don't like lying to people!" He told me to call Bob Jones and tell them he had decided to go to a secular college. Which was, of course, entirely true.

So the next day, I had Liz call and tell BJU the bad news. They were disappointed, but understood. And were extremely nice about it.

CUT TO: TeamFranken. Present day. A good idea never dies. I needed a kid without Joe's integrity. Fortunately, I was at Harvard. Among the fourteen members of TeamFranken, I had fourteen volunteers, including Owen Kane, a thirty-eight-year-old mid-career Kennedy School grad student.

But to maximize the chances of our little scheme working, it was important that my "son" or "daughter" be able to pass for a high school junior. Owen was out.

Andrew Barr was in. A sophomore at the college, Andrew was perfect. Fresh-faced, eager, he could easily pass for seventeen. Valedictorian at Boston Latin, the top public school in Boston, Andrew was razor sharp and quick on his feet. Only one problem. The Jewish thing. Neither Andrew nor I knew jack about Christianity, particularly the weird, freakish kind practiced by these incredibly nice people at Bob Jones University.

We decided to do our homework. Learning about Christianity would be too difficult and time-consuming. Also, boring. Instead, we checked out BJU's website, hoping not just to learn enough to pull off our scam, but also to find stuff to make fun of.

Unfortunately, we discovered that the interracial dating policy had been discarded altogether. Shit. There went the Tiger Woods joke.

But not to worry. There was plenty of other fodder. First of all, the "university" is not accredited. That's right. They have the same degree-granting power as Schlotsky's Deli. *They* claim it's because they don't *want* to be accredited. We think it's because they don't believe in *science*. You see, they stand without apology for the absolute authority of the Bible. God created the Earth in six days. And He didn't put gays in it, either.

Then, there's the BJU policy on student use of the Internet, which is "a source of much content antagonistic to Godliness." No argument there. Chat rooms, instant messaging, and web-based e-mail accounts are banned. Students are not allowed to access websites with "Biblically offensive material." In addition to the usual pornography and violence, this includes "crude, vulgar language or gestures, tasteless humor (excretory functions, etc.), and graphic medical photos." Fortunately, BJU has an automatic filter, updated *daily,* to block these websites. And since nobody's perfect (i.e., we're all sinners), if the filter picks up a student attempting to access one of these websites, the "incident" is logged for an Internet administrator. In fact, all Internet use is constantly monitored by the "university," giving parents real peace of mind. Like the incredible friendliness, "constant monitoring" would also become a theme of life at BJU.

And speaking of parents, Andrew and I found the linchpin for what would become "our elaborate ruse." On the BJU website is a letter telling parents that it is their "God-given responsibility" not to allow their children to choose their own college. The consequences of that are made clear in the vivid and terrifying stories of the "Three College Shipwrecks," written by Bob Jones, Sr., the founder of the "university."

The first two "shipwrecks," known as "His Only Daughter" and "The Pride of His Mother," come to alarmingly similar ends. In each, a promising, God-fearing student is allowed to go off to a secular university. After returning from their freshman years, both have lost their way, their faith shattered. The Only Daughter "rushed upstairs, stood in front of a mirror, took a gun, and blew out her brains." Whereas the Pride of His Mother, having contracted "an unspeakable disease," announces his intention to "buy a gun and blow out my brains."

The third shipwreck, "The Son of an Aged Minister," is less violent, though certainly just as tragic. He had been "a great boy, bright, clean, obedient, Christian." Unfortunately, although the boy makes the life-saving decision to attend a Christian school, it isn't BJU. "A skeptic had got in the Science Department" of the less-Christian Christian school, and when the boy returns home, he has lost his faith and becomes "a drunken, atheistic bum."

So. Parents could save their kids from suicide, alcoholism, and the clap by forcing them to go to BJU. Excellent. This was our key. Since neither Andrew nor I could pull off being devout evangelical Christians, it would be Andrew's *mother* who desperately wanted him to go to Bob Jones. Instead of being Andrew's father, I would be a friend of the family—in fact, the best friend of Andrew's father, who had died tragically of brain cancer—no wait, boating accident—three years ago. Andrew's mom had sunk into a deep depression, then miraculously found Christ.

It was perfect. Neither Andrew nor I would have to know anything. But why wasn't Mom there? Sick? No. Threw out her back carrying boxes of blood at a blood drive. At church. As you can see, we started putting *way* too much thought into the back story, and way too little into the fact that I have been on television for nearly thirty years.

Seeing as how we did spend the time on the back story, you really should hear it. Because it's pretty good. Andrew's father, Hank, my college roommate and financial advisor, ran an incredibly successful hedge fund. Andrew's mother, Ellen, therefore, was not just a stunningly beautiful widow—she looks like Naomi Judd—but also fabulously wealthy. Now for the delicious spin. I was more than just a family friend. I had my eye on the Widow Barr, and seeing to it that young Andrew would agree to attend Bob Jones would be a feather in my cap.

Andrew's part was equally delicious. Eager to please his mother, he had happily agreed to visit what he thought was just a typical, fun-in-the-sun Christian school. Our plan, as you can clearly see, was brilliant. Neither of us would have to know anything about either Christianity or Bob Jones University. We had thought of everything.

And, yes, I considered the possibility that I would be recognized. A disguise? Nah. I'd just cut my hair extra short. Yeah, that would do it.

"Hi, Mr. Franken! Big fan!" "Good to see you, Mr. Franken!" "Loved you on SNL!" These were the security guards at La Guardia. Nothing to worry about. We were still in New York. Didn't mean the haircut wasn't working.

We arrived in Greenville. The Hertz rent-a-car gal, also a big fan. That's good, I explained to Andrew. It's good to have a fan base. But this Hertz woman, she wasn't a nutcase evangelical. She watched secular TV. Don't worry.

So we got there around 11 A.M. Drove through the gates. Didn't set off the Jew alarm. We're in.

Took a look around. Not an unattractive campus. Buildings, grass—nice day. But the place was eerily devoid of human activity. We'd soon learn that everyone was at chapel, this being a weekday. Out of the car and into the Administration Building. At the desk, an extremely friendly, well-scrubbed, wide-eyed young man greeted us and sent us along into the admissions office, where we were met by an extremely friendly, well-scrubbed, wide-eyed female staffer. Like every woman at BJU, she wore a skirt that covered not just her upper thigh, but her lower thigh, and her knee, and her calf, and her either well-turned or not well-turned ankle. No real way of knowing. But she was *really* nice and showed us the official admissions video, which featured two miniature pirates who introduced themselves as "your guardians." At BJU, they told us, you're never alone. Remember I said "constant monitoring" would be a theme? The creepy mini-pirates weren't kidding.

We scheduled a 1 P.M. interview with "Gerald"[1] and decided to grab some lunch, joining the mass of students pouring out of chapel and into the dining commons. There were thousands of them, young men in shirts and ties and khakis, young women in their ankle-length skirts. You could say we stood out. We were about to face our first test.

His name was Doug, an intense, though extremely nice, finance major. In an effort to appear as if I had nothing to hide, I said hi. Doug squinted, looked me over skeptically, and decided to keep an eye on us. Very nicely, he offered to help us get lunch and sit with us, and then asked us lots and lots of questions about who we were and why we were there.

I took this as an opportunity to take our elaborate ruse out for a little test drive. Andrew's dad, dead. Mom, depressed. Mom finds Jesus. Wants Andrew at BJU. Throws out back carrying boxes of blood. Doug asked if Andrew wanted to go there. Andrew didn't know, but I pointed out that his mother really, *really* wanted him to. Doug said that Andrew shouldn't go unless he really wanted to. Hadn't Doug read "The Three Shipwrecks"?

Then things started getting sticky. Doug was asking *me* questions. Like, what did I do for a living? And why did I look familiar? I told him I was a writer, which is true, by the way. Remember, I lie only when it's absolutely necessary.

To get us off a potentially incognito-blowing line of questioning, I cleverly changed the subject to creationism. You really believe it? Doug said he did, and so did all his friends sitting around us. According to Doug, evolution made no sense at all. No mutation, he insisted, had ever been beneficial. I looked at my thumb, but said nothing, as I used it to hold my fork and shove the worst

---

[1] All names have been changed to protect me.

lunch I've ever had into my mouth. It was some kind of creamed broccoli on a bun. But then again, you don't go to Bob Jones for the food!

Doug told us that the chances of protoplasm evolving into a human being were infinitesimally small: one over ten to the 256th, or something like that. Duane, an intense, but extremely nice, business administration major, came up with a vivid analogy. "The chances," Duane said, "of protoplasm turning into a fully formed human being are worse than the chances of an explosion in a junkyard yielding an intact Boeing 747."

Doug could tell that I wasn't buying. "So, Alan," he said. Oh, I forgot. I had changed my name to "Alan" as part of our undercover operation. My name really is Alan—remember, only when absolutely necessary. "So, Alan," he said, "why do you believe in evolution?"

"Well, Doug, I'm not a scientist. But it seems that every scientist in this field at an accredited university [heh, heh] believes in evolution. You know, at M.I.T., Stanford, Wisconsin, Arizona State, Wake Forest, you know, everywhere."

Doug had a good answer. "So, just because everyone believes something, you think it's true. Well, remember, the Catholic Church taught for hundreds of years that the sun revolved around the Earth. Then they persecuted Galileo for saying the opposite."

"I think you're making my point, Doug. The Church based their conclusions on faith, just as you are. Galileo was an empiricist, like all those scientists at the accredited universities."

Andrew was growing more and more uncomfortable. Though he was thirty-two years my junior, he felt that I was exhibiting poor judgment by questioning the fundamental belief of the entire institution while attempting to remain inconspicuous. After a lot of eye contact between the two of us, we decided it was time to bail.

We told Doug and his friends that we had an appointment with an admissions officer, which again was true. Doug offered to walk us to the admissions office, but we told him that first we had to pick up something at a pharmacy, which while not true, was a necessary lie. We had to ditch Doug. Otherwise, our cover would be blown.

On the way to the "pharmacy," I was recognized by several students, some of whom yelled out, "Al Franken!" I waved. And gave out some autographs. The kids were very nice.

There was still thirty minutes until our appointment, so we did the only thing that made sense. We hid.

At 1 P.M. sharp, we slipped into the Administration Building for our appointment with Gerald Fortenberry. We were praying that Gerald hadn't been alerted to the presence of a liberal satirist on campus. It was our only hope.

We were unbelievably lucky. Gerald had no idea who I was. Clearly a recent graduate of the university, he was a sweet, almost innocent young man. A perfect patsy. He bought our elaborate ruse hook, line, and sinker.

Moved by the story of young Andrew's father's death (boating accident), he understood totally Mom's depression and subsequent salvation. "It sounds like your mother's life has been transformed."

"Yes," Andrew said. "And now she wants me to come here."

"Well, you're the one who really should want this."

Hadn't *anyone* read "The Three Shipwrecks"?! Even in the *Admissions* Department?

"Well," Andrew replied, "I'm not into the whole religion thing as much as my mother."

"That would be impossible," I offered. "She's very beautiful. She looks like Naomi Judd."

Gerald nodded.

"But I'm okay with it," Andrew continued. "I haven't really developed my own personal relationship with Christ, but I think it would be good to work on that. Plus, I'm really pumped about going off to college. I have a friend at Syracuse, and he's having a blast."

Gerald moved past the blast at Syracuse and came back to Mom. "She sounds like she's happier than she's ever been."

"Yeah," Andrew nodded. "Well, at least since Dad died."

I had a couple questions. Andrew was interested in premed. "I know you teach creationism as opposed to evolution. How does that work out with medical schools?"

"Oh, it's no problem," Gerald reassured. "In fact, we have a higher percentage of students accepted to medical school than the national average."

"Really? And what would that percentage be?" I wanted to know.

"I don't have that offhand," Gerald replied. "Perhaps I can get it for you."

Then Andrew pounced. At the airport in New York, we had picked up a *U.S. News & World Report Guide to the 1400 Top Colleges and Universities.* "Maybe it's in here," Andrew suggested innocently, pulling it out of his backpack.

Gerald blanched, knowing, as we did, that Bob Jones was not listed among the one thousand, four hundred top colleges and universities in the United States. Andrew flipped to South Carolina. "Hmmm . . . maybe it's under J."

"Give me that." I took the book and examined it thoroughly, as Gerald looked on uncomfortably. "It's . . . it's not here."

"No," said Gerald. "A lot of colleges pay to get in that thing."

"Really?" I asked.

"Yes." He nodded authoritatively.

Andrew understood. "So it's like an advertisement?"

"Yeah."

That was quite a relief for me. Until that moment, I had been feeling more and more guilty. But now that Gerald was lying about the college guide, I felt a lot better. Putting the book aside, I smiled at Gerald. "Well, at least we know Bob Jones is an accredited university."

"Uh . . . no."

"No?"

"No. Actually, we *choose* not to be accredited. I can give you a pamphlet on that."

Assured that the pamphlet would explain everything, we

moved on. Andrew expressed an interest in theater. Gerald got very excited. Every year Bob Jones's theater department presents what Gerald called a "Shakespeare-play." Gerald told us that before he came to BJU, "I wasn't much for operas and Shakespeare-plays."

One concern. Mom, the one that looks like Naomi Judd, was worried about a certain element that Andrew might be exposed to in the Drama Department. Did Gerald understand what I was getting at? To make it even clearer, I used the magic phrase, "alternative lifestyle." Any of that here at BJU?

"Oh, no, no, no, no." Gerald shook his head. "No, no, no, no. No." None of that here. We could be absolutely certain of that.

Good, good. Because Andrew was looking forward in particular to the heterosexual experience of college life.

"Yeah, my mom doesn't like me dating, because of, you know . . . but college is the time that, you know . . ."

"Oh, yes. We want you to meet girls here," Gerald smiled. "We encourage that."

"So, the dating scene," I asked on behalf of the boy, "what's that like?"

Before Gerald could respond, Andrew expressed some mild concern. "Yeah, I was talking to some guys outside and they said there were some . . . rules."

"Yes," Gerald nodded. "You cannot leave campus with someone of the opposite sex, unless you are accompanied by a chaperone."

Andrew raised his eyebrows. Then, looking for a ray of hope, "But on campus, you know . . ."

"We have a snack shop. You can sit and have a snack together."

Andrew and I looked at each other. How to put this?

I took it upon myself. "In terms of, um, you know, um—how far can he go?"

Gerald understood. "Well, obviously, there's absolutely no physical contact."

A numbed silence from the two of us.

"None?" finally came out of Andrew's gaping mouth.

"That's right. No holding hands, hugging, kissing, anything like that."

"Backrubs?" Andrew asked for clarification.

"No."

"Oh, you mean in public? Well, that's understandable," Andrew conceded.

"No. No physical contact anywhere. At all."

Andrew slumped.

Maybe Gerald had seen this reaction before. He knew just what to say. "Because, Andrew, you know what hand-holding leads to."

Andrew took a wild stab. "Sin?"

"That's right. You see, our rules are like guardrails that keep you on the path of Christ."

So far, our plan was working beautifully. Young Andrew, who at first seemed amenable to, even excited about, pleasing his mother, was now reeling. It was time to set up the kill.

"You know, Gerald, Andrew's mother really wants him to come here. I read that you have to be in the dorms by ten-twenty for the ten-thirty prayer group, and then lights out at eleven. But how about weekends?"

Andrew perked up. "Yeah, how far is it to Atlanta? Because my mom might let me bring my car, and a lot of the bands I like don't play here in Greenville."

"Well, you can have a car on campus, but you can only use it on weekends to go home or if you're going on a mission," Gerald explained helpfully.

"Oh, I see." Andrew nodded. "I guess it wouldn't be so bad to take the bus. Because Weezer didn't play in Greenville last time out."

"No, no. We don't want you going to rock concerts. There's no rock and roll."

"No rock 'n' roll?" I asked.

"No, we don't endorse that, obviously."

"What if I don't play it too loud?" Andrew said, becoming upset.

"No. We don't allow it in the dorms at all."

"I could use headphones," Andrew suggested.

"No."

Things were getting a little tense. "How about country music? That's good clean fun," I winked.

"No."

"*Christian* rock?" I tried. Certainly they must allow *Christian* rock.

Gerald shook his head. "We don't endorse that."

By now, Andrew was visibly shaken. No hand-holding. No road trips. No tunes. Lots and lots of prayer.

That's when I spoke up. "Gerald, could I have a word with you alone?"

"Sure, Alan."

I nodded to Andrew, who excused himself and stepped into the nearby men's room. I waited for the door to close, then turned to Gerald, suddenly in his face.

"Listen. This kid's mother is *extremely* wealthy. She has *tons* of money. She wants him to come here. If he comes here, I'm talking another *building*. Okay?! And you're blowing it!"

Gerald recoiled. His eyes opened wide. It was as if he had seen Satan himself.

I was pleading. "Don't tell him everything. You said before 'nobody's perfect.' Certainly there are kids who do stuff here."

"Well, I said that because we're all sinners. And the rules are guardrails to keep you on the path of Christ. I can't withhold anything from Andrew. That would defeat the whole purpose. Which is to live a life in Christ."

Aw, hell. Gerald was absolutely, totally, without question incorruptible. Screw it.


**W**e had our story. The place was weird, but the people extremely nice. A good honest day's work done, lying to God-fearing people. We'd sleep well tonight. But we decided to poke around a little more since we had some time to kill. Off to the museum, where BJU houses the largest collection of sacred art in the Western Hemisphere.

And let me tell you, it's a lot of sacred art: Botticelli, Granacci, Tintoretto, Dolci, Rembrandt, Ribera, Rubens, Van Dyck. Twenty-seven rooms full. A priceless collection. Donated by wealthy alums? Not quite. Most of it was purchased by Bob Jones, Jr., himself, the second of the three Bob Joneses.

You see, Dr. Bob II had spent some summers in the 1930s as a tour guide in Rome, Paris, and Vienna, and had acquired a taste for fine art. Luckily, when he returned to Europe in the late forties, he was able to acquire quite a bit of it at very reasonable prices. Hmmm, I thought. What do you suppose would be the chances of a white supremacist who came to Europe in the thirties knowing someone who knew someone who had recently come across some "misplaced" art in the late 1940s? In fact, I thought I recognized a couple pieces that used to belong to my grandfather, who was a big collector of sacred Christian art before he was hauled off to Buchenwald. Nah. Maybe I was jumping to conclusions.

Still with some time to kill, we decided to hop on the three o'clock tour with a delightful Christian family of four. We had a lovely time, even had some laughs, until we got to the theater, where our bluff was finally called. On the stage were several gigantic crosses, scenery for what they call "The Living Gallery." This involves recreating great works of sacred art using real people in tableaux. I was very excited about getting Andrew to take a picture of me hanging from one of the crosses. Then we met R.J. from the public liaison's office.

"I'll take them from here," R.J. told our tour guide. We didn't like the way he said that. Nor the way he said, "Let me tell you a little about the theater. The floor is from Rockefeller Center. But it's no *Saturday Night Live.*"

The jig was up.

"Can I just ask what you're down here looking for?" he inquired pointedly.

"Well, it's a long story," I said, willing, but not really eager, to go into the whole boating-accident-depression-salvation-boxes-of-blood thing again.

"Uh-huh. Look. We've had enough of being made fun of," R.J. said with more than a touch of bitterness. Then turning to Andrew, he added, "I hope this isn't awkward for you."

"Oh no," said Andrew cheerfully. "We've been getting this all day." Actually, we hadn't. But I thought it was a nice touch.

R.J. continued. "If you're legit, I'd be happy to show you anything you want to see. But we're not going to put our heads on the chopping block again." I had to admire his directness and his willingness to call us on what should have been obvious to everyone all day. And yet he had the manners to leave open the remote possibility that we were, as he put it, "legit." And even while being hostile, he was extremely nice about it.

Accompanied by R.J., we made a show of being interested in the alumni building, the least interesting building on campus, and then were walked to our car.

And as we bid farewell to old BJU, we realized that we had learned something, not just about Bob Jones University, but about ourselves. We'd come to Bob Jones expecting to encounter racist, intolerant homophobes. Instead, we found people who were welcoming, friendly, and extremely nice. A little weird, yes. And no doubt homophobic. But well-meaning. Kind of.

More important, we learned that while we were happy that we had successfully executed our ruse and relieved it had worked on Gerald, it was not something we were particularly proud of. Yes, we got a good story out of it. But while there's a certain subversive thrill in deceiving people, it also left us with an unsettled feeling in our stomachs that a trip to the Waffle House only exacerbated. It made us wonder what kind of person can lie like that every day of his life. How do the lying liars do it?

In a way, I was glad that R.J. had cut short our tour before I got up on one of those giant crosses. (Although if he hadn't, you'd be looking at a pretty cool picture right now.) I don't begrudge them their religion. Hell, I admire it. No, I don't. But it's their right to have it. Just as it's my inherent right to invade their privacy under false pretenses. No, it isn't.

Doug, Duane, R.J., and especially Gerald, when you finally read this—we're very sorry. Also, we stole some stuff from the gift shop. No, we didn't.

Yes, we did.

No, we didn't. We're not crooks.

# Thank God for Jerry Falwell

**As** you can imagine, it was hard for me to do my job after 9/11. I'm a comedian, and there wasn't much to laugh about.

Thank God for Jerry Falwell. On 9/13, Falwell went on Pat Robertson's *700 Club* and blamed certain Americans for the events of that horrible day. Americans like me, and probably like you.

Falwell was widely criticized for his remarks. He said he was quoted out of context. So, I did a LexisNexis search and got the exact transcript.

> I really believe that the pagans and the abortionists and the feminists and the gays and the lesbians who are actively trying to make that an alternative lifestyle, the ACLU, People for the American Way—all of them who have tried to secularize America—I point the finger in their face, and say, "you helped this happen."

To which Robertson responded: "Well, I totally concur."

Now, the only way I figure that could have been taken out of context is if it had been immediately preceded with, "I'd have to be a fucking nut to say . . ."

And by the way, Falwell and Robertson are kind of nuts. I know that's rough, but I think I can prove it.

In early 1999, just as the whole millennium fervor was beginning, Jerry Falwell felt it was important to go on television and announce that the Antichrist was alive and was a male Jew.

As a male Jew, I was, of course, curious about who it was. I knew it wasn't me. Fortunately, a few months later I was on Geraldo Rivera's show *Rivera Live* with the Reverend Falwell. The subject of that evening's program was not the identity of the Antichrist, but I couldn't help myself.

I said, "Reverend Falwell, you said earlier this year that you believe the Antichrist is alive and is a male Jew."

Falwell said, "The Antichrist is supposed to be the counterfeit Christ, and I think we'd all agree that Jesus was Jewish."

Of course, I nodded. Made perfect sense. "I was wondering who it is. Is it Marvin Hamlisch?"

Falwell said he didn't know whether or not the composer of "The Way We Were" and *A Chorus Line* was, in fact, the Antichrist. So Falwell's a nut.

Now over to Robertson. I don't know if you ever watch his show, *The 700 Club.* I still watch it every once in a while just to stay current. And when I do, the highlight is always when Pat does his faith healing. He'll say something like, "There's a woman in Ohio who's just been cured of her diverticulitis. Praise God!"

I watch that, and I think to myself, Pat Robertson doesn't think through everything he's saying. Think about it. Let's say for a minute that you're a woman in Dayton and you have diverticulitis. You turn on *The 700 Club* and you hear Pat Robertson say, "There's a woman in Ohio who's just been cured of her diverticulitis. Praise God!" And you think it's you!

Only, it's not you. It's a woman in Cincinnati. But you think it's you. So you eat a bowl of nuts. And you die!

See? That's why I don't think Pat Robertson thinks through everything he's saying. And frankly, it doesn't make any sense to me. I mean, if God can tell Pat Robertson that it's a *woman,* in *Ohio,* and it's *diverticulitis,* and *it's been cured*—why can't he tell Pat Robertson the woman's name? And her address? It makes no sense whatsoever.

So Falwell and Robertson are a little nuts, right? And what Falwell said was pretty disgusting. Everyone can agree on that. Even Robertson later apologized. He said he had been distracted by something in his earpiece and hadn't really been focusing on what was coming out of Falwell's mouth.

Ann Coulter wrote about this incident in *Slander.* So who did she go after? Walter Cronkite. The man she calls that "pious left-wing blowhard."

> In the wake of an attack on America committed by crazed fundamentalist Muslims, Walter Cronkite denounced Jerry Falwell. Falwell, it seems, had remarked that gay marriage and abortion on demand may not have warmed the heart of the Almighty. Cronkite proclaimed such a statement "the most abominable thing I've ever heard." Showing his renowned dispassion and critical thinking, this Martha's Vineyard millionaire commented that Falwell was "worshipping the same God as the people who bombed the World Trade Center and the Pentagon" (the difference being liberals urged compassion and understanding toward the terrorists).

Just another small taste of poison from *Slander*. There's no further description of what Falwell had actually said, that he had pointed his finger and accused other Americans of causing the deaths of three thousand people. Mentioning that would have blown another chance to distort and spew.

She also does a lot of spewing in Chapter Nine, "Shadowboxing the Apocryphal 'Religious Right.'" The whole chapter is devoted to denying the existence of the religious right in this country except insofar as it is a "boogeyman" for the left. The "Religious Right," she claims, is "a meaningless concept," "an inverted construct of the left's own Marquis de Sade lifestyle."

First of all, on this Marquis de Sade lifestyle. I've been married twenty-seven years, have two kids who've turned out fairly well, and a wife who runs my life. Ann, on the other hand, is forty-something, has never been married, and has the personality of a dominatrix. Who's kidding who?

Secondly, if Coulter doesn't think the religious right exists, she should really get out more. I've been to Christian Coalition events, and there are a lot of people there.[1]

On its website, the Christian Coalition makes no bones about its existence. Specifically, it claims to be "the largest and most active conservative grassroots political organization in America." According to their website, the Christian Coalition has fifteen hundred local chapters around the country. During the 2000 election, they distributed more than seventy million "voter guides."

A perhaps more objective source on the strength of the Christian right than either Ann or the Christian Coalition is *Campaigns and Elections,* a Washington magazine. According to a study they published in February 2002, Christian conservatives now exercise either "strong" or "moderate" influence in forty-four Republican state committees—compared with thirty-one committees in 1994, the last time the survey was conducted. They are weak in only six states. Guess what region of the country all those states are in? If you said "the South," you'd be so wrong. No, those six states are in the Northeast.

The point is, they're big and they're growing.

Ralph Reed, the former Christian Coalition executive director, is now chair of the Georgia Republican party and probably the second most powerful Republican operative outside the White House. The most powerful is Grover Norquist, head of Americans for Tax Reform, who once declared, "I don't want to abolish gov-

---

¹The only time I've ever been assaulted was at the Christian Coalition's "Road to Victory" celebration in D.C. in 1996. I'll explain. When Ralph Reed introduced William Bennett, Reed assailed then Surgeon General Joycelyn Elders for "advocating the legalization of drugs," something she had most certainly not done. At a National Press Club luncheon, in response to a question about whether the legalization of drugs might reduce violence, Elders responded that it should be studied. I'd seen Reed do this a number of times when introducing Bennett, because at one time Bennett had been drug czar. Bennett got up to the podium and said about Bill Clinton, "We don't have a president who understands what truth is." After Bennett spoke, I approached him and said, "Bill, I've seen Ralph Reed introduce you several times, and he always says 'Joycelyn Elders advocated the legalization of drugs.' And you've never corrected him. Why do you hold Ralph Reed to such a low standard?" Bennett literally harrumphed for a few seconds, and then a large Christian *shoved* me as hard as he could. Let me just say, however, that most of the Christians at these events are extremely nice. And let me also say that Bill O'Reilly repeats this lie about Joycelyn Elders on page 21 of the paperback edition of *The No Spin Zone:* "She advocates the legalization of hard drugs as way to 'reduce the crime rate.' "

ernment. I simply want to reduce it to the size where I can drag it into the bathroom and drown it in the bathtub." Tough talk, Grover. But not very Christian-sounding talk.

Bush has managed to form a coalition between Christian conservatives like Reed and mean antigovernment conservatives like Norquist. And hawkish Jewish neo-conservatives. The neo-cons and the Christian Right have formed a close bond on Israel. Though for slightly different reasons. Neo-cons support the Jewish state for the same reasons I do: because it is the only democracy in the region, and because they're Jewish. Evangelical Christians fervently support the survival of Israel in order to fulfill the prophecy of the Second Coming, which, of course, will lead to the fiery death of all Jews. At that point, Bush's coalition will collapse.

During Bush's first campaign for governor of Texas, he told an Austin reporter that only people who accepted Jesus Christ as their savior could go to heaven. While most of the press felt it was a gaffe, Rove knew it was the best thing his candidate had said so far. It let the people who like to exclude others from heaven know that he was one of them. That's why, in 2000, they kicked off South Carolina at Bob Jones University.

Rove likes to point out that four million Christian conservatives who voted in 1994 failed to vote in 2000. In a close political campaign, four million votes can mean the difference between winning and losing. That's why one of Bush's first acts as president was to cut off money for international family planning organizations that even mention abortions. And that's why Bush imposed restrictions on funding stem cell research, impeding the search for cures for Alzheimer's, Parkinson's, multiple sclerosis, and Lou Gehrig's disease, and in the process misleading everyone on how many viable stem cell lines existed. He said there were over sixty; there are fewer than ten.

It is why he is pushing abstinence-only sex education, which does more to prevent condom use than to prevent sex. It's why he appointed Dr. David Hager, an obstetrician/gynecologist who opposes prescribing contraceptives to single women, to chair the

Food and Drug Administration's panel on women's health policy. And it is why Bush continues to feed us his born-again story. Which I'm sure has some truth to it. But, Jesus, do you have to wear it on your sleeve?

And do we have to hear all this stuff about reading the Bible? Remember that conversation I had with Don Evans at the White House Correspondents Dinner where it became clear that he (and perhaps, by extension, Bush) had absorbed amazingly little from his Bible study boot camp? That story eerily parallels an excerpt from a January 2000 interview Bush did with Howard Fineman and Jonathan Alter of *Newsweek*.

At the time, the campaign had been making a big deal about Bush reading the Bible every day. So Fineman asked, "What Bible passage did you read this morning?"

At this point, according to Alter, Bush started "getting really peeved."

"You know something," Bush said, "I think you're trying to catch me as to whether or not I can remember where I was in the Bible . . . it's like that question when I was asked about tell me about Dean Acheson . . . I was asked that question because most of the press corps didn't think I read that book."[2]

Has Bush read the Bible? I'm sure he has. But from the little I know about the New Testament, Christ had a special place in his heart for the meek and the downtrodden. For the most publicly religious administration in memory, to me, anyway, this one seems the least Christian.

---

[2]The incident Bush was referring to is a funny one. In an early Republican presidential debate, Bush was asked what book he was reading. A biography of Dean Acheson (Truman's secretary of State), he answered. Twelve days later, in the next debate, moderator Judy Woodruff asked him what he had learned from the biography. Bush couldn't think of anything directly related to the life or work of Dean Acheson and went directly into his stump speech about how we have to be strong to keep the peace. When John McCain fielded his next question, he answered it quickly and used the rest of his time to talk in great detail about Acheson's role in the creation of NATO and the Marshall Plan.

# Abstinence Heroes

**President** Bush has pushed to fund abstinence-only sex education, saying that it is the only "surefire" way to prevent unwanted pregnancies, sexually transmitted diseases, and immoral, nasty, hot teen sex.

Abstinence, of course, does prevent all of these terrible things. Abstinence *education*, however, does not.

On a November 1999 *Meet the Press*, candidate Bush told Tim Russert, "The folks that are saying condom distribution is the best way to reduce teenage pregnancies obviously haven't looked at the statistics."

Interesting. Maybe he's referring to the statistics finding a huge decline in teenage pregnancy between 1990 and 1996. A study by the Alan Guttmacher Institute attributed 75 percent of that decline to increased use of contraception—the most frequently used being condoms. It's one of many studies that the American Medical Association, the National Institutes of Health, the Centers for Disease Control, the American Academy of Pediatrics, and the National Academy of Science's Institute of Medicine think about when they endorse comprehensive sex education. Comprehensive programs encourage abstinence, but also say that if you *do* have sex, you should use contraception.

Bush says that this "sends a contradictory message." He thinks that kids can't understand the message that abstinence is a good idea, but that if you do have sex, you should use birth control. I have two kids. I have to tell you, they find Bush's position more than a little patronizing. And honestly, I don't think there was ever a time when they were simultaneously too young to understand this concept, yet also physically old enough to have sex.

Brian Wilcox of the University of Nebraska looked at the statistics and found "mounting evidence" (that's right, he said "mounting evidence") that abstinence-only programs do not reduce pregnancies or sexually transmitted diseases. In fact, they may do more harm than good.

A Northern Kentucky University study showed that 61 percent of college undergraduates who had taken virginity pledges broke them—and were less likely to use condoms when they had sex for the first time than were those students who had never taken the pledge in the first place. By the way, my favorite part of the study was the finding that of those who did not break their virginity pledges, 55 percent had engaged in oral sex. The study did not explore the incidence of spooning.

A less interesting but more significant study by Peter Bearman and Hannah Bruckner at Columbia University found that students who had gone through "virginity pledge" programs were a third less likely to use contraceptives when they first had sex. A researcher explained that young people who have made a solemn pledge to God to remain chaste are less likely to carry condoms.

Bush might have gotten a clue from his term as governor of Texas, where he spent over $10 million on abstinence-only education. Texas has the forty-sixth-worst teen pregnancy rate in the country. While he was governor and Bill Clinton was president, teen birth rates went down throughout the country. But if you look at how much each state improved, Texas was ranked second to last.

Now, many people would look at all these statistics and conclude that it's time to stop funding abstinence-only education. I don't agree. I think the problem is not the programs themselves, but our cultural climate. TV and movies glorify sex. The cast members of *Friends* hop in and out of bed with one another. And just look at the Internet. There are whole websites devoted to *Friends*!

There's one way to make these abstinence-only programs work. We need to change the whole culture. We need to show these sex-crazed, hard-bodied teens that it's "cool" to be a virgin. And that's why I have sent the following letter to twenty-seven of our nation's most respected public figures.

Here's a copy of the one I sent to Attorney General Ashcroft.

April 21, 2003

Attorney General John Ashcroft
U.S. Department of Justice
950 Pennsylvania Avenue, N.W.
Washington, D.C. 20530-0001

Dear Attorney General Ashcroft,

  I am currently a Fellow at Harvard's Kennedy
School of Government, where I am working on a book
about abstinence programs in our public schools entitled, <u>Savin' It!</u>

  In these days of rampant immorality, unwanted
pregnancies, and dangerous sexual diseases, <u>Savin'
It!</u> will document how the Bush administration is
championing abstinence programs and setting the
right example for America's youth.

  The book's fourth chapter, "Role Modelin' It!",
will feature the personal stories of abstinence heroes for our nation's young people to emulate.
Isn't it about time for our young people to have a
chance to look up to leaders who truly walked the
walk—instead of just talking the talk—by not having
sex until they were married?

  I would very much appreciate it if you could
share your abstinence story. So far, I have
received wonderful testimonies from HHS Secretary
Tommy Thompson, William J. Bennett, White House
Press Secretary Ari Fleischer, Cardinal Egan,
Senator Rick Santorum, and National Security Advi-

sor Condoleezza Rice. (I'm still hoping to hear
back from the President!)

I have found that kids respond best to total
honesty. Don't be afraid to share a moment when you
were tempted to have sex, but were able to overcome
your urges through willpower and strength of character. Be funny! Did a young woman ever think you
were homosexual just because you wouldn't have sex
with her? Be serious! Were you ever taunted and
made to feel bad or "uncool" because of your
choice? But most of all, be real. Kids can sense a
phony a mile away.

I can tell by your passionate advocacy of
abstinence education that you will have a lot to
offer this book. Thank you for considering my project. I hope you can find time to inspire the next
generation of sex-free leaders.

Sincerely,

Al Franken

# Abstinence Heroes II

My letter went out to:

| | | |
|---|---|---|
| William J. Bennett | President George W. Bush | Rick Santorum |
| Ralph Reed | Condoleezza Rice | Bill Frist |
| Pat Robertson | Donald Rumsfeld | Roy Blunt |
| Tommy Thompson | Cardinal Edward Egan | Dennis Hastert |
| Rod Paige | Tom DeLay | Sean Hannity |
| Andrew Card | Newt Gingrich | James Dobson |
| Dick and Lynn Cheney | John Ashcroft | Ari Fleischer |
| Trent Lott | Don Nichols | Karl Rove |
| Arlen Specter | Phyllis Schlafly | General Norman Schwarzkopf |

Although I received a few polite regrets, no one had an abstinence story to share with the readers of *Savin' It!* Also, I got in trouble for using Harvard letterhead.

# "By Far the Vast Majority of My Tax Cuts Go to Those at the Bottom"

**You'll** remember from Chapter One that in the first debate with Gore then candidate Bush said of his tax cuts, "By far the vast majority of the help goes to those at the bottom end of the economic ladder." In the South Carolina primary debate with John McCain he said, "By far the vast majority of my tax cuts go to those at the bottom end of the spectrum." As you can see, he loved this line. He repeated versions of it everywhere.

Shall we parse this statement? Let's start at the end and work backward. "Bottom end of the spectrum." What's that gotta mean? At least the bottom 50 percent, right? Otherwise, the word "bottom" in this context is meaningless. He couldn't have meant the bottom 99 percent, could he? That would just be crazy.

How about "majority"? Well, that's unambiguous. It means more than 50 percent. So, so far, at the very least, the bottom half of the American people are getting 50 percent, plus a dollar, of Bush's tax cut.

Now let's add "vast." "Vast majority." "Vast" is big. Huge. Like the "vast" reaches of space. Very, very big. So, what's a "*vast* majority?" 90 percent? 85? It's subjective, I admit. So let's go with a very conservative 70 percent. At this point in our parsing, the bottom 50 percent are getting 70 (give or take) percent of Bush's tax cut.

But wait. It's not just a "vast majority." It's *by far* a vast majority. Okay, let's think about that. What does "by far" mean? When you say a restaurant is "by far" the best steak house in town, you're really saying something. When you tell your spouse that sex with her or him is "by far" the best sex you've ever had, you may not be telling the truth—much in the same way that Bush wasn't in this case—but you are definitely trying to score some points. So

I'm going to say that "*by far* the vast majority of my tax cuts go to those at the bottom" would mean that the poorest 50 percent were getting somewhere in the neighborhood of 85 to 99 percent of Bush's tax cut.

That's fair, right? That's a fair parsing.

As I said before, the bottom 60 percent got 14.7 percent of that tax cut.

**O**n the *Hannity and Colmes* episode immediately following the last State of the Union address, Sean Hannity described the President's 2003 tax plan (which contained Bush's third tax cut) in his confident, unequivocal way: "Ninety-two million Americans will get $1,100 back in their pocket."

Of course, he was lying. Or was he? Maybe he was just confused. Sean may be evil, but he's not smart. I don't dispute that ninety-two million Americans were getting an *average* tax cut of $1,083. It's not the seventeen bucks I'm quibbling about. It's the *average* part. Hannity had left that out. Averages can be tricky. You and Bill Gates probably have an average net worth of $32 billion. My daughter and I have an average gender of half-male, half-female. My daughter, my *wife,* and I have an average gender of female.

In fact, less than twenty-five million Americans would be receiving a tax cut of $1,100 or more. Sixty-two million taxpayers would be getting tax cuts of less than a thousand dollars—averaging about $302. And fifty million households would get no tax cut at all.

Colmes's next comment on that show was "Peggy [Noonan], thank you for being with us."

**P**ersonally, I think the President, like most Americans, is smarter than Sean Hannity. So when Bush, who, after all, is President of the United States, repeatedly says something that isn't true, it's not confusion. It's a lie.

Take these remarks by the President at a 2001 "Tax Family Event," in which he introduced America to the Yahngs. Talking about his first tax plan, the President of the United States said,

> It is a plan that significantly reduces taxes for people at the bottom end of the economic ladder. If you're a family of four making $35,000, you'll receive a one hundred percent tax cut. It's an average tax relief for families of $1,600. The Yahng family under the plan I submit will receive actually more than that. They now pay $2,000 in taxes to the federal government. If this plan is enacted by the United States Congress, they'll end up paying $150 of taxes.

There are actually four lies crammed into this little paragraph. Lie #1 is the "one hundred percent tax cut" part of the second sentence. The President could have told the truth by saying, "one hundred percent *income* tax cut." You see, a family of four making $35,000 pays, on average, $5,355 in payroll taxes.[1] Seventy-four percent of Americans pay more in payroll taxes than in income taxes, so this is kind of important. Especially if you're "at the bottom end of the economic ladder."

Lie #2 is tricky, because the "average tax relief for families of $1,600" is technically accurate in the same way that it is accurate to say his 2003 plan would give families an average tax cut of $1,083. But in the previous sentence, he said, "if you're a family of four making $35,000," so I'm calling this a "sleight of hand" lie. If you don't want to count it, fine. I respect that.

Lie #3 is "They now pay $2,000 in taxes to the federal government." Again, he's forgetting (or, rather, omitting) their payroll tax. Lie #4—"They'll end up paying $150 of taxes"—comes from the same dishonest non-payroll-tax-acknowledging place in Bush's soul.

You may remember that, during the 2000 campaign, Bush held

---

[1] Like the Heritage Foundation and every other conservative think tank does when it computes tax burdens, I am including here the employer's portion of the payroll tax.

quite a few of these Tax Family Events to deflect criticism that his plan was a giant giveaway to the wealthy.

The first few of these events with "working families" (Coulter's "families in which no one works") were disasters. After each one, the Gore campaign issued a press release showing how the working family would actually receive a larger cut under Gore's plan.

After a number of embarrassments, the Bush campaign realized it needed to take greater care in choosing its families. An e-mail sent out by the campaign to New Mexico Republicans seeking such a family laid out the criteria. A suitable family must make between $35,000 and $70,000, itemize its taxes, have no children in day care, no children in college, no one attending night school, no children younger than age one, and no substantial savings outside of 401(k).

No children in college? No one in night school? No children under one? No savings? Talk about living the American dream!

These highly selective criteria eliminated 85 percent of all couples in the income range. The 85 percent would have done better under the Gore tax plan. We can fairly conclude that a "vast majority" if not "*by far* a vast majority" of middle-income American families of four would be paying less taxes today if Gore had been inaugurated.

Rather than offering up an illuminating case of Mr. and Mrs. Joe Average, the Bush campaign was casting a political freak show in order to present a tiny minority as the norm.

The Bush campaign, however, would have had no problem finding families of four making between $350,000 and $700,000 who got a bigger tax cut under Bush's plan than under Gore's. In that income range, they all did.

---

There's a new sheriff in town, and he's dedicated to fiscal discipline.

—Ari Fleischer, of President George W. Bush,
October 18, 2002

The rationale for Bush's tax cuts was that, with a $4.6 trillion projected surplus, "I think it's fair, I think it's right that one quarter of the surplus go back to the people who pay the bills." (Not to quibble, but his tax cut was more than a *third* of the surplus. He was $450 billion off, enough to pay for all nonmilitary discretionary spending for a year.)

So, when we were expecting huge surpluses, Bush argued that it was our money, and if the government was taking more than it needed, we deserved to get some of it back. Specifically, we needed a $1.6 trillion tax cut, heavily tilted toward the wealthy.

But once evidence began to emerge that the economy was sputtering and the surplus was shrinking, this rationale no longer applied. There were new economic problems that needed new solutions. How could the economy be jump-started? Bush met with his top economic advisors and came back with an innovative answer: a $1.6 trillion tax cut, heavily tilted toward the wealthy.

It soon became apparent that we were headed back to deficit country. How would America's new fiscal discipline sheriff explain to the nation that he'd have to break his campaign promise never to go into deficit? The answer came on September 11, when terrorists struck the World Trade Center and the Pentagon, creating a national emergency and necessitating a war.

Not only did the tragedy provide a justification for deficit spending, it gave Bush a reliable laugh line for his speeches. Here's the joke. This is from a June 7, 2002, speech in Iowa. But he's told it on at least thirteen different occasions.

> I remember campaigning in Chicago and one of the reporters said, "Would you ever deficit spend?" I said, "Only—only—in times of war, in times of economic insecurity as a result of a recession, or in times of national emergency." Never did I dream we'd have a trifecta.

It got a laugh in Iowa. And a laugh in Georgia when he campaigned for Saxby Chambliss. It killed in Texas when he campaigned for gubernatorial candidate Rick Perry. They loved it at the Simon for Governor luncheon in Santa Clara. And he got laughter *and* applause at a meeting of the leaders of the Fiscal Responsibility Coalition in our nation's capital.

To me the joke itself is not as funny as the fact that it's based on a lie. He never said he'd allow a deficit "only in times of war, in times of economic insecurity as a result of a recession, or in times of national emergency." He'd never said anything remotely like it during the campaign. On June 9, 2002, Tim Russert interviewed Budget Director Mitch Daniels on *Meet the Press.*

> **RUSSERT:** Now, we have checked everywhere and we've even called the White House as to when the President said that when he was campaigning in Chicago, and it didn't happen. The closest he came was when he was asked, "Would you give up part of your tax cut in order to ensure a balanced budget?" And he said, "No." But no one ever talked about a war, a recession, and an emergency, the trifecta.

Daniels responded that he was not "the White House librarian," so he didn't have a record of Bush saying this during the campaign. A few weeks later, Russert told me that he'd heard that Ari Fleischer was hopping mad the following Monday morning and wanted to "go after Russert" for questioning Bush's credibility. Apparently, Karl Rove then took Fleischer aside and explained that they might want to let this one slide.[2]

Even after Russert exposed the lie, Bush continued to tell it.

**S**o now we have record deficits. But the good news is that, just as Bush promised, the 2001 and 2002 tax cuts have provided such a

---

[2]Funnily enough, one candidate *had* said something about a war, or a recession, or a national emergency being an acceptable reason for running a deficit. It wasn't Bush, though. Or Nader. It was Al Gore, who said at the Economic Club of Detroit on May 8, 1998: "Barring an economic reversal, a national emergency, or a foreign crisis, we should balance the budget this year, next year, and every year."

terrific stimulus to our economy that Congress passed another huge one in 2003.

Seriously, though, we have lost three million jobs in this country in the last two and a half years. It's gotten so bad it's even affected the children of semi-celebrities, who are usually immune to economic ups and downs. My daughter, Thomasin, just graduated from college, and she lost seventeen of those three million jobs. Four at Bear Stearns, two in the nonprofit sector, and one, ironically, in a job placement agency.[3]

I am a nut for statistics. Because numbers don't lie. Here's one that I think is particularly telling. During the six-plus years that the two Bushes have been president, there has not been one new net job created. Not one. Extrapolating from that, if the Bushes had run this country from its very inception to the present day, not a single American would have ever worked.

The idea that tax cuts for those at the very top will stimulate job creation is called supply-side, trickle-down, or "voodoo" economics. The concept is simple. By giving those at the top, who are, in theory, the most productive Americans, a tax break, you will motivate them to work even harder and create more wealth, more jobs, and a bigger pie for everyone.

That reasoning explains why, when Bill Clinton wanted to raise taxes on the top 1 percent in 1993 to deal with the then-record deficit, Republicans said his plan would cause a recession. Here's a sampling.

> I believe this will lead to a recession next year. This is the Democrat machine's recession, and each one of them will be held personally accountable.
>
> —Newt Gingrich, August 5, 1993

[3]Actually, she's an elementary school teacher in the Bronx, which I think is great. Though, given the state of the New York City economy, risky.

> The Clinton plan is a one-way ticket to recession. This plan does not reduce the deficit . . . but it raises taxes and it puts people out of work.
>
> Senator Phil Gramm, July 28, 1993

> This plan will not work. If it was to work then I'd have to become a Democrat and believe that more taxes and bigger government is the answer.
>
> Representative John Kasich, R-OH[4]
>
> July 28, 1993

So every Republican in Congress voted against Clinton's Deficit Reduction Act. It passed in both houses by one vote. (Gore broke the tie in the Senate.) The next eight years saw the longest period of economic growth in American history. Also, bolstered by the U.S., most of the world experienced an economic boom.

It's taken as gospel by conservatives that everyone will work harder when they're paying a 33 percent marginal tax rate than when they are paying a 39.6 percent rate. I heard Rush Limbaugh make a point that attempted to illustrate their logic. He said that if we taxed people at a 100 percent marginal rate, the government would get no revenue because no one would work. And, for once, I had to agree with him. I think the marginal tax rate should be somewhere between zero and 100 percent.

Bush made a point that I didn't find quite as compelling in his acceptance speech at the 2000 Republican convention, the same speech in which he lied about the army divisions not being ready for duty. He said, "On principle, no one in America should have to pay more than a third of their income to the federal government."

The crowd went nuts.

It struck me as odd that there would exist *on principle* such a specific number for the optimum top marginal rate. And that this

[4]Kasich, who is now presumably a Democrat, is substitute host on *The O'Reilly Factor.* Who says they aren't fair and balanced?

principle would somehow apply to every economic circumstance. I also thought it was lucky for Bush that this specific number was one third, rather than a messier or more complicated fraction. What if the Heritage Foundation had determined that the perfect top marginal rate was something slightly smaller than one third? Would Bush have gotten as rousing a cheer if he had said, "On principle, no one in America should have to pay more than nine twenty-ninths of their income to the federal government!"? Or worse, what if the optimum marginal rate were an irrational number, which cannot be expressed as a fraction?[5] How many digits beyond the decimal point would Bush have been willing to go?

No. I think the one third was actually kind of arbitrary. Also, I think people were cheering—not because of the principle of the thing—but because of the extra money they knew they'd be getting if Bush won.

Someone who seems to buy heavily into the supply-side ethos is my friend Bill O'Reilly. On his January 14, 2003, *Factor,* O'Reilly explained, in his typically modest way, how an increase in income taxes would cause him to fire several of his employees. The explanation came in his Talking Points Memo segment of the show.

> As far as the economy is concerned, "Points" continues to believe that putting more money back into the hands of Americans who earn it will help private enterprise. Raising taxes and increasing government spending is a surefire way to continue the economic doldrums. I'll back up that statement with my own story. Right now, I'm a busy guy, with TV, radio, books, a syndicated column, and a website. There are scores of people working with me, people who are making money and supporting their families. As I have mentioned, when my tax obligation is all added up, the government takes a bit more than 50 cents of every dollar

[5]Examples include $\pi$ or $\sqrt{2}$.

> I earn. And the Democrats want more. [I have no clue who he was talking about.] But I will tell you what. If my tax rate increases, I will cut back and do fewer things. It simply will not be worth my time, because I have enough money saved to live comfortably. I don't need to kill myself to pay the government. And if I do cut back, some of the people currently earning money under the *Factor* banner will stop earning that money.

The thought of O'Reilly cutting back is a frightening one. Not just for the employees he'd let go, and their families, who would suddenly have the wolf at their door. What scares me is the prospect that we could be deprived of thoughtful Talking Points like this one. Or that we'd see them only on TV, and not also get them on radio, in his syndicated column, and on his website. It's enough to make me want to fight for further tax cuts for the five-million-and-up bracket, even if it means that we'd have to cut back on Head Start and prenatal care for the poor.

It's also good to know that O'Reilly has enough money saved to live comfortably and that the only reason he's working so hard is pure greed.

In fairness, Bill is probably working extra hard so that his children can inherit enough money to live extravagantly without ever having to work or challenge themselves. That, of course, is every parent's dream.

And now, thanks to the visionary who coined the terrifying phrase "death tax" to describe the eminently reasonable estate tax, more Americans than ever will be able to see that dream come true. In 2001, Congress endorsed the deeply American idea of a permanent aristocracy by passing a phase-out, and eventual repeal, of the estate tax.

As Bush said in his acceptance speech: "On principle, every family, every farmer and small business person should be free to pass on their life's work to those they love. So we abolish the death tax."

By this "principle," every elementary school teacher should be able to pass on their life's work to the people they love. They should be able to pass on the lives they've touched, the children they've inspired, the futures they've changed. Logistically speaking, that would be hard to do. It is, however, easy to pass down money. As you can see, this principle breaks down very quickly.

Yes, a family farmer should be able to pass his farm down to his children. Fortunately, that hasn't been a problem. As the law existed before Bush took office, family farms had a $2.6 million exemption. For family farms worth more than $2.6 million, the heirs had a grace period of up to fourteen years to pay the tax bill at low interest rates. The fact is that neither *The New York Times* nor the American Farm Bureau Federation could find a single family farm that has ever been lost to the estate tax.

That didn't stop the Republicans from running extremely ugly ads about the issue in both the 2000 and the 2002 campaigns. My favorite was this radio spot run against Paul Wellstone in Minnesota:

60 SECOND SPOT: DEATH TAX

SOUND EFFECTS: SOUND OF FARM IMPLEMENTS. CHICKENS CLUCKING, COWS MOOING.

RUTH
Lloyd? We just got a letter from the IRS!

LLOYD
Ruth, what's wrong?

RUTH
They say we owe more taxes!

LLOYD
Bull! Dad always paid his taxes, even in the worst of times.

> RUTH
>
> We owe taxes 'cause he died?
>
> LLOYD
>
> He paid taxes when he worked! He paid taxes
> on this land, now he dies, and he has to pay—
> *more?* Who the hell thought up that doozy?
>
> RUTH
>
> Senator Wellstone just voted to keep the death
> tax.
>
> LLOYD
>
> Paul Wellstone actually voted to tax people
> 'cause they died?
>
> RUTH
>
> What's going to happen?
>
> LLOYD
>
> We're going to have to sell the farm.
>
> RUTH
>
> No, Lloyd, we're going to call Paul Wellstone
> and tell him our folks paid their fair share. And
> to keep his money-grubbing hands off our farm.
>
> ANNOUNCER (V.O.)
>
> Call Paul Wellstone. Tell him to protect small
> business and family farms, and to stop taxing
> the dead. Paid for by Americans for Job
> Security.

Wellstone *had* voted against the full repeal of the estate tax. But he
had also voted to exempt family farms and small businesses, and to
exempt all other estates up to $8 million. You know, if anyone
hated the small farmer, or, in fact, the little guy in general, it was

Paul "Moneygrubber" Wellstone. That's why they had to plant the crowd for his memorial.

Bush used the death tax issue in practically every stump speech he gave, lamenting the devastation it visited on family farmers and small business owners. The Republicans pushed the estate tax repeal as a middle-class tax-relief issue. With some success. Seventeen percent of Americans thought the estate tax would apply to them. In fact, the tax affects less than 2 percent of estates—and nearly half of the revenue it produces comes from taxes on 0.16 percent of estates, worth an average of $17 million, belonging to about 3,300 families each year. In 1999, fully a quarter of the estate tax revenue came from just 467 estates. As David Brooks, who works at the *Weekly Standard* but is nonetheless a terrific guy, wrote in *The New York Times,* the estate tax is "explicitly for the mega-upper class."

Bush has said that it is immoral to tax people when they die. Since we are currently experiencing a $450 billion deficit, the amount of the revenue being lost by the phase-out and eventual repeal of the estate tax will have to be made up by taxes on you and me. It is arguably more moral to tax an incredibly rich person who is dead than a middle- or working-class person who is still alive. The living person might use the money for medical care, food, travel, or other things that dead rich people don't have to think about.

The other bogus argument put forth by opponents of the estate tax is that it amounts to "double taxation." The idea is that you pay taxes as you accumulate your fortune, and then your children have to pay taxes on it again when you die. There are two problems with this argument. First, everyone pays double taxes all the time. Sales taxes, for example, are taxes on already-taxed income. Fees on things like your driver's license, a fishing license, a hunting license, and other licenses—that's all double taxation. Also fees on things that aren't licenses. Like permits. Let's say you want to open a business selling licenses. You need a license permit! That's triple taxation. I think.

Import taxes, excise taxes, bridge tolls, car registration, taxes on alcohol, gasoline, and tobacco are all double taxes. So are property taxes, which tax assets bought with already taxed income.

However, the repeal of the estate tax will create a way to avoid not just double taxation, but also single taxation. Here's how to do it. Buy an enormous amount of stock or property. Let it accumulate value. Die. Now the money goes to your kids, who escape both estate *and* capital gains taxes. Thanks to Bush, by 2010, only one thing will be certain in life. And that thing is either death, or taxes.

This new tax loophole is not a trivial matter. For estates worth more than $10 million, over 56 percent of their value comes from unrealized capital gains. Capital gains come from money making money without anyone actually working. Thus, our nation's most generous tax laws will now apply to the children of the very rich inheriting money even their parents didn't earn.

Instead of giving $60 billion a year[6] to our country's heirs and heiresses, we could be paying for things like after-school programs, schools on military bases, child vaccinations in Third World countries, prosecution of polluters, health care for veterans—all things which Bush has cut.

Take your pick. Which is more important? Making sure that Ivanka Trump will be able to live in the style to which she's grown accustomed even after The Donald has left our world? Or making sure that little Ivanka Average can go to a school that has toilet paper in the bathrooms?

Funny thing happened at the end of the Senate debate on this issue. Republicans, who knew they had the votes to win, kept spouting off about family farms and small businesses. So the Democrats gave them a chance to prove their sincerity. Instead of abolishing the estate tax altogether, how about exempting the first $4 million per couple? Nope. How 'bout the first $8 million? Sorry.

[6]That's what the yield would be in 2011 if the tax were in place.

Okay. Then how about this? Russ Feingold, Democrat of Wisconsin, offered an amendment that would exempt the first *one hundred million dollars* of a couple's net worth before a penny of estate taxes were paid. This would exempt all "family farms" and "small businesses" worth less than $100 million.

The amendment went down 48–51.[7]

In all this talk, one thing that gets lost is that there are forty-two million working Americans who have not gotten one cent in tax cuts. The *Wall Street Journal* refers to them as "lucky duckies" because they earn so little that they don't pay any income taxes. Many lucky duckies are deeply in debt to predatory lenders. Many of these lucky duckies couldn't afford college and cannot afford health insurance. Some of these lucky duckies, working Americans, will be homeless sometime during the year. Their children, the lucky ducklings, are far more likely than my kids, or Paul Gigot's, to be killed violently or die of a preventable disease.

Apparently, the *Wall Street Journal* thinks that the unluckiest thing in the world is paying taxes.

That's why they have been such vociferous supporters of the Bush tax cuts, more than half of which will eventually go to the top 1 percent of families.

> **Are You in the Top 1% of Earners?**
>
> 19% of Americans say "yes!"

In the last thirty years, those families saw their after-tax incomes rise 157 percent. The top one percent have incomes starting at $230,000. Their share of the national income has doubled, and is now as large as the combined income of the bottom 40 percent. The

---

[7]Kudos to Republicans who voted for the Feingold amendment: Chafee, Collins, Hutchison, McCain, Snowe, and Specter. Huge raspberries to the Democrats who crossed over: Baucus, Breaux, Cleland, Lincoln, Miller, Nelson of Florida, Nelson of Nebraska, and Wyden. Semi-kudos to Stevens of Alaska who did not vote.

thirteen thousand families at the very top have almost as much income as the poorest twenty million households in America, which is like the population of Bemidji, Minnesota, (home of Paul Bunyan) having more income than the country's six largest cities—New York City, Los Angeles, Chicago, Houston, Philadelphia, and Phoenix—combined.

You know who I think the real lucky duckies are? The residents of Bemidji, Minnesota. I mean the ones in my analogy. So why are they the ones getting the sweetest deal from the tax cuts?

**A**nytime a liberal points out that the wealthy are disproportionately benefiting from Bush's tax policies, Republicans shout, "class warfare!"

In her book *A Distant Mirror: The Calamitous Fourteenth Century*, Barbara Tuchman writes about a peasant revolt in 1358 that began in the village of St. Leu and spread throughout the Oise Valley. At one estate, the serfs sacked the manor house, killed the knight, and roasted him on a spit in front of his wife and kids. Then, after ten or twelve peasants violated the lady, with the children still watching, they forced her to eat the roasted flesh of her husband and then killed her.

*That* is class warfare.

Arguing over the optimum marginal tax rate for the top one percent is not.

# The Waitress and the Lawyer: A One-Act Play

**In** a radio address on February 3, 2001, President Bush said:

> Picture a diner in one of our cities. At the table is a lawyer with two children. She earns $250,000 a year. Carrying her coffee and toast is a waitress who has two children of her own. She earns $25,000 a year. If both the lawyer and the waitress get a raise, it is the waitress who winds up paying a higher marginal tax rate. She will give back almost half of every extra dollar she earns to the government.
>
> Both of these women, the lawyer and the waitress, deserve a tax cut. Under my plan, both of these women, and all Americans who pay taxes, will get one. For the waitress, our plan will wipe out her income tax bill entirely.

On May 30, 2003, Al Franken's *The Waitress and the Lawyer* was presented at the Belasco Theater in New York. It was directed by Mike Nichols, with the following cast:

| | |
|---|---|
| DONNA | Drew Barrymore |
| ALLISON | Helen Hunt |
| URBAN COWBOY | Brian Dennehy |

Scenery and lighting by Alex Jones, costumes by Edie Holway. The action of the play takes place in a diner in Houston, Texas, on April 14, 2003. It was performed without intermission.

The Waitress and the Lawyer
A One-Act Play

by Al Franken
(from an idea by George W. Bush)

---

*Set: A clean, well-lit diner. It's eleven at night.* ALLISON, *a slim, well-dressed lawyer in her middle thirties, sets herself down at the counter.* DONNA, *a plump waitress in her late twenties, approaches with a pot of coffee and a friendly smile.*

**DONNA:** Can I help you, sug?

**ALLISON:** Yes, please. Double cappuccino and a biscotti.

**DONNA:** Sorry. How 'bout coffee and a slice a pie?

**ALLISON:** No pie for me. I'm on a diet.

**DONNA:** You, on a diet! If I had your figure, I'd have pie for breakfast, lunch, and dinner.

*(They share a laugh.)*

**ALLISON:** Oh, what the hell! That lemon meringue looks great. Besides, it's gonna be a long night.

**DONNA:** You workin' the night shift, too?

**ALLISON:** Well, in a manner of speaking. I'm a tax attorney and April's my busiest month.

**DONNA:** Well, don't look for any business from me. Thanks to President Bush, I won't be paying any taxes this year.

*(*ALLISON *laughs as* DONNA *pours her a cup of joe.)*

**ALLISON:** You mean *income* taxes, Donna? Do you mind if I call you Donna? I read your name tag.

**DONNA:** Sure, sug.

**ALLISON:** Donna, how much do you make?

**DONNA:** Well . . .

**ALLISON:** C'mon, just between us gals.

**DONNA:** Twenty-five thousand.

**ALLISON:** Wow. That puts you in the top 10 percent of all waitresses. And how much in tips?

**DONNA:** That's *including* tips. I report every cent. In this country, if you play by the rules and work hard, you can make a better life for yourself.

(ALLISON *laughs again, spraying her coffee all over the counter.*)

**ALLISON:** I'm so sorry.

**DONNA:** Don't worry about it, sug. I'll wipe that up. But what's so funny?

**ALLISON:** It's just that what you said is so sweet and naive. Sure, you're getting a $365 cut in your income tax, but you're forgetting the $3,825 that was withheld in payroll taxes.

**DONNA:** Oh, I don't mind the payroll taxes, because I'll get back every cent in Social Security and Medicare when I retire.

**ALLISON:** Honey. Bush raided the Social Security and Medicare trust funds to pay for *my* tax cut.

**DONNA:** He did?

**ALLISON:** Yes. He took a $4.6 trillion ten-year projected surplus and turned it into a $1.8 trillion deficit. Let me show you what I'm talking about.

(ALLISON *empties the salt shaker onto the counter.*)

**ALLISON:** Let's say this pile of salt is the surplus that we had under Clinton. And . . .

(ALLISON *tears open a packet of sugar and pours it on the counter, as well.*)

**ALLISON:** And this pile of sugar represents the Bush defici—

(DONNA *eyes the growing mess, half listening.*)

**DONNA:** Would you mind not doing that?

**ALLISON:** Sorry. My point is that eventually someone is going to have to replace all that sugar in the packet and, well, clean up the mess. And I've got a feeling it's going to be you or your kids. You have kids?

(DONNA *starts cleaning up* ALLISON*'s mess.*)

**DONNA:** Two! Teddy's six. He has some learning disabilities, but he's the sweetest boy. And Debbi's two, and quite a handful, let me tell you. Especially for a single mom like me.

**ALLISON:** You know, I'm a single mom myself.

**DONNA:** No kidding!

(DONNA *stops cleaning up and leans forward to hear about* ALLISON*'s kids.*)

**ALLISON:** Yep. In fact, my oldest has a learning disability, too. Good thing I have him in private school, because the public schools are cutting back on special ed.

**DONNA:** Yeah, I know. They told me that next year Teddy's not getting special ed. Also, they're cutting the after-school program.

**ALLISON:** That's because Bush proposed cutting the Twenty-First Century Community Learning Centers by forty percent.

**DONNA:** Bush did that? Well, I still like him. Because he cut my taxes a *hundred* percent.

**ALLISON:** Yeah, but you only paid $365 in income taxes. That after-school program alone was spending $700 a student. So, in a sense, you're already down $335.

**DONNA:** You're good with numbers! No wonder you're a tax attorney.

**ALLISON:** But, you know, Donna, I'd be less worried about the after-school cuts, and more worried about losing your kids' health insurance. Here in Texas they're reducing eligibility in the SCHIP program from $30,520 down to $22,890.

**DONNA:** SCHIP? But that's how my kids get their Medicaid coverage.

**ALLISON:** Yes, you're losing—let's see, Medicaid coverage is worth . . . two kids—about $2,896 a year right there.

**DONNA:** Oh no! What if they get sick?

**ALLISON:** Just hope they don't. And you can blame George Bush. Because of the huge tax cut, the federal government can't fulfill its normal obligations to the states.

**DONNA:** Unfunded mandates.

**ALLISON:** Hey. You know the lingo.

**DONNA:** Yeah. We have Fox News on in here all the time. That's why I knew I was getting a hundred percent of my taxes cut.

**ALLISON:** Donna, mind if I ask you a personal question?

**DONNA:** If it's the recipe for the pie, no can do.

**ALLISON:** No, it's not the pie.

**DONNA:** Tell you the truth, we get it from a bakery.

**ALLISON:** Donna, do you live in subsidized housing?

**DONNA:** Why, yes. We get our Section 8 housing voucher in the mail every month.

**ALLISON:** Oh, dear. I'm afraid your Section 8 voucher is about to disappear. I'm guessing you live in a two-bedroom apartment with minimum amenities and rent in the fortieth percentile range—say, about $747 a month?

**DONNA:** That's right on target!

**ALLISON:** So your voucher is about $1,464 a year.

**DONNA:** Wow! If I ever have to pay taxes again, I'm coming straight to you.

**ALLISON:** Anyway, that's gone. So, let's see. After-school—$700. Medicaid—$2,896. Housing—$1,464. So, less your $365 tax cut, you're down $4,695.

**DONNA:** Well, Lord knows, I've been through hard times before. But as long as I have my child care, at least I can work without worrying about my kids. *(Pause)* What's that look?

**ALLISON:** Texas is getting less funding for its Temporary Assistance for Needy Families. So, they're cutting back on Child Care and Development Block Grants.

**DONNA:** But I don't get block grants.

**ALLISON:** Yeah. But your child care provider probably does. Or *did*, I should say.

*(Long pause.)*

**DONNA:** How's the pie?

**ALLISON:** Donna, how do you get to work?

**DONNA:** Are they doing somethin' to my bus?

**ALLISON:** Probably not. And that's the point. The state senate just cut public transit funding by 29 percent. They *were* going to upgrade the buses to cut down on the toxic emissions. Now they're keeping the old buses *and* raising the fares.

**DONNA:** Debbi does get asthma on bad smog days.

*(Long pause.)*

**ALLISON:** Pie's great.

*(Another long pause. In the background, we can hear SEAN HANNITY on the television.)*

**HANNITY** *(voice-over):* That's class warfare!

**LIBERAL GUEST** *(voice-over):* Sean, the top one percent are—

**HANNITY** *(voice-over):* I don't want to hear your talking points. Nearly four million Americans have been cut from the tax rolls!

*(The two women avoid each other's eyes. Finally DONNA raises the coffeepot.)*

**DONNA:** Can I top that off for ya?

**ALLISON:** No, thanks, Donna. I should get back to work.

**DONNA:** So, I take it you're not votin' for Bush next time.

**ALLISON:** Are you kidding? I make $250,000 a year. I love Bush.

**DONNA:** How big is your tax cut?

**ALLISON:** I'm gonna get $6,000. Which is about sixteen times as much as you. And, of course, the program cuts

**ALLISON:** (continued) don't affect me. But the big payoff comes when my mother passes away. She's on life support.

**DONNA:** I'm so sorry.

**ALLISON:** Are you kidding? If she can hang on till 2010, I'm getting $12 million. Tax free. That's about a six-million-dollar tax break.

**DONNA:** Oh, the repeal of the death tax. I saw that on Fox, too. I guess that's fair, because that money was already taxed once when it was earned.

**ALLISON:** My mom? Work? Oh, no no. It's mostly capital gains. Never been taxed, and now it never will be. Unlike your tips. Speaking of which, how much do I owe you?

**DONNA:** Well, let's see. They just raised the sales tax. I guess $4.87.

**ALLISON:** Change a fifty?

**DONNA:** Sure, darlin'.

(ALLISON *hands her a fifty.* DONNA *makes change.* ALLISON *gives her a ten.*)

**DONNA:** You don't have to do that.

**ALLISON:** Hey. We working moms gotta stick together, right?

(DONNA *smiles wanly.*)

**DONNA:** Right.

(ALLISON *gives her a wink, and she leaves, passing an* URBAN COWBOY, *who's just put a quarter in the jukebox.*)

*Music: "Cryin' Time"—George Jones and Tammy Wynette*

(DONNA *looks at the TV, then down at the half-cleaned-up piles of sugar and salt. Slowly she sweeps them into her palm, as the* URBAN COWBOY *sits down at the counter.*)

**DONNA:** Can I help ya, sug?

**COWBOY:** Just a cuppa joe, I guess. I just got laid off.

**DONNA:** Oh, I'm sorry to hear that. You work at the plant?

**COWBOY:** Naw. I'm a special ed teacher.

*(Curtain.)*

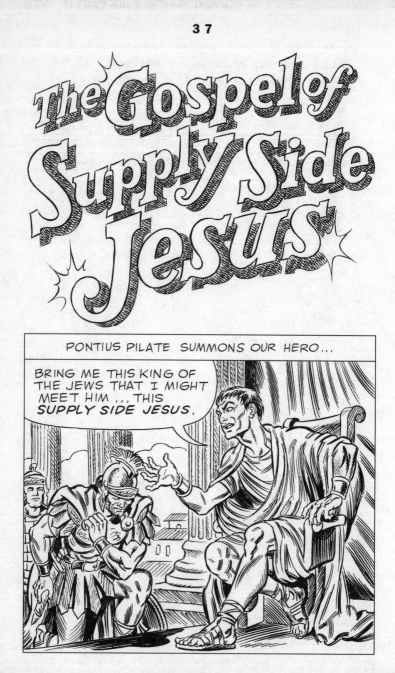

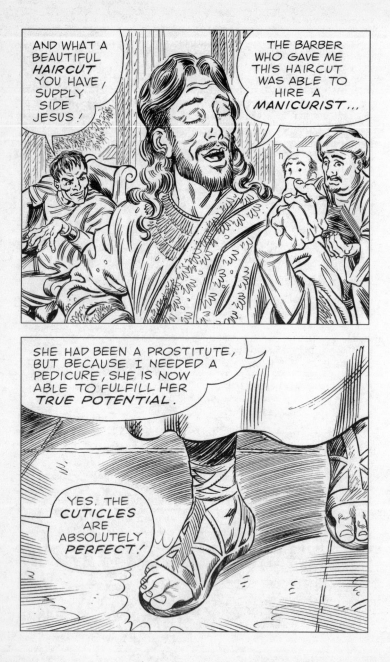

# I Challenge Rich Lowry to a Fight

**Rich** Lowry is an editor at the *National Review*. If you watch cable news, you've probably seen his head talking here or there, arguing the conservative position on some issue of the day. He's pretty young, I'd say about forty now. He's not bad, as these guys go. Fairly articulate. He even enjoyed a run as a semi-regular on *The NewsHour*.

One area where Lowry seems paleo-conservative, though, is in the realm of gender politics. When Massachusetts governor Jane Swift had twins, he called for her to step down. I agreed, but that was because she was a Republican.

As you may have figured out by now, I'm a bit of a C-SPAN junkie, and a couple of years ago, late at night, I caught Rich talking, I think, to some College Republicans. He was saying that Democrats had "feminized" politics. In fact, by making it okay for politicians to cry, Lowry said that we Democrats had "sissified" politics.

There seemed to be only one thing to do. The next day, I called the *National Review* and got Rich's direct line. I remember the conversation very clearly.

> RICH: Hello.
>
> ME: Rich, Al Franken. How do you do?
>
> RICH: Fine. To what do I owe the honor of your call?
>
> ME: Well, I saw you on C-SPAN last night talking about how we Democrats had sissified politics. So, I thought I'd challenge you to a fight.
>
> RICH: . . . A fight?

**ME:** Yeah. I figure the loser gives a thousand dollars to the winner's charity.

**RICH:** Where . . . where would we fight?

**ME:** In my parking garage.

**RICH:** Parking garage?

**ME:** Yeah.

**RICH:** What would the rules be?

**ME:** No rules. It's like *Fight Club*.

**RICH:** *Fight Club*?

**ME:** Yeah. No weapons or anything. The first to say "uncle" loses.

**RICH:** You want to fight me in a garage? With no rules?

**ME:** Yeah. If you win, I have to give to some nutty right-wing cause. If I win, you have to give to . . . I don't know, NARAL or Emily's List.

**RICH:** Can I ask you something?

**ME:** Sure.

**RICH:** Do you fight a lot?

**ME:** No, I have actually never been in a fight. But I wrestled in high school and I'm pretty confident I could beat you. Then again, I'm fifty and have a bad back. But I think I could take you. At any rate, I just don't want this "Democrats have sissified politics" to stand. So, I want to fight you.

**RICH:** Can I take a day or so to decide?

**ME:** Sure. Take your time. I just figured anyone who said that Democrats had sissified politics would kinda have to fight.

RICH: I understand. How about if I sleep on it?

ME: Absolutely. I'll call you tomorrow.

RICH: Okay, sure.

It was an extremely satisfying phone call. Sizing Lowry up on TV, he seemed just a tad on the wimpy side, which had only been confirmed by his reaction: terrified. I was just a decent high school wrestler, but I was convinced I could take him down, then basically punch his ears till he called "uncle."

Later that day, I happened to tell my son, Joe, about the call. He thought it was a bad idea. "Dad, if he turns you down, he's going to feel like a total wimp."

"That's the point, son. I couldn't allow him to challenge the manhood of us Democrats."

"Yeah, but it's not nice. If he says he won't do it, promise me you'll tell him you were kidding."

"Why?"

"It might make him feel like he's a little more off the hook."

"Okay, if he backs out, I'll tell him I was kidding."

"But if he accepts?"

"I'll kick his ass," I said. Frankly, I think Joe was kind of impressed.

I called Lowry the next day. As I expected, he said, "I've decided this is something I don't want to do." Then he said something about crying himself to sleep the night before, which was a joke, but, of course, he was kidding on the square. So, I did what I promised Joe, and told Lowry that I had been kidding, and then suggested we have lunch. We did and had a perfectly lovely time.

A few weeks later, Lowry was on *The NewsHour.* "Joe!" I shouted, "This is the guy!" Joe ran in from his room, and saw Jim Lehrer.

"Dad, he's like seventy."

"Not him. The guy he's talking to."

The shot cut to Lowry, and the moment my son saw him, Joe scoffed, "Aw, this guy? He's a wuss."

"Yeah, he is," I shrugged.

Joe just shook his head and went back to his room with, if possible, even less respect for his father.

But I'll tell you this. I've seen Rich Lowry on television plenty of times since then, and I think he's dropped the whole "Democrats have feminized politics" thing. But, if he hasn't, I'll be glad to meet him any time in my parking garage.

# 39

# Vast Lagoons of Pig Feces: The Bush Environmental Record

I want to draw you a word picture of a lagoon. This is not an azure lagoon trimmed with pearly beaches and wreathed with leafy palm trees, not the type of lagoon you may remember from *Gilligan's Island,* where a caged lion or an Indian in a canoe might wash up just to get that week's episode rolling. This lagoon is a rectangle the size of three football fields, lined with 40-mil high-density polyethylene and filled, to a depth of thirty feet, with pig shit.

Now imagine that, at the bottom of the lagoon, pebbles have punctured the liner, allowing the liquefied pig shit to seep under and ferment. A bubble is growing. The polyethylene liner rises like a creature from the brown lagoon. It breaks the surface, spilling a pungent stew of untreated feces and urine into a nearby creek. An undocumented Guatemalan worker is ordered to puncture the liner with a shotgun blast. Retching, he fires. The swollen liner retreats into the fetid depths. Mission accomplished.

The next day, however, one of the most magnificent sights in all of nature, a shit geyser, explodes into the afternoon sky. Those working nearby watch the pillar rise ten, then twenty, then thirty feet above the lagoon. It is as though the Earth itself is afflicted with a virulent case of projectile diarrhea.

Hold that image in your mind.

George W. Bush is the worst environmental president in our nation's history. As you read this, his self-interested coterie of industry shills are dismantling the protections that you and I take for granted.

Our air, water, and wildlife are under attack. How could this have happened under the watch of a man who spoke so passionately and with such quiet eloquence to this very issue in his very first presidential Earth Day speech?

> Each of us understands that our prosperity as a nation will mean little if our legacy to future generations is a world of polluted air, toxic waste, and vanished forests. . . . I encourage Americans to join me in renewing our commitment to protecting the environment and leaving our children and grandchildren with a legacy of clean water, clean air, and natural beauty.

I know *I* joined him in renewing my commitment. Not too many people realize how much celebrities can do to improve the environment. Remember how I'm a nut for statistics? Well, not too many people realize this, but show biz celebrities make up just .000000001 percent of the world's population, and yet consume nearly 37 percent of its resources. For example, every day, seventeen acres of rain forest are consumed by Barbra Streisand alone.

After Bush's speech, determined to do my part, I wasted almost twenty minutes trying to persuade my son to accept a Prius as a graduation gift, in place of the 280-horsepower Infiniti G35 coupe I had promised him in a weak moment.

So I'm pulling my weight. I wish I could say the same for J. Steven Griles, the deputy secretary of the interior. Instead of renewing his commitment, like the President told him to, Griles has opened public lands to oil, gas, and mining interests, all while still receiving money from his former employers in the oil, gas, and mining industries. Griles's appointment has been a particular boon to a sector of the coal mining industry that is not afraid to think big: the mountaintop removal sector.

You see, when you remove the top of a mountain, you can gain ready access to what is inside, be it diamonds, molybdenum, or most commonly, bituminous (or "dirty") coal. The thing is, a removed mountaintop doesn't just vanish. The top of the mountain has to go somewhere. And that somewhere is usually a nearby valley.

Griles himself has had plenty of experience removing unnecessary mountaintops. As an executive at United Company, he oversaw the Dal-Tex mine in West Virginia, which occasioned one of the largest mountaintop removals since Krakatoa. The mine was not what you would call a good neighbor. When miners detonated mountain ridges, filling in valleys and burying streams with trees, rocks, and thirteen species of songbird, they also sent boulders flying into local houses. As you can imagine, neighbors complained, not just about the boulders, but also about the choking dust.

Griles's inconsiderate behavior did not end with the boulders or the asthma-inducing debris. United Company set up huge coal-loading machines that ran twenty-four hours a day, right next to homes.

For years, a number of regulations have interfered with the ability of mining companies to remove mountaintops. For example, until recently, it's been illegal to dump the mountaintop into a nearby stream or river. The Bush administration has changed all that, by rewriting the Clean Water Act's rules to allow mining waste to be dumped directly into many heretofore off-limits waterways.

The President would argue that our natural resources are best managed by people intimately familiar with all the relevant regulations and statutes, and the tricks polluters use to evade them.

I agree. Such people include academics, regulators, and environmental advocacy groups. Experts all. Oh, but let's not forget the lobbyists for the polluters themselves. In their own way, they are every bit as expert. This last group seems to be disproportionately represented in this administration. There's people like:

| Name | Position | Currently in charge of | Previously lobbied for polluters of |
|------|----------|------------------------|-------------------------------------|
| Mark Rey | Undersecretary of Agriculture for Natural Resources and Environment | Forests | Forests |
| Bennett W. Raley | Interior Assistant Secretary for Water and Science | Water | Water |
| Rebecca Watson | Assistant Secretary of the Interior for Land and Minerals Management | Land that contains minerals | Land that contains minerals |
| Carmen Toohey | Special Assistant to the Secretary of the Interior for Alaska | Alaska | Alaska |
| Patricia Lynn Scarlett | Assistant Secretary of the Interior for Policy, Management, and Budget | Government regulations | Everything |

I am not going to put you through a long list of horrible environmental actions taken by this administration. Instead, I refer you to what TeamFranken calls the Internet. For instance, a Google search of the terms "Bush, horrible, environment" yields 42,500 websites, some of which discuss Bush's environmental record without any reference to horny, barely legal coeds.

Instead, I want to focus on what, for me, is the symbol of the Bush administration's relationship to the environment: the sky-scraping pig shit geyser.

The scene I described at the beginning of this chapter was not from some science fiction movie. It's very real. It happened on one of the growing number of factory farms that are despoiling vast tracts of America. It's a very, very shitty story.

Before we start, allow me to make it clear that I love meat. In fact, I am eating meat right now. Sitting to my right are two members of TeamFranken. Sitting to my left are two pounds of summer sausage.

Twenty years ago, the hogs produced in this country were raised by family farmers. Today, three companies produce 60 percent of all the hogs in America. And they do it in factory farms, or CAFOs: Concentrated Animal Feeding Operations.

Concentrated Animal Feeding Operations are, perforce, Concentrated Animal Shitting Operations. Every hog produces ten times as much feces as a human being. Imagine if you produced ten times as much shit as you do right now. You'd probably be able to read this entire book on the can, instead of just this one chapter.

A single CAFO in Utah is home to 850,000 hogs, producing as much shit as the city of New York. New York City has fourteen sewage treatment plants. CAFOs have none. This presents something of a problem.

In order to dispose of hog waste, farmers have, since time immemorial, used it as fertilizer. It's a nice idea. The pig eats an ear of corn and, two or three minutes later, takes a dump. The shit is then used as fertilizer to grow more corn, which is then fed to the pig, producing more shit, and so on and so forth. It's the circle of life.

The concentration of hundreds of thousands of animals in a small area has disrupted this delicate balance by overloading the shit side of the equation. The waste from a hundred thousand pigs cannot be recycled in the same way. This is where our lagoons come into play.

A typical factory farm lagoon holds anywhere from five to twenty-five million gallons of untreated pig shit. As you might imagine, it smells a bit. In fact, according to pilots, you can smell a CAFO shit lagoon from an altitude of three thousand feet. The smell also travels horizontally. People lucky enough to live in the vicinity of an industrial hog farm are, with each breath, made keenly aware of the cause of their declining property values. If you live downwind of a CAFO, the value of your property drops thirty percent. If you drink a glass of orange juice, it tastes like hog shit.

"I've seen grown men cry because their homes stank," says Don Webb, a very sad retired hog farmer.

The shit stink is exacerbated by the practice of spraying excess shit into the air and onto fields of Bermuda grass when the lagoons threaten to overflow. The industry maintains that spraying the shit onto Bermuda grass is a productive way of recycling the sewage, although the grass is so toxic that it will kill any animal that eats it. At any rate, most of the sprayed shit just goes into the environment, seeping into the groundwater, into the air, and into rivers and streams.

In 1995, a spill from one of these lagoons killed a billion fish in the Neuse River of North Carolina. Every year since, dead fish have continued to wash up onshore by the tens of millions. They're not dying from the smell. No, these fish are falling prey to a previously unknown life form spawned in the pig shit basins and carried into the river waters: the *pfiesteria piscicida*. This dinoflagellate is a microscopic free-swimming single-celled organism that can mutate into at least twenty-four different forms, depending on its prey. It attacks the fish, stunning them with one toxin, then liquefying their flesh with another, then feasting on the liquefied skin and tissue. This is why so many of the fish in the Neuse (dead and alive) sport horrible, bloody lesions.

The fishermen and bridge keepers of the Neuse have also developed these ugly sores, which is why they don't wear shorts on a first date. Of course, it's hard to get a date when you suffer from lethargy, headaches, and such severe cognitive impairment that you can't remember your own name or dial a telephone number. Which *pfiesteria* also causes.

Because the meat industry in this country has become vertically integrated, Big Meat has put the small independent hog farmer out of business. Twenty years ago there were 27,500 family hog farmers in North Carolina alone. Now there are none. Today, a single company named Smithfield owns more than 70 percent of the state's hogs. Small farmers are learning that you can't beat Big Meat.

Nobody claims that factory farming is pretty. But its defenders say that it brings economies of scale that drive down the price of meat for consumers. This is true as long as you don't factor in the shit. Bobby Kennedy, Jr., president of the Waterkeeper Alliance, told me that, if the waste were disposed of legally, the cost of pork from factory farms would be higher than pork from family farms.

> They cannot produce hogs, or pork chops, or bacon more efficiently than a family farm without breaking the law. They aren't about the free market, because they can't compete without committing criminal acts every single day. Their whole system is built on being able to disable or capture government agencies.
>
> They're not in favor of responsibility, or democracy, or private property. It's just about privatizing the air, water, all the things that the public's supposed to own. They are trying to take them away from us, privatize them, and liquidate them for cash.
>
> That's the only coherent philosophy they have. That's it.

Yeah!

To be totally honest, I wish the Clinton administration had done more to address the pig shit problem. But at least he was pushing in the right direction. Toward the end of his administration, the EPA issued stringent new CAFO regulations, requiring hog factories to take responsibility for their waste and initiating suits against some of the violators.

When Bush took office, his appointees gutted the regulations. Eric Schaeffer, head of enforcement for the EPA, resigned in disgust after being told to drop the agency's cases against the offending conglomerates. The administration cut a deal granting immunity to factory farm air polluters, and its Republican allies in Congress defeated a proposal by Paul Wellstone to bar hog producers from also owning the slaughterhouses. As Bush's stance on pig shit became clear, you could hear the squeals of joy at Smithfield.

They say that a rising tide lifts all boats. But in a pig shit lagoon, the only boat that rises is the one on top of the geyser.

Perhaps there is someone reading this who is saying, "Give me a break, Al. I don't care about pigs, or pig shit, or family farms, or mountaintops, or this pfiest-a-mahoosey, or the environment." To you, I have this to say: You were not legitimately elected president, sir.

But I respect the office you hold, and I'm honored that you're reading my book.

## 40

# I Meet Former First Lady Barbara Bush and It Doesn't Go Well

**During** my adult life, the most popular First Lady by far has been Barbara Bush. There was something about the ease of her matronly bearing that made us all feel comfortable. She was everyone's grandmother. Even, it sometimes seemed, her husband's. And for those of us on the liberal side, there was always the niggling suspicion that she was secretly pro-choice but had chosen to keep that between herself and George. Barbara Bush was the benevolent matriarch, somehow above the fray. Oh, an occasional unpleasantry might slip out, like when she called Geraldine Ferraro a "bitch." But that was to be expected in the rough and tumble. All in all, Barbara Bush was a role model for wives and mothers throughout the land.

That's why I was thrilled when I found myself on a flight from Houston to Washington, D.C., sitting across from our former First Lady. It was January of 2000, just a week or two before the primary season was beginning, and this would be my chance to charm her.

I was flying first class because I had just given one of my hilarious and well-received corporate speeches. Mrs. Bush had a window seat, so I was sitting directly across from a Secret Service man, who checked me out when I stood up to say hi. I gave him a smile that said, "Don't worry, I'm all right." See, I consider myself a people person, and I know how to handle myself. Anyway, I guess I checked out because he let me lean in and say, "Excuse me, Mrs. Bush. My name is Al Franken and I'm a friend of Dana Carvey's."

"Oh. Well, Dana's a good man." Yes, Dana is. Dana had done the hilarious, if at times somewhat unflattering, impression of Bush

**345**

Sr. on *Saturday Night Live*. Quite generously, the Bushes had invited Dana to the White House after the 1992 election, and I knew they had gotten along famously. See? People person.

"I'll bet Dana misses my husband," she said with a wry smile.

"Yes. But I'm sure he's working on your son," I responded jauntily.

Her smile disappeared. "Well, I don't know of any characteristics that he has that anyone could possibly make fun of."

As it so happens, I had found a small Dubya quirk and decided it might be fun to show it to his mother. I was sure she'd get a kick out of it. "Well, when he laughs sometimes, his shoulders go up and down like this." Then I did my little impression: Dubya laughing, "heh, heh, heh," his shoulders shooting up and down.

Her face darkened noticeably. "I've never seen him do that."

"Well, I'm sure Dana will do it better. And, of course, it's going to be a *very* valuable impression," I said. That lightened the moment. So much so, that I made what was, in retrospect, an unwise decision. I decided to kid. "You know, until November."

A scowl flashed across her face. And, dismissing me with an imperious wave of her hand, she issued a stern "Well, I'm through with you!"

It was so over the top, I was convinced she was kidding.

"Oh, c'mon, I'm a Democrat," I said, all in good fun.

"I gathered that. And I'm through with you!" Another wave of the hand.

Suddenly, I was dealing with the Queen of Hearts. But I honestly couldn't tell whether she was being serious or just having a bit of fun—in which case, I would have been selling her short just to go back to my seat. So I tried again. "I was just kid—"

"I told you. I'm through with you."

So I nodded and backed away, looking to the Secret Service man for some clue. She's kidding, right? I got nothing from the guy. But they're trained that way.

I spent the next couple of hours reliving the conversation, becoming more and more convinced that Mrs. Bush had the most fabulous sense of humor and the whole "I'm through with you" thing was just a hilarious bit of playacting. After dinner was served and cleared, I decided to try again.

"Here's something you'll like about me," I said as I approached.

Which was met with a severe "I told you. I'm through with you."

"Ah, yes. But I'm a friend of John Ellis." (This was true, and, in retrospect, a little sad. You may remember John Ellis as the Bush relative who manned the Fox News Decision Desk on election night and called Florida for his first cousin. I had known John since his days as a political analyst at NBC, though I've lost touch with him since he helped steal the election for his family.)

"Well, John Ellis is a good man."

We discussed Ellis for a couple of minutes. Then I took my leave *before* she was through with me. Success. I was back in Barbara Bush's good graces.

After we landed and were getting our coats, I thought I'd take one last stab at jollying her up. Knowing that Mrs. Bush had always been a champion of literacy programs, I decided to brag on my daughter.

"Here's another thing you'll like about me," I said, reaching into the overhead bin above her.

"I told you. I'm through with you." Somehow, we had regressed.

"I know, I know. But my daughter teaches kids to read."

"We can't take credit for our children," she scolded.

"We can't? Sure we can. Look at you. You've got two governors."

"I have *five* children," she said with a stern look. "And I'm proud of every one of them."

"Even Neil?" I thought of saying. (He's the one who got mixed up in a sleazy S&L deal in the eighties.) But I didn't. Instead, I said, "Well, if you're proud of them, that's kind of like taking credit for them, isn't it?"

She just scowled at me one last time and said, "I'm through with you." Then she turned and walked off the plane.

I had flown to Washington, instead of home to New York, to attend the Bat Mitzvah of my friends' daughter. The dad is an extremely well-regarded political journalist who had written about the Bushes for years, sometimes in glowing terms. Many of the guests would be other Washington insiders, Democrats and Republicans alike. *They* would know whether Mrs. Bush had just been kidding.

I must have told the story twenty times at the Bat Mitzvah (not during the service). Huge laughs each time. Every "I'm through with you"—big laugh. But what everyone who knew Barbara Bush thought was funniest—by far—was that I had kept thinking that she had been kidding.

I kept hearing things like: "On no, she's a *horrible* bitch." "Omigod, she's the worst bitch on earth." "She can be *very* charming, but Barbara Bush is *the Queen Bitch*."

Understand. This was absolutely universal. And not always said in an unadmiring way. "She's the enforcer." "Barbara's the tough one." "She's mean, but she keeps everyone in line."

But another, even more interesting, insight came from everyone who knew the Bushes. They all agreed. "Dubya is *her* son." He's mean.

Now, I don't know George W. Bush. I met him once briefly, and I found him charming and likeable. I wrote about it in the paperback edition of *Why Not Me?*, but I think, in the context of this book, it bears repeating.

It was August 1999, and I was covering the Iowa Republican straw poll for *George* magazine, at a front-porch event in Indianola, a small town about fifteen miles south of Des Moines. As he was giving the short version of his standard "compassionate conservative" stump speech, literally on a front porch, he caught a glimpse of me standing among fifteen or so members of the press. He looked a bit surprised, then gave me a little wink. Which, I thought at the moment, was kind of charming. I mean, he knew who I was!

After the speech, he glad-handed the good Iowa neighbors who had come to see him. And then, on the lawn, held a press availability. I was going to get to ask him questions!

We gathered around him, and the first thing he did was point to me and say, "I see they're lettin' anyone in these days." Light, funny. After a few other questions, he called on me.

Now, this was the period when the rumors about his cocaine use had first come out. So I said, "Governor, I personally don't care about whether or not you did cocaine years ago when you were a young man. But since we're in Iowa, I feel I have to ask you: Have you ever manufactured any crystal meth?"

Everyone laughed, including Bush. Again, charming. But, and I think this is the important part, he did not answer. Important not because I think George W. Bush ever cooked a tub of methamphetamines. But because, if Bush *had* answered the question, I would have trapped him. Because he had been refusing to answer the coke question. By laughing instead of answering, he had outsmarted me.

I talked to him about a couple of other things. If you're curious, *Why Not Me?* is still in print. But the point is, I came away from my one interaction with the guy kind of, well, charmed. And that, I understand, is a very common experience.

Don't get me wrong. As you've probably figured out by now, I don't like this president. I don't like his policies. He gives me the willies whenever he speaks. I don't like him.

It's because I think he is his mother's son. I think he's mean. I think we're all too ready to blame Karl Rove, or Dick Cheney, or Ari Fleischer, or Gale Norton, or Donald Rumsfeld, or John Ashcroft when this administration does something despicable. When South Carolinians get push polls saying John McCain fathered an illegitimate black child, you know Karl Rove had something to do with it. But it's really Bush. When our energy policy is set by cronies from the oil, coal, and automobile industries, you can shake your fist at Dick Cheney. But it's Bush. When Ari Fleischer feeds rumors that the Clinton people vandalized the White House, doing $200,000 worth of damage, but months later a GAO report says that ain't true, you can say that Ari Fleischer is a chimp. And he is. But it's Bush. When this administration reinterprets the Clean Water Act to allow polluters to dump into creeks and streams, you can blame Gale Norton or Christie Todd Whitman all you like. But it's Bush. When Donald Rumsfeld refuses to apologize for our military accidentally killing a wedding party of fifty in Afghanistan, you can bet that swaggering callousness emanates from the Oval Office. When an American citizen can be put in prison indefinitely without charges being filed and without access to a lawyer or a judge, you may think "John Ashcroft is out of control." And you'd probably be right. But the rest of the time, don't kid yourself. It's Barbara Bush's son.

And I'm through with him.

# 41

# My Personal Search for Weapons of Mass Destruction

**This** is the chapter I've been putting off for the whole book. At one point I told TeamFranken that I was going to wait until the reconstruction of Iraq was complete to write it, but they said they wanted to read what I had to say while they were still alive.

Deep breath. Okay. Here's the thing.

I was genuinely torn about the war. On the one hand, I'm not a believer in the Bush Doctrine of preemption. I think it could be used to justify wars of aggression, not just by us, but by the Japs.

On the other hand, it would be silly to deny that, on 9/11, the world changed. On that day, we learned that America was vulnerable to attack. There were hard choices to be made. We were confronting an enemy that was everywhere and nowhere. The person who had to make those choices was the man with all the facts: George Herbert Walker Bush. And his son—the President.

So, reluctantly, I became a supporter of the war against Saddam. In my own defense, I should say that I wasn't thinking clearly. I was terrified by the imminent threat to me and my family posed by Iraq's arsenal of weapons of mass destruction.

I was especially frantic about the nuclear device Saddam was building with enriched uranium obtained from Niger. The President had told the entire nation about that in his State of the Union address.

My wife was not so worried about the nuclear threat. She was more concerned about a chemical attack on the Frankens. They're doing some construction across from our apartment, and my wife was convinced that the large cement mixer was one of those mobile chemical weapons laboratories that Colin Powell told the U.N. about.

My son, Joe, who is normally very levelheaded, was less worried about a chemical attack than a biological one. He thought the cement mixer was mixing up a potent batch of ricin, a powerful neurotoxin made from castor beans, and that Saddam was planning to use it on us and the Bellers in 9B.

My daughter, Thomasin, shared her brother's concern about biological weapons, but she was less worried about neurotoxins, which kill reasonably quickly through acute hypoxic respiratory failure, and more worried about lethal viruses, which condemn you to a slow and painful death.

All this came out at an emotional family meeting about whether I should speak at a Clear Channel rally supporting the war. Clear Channel owns over twelve hundred radio stations (four times as many as the next biggest media conglomerate), many of which were boycotting the Dixie Chicks and sponsoring pro-war rallies around the country. I'd been thinking about doing a radio show, and I knew that Clear Channel was in 247 of the nation's 250 largest radio markets.

Franni paced the living room, nervously eyeing the cement mixer. "Is it normal to mix cement at 10 P.M.?" she asked.

"Mom," Joe said, "the truck isn't mixing, it's idling. Probably waiting till the temperature is right to ferment the ricin."

"You and your ricin!" Thomasin shouted. "How are they going to weaponize it, butthead?! An *aerosol*? I'm telling you, it's a highly infectious virus, such as Lassa, white pox, or any number of the hemorrhagic fevers. There are eight million delivery systems right here in New York."

"Everybody! Hello!" I broke in. "This is a family meeting to decide whether Daddy should speak at a Clear Channel rally for a cause he's not sure he really believes in."

"It's all about *you*, Dad, isn't it? *It's always about you*," Thomasin said, her voice dripping with the sort of sarcasm I've used italics to indicate throughout this book.

I faked a sneeze, sending her fleeing to her bedroom, where she slammed the door and wedged a wet towel in the crack under it.

"That's not going to save you!" her brother taunted maliciously.

"Okay, focus. What about the speech?" I asked.

"You know you're going to do it, Al. You've already made up your mind." Franni said. "Why are we even having this meeting? You always do this. Do you want me to say I think you should do the speech? Fine, I think you should do the speech."

"Ladies, gentlemen, SportsRadio 640 WGST contest winners, and Lee Greenwood — welcome to Clear Channel's 'Let's Iraq 'n' Roll' rally! A special thanks to retired Air Force Major Dave Cranepool for his flyover in that vintage F-102 Delta Dagger. Wow!

"Today we are not just SportsRadio 640 WGST listeners, or listeners of WKNR, the channel for classic rock, or Hot 92.7 fans, or inmates of the *Morning Asylum with Dave and the Donut Lover.* No, today we're all Americans. *(Cheers, applause)* Except for NPR listeners, who always seemed a little French to me. *(Laughter, boos).* Lee Greenwood liked that one.

"If I could just be serious for a minute. I know your prayers are with our men and women fighting in Iraq, who are there protecting us from Saddam Hussein and his weapons of mass destruction. *(Mix of boos and cheers for Saddam and troops, respectively)*

"You know who really honks me off? Hans Blix. *(Boos)* Hans Blix says he can't find weapons of mass destruction in Iraq. Well, after Saddam Hussein nukes the U.N., it's going to be pretty hard to find Hans Blix! Right, Lee?

"Hey. Did you hear the Dixie Chicks changed their name? They're now the Blixie Chicks! *(Huge cheers)* Am I right? *(Laughter, applause)*"

It was not my proudest moment. And not just because it wasn't my A-material. (Although TeamFranken is great at crunching budget numbers, they're not so hot with the Dixie Chicks jokes.) No, my shame was that I had allowed fear to cloud my normally robust skepticism regarding the veracity of the Bush administration.

Many of the things they had told us about weapons of mass destruction had turned out not to be so true. The uranium from Niger, the aluminum tubes for atomic weapons that Colin Powell told the U.N. about, Bush's references to a nonexistent International Atomic Energy Agency report saying Iraq was six months from having a nuke. All the compelling arguments that Iraq posed an imminent threat to the Frankens. All lies.

Remember the fleet of manned and unmanned aerial vehicles Saddam was building? Bush told us, "We are concerned that Iraq is exploring ways of using these UAV's for missions targeting the United States." This turned out to be about as plausible as the Malawi space program, which consists of a bucket and one man's dreams.

As of this writing no weapons of mass destruction have been found. What has been discovered is that the Bush administration made its case to the American public on the basis of selectively chosen evidence that they knew was shaky. Or worse. In the case of the Niger uranium, for example, the CIA had been telling the White House for a year that the evidence was an obvious forgery.

Nevertheless, as I write this, 34 percent of Americans believe that we have already found weapons of mass destruction in Iraq. I wish I were among this 34 percent. Then I wouldn't feel so guilty about whoring myself out to Clear Channel.

Perhaps so many Americans believe this because they are watching "the number one show on television" (not *CSI: Miami*, but *Hannity and Colmes*). During and after the war, Sean Hannity excitedly announced the discovery of actual weapons of mass destruction or things that seemed to be weapons of mass destruction or the items that proved that weapons of mass destruction were about to be found.

> **HANNITY:** I think the weapons of mass destruction will be found. I don't think we have any doubt about that. What are we to make . . .

COLMES: None whatsoever, Sean.

HANNITY: What are we to make of the reports that they've discovered these large concentrations of cyanide agent, mustard agents in the Euphrates, and the fact that our Marines have found these boxes of suspicious white powder, nerve agent, antidote, Arabic documents on how to engage in chemical warfare?

FOX MILITARY ANALYST LIEUTENANT COLONEL BILL COWAN: Sean, I'm right there with you. No surprises whatsoever that all these things are being found, maybe even no surprises that the U.N. inspection team, Hans Blix and company, had been into some of these places and not found anything . . .

COLMES: Colonel, senior defense officials are telling Fox News at this hour that that white substance found in an industrial plant near Baghdad is not a chemical weapon.

There was tons of this. Every time I watched *Hannity and* Colmes, Sean was certain they had just found the smoking gun. And then someone, in this case, an unusually feisty Colmes, would update the story with the information that what had, in fact, been found was a box of Tide.

Or maybe Americans got the impression that we'd already found weapons of mass destruction because they'd heard it from a high-ranking source in the White House, namely the President. On May 29 of this year, President Bush said on national television, "We found the weapons of mass destruction."

It was on *Polish* national television. The President was in Poland to thank them for joining Eritrea, Tonga, and the Solomon Islands in the Coalition of the Willing. If it turns out that the administration deliberately misled Americans and the rest of the world, next time countries like Tonga might not be so willing lend their support.

There are serious questions about the possible deceptions used to win public support for the war. It is increasingly clear that the disinformation campaign, particularly regarding the much-hyped uranium from Niger, emanated from the highest reaches of the government. The question must be asked: What did the President know? And, if not, why didn't he know it? If, as may be the case, the President did not understand his intelligence briefings, why didn't he ask to have them explained to him? And did he know that he didn't understand them?

When President Clinton left office, America enjoyed tremendous respect and admiration around the world. As a candidate, Bush repeatedly emphasized the need for humility in the conduct of our foreign affairs. What would he have done differently in Kosovo? Been more humble. How would he approach the Middle East? With humility.

But as soon as he became president, Bush managed to spend Clinton's surplus of international goodwill in astonishingly short order. He ditched Kyoto, the anti-ballistic missile treaty, the germ warfare protocol to the Biological Weapons Convention, the Comprehensive Test Ban Treaty, the International Criminal Court, and the land mine treaty.

And did it all with a decided lack of humility. He didn't say, "We hope you don't mind, we're very sorry, but we have to withdraw from the Kyoto Protocol. I feel terrible that we're not able to live up to our responsibility to take a leadership role in addressing the impending global warming crisis." Or something like that. I'm no diplomat. But there must have been some way to be nicer about it.

No. He had to go piss the world off. Not once. But twice.

You see, the day after 9/11, we got the world back on our side. All over the planet, there were spontaneous outpourings of sympathy, support, and genuine affection for the United States. It was a terrible way for it to happen. But it gave Bush a second start.

Then he pissed them all off again. His administration showed an almost reflexive contempt for even the idea of listening to the rest of the world. Like when Cheney told the world that he "didn't give a shit" (quotation marks mine) about weapons inspectors. And Bush's response to whether the largest simultaneous antiwar protests in human history had made any sort of impression on him. "Size of protest," he said, "it's like deciding, well, I'm going to decide policy based upon a focus group." A ten-million-person focus group.

Several months ago, I saw former President Clinton on C-SPAN giving a speech about globalization to the Council on Foreign Relations. He spoke for a couple of hours, with just a few notes, displaying an incredible depth and breadth of understanding. In a way, it made me miss him.

But to be fair to Bush, there's more to being president than simply being articulate, intelligent, and knowledgeable.

I still really hope we find weapons of mass destruction. Not just because my Clear Channel fiasco is on tape. But because if we don't, the rest of the world will trust us even less than they do now. I'm not sure why that matters. Maybe terrorism or the international drug trade or global ecological disasters or emerging infectious diseases or transnational cyber-crime. I don't know. It's just that maybe, someday, one of those things might involve working with a foreign country.

# 42

# The No Child Left Behind Standardized Test

*In compliance with the President's recent educational initiatives, teachers using this volume as a textbook are encouraged to "teach to the test." The practice questions below are the questions that will appear on the test and determine whether your school will receive federal, state, and local funding. In accordance to the Texas model, please ensure that your lowest performing students have dropped out prior to the test date.*

## SECTION ONE—MATH SKILLS

1. In the No Child Left Behind Act, Congress authorized a $5.6 billon increase in Title One spending for low-income children. However, President Bush budgeted only $1 billion for Title One. If Title One calls for $2,800 per poverty-level student, how many children are left behind?
   a. 0
   b. 1
   c. 7
   d. 1,642,857

2. In the No Child Left Behind Act, Congress authorized an expansion of transportation and other support services to an additional 130,000 homeless children. Instead of an increase, the President's budget froze funding for the homeless education program. Because of inflation, this meant 8,000 fewer homeless children could be served than in the previous year. Assuming there is no increase

in homelessness this year, how many homeless children are left behind?

a. 0

b. 8

c. 13

d. 138,000

3. In the No Child Left Behind Act, Congress authorized increased funding to help school districts meet the mandate that all teachers in core academic subjects be "highly qualified" by the end of the 2005–2006 school year. By freezing funding for the Teacher Quality State Grant Program, the Bush budget trains 92,000 fewer teachers than were promised by the act. Assuming each teacher teaches four classes a day of twenty-five students each, and does guidance counseling for eight additional students, how many children are left behind?

a. 0

b. 25

c. 33

d. 9,936,000

4. There are seventy-two million children in the United States. If George leaves 1,642,857 children behind by cutting Title One programs, and leaves 138,000 children behind by freezing spending for homeless education programs, and leaves 9,936,000 by slashing teacher training, what percentage of America's children has George left behind?

a. 0%

b. 1.63%

c. 16.3%

d. 163%

## SECTION TWO—VERBAL SKILLS

1. Teddy agreed to throw his support behind the No Child Left Behind Act because George had promised to fully _____ it. When George presented his budget, Teddy felt _____. *Which pair of words best fills in the blanks?*
   a. undermine; excited
   b. comprehend; appreciative
   c. transcribe; Betsy
   d. fund; betrayed

2. George W. Bush said, "Education is my top priority," he was being . . .
   a. mendacious
   b. rebarbative
   c. risible
   d. all of the above

3. Sometimes in life, it is okay to tell a little _____, but you should always avoid _____. *Which pair best fills in the blanks?*
   a. white lie to the American people; getting caught
   b. story that tugs at the heartstrings; being mawkish
   c. joke to lighten the mood; running with scissors
   d. kid that you're going to fund his education; following through

4. Correct the punctuation in the following sentence: "George W. Bush is the President who, in God's name, will protect our children."
   a. The sentence is correct.
   b. George W. Bush is the President who in God's name will protect our children.
   c. George W. Bush is the President. Who, in God's name, will protect our children?
   d. George W. Bush is the President. Who, in God's name, will protect our children?!

# 43
# What Is a Lie?

**Throughout** this book I've used the terms "lie," "liars," "lying," and "O'Lie-lly" rather, you might say, liberally. Calling someone a liar is a serious charge. It's not quite as bad as calling someone a "traitor," as Ann Coulter does in her new book, *The Treason Diet*, but it's serious.

Telling the truth is something I take seriously, and I try to hold myself to an impossibly high standard. For example, Coulter's book isn't really titled *The Treason Diet*. It's titled *Treason: Liberal Treachery from the Cold War to the War on Terrorism*.

Yes. Lying is a serious matter. And calling the President of the United States a liar is not something I say with any relish or self-satisfaction. I wish with all my heart that our president wasn't a liar, or if he were, that he was more like President Clinton.

Bush lies about important things. Like the economy, his tax cuts, education, our reasons for going to war, and drunk driving. But I think he lies only when he feels he has to. He knows that, most of the time, Fox News, the *Wall Street Journal*, and Rush Limbaugh are only too glad to do it for him.

And all the lies, small and large, add up. They create a worldview in which the mainstream media is a liberal propaganda machine. In which Democrats are ruthless, manipulative power grabbers. And also sissies. Where if you're poor, you should blame yourself, and for everything else, blame Clinton. Where Democrats feed a culture of victimhood, but where the real victims are decent, hardworking white males. The right-wing media's lies create a world in which no one needs to feel any obligation to anybody else. It's a worldview designed to comfort the comfortable and further afflict the afflicted.

In a surprising moment of candor, the *Weekly Standard*'s Matt Labash told an interviewer:

> The conservative media likes to rap the liberal media on the
> knuckles for not being objective. We've created this cottage
> industry in which it pays to be unobjective. It pays to be
> subjective as much as possible. It's a great way to have
> your cake and eat it, too. Criticize other people for not being
> objective. Be as subjective as you want. It's a great little
> racket. I'm glad we found it, actually.

It is a great racket. And not just for their media, but for Bush and
everyone around him. Bush is good at make-believe. He says what
he has to say. But he gives tax cuts to his supporters, throws business to his cronies, quietly guts environmental protections, and
leaves millions of children behind. He calls himself a compassionate conservative. That's the biggest lie of all.

The right-wing media racket lets Bush get away with it. When
the mainstream media dares to tell the truth about Bush, they're
called biased. This book, no doubt, will be accused by some of
having a liberal bias. See how shameless they are? They'll stop at
nothing.

Yes, I'm a liberal, and I'm proud of it. It's a term we need to re-
claim. Because I believe most Americans are liberals just like me.
Most Americans believe in helping people. And most Americans
believe that the government has a role to play—to create opportunity, to protect the environment, to provide for the common good.

We are the country, but they control it. Only 7 percent of
Americans say they want to *weaken* environmental regulations.
But the 7 percent are in charge.

How do we get it back? We have to fight. But we can't fight like
they do. People say that Rush and Fox and their ilk are popular because they're entertaining. And if you can stomach that stuff, I
suppose they are. But a part of their entertainment value comes
from their willingness to lie and distort. They fight with lies.

We can't do that. We have to fight them with the truth. Our
added entertainment value will have to come from being funny
and attractive. And passionate. And idealistic. But also smart. And

not milquetoast-y. We've got to be willing to throw their lies in their face.

When we say, "Hey, Dr. Wolfowitz, didn't the Clinton military do a great job in Iraq?"

And they say, "Fuck you!"

We've gotta come right back and say, "No. Fuck *you*!" That's how we're going to win this thing.

Truth to power, baby.

**R**ecently, flying back from one of my widely acclaimed corporate speeches, I sat next to an avuncular Methodist minister. I told him about my book. He smiled warmly and responded with an interesting nugget from the New Testament. "Do you know what God's punishment is for liars?" he asked me.

Guessing wildly, I tried, "They're turned into donkeys?"

"No," he said. "God's punishment for liars is that they believe their own lies."

I thought that would be a great ending for this book. They believe their own lies. How fitting. That's just the kind of thing God would think of.

So I asked God where exactly in the Bible he said that. God told me that the Methodist minister had had his head up his ass. It doesn't say that in the Bible.[1]

And, in a way, that's an even better ending. Because I don't think they *do* believe their own lies. Anybody, even a Methodist minister, can make an innocent mistake and say something that isn't true. But lying is when you intentionally deceive.

While it might not seem like I'm changing the tone when I accuse my friends on the right of being liars, my hope is that, if we

---

[1] As it turned out, the minister was right. A reader sent me the following from 2 Thessalonians 2:10–11: " . . . and with all the deception of wickedness for those who perish, because they did not receive the love of truth so as to be saved. For this reason God will send upon them a deluding influence so that they will believe what is false. . . ." I guess it was God who had his head up his ass.

keep calling them on their calculated dishonesty, their dishonesty will lose its effectiveness.

Then O'Reilly and company will have to resort to Plan B: name-calling. Which, I think, will expose them for what they are. Stupid bastards.

## 4 4

# I Win

**The** hardcover edition of this book was an enormous success. I like to think it was because I wrote a funny, well-researched book that gave expression to the anger that many Americans were feeling toward George W. Bush and the right-wing media that had been shilling for his administration.

But we all know I owe everything to Bill O'Reilly.

A couple days after our dustup at the Los Angeles BookExpo, a friend of mine who's an NBC News executive overheard O'Reilly while they were standing in line for the New York-Washington shuttle. According to my friend, O'Reilly was "rip-roaring mad" and didn't seem to care who could hear him. "He was talking in a rather loud voice to Shephard Smith, complaining vociferously. 'He can't do that! I'm gonna have to sue him! I mean it! I'm going to sue him! You can't stand by while people do that! I'm going to sue him!' "

About a week after the BookExpo, my publisher Carole Baron received a letter from Fox threatening to sue. Carole called to let me know. I told her not to worry. "I've been doing this for thirty years, and they have no case," I reassured her. "In this country satire is protected speech even if the object of the satire doesn't get it."

"Our letter to Fox," I said, "should be: 'Dear Fox, Please, please, *please* sue us!' "

My publisher got Floyd Abrams, the nation's preeminent First Amendment lawyer to look at Fox's letter and my book. Floyd didn't end up writing the "Please, please, *please*" letter to Fox. He wrote them the "This is the United States of America" letter.

I frankly thought that was the end of that. I still had to do a tremendous amount of work to get the book done, including rewriting the O'Reilly chapter to chronicle his meltdown at the BookExpo.

After putting the book to bed, I recorded the book-on-tape, for which I would win my second Grammy. (Hillary was also nominated, but I kicked her ass.)

Then it was off to Italy for a well-deserved vacation with my family. We stayed at a villa rented by the father of one of my Harvard students—the ridiculously wealthy one, whom we will call Horace Rockefeller.

Italy was extremely hot last summer, so my wife and I slept above the sheets with our bedroom door open. Fabulous wealth doesn't necessarily buy air-conditioning in Italy. One morning, about a week into our vacation, Horace walked into our bedroom and woke me by tapping my shoulder. As I blinked awake, Horace told me, "Al, you're being sued by Fox."

It took a moment to sink in. Then I said: "Good." And went back to sleep.

About an hour later I woke up and checked my e-mails. A number were from TeamFranken members: "This is huge!!!" "Can you believe they were this stupid?!"

I checked Amazon. The book had moved from number 489 to number 12. Now this was August 12, over a month before the scheduled publication date. An hour later the book was number 4. An hour later number 1!

As my friend Arianna Huffington would later say to me, "It was as if Bill O'Reilly walked up to you and handed you a million dollars."

There was some price to pay. The complaint, written by Dori Ann Hanswirth, an attorney from the law firm of Hogan & Hartson, (with, I suspect, some help from O'Reilly), was filled with personal invective that had nothing to do with the case and was quoted widely in newspapers throughout the country.

> Franken has recently been described as a "C-level political
> commentator" who is "increasingly unfunny" . . . and was re-
> ported to have appeared either intoxicated or deranged . . .
> he appears shrill and unstable. . . . One commentator has

referred to Franken as a "parasite" for attempting to trade
off of Fox News' brand and O'Reilly's . . ."

The description, and the report, and the commentator to which
Ms. Hanswirth referred all came from two right-wing websites,
including one to which O'Reilly is a contributor. The other had
posted the following invitation to prospective contributors: "Even
if you're an amateur writer your piece has a far greater chance of
being published here than on almost any other website." The complaint confirmed everything I had written about Fox in the book.
No journalist (let alone lawyer) even vaguely interested in main-
taining a reputation would cite a source so wholly without merit.

Fox was attempting to stop the publication of my book because of my use of their trademarked slogan "Fair and Balanced"
in the book's subtitle. To tell you the truth, at first I didn't know if
Fox was suing me because I was infringing on their trademark or
because I had stolen their idea of using "Fair and Balanced" ironically.

Actually, irony would be an issue in the case itself. When I returned home, I learned a little about trademark law from Floyd and
his team. American case law holds that the First Amendment protects "wordplay, ambiguity, irony and allusion in titling." The use
of *any* of those literary tools allows a writer to use a trademarked
phrase in a title. And ironically, my title contained them all.

Further, Fox had to prove that potential consumers would be
confused by the cover into thinking that this was a Fox book. We
already had dispositive proof that consumers weren't confused.
People who had been preordering the book on Amazon were buying books exclusively by other liberal authors. Plus, we had going
for us the fact that any moron could tell this wasn't a book endorsed by the Fox News Channel.

When I returned home to New York, I Nexused all the
columns and editorials about Fox's suit against me. There were
nearly two hundred and only one sided with Fox. It was written by
a fellow named Bill O'Reilly.

Nevertheless, Fox persisted, and went to federal court seeking an injunction against the publication of the book. As could have been predicted, Fox and their attorneys were literally laughed out of court. Now, normally when you say *literally* laughed out of court, what you mean is *figuratively* laughed out of court. Not here. Fox and Dori Ann Hanswirth were literally laughed out of court.

Ms. Hanswirth didn't do herself any favors by opening with "The Fox News Channel has 80 million subscribers."

Judge Denny Chin interrupted, "When you say there are 80 million subscribers, by the way, I'm not sure what that means . . . On my basic cable I get the Fox cable station. . . . So am I a subscriber to Fox?"

There was a pause, then, a soft: "Yes." The courtroom exploded with laughter.

The headline the next day on the front page of *The New York Times'* metropolitan section read: "In Courtroom, Laughter at Fox and a Victory for Al Franken." You see, people had shown up from miles around to see this landmark First Amendment case, and, as the *Times* put it:

> (Fox's) arguments were met by laughter in the crowded courtroom. . . . One round of laughter was prompted when Judge Chin asked, "Do you think that the reasonable consumer, seeing the word 'lies' over Mr. O'Reilly's face would believe Mr. O'Reilly is endorsing this book?"
>
> The giggling continued as Dori Ann Hanswirth, a lawyer for Fox, replied, "To me, it's quite ambiguous as to what the message is here." She continued, "It does not say 'parody' or 'satire.' "
>
> Ms. Hanswirth said Fox's "signature slogan" was also blurred because people who were not associated with the network, which owns the Fox News Channel, also appear on the cover with Mr. O'Reilly.

Judge Chin said, "The President and the Vice President are also on the cover. Is someone going to consider that they are affiliated with Fox?"

The courtroom broke into laughter again.

By the way, Ms. Hanswirth's answer to that last question was fabulous. "I think Mr. Franken does." That was met with howls. Dori Ann Hanswirth had stepped into a lawyer's nightmare. It was a miracle she wasn't arguing the case in her underwear.

Finally, she was done, and Floyd came up and eviscerated the poor woman. When Judge Chin returned from a short recess, he told Ms. Hanswirth, "There are hard cases and there are easy cases. This is an easy case, for in my view the case is wholly without merit, both factually and legally."

Chin scolded Fox for bringing its complaint to court at all. "It is ironic," he said, "that a media company that should be seeking to protect the First Amendment is seeking to undermine it."

And he signaled to Fox that their best strategy would be to withdraw the suit as quickly as possible. During the hearing, Floyd had threatened to challenge their trademark if the case went any further, and Judge Chin let Fox know that "I think it is highly unlikely that the phrase 'fair and balanced' is a valid trademark."

So Fox withdrew their suit the next business day. And if you watch Fox (which I would not recommend), you'll notice they don't use "fair and balanced" as much as they used to. But I think that Judge Chin may have given them their new slogan: "The Fox News Channel—Wholly Without Merit."

Even though we had known we would win the case all along, the Frankens still celebrated. But as I told my family, it wasn't just a victory for me. It was a victory for satirists everywhere, even bad ones.

Since the humiliating defeat, O'Reilly has often denied having anything to do with the suit. Take this exchange with Terry Gross on the October 8, 2003, edition of her NPR show *Fresh Air:*

**GROSS:** As you probably know, Al Franken was on the show when his book came out. Are you sorry you sued him?

**MR. O'REILLY:** I didn't sue him.

**GROSS:** I know. Fox sued him. But I assumed you—

**MR. O'REILLY:** I had no control over that. And I—they ran it by me in the beginning. And I said, "Look, if you can hold this guy accountable, that's fine with me. I'm looking into suing him myself for defamation." And that's all the input that I had into that. I didn't see the brief. I didn't know what they were doing. And, you know, that's how it went down.

**GROSS:** A lot of people have speculated that you convinced Fox to go with this lawsuit. You're saying that's not the way it happened?

**MR. O'REILLY:** That's correct. That's what I'm saying.

Of course, that was slightly at odds with what O'Reilly had told *Time*'s Rick Stengel in the magazine's October 6, 2003, "Ten Questions" feature.

**TIME:** Do you regret pushing the lawsuit against Al Franken?

**O'REILLY:** Not at all. This man is being run by some very powerful forces in this country, and we needed to confront it. I was ambushed at a book convention. He got up in front of a national audience and called me a liar for twenty minutes. President Andrew Jackson would have put a bullet through his head.

If you remember back to Chapter 13, you might note the charming *leitmotif* of the bullet in my head that was so delighted by my wife and kids. And the "very powerful forces" that O'Reilly alluded to presumably are the fourteen lovable misfits who made up TeamFranken.

Back to O'Reilly and his plucky attempts to skirt responsibility for the dumbest lawsuit since *Neanderthal v. Homo Erectus*. In the September 4, 2003, *New Yorker*, Ben McGrath wrote:

> According to someone close to the situation, Fox executives were not at all in favor of suing, correctly anticipating a P.R. debacle. They told O'Reilly as much in a series of meetings, but he continued to lobby aggressively for bringing a suit, pressing his case with Roger Ailes, the Fox News chairman, and others.

Speaking of Ailes, I ran into him at a restaurant in Midtown this January while I was having lunch with *New York Daily News* reporter Lloyd Grove. Here's Lloyd's report:

> "Will you go on my radio show?" demanded Franken, who's launching a liberal, talk-radio venture in a couple months. "Remember, I helped you out once when you asked me to come on your radio show."
>
> "I really don't do those things anymore," replied Ailes, who had dropped by the table on his way out of the restaurant. "I haven't done it in two years."
>
> "Here, I do you a favor, and that's the thanks I get?" Franken persisted.
>
> "Yeah," Ailes fired back, "but you were the only guest who ever demanded to be paid. I think we had to give you $12."
>
> "That was for cab fare," the comedian insisted.
>
> Franken, my lunch partner, also interrogated Ailes about the cable network's notorious lawsuit against him for appropriating the Fox News slogan in his book, *Lies and the Lying Liars Who Tell Them: A Fair and Balanced Look at the Right*. The publicity over the unsuccessful suit helped turn Franken's book into a huge best-seller.
>
> "Whose idea was it to sue? Was it O'Reilly's?" Franken

probed, referring to Fox News' Bill O'Reilly, star of *The O'Reilly Factor,* whose photograph is prominent on the cover of Franken's book.

"I can tell you that it was August, and I was on vacation," Ailes parried. "I think I said, 'Let's send this over to the legal department,' and somebody there must have thought that meant sue. That's not what I meant."

"But it was O'Reilly who asked for the suit?" Franken repeated.

"Let me put it this way: It wasn't my idea—and it wasn't the legal department's," Ailes said. "Listen, talent always wants to sue about everything. . . . It's the sort of thing that happens in August."

So, really, I have O'Reilly to thank.

## THE FOX NEWS CHANNEL: WHOLLY WITHOUT MERIT

On August 26, 2003, Brit Hume said this on the "Grapevine Segment" of his FNC show *Special Report.*

> Two hundred and seventy-seven soldiers have now died in Iraq, which means that statistically speaking U.S. soldiers have less of a chance of dying from all causes in Iraq than citizens have of being murdered in California, which is roughly the same geographical size. The most recent statistics indicate that California has more than 2,300 homicides each year, which means about 6.6 murders each day. Meanwhile our U.S. troops have been in Iraq for 160 days, which means they are incurring about 1.7 deaths, including illness and accidents, each day.

Of course, Hume was lying. Statistically speaking, U.S. soldiers do *not* have less of a chance of dying than citizens have of being murdered in California. You see, "the most recent statistics" also indicate that over 34 million people live in California, while at the time Hume made his report, we had about 140,000 troops in Iraq. That would make it about 63 times *more* likely that a soldier would die than a citizen of California.

When this was pointed out to Hume by *The Washington Post,* what do you suppose he said? Did he say: "Oh my God! I am so sorry! An overzealous staffer must have stuck it in front of me and I read it without thinking. But that's no excuse. How can I apologize to the men and women who have lost their lives or been wounded? And to their families? And to the soldiers serving there now who are sacrificing every day so that I have the freedom to sit in my comfortable studio and say garbage like that? Oh my God! I am so sorry! Please forgive me!"

No. He didn't say that. Hume said, "Admittedly it was a crude comparison. But it was illustrative of something."

I agree. It *was* illustrative of something. How big an asshole Brit Hume is. And how shameless Fox is. The point of the Grapevine item was to show how well things were going in Iraq. After all, it's safer than in Santa Clara. Hume was shilling for the Bush administration.

Brit, I'm sorry to call you an asshole. But I went to Iraq this past Christmas season on a USO tour. It was my fourth USO Tour, but my first in such a dangerous war zone. I saw soldiers there that were my kids' age and I was moved to tears by their bravery and their spirit and their patriotism. If you have any decency at all, Brit, you will apologize to our soldiers and to their families.

(When I said goodbye to my wife before leaving for Iraq, my wife was worried. She said to me, "You don't see Bill O'Reilly going on a USO Tour." I said, "Honey, that's not fair. He has no talent.")

To give you another idea of how the "wholly without merit" slogan fits Fox like a glove, let's take a look at a study conducted by the Program on International Policy Attitudes at the University of Maryland. The study correlated people's misperceptions on Iraq with where they got their news. The poll focused on three widely held misperceptions:

1. That evidence of links between Iraq and al Qaeda had been found.

2. That weapons of mass destruction had been found in Iraq.

3. That world public opinion had favored the U.S. going to war against Iraq.

Of people who get their news primarily from Fox, 80 percent held at least one of these three misperceptions.

Of people who get their news primarily from NPR and PBS, 23 percent held one of these three misperceptions.

My favorite finding in the study, however, was that among those who primarily watch Fox, the more they watched, the more likely they were to have one of the misperceptions.

In other words, the more you watch Fox, the stupider you get.

Unfortunately, it wasn't just Fox. The fact is that the entire "liberal media" failed us in their coverage of Iraq.

|  | FOX | CBS | ABC | NBC | CNN | Print Sources | NPR/ PBS |
|---|---|---|---|---|---|---|---|
| None of the 3 | 20% | 30% | 39% | 45% | 45% | 53% | 77% |
| 1 or more misperceptions | 80 | 71 | 61 | 55 | 55 | 47 | 23 |

Source: Program on International Policy Attitudes at the University of Maryland, October 2, 2003.

In his February 26, 2004, *New York Review of Books* article, "Now They Tell Us," Michael Massing chronicles the disgraceful story of how the media failed to cover the debate over weapons of mass destruction that had been raging within the intelligence community during the lead-up to the war. *The New York Times, The Washington Post,* and for most part, the entire mainstream media,

Massing shows, gave far too much credence to administration officials and Iraqi defectors who invented or exaggerated their credentials while dismissing dissenters who, we would ultimately learn, had been right.

On August 26, 2002, Vice President Cheney told us that "[t]here is no doubt that Saddam Hussein now has weapons of mass destruction [and is preparing to use them] against our friends, against allies, and against us." According to Cheney, Saddam had not only biological and chemical weapons, but had "resumed his efforts to acquire nuclear weapons." There was no choice but to take preemptive action against him.

Over the next several months we got similarly definitive statements from Condoleezza Rice, Don Rumsfeld, Paul Wolfowitz, Colin Powell, and the President of the United States. These statements were not—what's the word? Oh yeah. They were not true.

Since the invasion of Iraq, we have learned from David Kay, head of the Iraq Survey Group, that there were no weapons of mass destruction in Iraq. Only, as the President would tell us in his latest State of the Union Address, dozens of weapons of mass destruction–*related program activities.* Twelve of these were coloring books. And one of the weapons of mass destruction–related activities was a candy drive by middle schoolers in Mosul to raise money for scientists who were laid off when Iraq discontinued its weapons of mass destruction programs. Also, some cheerleaders from a high school in Sumara had a camel wash for the same purpose.

It is clear now that this was not just an intelligence failure. This administration deliberately massaged cherry-picked information, pressured analysts at the CIA, and circumvented the Agency by "stovepiping" faith-based intelligence gathered by the Pentagon's Office of Special Plans directly to the White House.

As I wrote in the hardcover edition, I fell for it. I can point to the exact moment when I became convinced that we had to attack Iraq. It was on February 5, 2003, during Colin Powell's testimony at the United Nations. I trusted Powell. I believed he was the only high-level official in the Bush administration that I could trust.

Powell told the General Assembly and the rest of the world that Saddam was reconstituting his nuclear program. As Rice, Rumsfeld, and Bush had said in the weeks prior, we didn't want the smoking gun to be a mushroom cloud. Powell's evidence? Powell wasn't stupid enough to use the uranium-from-Africa story the President had tried to feed us in his State of the Union Address. No, Powell's proof was the aluminum tubes.

These were the aluminum tubes that Saddam had been importing, the Iraqis claimed, to make rockets. But the Bush administration told us they were to be used for centrifuging uranium (presumably from Africa) to turn it into weapons-grade uranium, a key step in manufacturing a nuclear bomb. There were many in the intelligence community (experts on centrifuging uranium, for example) who dissented. Not that you would have known that if you were reading the front page of *The New York Times*.

So Powell told us about the tubes.

> What we notice in these different batches is a progression to higher and higher levels of specification, including in the latest batch, an anodized coating on extremely smooth outer and inner surfaces. Why would they continue refining the specifications, go to all that trouble for something that, if it was a rocket, would soon be blown into shrapnel when it went off?

That was the moment. My God! They have an anodized coating!!! Why, *why* would these tubes have an anodized coating *unless* they were making a bomb?! Holy shit!

Six months later, on August 10, I read an article in *The Washington Post* by Barton Gellman and Walter Pincus. It was a little late, considering, you know, that we had already invaded and were occupying Iraq, losing about 1.7 guys a day. But Gellman and Pincus interviewed the government's centrifuge scientists at the Energy Department's Oak Ridge National Laboratory and at its sister institutions.

Speaking publicly for the first time, Houston G. Wood III, founder of the Oak Ridge centrifuge physics department, who is widely acknowledged to be among the most eminent living experts on centrifuging uranium, said of the aluminum tubes in question: "It would have been extremely difficult to make these tubes into centrifuges. It stretches the imagination to come up with a way. I do not know any real centrifuge experts that feel differently."

It turns out that the aluminum tubes were the wrong size to be used in centrifuges. They were the right size for rockets, but *not* for centrifuging uranium. And the anodized coating? Well, the scientists interviewed by Gellman and Pincus said that the anodized coating was actually a strong argument *for* use in rockets. Anodized coating resists corrosion of the sort that ruined Iraq's previous rocket supply. Ready for the kicker?

If aluminum tubes were going to be used for centrifuging uranium, the *first* thing you'd have to do is mill off all the anodized coating.

They lied. They lied about the weapons of mass destruction. They lied to us and to the rest of the world.

Saddam Hussein is an evil fuck. I'm glad we got him. The Iraqi people are better off without him. When I was in Baghdad, I stayed at one of his palaces. It was the second night of Hanukah, and an army chaplain in Tikrit had given me and my brother a menorah. At one of Saddam's central command headquarters, I was told, there is a huge mural of SCUD missiles flying from Iraq to Tel Aviv and destroying Israel. We celebrated Hanukah in the obscenely large foyer of Saddam's palace. Under the largest cut-glass chandelier I've ever seen—by a factor of ten—my brother and I lit the candles as a "fuck you" to Saddam Hussein.

Our military is in Iraq now and will be there for a long time. We have no choice. It will cost hundreds of billions of dollars, even though Paul Wolfowitz told the House Appropriations Committee on March 27, 2003, that the reconstruction of Iraq would cost you and me next to nothing. "It doesn't have to be U.S. taxpayer money. We are dealing with a country that can finance its own reconstruction, and relatively soon."

On April 23, administration official Andrew Natsios told Ted Koppel on *Nightline* that the entire bill, the *entire* bill, to the American people for the reconstruction of Iraq would be $1.7 billion. That's right. $1.7 billion.

In reality, the war is costing us a billion dollars a week. And we will have to be there for years.

In February, after David Kay made his no WMD announcement, Colin Powell was asked by *The Washington Post* whether he would have recommended an invasion of Iraq if he had known that it had no stockpiles of banned weapons. Powell said, "I don't know."

He took that back later. But this is kind of like a wife asking her husband in an unguarded moment, "If you had to do it all over again, would you still marry me?" Somehow, "I don't know" doesn't cut it.

I mean, even I know enough to say, "Yeah, honey, it was the best decision I ever made in my life."

Powell's married. He should know how this works. Someone asks him if he still would have recommended invading Iraq, the right answer was, "Absolutely! Saddam Hussein is a dangerous man in a dangerous part of the world." At least have some respect for the guys over there dodging bullets as he was speaking. I mean, Jesus Christ!

Because of the massive diplomatic failure by this administration, American taxpayers and American troops are bearing the burden in Iraq virtually alone. And even worse, our guys and women are dying and being wounded because Rumsfeld and Wolfowitz and Cheney *willfully* ignored the massive planning for post-invasion Iraq developed by the CIA, the Army War College, and the State Department's Future of Iraq Project.

The latter group's final report contained thirteen volumes of recommendations on specific topics, plus a one-volume summary and overview. James Fallows, whose article in the January/February 2004 issue of *The Atlantic Monthly* recounts this scandalous story in harrowing detail, read over two thousand pages of the report, which so presciently predicted the challenges of postwar Iraq: Establish order. Prevent looting. Get the electrical grid up and running immediately. Disarm, demobilize, but then reintegrate the military.

Says Fallows, "All the working groups concluded that occupying Iraq would be far more difficult than defeating it. Wolfowitz either didn't notice this evidence or chose to disbelieve it."

In late May of 2002, the CIA began a series of war games to simulate best- and worst-case scenarios after the overthrow of Saddam. "One recurring theme in the exercises," writes Fallows, "was the risk of civil disorder after the fall of Baghdad." After Rumsfeld found out that representatives of the Defense Department had attended the war games, he reprimanded them and told them not to participate further. Why?

> Because detailed planning for the postwar situation meant facing costs and potential problems. It weakened the case for a "war of choice" and was seen by the war's proponents as an "antiwar" undertaking.

Instead, we were told the Iraqis would welcome us with flowers. And instead of the two extra divisions requested by generals inside the Pentagon, as Army Secretary Thomas White told Fallows, "we went in with the minimum force to accomplish the military objectives, which was a straightforward task. . . . And then we *immediately* found ourselves shorthanded in the aftermath. We sat there and watched people dismantle and run off with the country, basically."

When the administration chose Jay Garner to lead our postwar effort in Iraq, he came in cold, totally unfamiliar with the planning the rest of the government had already done. Working under Pentagon control, Garner was told by Rumsfeld not to waste his time reading the report created by the Future of Iraq Project. When Garner hired the project's director, Thomas Warrick, Rumsfeld ordered Garner to fire him.

After our successful invasion of Iraq, the country soon disintegrated into chaos. On April 11, Rumsfeld was asked why U.S. soldiers were taking no action to stop the looting. "Freedom's untidy, and free people are free to make mistakes and commit crimes and do bad things." Had Rumsfeld read any of the prewar planning for the occupation of Iraq, he would have known that looting was a prelude to the unraveling of civil society and to the deaths of American soldiers.

It is the hubris of Donald Rumsfeld, Paul Wolfowitz, Condi Rice, Colin Powell, and George W. Bush, plus his total lack of curiosity and attention to detail, combined with maybe just a touch of stupidity, that have led to the needless death and wounding of our troops.

Republicans have accused Democrats of being angry at President Bush.

Yuh.

As I traveled this great country, flogging my book in state after state, I spoke with a lot of angry Americans—Democrat, Independent, and, yes, Republican. I tried to figure out why we're so angry, where it comes from. And about halfway through my tour, I think I figured it out. Maybe I'm wrong. But I really believe it comes from 9/11. As I said in Chapter 22, after that horrible day, our country was more united than I have ever seen it. *And* we had the world behind us. George W. Bush had an opportunity to lead us into a new American century, and instead he hijacked 9/11 for his own political purposes, to reward his base, and alienate the rest of the world.

On February 8, President Bush opened his 2004 campaign with a disastrous appearance on *Meet the Press,* reminding Tim Russert that he is a "war president." Yet, never before has this country cut taxes in a time of war. I ran this by Paul Krugman, the *New York*

*Times* columnist and Princeton economist, who told me he can't find a *civilization* in the *history of mankind* that has cut taxes while at war.

The funny part is that even George W. Bush kind of got it. For about a minute. In Ron Suskind's book, *The Price of Loyalty,* about Paul O'Neill's tenure as Bush's Secretary of Treasury, there is the description of a November 26, 2002, meeting to discuss the second round of tax cuts, which heavily emphasized cutting taxes on stock dividends. At one point, Bush asks, "Won't the top-rate people benefit the most from eliminating the double taxation of dividends? Didn't we already give them a break at the top?"

Karl Rove spoke up. "Stick to principle," he told the President. Principle. The high earners are where the entrepreneurs are. Just like the principle behind eliminating the estate tax, which punishes the most productive people—the children of the very wealthy.

It didn't take much to steer Bush back on course. The tax cuts would go to his contributors while the deficits just continue to grow. Meanwhile, job creation remained stagnant. For those at the bottom, life has become harder. Single mothers lose health coverage for their children in state after state. No Child Left Behind remains an underfunded mandate, forcing states to increase class size and cut off teacher training and after-school programs. No Child Left Behind is the most ironically named piece of legislation since the 1942 Japanese Family Leave Act.

This February, the President signed and submitted his annual economic report to Congress, predicting the creation of 2.6 million new jobs. The administration immediately backed off that prediction, now estimating a million new jobs—some of which may actually employ workers here in the United States.

It's funny. During the 2000 campaign, when Bush said he was against nation building, I didn't realize he meant only this nation.

# SOURCES AND NOTES

## 1—Hummus

A Nexis search for "Gore AND James Lee Witt AND lie OR mislead OR inaccurate" between 10/3/00 (the debate) and 11/5/00 (Election Day) results in sixty-eight hits. A search using the same dates for "Bush AND vast majority w/s tax cuts AND lie OR mislead OR inaccurate" results in two hits, each of which is a wire service transcript of a Gore campaign press release, and neither of which refers to Bush's lie in the debate.

Information regarding the shape of Bush's 2001 tax cut comes from Citizens for Tax Justice: *http://www.ctj.org/html/gwbfinal.htm.*

## 2—Ann Coulter: Nutcase

In an August 26, 2002, *New York Observer* article, Ann said she was "friendly with MSNBC commentator and *West Wing* writer Lawrence O'Donnell and *Saturday Night Live* political satirists Jim Downey and Al Franken." For what it's worth, she also said that "only two minor, irrelevant errors" had been found in *Slander.*

Frank Rich's column on John Ashcroft and Planned Parenthood appeared in the October 27, 2001, *New York Times* under the headline, "How to Lose a War."

The November 12, 2001, *Washington Post* article regarding the media consortium study was titled "Florida Recounts Would Have Favored Bush; But Study Finds Gore Might Have Won Statewide Tally of All Uncounted Ballots." The distinction is that Bush would have won on any of the specific recount methods proposed by Gore, but had there been a full recount of all undervotes, Gore could have ended up with more votes.

The articles that Coulter claims reveal the *Times*'s anti-Christian bias are "The Wrong Passions," appearing on July 9, 2000, and "John Paul's Jewish Dilemma," appearing on April 26, 1998.

## 3—You Know Who I Don't Like? Ann Coulter

Coulter wrote the "kill their leaders and convert them to Christianity" line in her September 13, 2001, column, which got her fired from National Review Online. She made the Timothy McVeigh comment in the August 26, 2002, *New York Observer* article. And her contribution to the national debate about Trent Lott was published in *The New York Times* on December 18, 2002, under the headline "Conservatives Are Differing Over Role in Controversy."

## 6—I Bitch-Slap Bernie Goldberg

The *Editor & Publisher* survey of newspaper endorsements was published in the November 2, 2000, issue.

A Nexis search for "latchkey" through December 2001 reveals eleven relevant mentions for CNN, eleven relevant mentions for CBS News, ten relevant mentions for ABC News, and three relevant mentions for NBC News. There were also quite a few irrelevant mentions, many of which referred to something called "latchkey dogs."

The popularity of "I Hate Israel" was reported on March 12, 2001, by the *Philadelphia Inquirer*; on May 3, 2001, by the *Baltimore Sun*; on May 20, 2001, by the *Pittsburgh Post-Gazette*; on May 27, 2001, by the *Milwaukee Journal Sentinel*; on May 30, 2001, by the *Buffalo News*; on June 22, 2001, by the *Chicago Sun Times*, *Washington Post*, and *Atlanta Journal and Constitution*, and on September 17, 2001, by the *Boston Globe*.

### 7—The 2000 Presidential Election: How It Disproved the Hypothetical Liberal Media Paradigm Matrix

If you'd like to read the Pew Charitable Trusts Project for Excellence in Journalism report on the media's coverage of the 2000 campaign, go to *http://www.journalism.org/resources/research/reports/campaign2000/lastlap/default.asp*.

For more information on Gore's exaggerated exaggerations, read Robert Parry's piece entitled "He's No Pinocchio," published in the April 2000 issue of *Washington Monthly*. It's also available online at *http://www.washingtonmonthly.com/features/2000/0004.parry.html*.

Bush's military record was most prominently covered in the May 23, 2000, *Boston Globe*, in a story by Walter V. Robinson.

### 12—The Chapter on Fox

For more on Rupert Murdoch's riches, media holdings, and adventures in China, see Eric Alterman's *What Liberal Media?*, pp. 234–242.

Roger Ailes's Willie Horton comment has been reported in multiple publications, including in the November 14, 1988, issue of *Time*, under the headline "Bush's Most Valuable Player."

Tucker Carlson made his comment in an op-ed that appeared under the headline "Memo to the Democrats: Quit Being Losers!" in the January 19, 2003, *New York Times*.

### 13—Bill O'Reilly: Lying, Splotchy Bully

If you'd like to watch the BookExpo America panel, check out C-SPAN's online coverage: *http://booktv.org/ram/feature/0503/btv053103__4.ram*. The best parts are also all over your major file-trading services.

For the record: *Inside Edition* won a George Polk Award in 1996 for an investigative report on insurance scams. Bill O'Reilly left the show in 1995.

O'Reilly's childhood is discussed by him (Levittown) in the *New York Observer* under the headline "Fox News Superstar Bill O'Reilly Wants to Oppose

Hillary in 2006!" on October 9, 2000. His mother's version (Westbury) appears in "The Life of O'Reilly," in the December 13, 2000, *Washington Post*. The real version (Westbury is not part of Levittown) appears on any good map of Long Island.

I looked up Sweden's population in the encyclopedia.

O'Reilly called for the Ludacris boycott on August 27, 2002. He reveled in its success on August 28, 2002. And he denied it on February 4, 2003.

To see the O'Reilly vs. Ludacris obscenity count in chart form, visit *http://www.soundbitten.com/archives/week__2002__09__22.html*. Thanks, guys!

## 14—*Hannity and* Colmes

The article in which Sean Hannity was unable to perceive a rhetorical question is "City's Kids Flunk the Basics," from the March 15, 2001, *New York Post*.

Hannity cites a 1996 study by Paul E. Peterson of Harvard and Jay P. Greene of the University of Houston. According to "Researchers Counter Flawed Milwaukee Voucher Study," which appeared in the November 1996 issue of *On Campus* magazine, Peterson and Greene failed to control for family background. When another researcher performed a similar study controlling for family background, the voucher students did not outperform the public school students. Peterson and Greene also ended up basing their conclusions on an exceedingly small sample size.

Hannity also cites a 2002 study by researchers (including Paul Peterson) at Harvard and the University of Wisconsin that looked at the Children's Scholarship Fund in New York City. The study claims that while Latino students did not seem to benefit from vouchers, African-American students did. According to "Results An Open Question," published on June 15, 2003, in the Baton Rouge *Sunday Advocate*, Peterson et al. left out 44 percent of the children in the test sample because they had not taken a state test as kindergartners and therefore did not have convenient baseline scores. He also used a child's mother's race to determine the child's race. When a pair of Princeton researchers analyzed the data correctly, they found that the gains for African-American students all but disappeared.

If you're looking for grist for your humor mill with regards to President Clinton's impressive economic record, you could start by visiting *http://clinton3.nara.gov/WH/Work/020700.html*.

## 15—*The Blame-America's-Ex-President-First Crowd*

For more on conservatives, including Dana Rohrabacher, blaming Clinton after the terrorist attacks, see "Conservatives Sound Refrain: It's Clinton's Fault," in the October 7, 2001, *Washington Post*.

The Byron York piece that came within one word of describing the Clinton counter-terrorism record is "Master of His Game," appearing in the October 15, 2001, *National Review*.

Robert Oakley's comments were printed in "Planned Jan. 2000 Attacks Failed or Were Thwarted," in the Christmas Eve 2000 *Washington Post*. As were Paul Bremer's.

Barton Gellman's exegesis of Clinton's counter-terrorism efforts appeared in a series in the *Washington Post* under the headlines "Broad Effort Launched After '98 Attacks," on December 19, 2001, and "Struggles Inside the Government Defined Campaign," on December 20, 2001.

For more on the Sudan story, see Gellman's article in the October 3, 2001 *Washington Post*, entitled "U.S. Was Foiled Multiple Times in Efforts to Capture bin Laden or Have Him Killed." Sandy Berger wrote an op-ed in the *Washington Post* about the Mansoor Ijaz story. The piece, "Skeptical About Sudan," was published on July 13, 2002. And for more on Mansoor Ijaz, see Daniel Benjamin and Steven Simon's *The Age of Sacred Terror*.

## 16—Operation Ignore

The stories which reveal Condoleezza Rice's lie, as well as the specifics of Operation Ignore, are: "Special Report: The Secret History," in the August 12, 2002 issue of *Time*, and "Planning for Terror but Failing to Act," in the December 30, 2001 issue of *The New York Times*.

For more on Operation Ignore, also see: "The 9/10 President," in the March 10, 2003, issue of *The New Republic*, "Say Nothing and Do It," in the January 19, 2002, *Washington Post*, "A Strategy's Cautious Evolution," in the January 20, 2002, *Washington Post*, "Slow-walked and Stonewalled," in the March 1, 2003, *Bulletin of the Atomic Scientists*, and "White House Defends its Action on Hijack Warnings," in the May 17, 2002, *USA Today*.

The Bush administration's counterterrorism cutbacks and freezes are described in "How Sept. 11 Changed Goals of Justice Dept.," appearing in the February 28, 2002, *New York Times*.

Bush's extended vacation at his Crawford ranch is detailed in the May 19, 2002, *New York Daily News*, in a great article by Michael Daly entitled "W's Mind Was on Vacation."

## 18—Humor in Uniform

For more on Halliburton and its taxpayer-funded contracts and loans, check out the Center for Public Integrity's report, "Cheney Led Halliburton to Feast at Federal Trough," accessible on their website at *http://www.public-i.org*.

The information regarding Halliburton's dealings in Iraq and Iran comes from a letter sent by California Representative Henry Waxman to Donald Rumsfeld, which can be viewed at the following link: *http://www.house.gov/reform/min/pdfs/pdf__inves/pdf__admin__halliburton__contract__april__30__let.pdf*. Representative Waxman cites the following articles, among others: October 5, 2000, *Financial Times*, "U.S. Companies Move Quietly into Iranian Markets"; March 31, 2001, *Washington Post*, "Iran Throwing Off Its Isolation"; February 8,

2001, *Wall Street Journal*, "Halliburton Connected to Office in Iran"; and June 23, 2001 *Washington Post*, "Firm's Iraq Deals Greater than Cheney Has Said."

### 19—Who Created the Tone?

Richard Mellon Scaife's confrontation with Karen Rothmyer is detailed in Eric Alterman's *What Liberal Media?*

Scaife's profile in the *Wall Street Journal* ran on October 12, 1995, under the headline "Citizen Scaife: Heir Turned Publisher Uses Financial Largess to Fuel Conservatism."

The *Wall Street Journal* does not archive its material on LexisNexis, so its collection of Vincent Foster editorials was accessed on Factiva.com.

The phone number for "The Clinton Chronicles" was printed in the *WSJ* editorial "The Falwell Tape" on July 19, 1994.

Joseph Sobran's column, "Inductive Reasoning . . . and Moldering," ran in the *Washington Times* on March 5, 1999.

### 21—Why Did Anyone Think It Would Change?

Some information about the Republican primary campaign in South Carolina came from Rick Davis, who ran the McCain campaign.

Information about Karl Rove's history comes from *Bush's Brain: How Karl Rove Made George W. Bush Presidential* by James Moore and *Boy Genius: Karl Rove, the Brains Behind the Remarkable Political Triumph of George W. Bush* by Lou Dubose et al.

### 22—I Grow Discouraged

Ari Fleischer's comments about the alleged vandalism were made during his press briefing on January 25, 2001, and in a *Boston Herald* article, "White House Staffers Left Trail of Trash," published January 26, 2001. The administration's efforts to inflame the story were detailed in a January 29, 2001, *Slate* article, "Was the White House Trashing Story Garbage?" The *Washington Times* story detailing the porn bombing of the White House, published on January 26, 2001, was entitled "Clinton Aides Accused of Theft, Vandalism."

A Nexis search of "Fox News Network AND vandalism" from January 24, 2001, to January 31, 2001, reveals that the topic was brought up in at least thirteen different segments. Grover Norquist made his comments on *CNN Talkback Live* on January 26, 2001.

The GAO report was detailed in several publications, including *The New York Times,* which ran "White House Vandalism Caper Was Overblown, A Report Finds" on May 19, 2001; and was quoted on Salon.com, which ran "The White House Vandal Scandal That Wasn't" on May 23, 2001.

The Bush administration's actions toward Dana Milbank and Thomas Ricks are detailed in *The American Prospect*'s March 11, 2002, issue, under the headline, "Beat the Press."

John DiIulio's memo, reported on in the article "Why Are These Men Laughing?" in the January 2003 issue of *Esquire*, was obtained in full from the Drudge Report.

Information about the attacks on Tom Daschle comes from *The New Republic*'s May 12, 2003, article, "Hard Target."

ABC reported on John Ashcroft's draping of the statue on January 29, 2002.

### 23—I'm Prudenized

The Reverend Moon's self-aggrandizing comments appeared in the November 11, 1995, *Ottawa Citizen* and the September 8, 2002, *Melbourne Sunday Herald-Sun*.

John McCaslin's column in which I was Prudenized ran on May 11, 1999.

### 24—Paul Gigot Is Unable to Defend an Incredibly Stupid Wall Street Journal *Editorial*

The editorials cited are as follows: "Gun Control, Ashcroft Style," February 3, 2003; "Dick Tracy Wins," January 26, 1994; "Civil Liberties or Civil Security?" December 10, 1993; and "Missing the Target," May 11, 1994.

Crime statistics are from the FBI's Uniform Crime Reports. You can view them yourself at *http://www.fbi.gov/ucr/ucr.htm.*

Paul Gigot became editorial page editor of the *Wall Street Journal* in 2001. Thus, the last three editorials listed above were published during the tenure of Robert Bartley.

### 25—"This Was Not A Memorial to Paul Wellstone": A Case Study in Right-Wing Lies

For more information about the events following Wellstone's death and surrounding the memorial, see "13 Days," in the April 2003 issue of *Mpls.St.Paul Magazine.*

When we entered "Mondale Social Security" into Google, not only was the first hit an article entitled "Mondale Condemns Social Security," but the second hit was an August 28, 2002, *Washington Post* article called "Gingrich Accusations Come Under Scrutiny." The third was a piece about Gingrich's lie entitled "Why Don't These People Use Google?"

An October 31, 2002, article in the *Minneapolis Star Tribune* quotes Daniel Williams, research manager for KSTP-TV, as estimating that "more than 630,000 people tuned in for at least part of the event."

During the campaign, Norm Coleman liked to boast that he had "created" 18,000 jobs as mayor of St. Paul. The Wellstone campaign thought it was only fair to point out that, during Paul's tenure in the Senate, Minnesota had gained 428,400 new jobs. During his twelve years as a senator, Paul helped pass an economic stimulus law providing tax incentives for small businesses to expand and create jobs, worked to cut red tape for Minnesota's medical technology industry, pushed for broadband Internet access throughout rural Minnesota in order to attract business, introduced a bill to provide $2 billion in job training services, championed micro-loan programs that provide capital to start-up businesses, and supported renewable bio-fuels that produced new work opportunities.

According to Senator Clinton's office, she attended the following events after the terrorist attacks of September 11, 2001:

- 9/15—Attended and spoke at funeral service for FDNY Chaplain Michael Judge

- 9/15—Visited 69th Regiment Armory, where families of missing persons gathered to find information about lost loved ones

- 9/19—Visited Family Assistance Center at Pier 94

- 9/20—Toured Ground Zero and Family Assistance Center with fellow members of Congress

- 9/23—Attended Yankee Stadium vigil

- 9/27—Visited family members and spoke at memorial service for Windows on the World employees

- 10/6—Attended and spoke at funeral of a friend in Boston who died in the World Trade Center attacks and met with the family

- 10/6—Met with people who lost loved ones in attack, at Human Rights Campaign event in Washington

- 10/11—Attended Pentagon Memorial service

- 10/19—Privately visited woman still recuperating from wounds suffered after being struck by landing gear from one of the planes that hit the World Trade Center

- 10/20—Attended Madison Square Garden concert for families

## 26—White House Correspondents Dinner

There is no factual basis for my claim that "Fox and Friends" sports anchor Brian Kilmeade was born Leslie Hochswenderson.

Howard Fineman's cover story "Bush and God" was published on March 10, 2003. According to sources at *Newsweek*, it was the highest-selling issue of the magazine since 9/11.

Seymour Hersh's piece in *The New Yorker* describing Richard Perle's shady dealings appeared on March 17, 2003.

My interaction with Paul Wolfowitz is detailed in several publications, including *Slate* (May 2, 2003), the *New York Post* (April 28, 2003), and the *Irish Times* (May 3, 2003).

## 27—The Lying Years

A Nexis search for "Cheney AND crosses row on row" for July 2000 through November 2000 reveals a total of three mentions of Cheney's mistake. And in only one instance, a UPI wire story from August 3, 2000, was his gaffe the main focus of the story.

## 28—Bush Can't Lose with the Clinton Military

Information regarding military budgets comes from the Council for a Livable World. Check out *http://www.clw.org/milspend/dodbud01.html* and *http://www.clw.org/milspend/fy02appropupdate.html*. The numbers regarding the current-dollar budgets of 1986 and 1996 comes from a report available at *http://www.whitehouse.gov/omb/budget/fy2003/pdf/hist.pdf*.

According to OnWar.com, the Third Anglo-Afghan War of 1919 lasted about a month. As Britain was unable to quell the Afghan uprising, it led to full Afghan independence—at a cost of roughly one thousand Afghan lives and two thousand British lives.

Fred Kaplan's *Boston Globe* article appeared on December 9, 2001, under the headline, "Fighting Terror; High-Tech US Arsenal Proves Its Worth."

Captain O'Brien's comments, along with Condoleezza Rice's comments downplaying the worth of peacekeeping, appeared in the *International Herald-Tribune* on April 19–20, 2003, under the headline "From Fighting a War to Keeping the Peace."

Lawrence J. Korb's op-ed appeared under the headline "Thank Clinton for a Speedy Victory in Iraq," in the May 13, 2003, *Boston Globe*.

## 29—Operation Chickenhawk: Episode One

Ari Fleischer made the claim that the USS *Abraham Lincoln* would be "hundreds of miles from shore" in comments printed, among other places, in the May 1, 2003, *New York Post*. The actual story was told in the May 8, 2003, *Washington Post*, under the headline "Ship Carrying Bush Delayed Return."

There are many websites devoted to exposing the chickenhawks. One of the best is *http://www.nhgazette.com/chickenhawks.html*. Another is *http://awol-bush.com/whoserved.html*.

Tom DeLay's bizarre explanation for his failure to serve in Vietnam is detailed in a January 7, 1999, *Houston Press* article entitled "Which Bug Gets the Gas?"

## 30—Fun with Racism

NPR's *Weekend Edition* "coverage" of Senator Lott's speech aired on December 8, 2002. Big props to Sidney Blumenthal, ABC's *The Note,* Atrios, Josh Marshall, Tim Noah, Andrew Sullivan, *Instapundit,* and the rest of the bloggers who broke the "segregationist-sympathizing" angle.

Sean Hannity commented on Fox that "segregation is the legacy of the Democratic Party" on December 10, 2002. Then he did it again on December 18, 2002. Also, he's said it on his radio show.

Shannon Reeves made his comments regarding African-Americans and the Republican Party in the January 8, 2003, *Contra Costa Times,* under the headline "State GOP Leader Blasts Party Racism."

Several blogs reported on voter suppression in the 2002 campaign in great detail, as well as *Slate* on November 4, 2002 (see it online at *http://slate.msn.com/id/2073522/*). If you'd like to see a copy of the Maryland flier, check out the Talking Points Memo. Here's the address: *http://www.talkingpointsmemo.com/docs/balt.vote.suppress.html.*

Condoleezza Rice was referred to as one of the "prime movers" in the Bush decision in a January 17, 2003, *Washington Post* article, "Rice Helped Shape Bush Decision on Admissions." And she contradicted that characterization in a January 18, 2003, *New York Times* article, "Bush Adviser Backs Use of Race in College Admissions."

The M.I.T./University of Chicago study was reported on in *The New York Times* on December 12, 2002, under the headline "Sticks and Stones Can Break Bones; But the Wrong Name Can Make a Job Hard to Find."

The statistic on African-American youth poverty comes from "16% of Children Live in Extreme Poverty," in the May 1, 2003, issue of the *Los Angeles Times.* There are almost one million black youths living in poverty.

Gene Weingarten reported on the African-American Republican Leadership Council in his Below the Beltway column in the *Washington Post* on February 2, 2003.

## 32—Thank God for Jerry Falwell

Joycelyn Elders made her comments at the National Press Club luncheon on December 7, 1993. Her exact words were "I do feel that we need to do some studies."

## 33—Abstinence Heroes

The Guttmacher Institute attributed one-fourth of the decline to increased abstinence and three-quarters to decreased pregnancy among sexually active teenagers as a result of improved patterns of contraception use. It also reported that condoms were the most commonly used contraceptive.

The Northern Kentucky University study was detailed in a Reuters report on June 23, 2003.

### 35—"*By Far the Vast Majority of My Tax Cuts Go to Those at the Bottom*"

During a February 15, 2000 debate with John McCain before the South Carolina Republican primary that aired on Larry King Live, Bush said that "by far, the vast majority of my tax cuts go to those at the bottom of the spectrum."

Information regarding the shape of Bush's 2001 tax cut comes from Citizens for Tax Justice: *http://www.ctj.org/html/gwbfinal.htm*.

The statistics regarding the shape of the 2003 tax cut (the ones refuting Sean Hannity's inference) come from the Urban Institute–Brookings Institution Tax Policy Center (UIBITP). Check them out for yourself at *http://www.tax policycenter.org/commentary/admin__stimulus/section2/table2__1.pdf*.

The Yahngs' moment in the sun came at a February 20, 2001, Tax Family Event that the White House was kind enough to transcribe and post at *http://www.whitehouse.gov/news/releases/2001/02/20010220-5.html*.

Payroll tax information comes from UIBITP: *http://www.taxpolicy center.org/UploadedPDF/1000456__payroll__income.pdf*.

The *Washington Post* ran a story about the New Mexico tax family recruitment on September 13, 2000, entitled "For Bush's 'Typical' Family, Lots of Restrictions."

One quarter of the surplus would have been $1.15 trillion. Bush's tax cut was $1.6 trillion. That's a difference of $450 billion. According to the Center for Budget and Policy Priorities, the net increase in discretionary spending in Bush's plan was $330 billion. Check it out for yourself: *http://www.cbpp.org/10-19-00bud.htm*.

According to Salon.com (June 18, 2002), Bush told his "trifecta" joke this way in Iowa on June 7, 2002. And the White House recorded him saying it a dozen other times in the previous four months. In the *Washington Post* article "Karl Rove, Adding to His To-Do List," published June 25, 2002, it was reported that Bush continued to use the line after its lie was exposed on *Meet the Press*. And the *Washington Post*, in an article entitled "A Sound Bite So Good, the President Wishes He Had Said It" on July 2, 2002, revealed that Gore had actually made the statement, not Bush.

For more on the big lie about family farms being lost due to the estate tax, and to see for yourself that I didn't make up the statistics about its perceived and actual effects, see the April 8, 2001, *New York Times* article instructively titled "Talk of Lost Farms Reflects Muddle of Estate Tax Debate."

The amendment that Wellstone voted for that would have exempted all family farms was Senate Amendment 3832 to H.R. 8, proposed by Senator Dorgan of North Dakota.

To hear the "Money-Grubbing" ad, go to *http://news.mpr.org/features/ 200206/21__mccalluml__adwatch/index.shtml.*

Figures on who pays the estate tax come from Paul Krugman's excellent October 20, 2002, *New York Times* essay, "For Richer." Also taken from this piece, which you really should read, are the statistics about the top 1 percent of earners at the end of the chapter. Except for the population of Bemidji. Which, like that of Sweden, I got from an encyclopedia.

David Brooks's *New York Times* piece on the estate tax, "The Triumph of Hope Over Self-Interest," was published on January 12, 2003.

The fact that estates worth upward of $10 million consist of at least 56 percent capital gains comes from the Center for Budget and Policy Priorities. Here's another link that you could click on if you were using some sort of hybrid book-computer: *http://www.cbpp.org/3-15-01tax2.htm.*

The Democrats' futile attempt to raise the estate tax exemption is detailed in "Hatch Withdraws Research Tax Credit During Senate Votes," the *National Journal*'s *Congress Daily* report for May 22, 2001.

The *Wall Street Journal* was so proud of introducing the concept of "lucky duckies" in its November 20, 2002, editorial "The Non-Taxpaying Class" that the concept was brought back for its "Lucky Duckies Again" editorial on January 20, 2003.

## 36—The Waitress and the Lawyer: A One-Act Play

Thanks to the help of Andrew Lee and Richard Kogan at the Center for Budget and Policy Priorities, William Gale at the Brookings Institution, and Jeffrey Liebman at Harvard, the figures in this play are derived from actual numbers and events.

Donna's payroll tax burden was computed based on a 15.3 percent rate, multiplied by her $25,000 income.

Information regarding projections of budget surpluses or deficits taken from Congressional Budget Office (CBO).

Information regarding Twenty-First Century Community Learning Centers comes from the U.S. Department of Education report "When Schools Stay Open Late: The National Evaluation of the 21st Century Community Learning Centers."

Information regarding SCHIP comes from the Center for Budget and Policy Priorities: *http://www.cbpp.org/3-20-03sfp.htm.* In Texas, a proposed cut would reduce eligibility for the program from 200 percent of the federal poverty line ($30,520) to 150 percent ($22,890), according to the March 20, 2003, *Houston Chronicle* article "Measures Call for Permanent Cuts in Budget."

According to a fact sheet produced by the American Academy of Pediatrics and the National Association of Children's Hospitals and Related Institutions, it costs Texas $1,448 to insure a Medicaid-eligible child. Of course, now that Donna is losing that coverage, she'll be paying a lot more for private health insurance for her kids.

Section 8 housing vouchers, according to the Department of Housing and Urban Development, make up the difference between 30 percent of the family's income and the yearly rent for an apartment meeting the qualifications Allison lists. In other words, Donna's voucher consists of her yearly rent ($8,964) minus 30 percent of her income ($7,500), or $1,464. For more information, check out *http://www.hud.gov* or *http://www.texashousing.org*.

Information regarding TANF reductions and reductions in Child Care and Development Block Grants comes from a report by the Children's Defense Fund entitled "State Budget Cuts Create a Growing Child Care Crisis for Low-Income Working Families."

While Houston does, in fact, have a clean and efficient bus system, other communities in the area may not be so lucky after the funding cut: *http://www.texastransit.org/archives/000629.html*.

Allison's tax cut was computed for us by Andrew Lee and Richard Kogan at the Center for Budget and Policy Priorities. If Allison had had $10,000 in dividend income and $10,000 in capital gains, her tax cut would be even greater—$8,000.

### 38—I Challenge Rich Lowry to a Fight

This chapter, unlike "Operation Chickenhawk," is a real story. Rich wrote about our interaction in his August 28, 2000, *New York Post* article entitled "Why I Won't Fight Al Franken."

### 39—Vast Lagoons of Pig Feces: The Bush Environmental Record

An invaluable resource in writing this chapter was Bobby Kennedy, Jr., president of Waterkeeper Alliance and senior attorney at the Natural Resources Defense Council.

For more information on lagoons, see the following: "Why the Fish Are Dying," *New York Times*, September 22, 1997; "Neighbors of Vast Hog Farms Say Foul Air Endangers Their Health," *New York Times*, May 11, 2003; and *60 Minutes*, June 22, 2003.

For more on the Bush administration and mountaintop removal mining, see the May 19, 2002, *New York Times* article "Judge Takes On the White House On Mountaintop Mining."

Information about J. Steven Griles was compiled from a May 16, 2001, *Washington Post* article, "Symbol of a Shift at Interior; Griles Represents Movement of Pro-Industry, Anti-Regulation Conservatives."

The information in the table of former lobbyists now in charge of the environment comes from a February 23, 2002, *National Journal* article, "Recruiting from Industry."

If, for some reason, you want to know more about *pfiesteria*, there's a website devoted to it: *http://www.pfiesteria.org/pfiesteria.*

## 41—My Personal Search for Weapons of Mass Destruction

For more on Clear Channel, read the April 14, 2002, article in the *Chicago Tribune* entitled "Rocking Radio's World."

Bush's remarks on Polish television were documented by the *Washington Post* in a June 15, 2003, op-ed by David Wise entitled "If Bush Is Lying, He's Not the First."

Bush mentioned Iraq's UAVs in a speech broadcast on CNN (among other places) on October 7, 2002.

The poll in which 34 percent of respondents insisted that we had found weapons of mass destruction was from the Program on International Policy Attitudes, released in May 2003. You can read it online at *http://www.pipa.org/OnlineReports/PostWarIraq/PReleaseIraq5-03.pdf.*

## 42—No Child Left Behind Standardized Test

Question 1: The Congressional Research Service estimates that 40 percent of the national average per pupil education cost (the target for federal support established by NCLB) is $2,827. Bush's budget contained a $1 billion funding increase for Title 1, but NCLB called for a $5.65 billion funding increase.

Question 2: The numbers are based on Congressional Budget Office projections of cost per child, based on FY2000 program data and adjusted for inflation.

Question 3: Based on a National Commission on Teaching & America's Future estimate of roughly $4,000 for funding the training of one teacher, adjusted for inflation according to Congressional Budget Office projections to $4,295, Bush's budget request would fund approximately 316,000 teachers, or 92,000 fewer than were supported under NCLB.

# MEET TEAMFRANKEN

**The** fourteen members of TeamFranken received no course credit for their work. While carrying full course loads at either the Kennedy School or the College, they did their research out of dedication to the truth and for a home-cooked meal provided by my wife Franni every Wednesday night at the Cambridge apartment we rented. We had a great time.

1. Me.

2. Owen Kane—Mid-career Kennedy School '03. An actual adult and a great guy. Also, an attorney with fifteen years experience in private and public sectors. Owen actually worked with a Republican, Massachusetts Governor Jane Swift, as her general counsel of legislative affairs. I held that against him so I made Owen listen to Rush Limbaugh.

3. Joan McRobbie—Mid-career Kennedy School '03. An award-winning journalist. A mom/Bay Area feminist in the best way possible. Joan brought a maturity and sense of calm to an otherwise green and excitable group. Joan helped on taxes and found that all the voucher studies cited by Sean Hannity were either suspect or entirely discredited.

4. Andrew Barr—College '05. Brilliant kid. Valedictorian of Boston Latin, the oldest public school in Boston. Andy became my personal assistant in Cambridge, and came to New York for the killer wrap-up of the book. You'll remember him as my fellow conspirator at Bob Jones.

5. Ryan Friedrichs—Kennedy School '03. University of Michigan '99. Passionate Democrat. Michigan organizer

through and through. Ryan brought tremendous emotion to the Wellstone memorial and to his distaste for O'Reilly. He found the invaluable passage in *Those Who Trespass.* A fighter.

6. Ryan Cunningham—Kennedy School '04. University of Texas Phi Beta Kappa. Taught poor kids as a Teach America Volunteer. Very funny guy. Wrote Kharap Jhuta's first line: "My job in the factory is very hard." Ryan also worked on "Who Created the Tone?"

7. Ben Mathis-Lilley—College '03. Wry, brilliant. Ben was perhaps the least political of all TF members, and it was wonderful watching his amazed reaction to each fresh conservative lie. I'll always cherish Ben's smile when he found Ari Fleischer's "There's a new sheriff in town" quote.

8. Ric Arthur—Kennedy School '03. '93 Annapolis grad. Two tours in the Navy. Ric and I spent a couple hours on the phone with former Swift Boat commander Wade Sanders and together the three of us hashed out the story line for "Operation Chickenhawk." Ric also was invaluable on other military matters.

9. Ben Wikler—College '03. Ben took the term off and was with me through every step of the process. A brilliant, committed activist, Ben was cofounder and national coordinating committee member of the Student Global AIDS campaign, which has done incredibly effective work. Ben contributes to *The Onion*, source of the most consistently funny stuff anywhere. An amazing intellect and talent.

10. Karl Procaccini—College '05. Karl took tremendous delight in ferreting out the oddest stuff, including figuring out some of Ann Coulter's techniques for lying with footnotes. Among others, Karl discovered the "overloading

Nexis" method. He found one I didn't use which he just loved: Coulter savages a writer for using "not the sharpest knife in the drawer" to describe Bush twice in a month, but it turned out it was just the same article published in two newspapers. Sorry I didn't use that, Karl. He also did a lot of the groundwork for "The Lawyer and the Waitress."

11. Steve Rabin—Kennedy School '04. *Summa cum laude* grad from Brandeis. Passionate, committed, my wife called Steve "the catch" from TeamFranken. Steve is a committed activist with a great sense of humor. The Kharap Jhuta chapter was Steve's idea. Tremendous help on issues of bias. I wish I had used more of Steve's stuff on Bush's crony capitalism. It'll be in the paperback.

12. Madhu Chugh—Kennedy School '04. As you can tell from her name and picture, a Texan. A Democrat who has worked for Iowa Governor Tom Vilsack and in the Senate doing health care policy for Senator Ted Kennedy. Winner of all kinds of awards, including University of Texas Outstanding Female Student of the Year 1997–8. Madhu covered the health care front, also the effect of tax cuts in states.

13. Noah McCormack—College '04. At first Noah was slightly disruptive because he knows so much about everything that it was unnerving to all of us. Soon, Noah and we adapted and he became an invaluable instant resource when we couldn't get Norm Ornstein on the phone. A passionate intellectual, Noah's areas of interest knew no bounds. Though he was particularly helpful on taxes, the estate tax in particular.

14. Bridger McGaw—Kennedy School '04. Deputy director of press advance for Al Gore in 2000. Bridger had a gen-

uine dislike for the Bushies and especially their press operation. Worked on 2000 election and changing the tone chapters. He called me "chief" a lot, which made me feel like I knew what I was doing.

15. Emily Berning—Kennedy School '03, UC Berkeley Law '03. *Summa cum laude* from Wellesley. Emmy is *not*, as I suggested, a super-feminist. In fact, she's assembling a cookbook for TeamFranken of Franni's recipes. Also, she's not type-A, just amazingly organized, effective, and smart. Emmy worked on the Religious Right, on Ashcroft, and was forced to listen to and watch Sean Hannity. (Also, notice Ben's hand very low on Emmy's lap).

x. The small figure in silhouette in the entryway behind the steps is the spy from Karl Rove's office that always tailed us.

## ACKNOWLEDGMENTS

**This** is my fifth book. And it's my fifth book published by Carole Baron. Thanks for your faith and support. Mitch Hoffman, my editor, is the nicest man I know. Is he a great editor? Read the book. You tell me. Lisa Johnson, publicity director at Dutton—sorry Bill O'Reilly intimidated you. Jean Anne Rose, the Dutton publicist assigned to me—we haven't worked together yet, but I'm assuming the best. Art director Richard Hasselberger made the beautiful cover and wanted badly to de-splotch O'Reilly. Design director Jaye Zimet made the interior of the book what it is. Production director Bob Wojciechowski turned this thing around in unbelievable time. Managing editor Susan Schwartz held everything together. Editorial director Brian Tart, thank you for your editorial direction. And Rick Willett did the copyediting. Which is why any mistakes are his.

Jonathon Lazear, my agent—I hope this caps off what has been just a great year for you. Gunnar Erickson, my lawyer, had to jump off some rocks to avoid getting bitten by a rattlesnake in Yosemite and landed face-first on a boulder. He's been useless to me since.

To Alex Jones and all my friends at the Shorenstein Center, thank you. Alex was someone I could always come to for advice. To Edie Holway, who supervises the Fellows, you made my life so much easier while I was at Harvard. Jonathan Moore, who travels the globe doing development work in the Third World and is an inspiration, was my squash partner in Cambridge. He's seventy and is almost blind in one eye. Guess who usually won? Me! Michael Waldman—great having you next door. Tom Patterson—calm down. Richard Parker—for helping me with Jesus. Nolan Bowie—

you gave me too many books. Bob Blendon—could you analyze the reaction to my book? Nancy Palmer—thanks. Parker, Danielle, Allison, Karen, and Jamieson, and all the other Shorenstein people whom I've forgotten, I'll always remember you.

My fellow Fellows. Esteban Lopez-Escobar, I didn't understand a word you said. Margie Reedy, great documentary. Terry Samuel, see you on the Hill. Mike Tomasky, thanks for your help and friendship.

The joke at TeamFranken when we needed to know something quick was "Norm!" That's Norm Ornstein at the American Enterprise Institute. Though AEI is considered a conservative think tank, Norm is actually further to the left than Noam Chomsky and just fools them over there. That's not true. But he's a great friend, an amazing repository of knowledge, very funny, and a great sounding board.

The most emotional chapter to write was, of course, the case study of the Wellstone memorial. Thank you, David Wellstone, for your help. You know how I felt about your parents. And Marcia did have a smile that lit up a room. Jeff Blodgett, Paul's campaign manager, thank you for all your help and all your work. I'll be seeing you and David and Mark at Wellstone Action events. David McLaughlin, thank you for allowing me to use your beautiful words about your brother. And thank you, Ann Mulholland and Robert Richman.

Don Simpson, thank you for your unbelievable work on the illustrations. You are a joy to work with and a real artist.

Wade Sanders was my consultant on "Operation Chickenhawk." A Swift Boat commander in Vietnam himself, and former deputy assistant secretary of the Navy, Wade gave so generously of his time. Thank you for that and for your service to our nation. And thanks to John Kerry for hooking us up.

Max Cleland. Thank you for speaking with me. You are a hero.

Bobby Kennedy, Jr., spent a morning with me and three members of TeamFranken and told us pig shit stories that we will never forget. Thank you for your commitment and your fight. You are an inspiration.

Supply Side Jesus was Bradley Whitford's idea. That's right. The same guy who plays Josh Lyman on *The West Wing*. He didn't write it, though. He's just an actor. Bob Gunn, thank you for your help with Jesus and for the emotional support.

Rick Davis, John McCain's former campaign manager, thank you for sharing your insights into the South Carolina campaign.

Joe Lockhart, Howard Fineman, Jonathan Alter, Walter Isaacson, George Stephanopoulos, Mike McCurry, Susan Zirinsky, Joe Peyronin, Andrew Heyward, Erik Engberg, Mark Halperin, Dan Radmacher—thank you for allowing me to understand your worlds a little better.

Thanks to my national security team: former National Security Advisor Sandy Berger; former Secretary of Defense William Cohen; Jim Walsh, executive director of Managing the Atom at Harvard; former Assistant Secretary of Defense for International Security Policy Ashton Carter, now codirector of the Belfer Center for Science and International Affairs at the Kennedy School; former director for counterterrorism on the National Security Council Daniel Benjamin, now senior fellow at the Center for Strategic and International Studies. And my old classmate from college former Deputy National Security Advisor James Steinberg, vice president and director of Foreign Policy Studies at Brookings.

To my economic team: Bob McIntyre at Citizens for Tax Justice, Andrew Lee, Joel Friedman and Richard Kogan at the Center for Budget and Policy Priorities, Jeffrey Liebman from the Kennedy School, William Gale and Thomas Mann at Brookings.

Paul Krugman, thanks for being an inspiration.

Margie Kriz of the *National Journal*, thank you for your insight on Bush's environmental policies.

Karl Struble, Max Cleland's media consultant—thank you for your insight into the 2002 Georgia campaign.

Jim Kennedy from President Clinton's office, thanks for your help and friendship.

Thanks to friends Hazel Lichterman, Bob Franken, Eli Attie, and Geoff Rodkey, who gave a read or two along the way.

A special category to Republicans who either called me back or just stopped long enough to talk to me in person. Tucker Carlson, who spent the most time on the phone, then in descending order of time spent: Vin Weber, Peggy Noonan, Commerce Secretary Don Evans, Christopher Caldwell, Karl Rove, Barbara Bush, Paul Gigot, and Paul Wolfowitz. As Bill Frist said to David Wellstone, "It wasn't personal."

And boos to William Kristol of the *Weekly Standard* for not returning multiple calls even after I left the message that he might have a Jayson Blair problem with Christopher Caldwell.

Eric Alterman, thanks for writing a book on bias that I could just add jokes to.

Sidney Blumenthal, Joe Conason, Mike Pesca, David Sirota, Molly Rowley, Peter Koechley; FAIR, Ralph Neas and everyone at People for the American Way, Bob Somerby at DailyHowler.com, SpinSanity, Buzzflash, Talkingpointsmemo.com, MediaWhores online.com, and Truthout.org were all great resources. Thank you.

To Al Gore. A good man. A funny man. My friend.

To Andy Breckman and John Markus, great comedy writers and great friends who gave me moral support when I needed it. And Roger Rosenblatt, who did the same.

To Liz Topp, my personal assistant and friend. Thanks for handling my life for two years. When Franni wasn't.

To Marie Evans, Franni's assistant, meaning also mine. Thanks for making my life easier and brighter.

To my kids, Thomasin and Joe. Especially Joe, who bore the brunt of my semester in Cambridge. I love you both, and I'm proud of you to boot.

To Andy Barr, who was not just a key member of Team-Franken, my Bob Jones cohort, but also my assistant at Harvard.

Andy also came down for the final push of the book and did heroic work.

Billy Kimball, who, as always, lent his inspiration and brilliance to this project, is a great friend and an enormous comedic talent.

And to Ben Wikler, who, thank God, took the final term off senior year—could not have done this without you. To your parents—you have a brilliant son and he *will* graduate.

And to all the people who helped me that I forgot to acknowledge, it's Andy's fault.

# ENDNOTES

[i]Evan Thomas is the grandson of Norman Thomas. Did you find this endnote? Congratulations.
[ii]See how hard it was to find?

# INDEX

# AL FRANKEN

## WHY NOT ME? THE INSIDE STORY OF THE MAKING AND UNMAKING OF THE FRANKEN PRESIDENCY

'Hilarious throughout ... Franken has perfect pitch' P. J. O'Rourke, *The New York Times*

'Franken keeps you in stitches' *Independent on Sunday*

Could an inept, coke-addled, mentally deficient, oversexed fool become the most powerful leader in the world? Only in America ...

Join outrageous satirist Al Franken on the campaign trail, as he imagines just what would happen if the American people lost all sense of reason and voted him into office.

Meet President Al's dream team, including his loyal wife Franni, disgraced foot-fetishist Dick Morris and his alcoholic brother Otto, who eliminates political rivals by hitting them with a large board. Go behind the scenes of the Franken campaign, as he stuns the pundits by sweeping into office with his visionary 'lower ATM fees' campaign. Witness triumph turn to tragedy, as the new leader makes the ill-advised decision to have himself cloned and descends into a bed-ridden hell of depression, self-loathing, TV movies and prescription drugs. Cringe as the Joint Committee on the President's Mood Swings releases his secret personal diaries to the public, disclosing the embarrassing truth about the pay-offs, the hookers, the lesbian sex phone line ...

*Why Not Me?* is a riotous lampoon on the improbable rise and scandalous downfall of a man who believed *anyone* could become President – and paid the price for proving he was right.

'Al Franken blazes a side-splitting, scathing campaign trail ... "Genius" might be too strong a word, but when a book has sucked you in to the point where you don't even know whether to take the acknowledgements seriously ... you know you're in the presence of great satire' *Dallas Morning News*

# AL FRANKEN

## RUSH LIMBAUGH IS A BIG FAT IDIOT AND OTHER OBSERVATIONS

From the bestselling author of *Lies (and the Lying Liars Who Tell Them)*

'Funny, angry and intelligent' *The New York Times*

Al Franken – riler of the right wing and crusader against corruption – dukes it out with the dinosaurs, warmongers, racists and nutcases of conservatism, starting with his favourite: talk-radio bully-boy and drug addict Rush Limbaugh: self-styled voice of Middle America, rabid liberal-hater and factually challenged lardbutt. But that's not all. Al also chronicles his early adventures in politics and as a writer for *Saturday Night Live*; turns his guns on other adversaries including Reagan, Ross Perot and 'Pat Buchanan: Nazi Lover'; and joins the crackpots and creationists of the Christian Coalition on their 'Road to Victory' conference.

The book that established Al Franken as one of the US's most hilarious political humourists, this is a searing satire on the breakdown of civility and rational argument in today's public discourse – and a well-aimed kick in the (extremely chunky) behinds of big fat idiots everywhere …

'Wickedly funny' *Newsweek*

'A master of political humour … a delight to read and certain to appeal to readers of any political persuasion whose spirit hasn't been completely broken by the state of current US politics' *Washington Times*

'Very funny … this book destroys Limbaugh' *USA Today*